*Flannery O'Connor and the*

*Christ-Haunted South*

# Flannery O'Connor and the Christ-Haunted South

Ralph C. Wood

*William B. Eerdmans Publishing Company*
*Grand Rapids, Michigan / Cambridge, U.K.*

Wm. B. Eerdmans Publishing Co.
255 Jefferson Ave. S.E., Grand Rapids, Michigan 49503 /
P.O. Box 163, Cambridge CB3 9PU U.K.

Printed in the United States of America

09  08  07  06  05  04      7  6  5  4  3  2  1

**Library of Congress Cataloging-in-Publication Data**

Wood, Ralph C.
    Flannery O'Connor and the Christ-haunted South / Ralph C. Wood.
      p.    cm.
    Includes bibliographical references and index.
    ISBN  0-8028-2117-0 (alk. paper)
    1. O'Connor, Flannery — Criticism and interpretation.  2. Christianity
and literature — Southern States — History — 20th century.
3. Christian fiction, American — History and criticism.  4. Southern
States — In literature.  5. O'Connor, Flannery — Religion.
6. Southern States — Religion.    I. Title.

PS3565.C57Z97   2004
813'.54 — dc22

                          2004044125

www.eerdmans.com

# Contents

# Preface

There are turnings in one's life which, once taken, remain irreversible. My own life took such a turning in 1959 when I enrolled at East Texas State College in the blackland prairie town called Commerce. I had wanted to attend Baylor University in Waco. As the ultimate place to prepare for Baptist ministry, Baylor was called "Jerusalem on the Brazos River" with good cause. I believed that I had been called to become a Baptist preacher; in fact, some folks think that I'm still seeking to become one. But total Baylor expenses were $2000 in 1959, and my parents were public school teachers earning $300 a month. Because they had worked diligently to stay clear of ruinous debt since their marriage in 1930, I did not want to put the modest family bank account in arrears.

There is little doubt that I would have received a considerably superior education at Baylor — the school where I finally arrived almost forty years later. Yet one vital thing would have been missing: I would never have encountered a Roman Catholic professor. For in those shamefully anti-ecumenical days, Catholics could not teach at schools such as Baylor. As a Baptist youth, I had even heard dark mutterings that Catholics were those potentially demonic creatures whose church was to be identified as the Scarlet Whore of Rome described in Revelation 17. Even the more charitable Baptists, at least many of them, still did not regard Catholics as Christians. This hostility should not be surprising, for in 1959 I had never met a Catholic, though I had been made curious, and perhaps a little perplexed, by the sight of habited nuns serving as splendid nurses at St. Michael's Catholic Hospital in the neighboring city of Texarkana. But in my own hometown of Linden — in fact, in the whole of Cass County — there was not a single Catholic church. Our Roman fellows in the Faith had not much better regard for us Protestants, looking upon us not as "separated brethren" (the felicitous phrase adopted by the Second Vatican Council to describe Protestants) but as outright heretics.

My snail-shell world was happily burst open in the autumn of 1959 when I arrived on the East Texas State campus. Almost immediately I began to hear stories about an English professor named Paul Barrus. A Yankee from the Deep North state of Iowa, a cosmopolitan fluent in French and German, a scholar learned in Latin no less than American and English literature, Barrus was a teacher whose courses were reported to be electric with religious no less than literary interest. Yet there was also a huge caveat: Barrus was a Roman Catholic, the only one on the faculty. I might have persisted in my belief that this final disqualifier canceled Barrus' other merits if Richard Norton had not been my collegiate mentor in the Christian life. A scholarly and gifted minister in his own right, Norton was the ecumenically-minded director of the campus Baptist Student Union, and he invited Barrus to speak at one of our daily vesper services. Far from being an agent of the Anti-Christ, Barrus proved to be a transparently Christian man. He was not our enemy, I saw, but our friend, our brother in Christ. I can still recall how he sought to explain to us Baptists — not hectoring or berating, but dealing with us ever so gently and patiently — the meaning of the word "sacrament." It's a central Christian reality whose mystery I am still seeking to fathom.

When finally I entered Barrus' classes as an English major in 1961, I found that his reputation as a teacher was not too large but too small. To be his student was nothing less than transforming. He taught Milton as well as the masterpieces of American literature, not merely as interesting texts having their own intrinsic and historical merits, but also as novels and poems and dramas that grappled with the deep things of life and death, even eternal life and eternal death. It soon became evident to me that, rather than remaining a second-rate Baptist preacher, I was called to seek Barrus' kind of excellence: to teach the great works of English and American and European literature as he taught them.

There was nothing denominational about Paul Barrus' teaching. He did not seek to make Catholics out of us Baptists. But when in the spring of 1962 Barrus heard Flannery O'Connor address the Southern Literary Festival in Spartanburg, South Carolina, he asked if she would be willing to speak at East Texas State. Always pressed for cash and ever willing to set forth the prime concerns of her fiction — which were still grossly misunderstood in those early years of her public reception — O'Connor agreed to come. It turned out to be her only trip to Texas. In November of 1962 she lectured on "Some Aspects of the Grotesque in Southern Literature" at our modest little college. I can't boast of having asked O'Connor intelligent questions; in fact, I didn't even have the chance to meet her. Yet I do recall a few eccentric professors worrying that they might soon appear in her stories. I also remain impressed, listening to the tape recording of her lecture more than forty years later, that this audience made up of unsophisticated Southern students was fully attuned to what she had to say, and that we laughed raucously at her one-liners. A little old lady from a California insane asylum had written to complain, O'Connor reported, that her books had left a bad taste in the woman's mouth. O'Connor replied that she was not supposed to eat them. When asked about the significance of The Misfit's hat, O'Connor answered flatly: "The significance of The Misfit's hat is to cover The Misfit's head."

We were well prepared for O'Connor's visit because all the classes in the Hall of Languages had studied *A Good Man Is Hard to Find,* her first collection of stories. It would be extremely foolish to suggest that, as a greenhorn English major, I understood them at any great depth, but there is no doubt that they created the chief turning point of my entire academic and religious life. For I saw in her work the integration of two worlds that I had theretofore thought to be not only separate but opposed, even divorced: uproarious comedy and profound Christianity. I had thought that the sour saint was the model of the Christian life, and that somberness was the ultimate sign of serious faith. O'Connor taught me, exactly to the contrary, that the deepest kind of Christianity, as well as the best kind of literature, is finally comic and joyful, glad-spirited and self-satirizing. For the Cross and Resurrection, because they free us from taking ourselves with a damnable seriousness, enable us rightly to delight in all of the good things of the good creation. I also discerned, no less remarkably, that O'Connor had made world-class art from the stuff of my supposedly retrograde region and its seemingly small-minded Christianity.

When, after finishing my B.A. in 1963 I proposed staying on to take a master's degree in English and to write a thesis on Flannery O'Connor, Paul Barrus suggested that I first learn a good deal about the Catholic Renascence that was then in full flower. He thus put me in pursuit of Graham Greene and Evelyn Waugh, François Mauriac and Georges Bernanos, J. F. Powers and Walker Percy, Jacques Maritain and Etienne Gilson. Though it seems utterly unexceptional in hindsight, this was a revolutionary moment for a Baptist youth from the piney woods of eastern Texas. For it meant that my rapidly widening world was opened to a yet grander realm. Again without any conversionist intent — urging me, instead, to remain faithful to my own Baptist tradition — Barrus brought me into the expansive terrain of Catholic Christianity. Far from threatening to undo my Protestant faith, it has immensely enhanced both my belief and my practice. Thus have I spent my thirty-three years in the classroom seeking to enrich the lives of my mainly Protestant students by exposing them to the riches of the same Catholic world of art and theology that I first learned with revitalizing power from Paul Wells Barrus. This book is thus dedicated to his blessed memory.

I am ever so grateful to Reinder Van Til and Jon Pott, my editors at Eerdmans, for inviting me to write it. They have given me *carte blanche* to speak not in an allegedly neutral academic voice, but to write an openly confessional work, to engage my readers with an unapologetically Christian argument, and thus to enter the postmodern "tournament of narratives" (as our late baptist theologian James Wm. McClendon called it) by putting a Christian account of things in contest with countervailing claims and traditions. This is not to say, of course, that I want my fellow Christians to feel "at ease in Zion" or that I have sought to make non-Christians into villainous creatures. On the contrary, I have sought to show that Flannery O'Connor's work constitutes a massive assault on Christian presumption, even as it serves as a splendid summons to skeptics, half-believers, and unbelievers alike to join the glad way of the gospel.

The debts one incurs in taking a largely untravelled road are too countless to list, but it's an occasion for immense gratitude to name a few of the folks who have helped me along the way. My graduate assistant Brenda Welch was cheerfully patient in tracking down and checking all the quotations. My wife Suzanne and my daughter Harriet were equally eagle-eyed as proofreaders. And in taking my son Kenneth to his nightly meetings, I was able to return to the office every evening and thus to do work on this book that had been put aside during the day. These outward signs of familial support betoken an inward grace and love for which I can never be sufficiently thankful. They are literally my *sine qua non*.

Tom Gossett invited me to team-teach a winter-term course on Walker Percy and Flannery O'Connor in 1973 and, together with his scholar-wife Louise, we have shared our love for O'Connor ever since. Among other Wake Forest University faculty who stimulated my understanding of the Southern Mystique, as we once called it, I am happy to single out Pat Johansen, who in 1978 joined me in teaching a continuing-education course at Reynolda House in Winston-Salem. It included a splendid trip to Nashville and Oxford, to New Orleans and Milledgeville. The many fine students who have studied O'Connor with me at Wake Forest and Samford and Baylor are far too numerous to name, but a few stand out as my main helpers and critics: Steve Blakemore, Pete Candler, Marti Greene Eads, John Hayes, the late John Millis, Jim McCoy, Araminta Stone Johnston, Ben Salt, and John Sykes. Among fellow O'Connor scholars, I offer special thanks to Richard Giannone and William Sessions for their many kindnesses. It has been a pleasure also to labor for nearly three decades with the editors of the *Flannery O'Connor Bulletin* (now renamed and expanded as the *Flannery O'Connor Review*). First there was the late Mary Barbara

Tate, and then the recently retired Sarah Gordon, to whom I offer my unstinted gratitude. In an exchange of more than a hundred and fifty letters, she has adopted the persona of Sally Virginia Cope (from "A Circle in the Fire"), while I have enacted the role of Asbury Fox (from "The Enduring Chill"). Sarah has been my faithful antagonist and thus my ever so faithful friend.

It is also an honor to cite the original places where many of these chapters, now drastically revised and totally transformed, first appeared.

CHAPTER ONE

"The Catholic Faith of Flannery O'Connor's Protestant Characters: A Critique and Vindication," Third Flannery O'Connor Symposium, Milledgeville, GA, April 1984. Panel discussion with Sally Fitzgerald, J. O. Tate, and Frederick Asals, *Flannery O'Connor Bulletin* 13 (1984): 59-72; and "Flannery O'Connor's Strange Alliance with Southern Fundamentalists," in *Flannery O'Connor and the Christian Mystery,* ed. John J. Murphy (Provo, UT: Brigham Young University Center for the Study of Christian Values in Literature, 1997): 75-98.

CHAPTER TWO

"Eugene Genovese and the Biblical Tragedy of the South," *Perspectives in Religious Studies* 28, 1 (Spring 2001): 99-113; and "Flannery O'Connor, H. L. Mencken, and the Southern Agrarians: A Dispute over Religion more than Region," *Flannery O'Connor Bulletin* (1991): 1-21.

CHAPTER THREE

"'Where Is the Voice Coming From?' Flannery O'Connor on Race," *Flannery O'Connor Bulletin* 22 (1993-94): 90-118, followed by a critical letter from Sally Fitzgerald and a reply from the author, *Flannery O'Connor Bulletin* 23 (1994-95): 175-83; and "Flannery O'Connor's Racial Morals and Manners," *Christian Century* 111, 33 (November 16, 1994): 1076-81.

CHAPTER FOUR

"From Fashionable Tolerance to Unfashionable Redemption: A Reading of Flannery O'Connor's First and Last Stories," in *Flannery O'Connor: Modern Critical Views,* ed. Harold Bloom (New York: Chelsea House, 1986), pp. 55-64; and "'Obedience to the Unenforceable': Mystery, Manners, and Masks in 'Judgment Day,'" *Flannery O'Connor Bulletin* 25 (1996-97): 153-74.

CHAPTER FIVE

"Flannery O'Connor's Preachers and Mikhail Bakhtin's Dialogical Understanding of Truth," *Flannery O'Connor Review* 1 (2001-2002): 56-73; and "On

Not Speaking of Man in a Loud Voice: Flannery O'Connor's Grotesque Preachers of the Gospel," *The Cresset* LXVI, 2 (November 2002): 11-18.

**CHAPTER SIX**
"Flannery O'Connor, Martin Heidegger, and Modern Nihilism: A Reading of 'Good Country People,'" *Flannery O'Connor Bulletin* 21 (1993): 100-18; and "Talent Increased and Returned to God: The Spiritual Legacy of Flannery O'Connor's Letters," *Anglican Theological Review* 102 (April 1980): 153-67.

All parenthetical references to Flannery O'Connor's *Collected Works* (New York: The Library of America, 1988) will be indicated as CW. The letters HB refer to *The Habit of Being*, ed. Sally Fitzgerald (New York: Farrar, Straus & Giroux, 1979), while MM designates *Mystery and Manners*, ed. Sally and Robert Fitzgerald (New York: Farrar, Straus & Giroux, 1970).

> The Feast of the Conversion of St. Paul
> January 25, 2004
> Baylor University
> Waco, Texas

# Introduction

No one understood both the promise and the failure of the modern church better than Flannery O'Connor. In a letter written in July 1955 to her new friend Elizabeth Hester,[1] O'Connor specified both qualities: "I think that the Church is the only thing that is going to make the terrible world we are coming to endurable; the only thing that makes the Church endurable is that it is somehow the body of Christ and that on this we are fed. It seems to be a fact that you have to suffer as much from the Church as for it but if you believe in the divinity of Christ, you have to cherish the world at the same time that you struggle to endure it" (HB, 90). This is the judgment of no abstract thinker or writer, but of a thoroughly engaged Christian. Though safely situated in a Georgia hilltop farmhouse, seemingly sequestered from the terrors of history, O'Connor detected the demonry that was everywhere in the air. The racial bitterness and violence that would strafe her own native region served as but one of the many shocks that made up O'Connor's "terrible world." She saw racism as a species belonging to a much deeper and more pernicious genus of evil. In a letter she wrote just a month later to the same correspondent, O'Connor called this evil by its rightful name, and she rightly saw it as the pandemic of our age: "[I]f you live today you breathe in nihilism. In or out of the Church it's the gas you breathe. If I hadn't had the Church to fight it with or to tell me the necessity of fighting it, I would be the stinkingest logical positivist you ever saw right now" (HB, 97).

It was a religious void, a cultural abyss, a moral nothingness that O'Connor sniffed as surely as Nietzsche did when, a century earlier, he de-

---

1. Since the identity of the anonymous "A." in O'Connor's letters has long been known, I will refer to her by name. For a full interpretation of Elizabeth Hester's complex relationship with O'Connor, we must await William Sessions' forthcoming study of her troubled and tragic life.

clared that he could detect the odor of God's rotting body in his nostrils. Like Nietzsche, O'Connor located the evil not in some remote ethereal realm, nor in her circumambient culture alone, but also in the "one holy catholic and apostolic church." She confessed that the church's feeble and often noxious witness causes Christians as much grief as does the world's mad plunge over the cliffs of self-destruction. The Catholic theologian Romano Guardini went even further: he described the church as the cross on which Christ was crucified. Unlike Nietzsche, O'Connor agreed with Guardini that the church contains the one Solution even as it constitutes a terrible part of the problem. For O'Connor, the church is the body of the risen and reigning Christ. As such, it cannot decay into final decrepitude and death, even if it remains scrofulous and sclerotic. Hence the frequent likening of the church to Noah's ark: only the storm without exceeds the stench within. Yet insofar as Christ remains its animating center, the church provides everlasting life amidst the all-encompassing death. Thus does it justify believers in laying down their lives in behalf of its Lord, even as it calls all and sundry unbelievers to take up the way of the Cross. The path of Calvary is the only way that leads home, even if both tired veterans and fresh converts must traverse it together while laughing at our malodorous condition.

The summons to the sweet incense of the nonpositivist gospel — to the Good News that refuses to reduce everything to empirical evidence and material causation — rings clearly throughout the whole of Flannery O'Connor's work. It is not a vague or generalized call to embrace suffering humanity or to recover damaged nature or even to repair the decaying commonweal, though the gospel trenches deeply on all of these worthy concerns. O'Connor approaches such matters as she said Dr. Johnson's blind housekeeper poured tea: she kept her finger inside the cup. Not until the hot liquid scalds her thumb is O'Connor assured that she is dealing with real rather than theoretical matters. So do her stories and novels cause readers to feel the sting of moral and spiritual realities as they splash, often painfully, against our calloused sensibilities.

This book seeks to demonstrate the immense social and religious relevance of Flannery O'Connor's work. It does not offer yet another close literary examination of O'Connor's individual stories and novels. Nor is it an attempt to set forth, in a systematic way, the theological vision embodied in her fiction. Both of these tasks have been performed often and well.[2] On the con-

---

2. I have undertaken this effort myself in two chapters of an earlier book, *The Comedy of Redemption: Christian Faith and Comic Vision in Four American Novelists* (Notre Dame, IN: University of Notre Dame Press, 1988), pp. 80-132.

trary, this is a study of O'Connor's work as it bears on the life of the contemporary church and one of its regional cultures, specifically the church that is situated in her own native realm — the Christ-haunted South.

Chapter One, "A Roman Catholic at Home in the Fundamentalist South," deals with O'Connor's insistence on a radically unapologetic gospel as it is mediated by a no less radical sacramentalism. Here we will focus on one of the strangest anomalies of modern cultural life: how this nation's most benighted and backward region, the South that H. L. Mencken derisively dismissed in 1917 as "the Bible Belt," produced the most important imaginative literature of twentieth-century America. It did so, I will argue, because of the very thing that Mencken despised: its sweated and hard-edged Christianity, its old-fashioned fundamentalism. Though they would seem to stand at the polar antipodes to O'Connor's own Roman Catholicism, Southern fundamentalists won O'Connor's ungrudging admiration because of their refusal to compromise the church's angular message for smooth secular nostrums. In "A Good Man Is Hard to Find," O'Connor's most famous story, the protagonist is a serial killer who earns O'Connor's undying regard because his church-rearing taught him the most basic of distinctions: the divide between Christ and nothingness. Yet in her last published story, "Parker's Back," O'Connor offers a strong critique of Southern antisacramentalism. Hence her call to the contemporary church to maintain the drastic distinctiveness of the gospel rather than putting it into the service of other things — no matter how worthy — and thus to retain its radicalism by holding hard to the sacraments that evangelical Protestants are prone to neglect.

Chapter Two, "The Burden of Southern History and the Presence of Eternity within Time," focuses on O'Connor's relationship with the chief defenders of Southern civilization, especially against its chief Northern detractor, H. L. Mencken. We know that O'Connor was no aficionada of the Civil War, that she ridiculed the Secession Day pageants in Milledgeville, and that she read the Southern Agrarians fairly late in her short life. Yet she shared much of their concern about the unique value of Southern civilization, and she did not want its virtues to be destroyed along with its vices. O'Connor would seem, therefore, to have been the natural ally of Allen Tate, John Crowe Ransom, and Robert Penn Warren, as well as the sworn enemy of Mencken. This judgment holds true in obvious ways. Yet the chief burden of this chapter will be to show — chiefly by recourse to the work of Eugene Genovese — that the old South was not the conservative culture that Tate imagined it to be, since its traditionalist goals were undermined by its modernist economics. Unlike the Agrarians, moreover, O'Connor shared Mencken's obsessive concern with religion as the real issue confronting Southern society. She was less concerned, as we shall see, to preserve Southern civilization than to reclaim Christian radicalism, even the grotesque variety embodied in the Pentecostal figure of Mrs. May in O'Connor's story entitled "Greenleaf."

Chapter Three, "The Problem of the Color Line: Race and Religion in Flannery O'Connor's South," will treat O'Connor's fictional assessment of the single question that has vexed the American nation and its churches more than any other. Here the emphasis will fall on her conviction that the real roots of racism lie very deep — in the pandemic sinfulness of human nature. O'Connor locates racial evils not only in the denial of civil rights and elementary justice to black people, outrageous though these remain, but also in the smugness that animates certain kinds of racial reformers. In "Everything That Rises Must Converge" and "The Enduring Chill" she shows how secular liberators can be guilty of their own heinous sins, especially when they deny the humanity of their own unenlightened parents. With uncanny foresight, O'Connor warned against the church's aligning itself uncritically with the mores of its time and place, not only those of the racist right but also those of the self-righteous left.

Chapter Four, "The South as a Mannered and Mysteriously Redemptive Region," treats O'Connor's two most liberating stories concerning race. Because the South has been a region characterized by its elaborate set of manners, O'Connor's story entitled "Judgment Day" shows how a fundamental respect and regard can prevail between peoples who are otherwise divided by race and experience: a black man and his white "superior" come to live together in lifelong amity. Yet manners will not finally suffice for a church whose gospel calls for reconciliation rather than toleration. O'Connor's most controversial story, "The Artificial Nigger," thus points toward the one true basis for human commonalty: a cruciform mercy and forgiveness. Here O'Connor corrects the inveterate Southern use of Scripture to justify slavery and segregation, as she has recourse to a sacramental understanding of black suffering. Thus does she offer deep Southern wisdom for a nation still vexed by racial antagonism. At the same time, she remains implicitly critical of her region and its religion, for her characters have access to no Christian community wherein they might live amidst racial reconciliation.

Chapter Five, "Preaching as the Southern Protestant Sacrament," deals with the Southern church's chief compensation for its antisacramental barrenness, namely, its Pauline sense that the gospel is not something to be preached so much as it is preaching itself. Here our guide will be the theology of Karl Barth, which holds that the proclaimed Word is God's own speech-act. O'Connor's first novel, *Wise Blood,* demonstrates that Hazel Motes is not satisfied in his solitary conversion to nihilism; he must make fellow adherents to the gospel of nothingness. Since anything worth believing must also be worth evangelizing, Motes proclaims his nihilistic gospel in a nihilistic way. Yet we will also examine O'Connor's two positive Christian preachers, the boy Bevel Summers in "The River" and the girl Lucette Carmody in *The Violent Bear It Away.* In their refusal to palliate the scandal of the gospel, they summon the contemporary church to overcome its neglect of the boldly proclaimed Word.

Chapter Six, "Demonic Nihilism: The Chief Moral Temptation of Modernity," wrestles with what O'Connor regarded as the chief ethical seduction of our age: the temptation to deny the God of the gospel because of unexplained human suffering and, having done so, to justify the elimination of the unneeded and the unwanted, the "useless." Because of her own unjust suffering, Hulga Hopewell, the protagonist of "Good Country People," attempts to enact the nihilism of Dostoevsky's Ivan Karamazov, who famously declared, "If God is dead, all things are permitted." For Hulga, as for Ivan, we inhabit a godless world. Not meant to be conformed to any moral or spiritual order transcending ourselves, we remain as malleable as clay. Thus does Hulga seek to reshape a Bible salesman, a youth whom she regards as a virtual child, into her own nihilist image. Children are almost always the object of O'Connor's reformers. But when these children prove unworthy or incapable of such improvement, they must be done away with. Against such moral nihilism, we shall see that O'Connor offers a eucharistic vision of solidarity with the outcasts and rejects of the world, a vision rooted, I shall argue, in what Pope John Paul II calls "the gospel of life."

Chapter Seven, "Vocation: The Divine Summons to Drastic Witness," explores O'Connor's perpetual concern with the call of God — in both its specific and its general sense. While her preachers and prophets are summoned to make direct proclamation of the gospel, nearly everyone in her fiction is called to conversion. They are beckoned to a holiness of life that consists not of privilege and power but of suffering and sacrifice. Christian vocation comes to clearest focus in O'Connor's treatment of the two universal Christian sacraments: baptism and the Eucharist. In "The River," O'Connor seeks to astonish her readers into the recognition that baptism is not an outworn symbol or insignificant act held over from an antique age of belief, but the very fundament of life. It enables the death and burial with Christ that forms the lifelong pattern of Christian existence. Images of hunger and thirst also pervade the whole of her fiction, as her characters yearn unwittingly for a sustenance that the world cannot give, for a Eucharistic feeding from the slain body and drained blood of Christ. Especially in *The Violent Bear It Away* do we discover that O'Connor emphasizes the utter objectivity of both sacraments: they do not represent subjective acts of human commitment and remembrance so much as God's own bestowal of his unbidden grace. Their efficacy lies, on the contrary, in what they do to and for those who receive them, calling ever so reluctant souls to repeated and lifelong conversions to Christ, enabling them to make a radical countercultural witness concerning such fiercely contested matters as homosexuality and abortion.

Chapter Eight, "Climbing into the Starry Field and Shouting Hallelujah: O'Connor's Vision of the World to Come," is devoted to O'Connor's vision of eternal life as it bears on our present existence. She espoused no soupy eschatology wherein everyone is slouching toward a beneficent eternal destiny, following a sort of granddaddy God who wishes all souls well. On the contrary, she depicts in George Rayber, the antagonist of *The Violent Bear It Away*, a thoroughly self-damned man. Yet the final word her fiction utters is not No but Yes. In the figures of Francis Marion Tarwater and Ruby Turpin, we meet two characters who, though on the verge of damnation, are eschatologically transformed by their wrenching encounter with divine judgment. They discover that in the kingdom of heaven the last always enter first, and that limited virtues must be painfully purged. What is so remarkable about O'Connor's beatific vision is that, in an age rent by enmities and divisions of all kinds, it remains inclusive in the truest sense. No souls are excluded from this heavenly company, except by their own recalcitrance; for this is the community whose citizenship is divinely invited and whose borders lie beyond the walls of the world.

*    *    *

In the course of an essay on O'Connor criticism published in 1990, Frederick Crews diagnosed an American academic malaise whose fevers have not abated. Himself no sort of Christian, Crews confessed the thorny quality of O'Connor's theological imagination. Yet her angular orthodoxy troubled him far less, he admitted, than the attempt by certain critics to sanitize the scandal at the center of her work. O'Connor's "penchant for settled judgments is being treated as a worrisome problem," Crews wrote. Critics made nervous by the theological incorrectness of O'Connor's vision must resort to desperate means: "The professorial instinct when a difficulty looms is not to face it squarely but to reach for a methodological wand that can make it disappear." The favored academic magic, Crews contended, usually entails "some form of deconstructive loosening whereby the offensive content [of O'Connor's work] can be represented as neutralized or altogether negated by subversive textual forces."[3]

My reading of O'Connor's fiction and its Southern milieu offers no sophisticated sterilizing of their Christian offense. Yet in dealing with O'Connor's stories and novels in an overtly theological and ecclesial fashion, I do not intend to use them as fodder for an argument that could be made just as well without them. On the contrary, I will seek to honor the integrity of her characters and her stories by refusing to reduce them to mere theme or statement. When O'Connor herself was asked to explain the meaning of her work, she would answer sternly that, if she could thus state its significance, there would have been no need for the stories themselves: "A story is a way to say something that can't be said any other way, and it takes every word in the story to say what the meaning is" (MM, 96). What makes a story work, she adds, is

> some action, some gesture of a character that is unlike any other in the story, one which indicates where the real heart of the story lies. This would have to be an action or a gesture which was both totally right and totally unexpected; it would have to be one that was both in character and beyond character; it would have to suggest both the world and eternity. . . . It would be a gesture that transcended any neat allegory that might have been intended [by the author] or any pat moral categories a reader could make. It would be a gesture which somehow made contact with mystery. (MM, 111)

O'Connor's work plumbs the depths of mystery — which she defined as "the Divine life and our participation in it" (MM, 111) — in the awful inevitability of her plots; they reach their climacteric in shocking, often deadly vi-

---

3. Frederick Crews, "The Power of Flannery O'Connor," *New York Review of Books* (26 April 1990): 49. Twenty years earlier, the very first book-length treatment of O'Connor was already seeking to dodge the pistol-shot directness and thorny integrity of her work. Josephine Hendin contended that there is not one singular O'Connor but two disparate ones, the dutiful Catholic daughter and the complex literary artist. While the public persona appeared faithful and patient, the private writer was exploding with rage: "Flannery O'Connor seems to have lived out a fiction and written down her life." *The World of Flannery O'Connor* (Bloomington, IN: Indiana University Press, 1970), p. 13. More than three decades later, Hendin's thesis continues to be given currency, though now with a feminist twist: see Sarah Gordon, *Flannery O'Connor: The Obedient Imagination* (Athens, GA: University of Georgia Press, 2000) and Katherine Hemple Prown, *Revising Flannery O'Connor: Southern Literary Culture and the Problem of Female Authorship* (Charlottesville, VA: University Press of Virginia, 2001).

olence. While totally unexpected, these appalling consummations are completely necessary to clarify the action. In a very real sense, what happens had to happen, as it does in *Oedipus the King*, the Greek tragedy whose ending so deeply influenced O'Connor. We cannot anticipate that Oedipus will tear out his eyes in horror at discovering the terrible truth he had failed to discern. Yet when at last he sees, we know instantly that everything else in the play both leads up to and follows from Oedipus' self-blinding. O'Connor's stories usually end with a culmination that is mysterious in this Sophoclean sense: "The reader [is left] with a deeper mystery to ponder when the literal mystery has been solved."[4]

The mystery pervading O'Connor's fiction also springs from its Sophoclean dramatic unity. Her narrative sense coincides with her moral sense, so that the meaning of her stories emerges from the imaginative world they create and from the characters who inhabit it:

> The novelist makes his statements by selection, and if he is any good, he selects every word for a reason, every detail for a reason, every incident for a reason, and arranges them in a certain time-sequence for a reason. He demonstrates something that cannot possibly be demonstrated any other way than with a whole novel. (MM, 75)

O'Connor could have ended her stories less harshly and more "happily," of course, but only if she had been untrue to her characters and their complex motives. Such fudging of dramatic and religious truth makes for the sentimentality that O'Connor so starchily scorned, especially when it was prompted by allegedly Christian concerns. She likened such saccharine religion to pornographic literature: the achieving of cheap and easy ends at the expense of valuable and difficult means.

Yet if O'Connor's art is an act of imaginative creation rather than a sermonic preachment — so that its "message" is found in its form and its method of telling — it is also a telling of the truth. There is absolutely nothing precious about O'Connor's art, as if it existed for the sake of its own well-wrought perfection. Not for nothing was O'Connor a satirist, and satire is indisputably a reforming art. A satirist seeks to deflate pretenders and poseurs, to prick the bubble of all things falsely inflated, to name the illness that makes us sick unto death. There is a diagnostic quality about O'Connor's fiction in the precise sense described by Walker Percy:

4. *"The Presence of Grace" and Other Book Reviews by Flannery O'Connor*, compiled by Leo J. Zuber (Athens, GA: University of Georgia Press, 1983), p. 89.

Something, it appears, has gone wrong with the Western world, and gone wrong in a sense far more radical than, say, the evils of industrial England which engaged Dickens. It did not take a diagnostician to locate the evils of the sweatshops of the nineteenth-century Midlands. But now it seems that whatever has gone wrong strikes to the heart and core of meaning itself, the very ways people see and understand themselves. What is called into question . . . now is the very enterprise of human life itself. Instead of writing about this or that social evil from a posture of consensus from which we agree to deplore social evils, it is now the consensus itself and the posture which are called into question.[5]

O'Connor's stories are stark and often grotesque because they cast doubt on the consensus assumptions of the modern age. She agrees with Percy that the Enlightenment project has fallen apart, that its center has not held, in Yeats's famous phrase, and that a monstrousness has been loosed upon our moral and religious landscape. Drastic cultural conditions require drastic literary means. We have to push as hard, O'Connor once said, as the age that pushes against us.

> The novelist with Christian concerns will find in modern life distortions which are repugnant to him, and his problem will be to make these appear as distortions to an audience which is used to seeing them as natural; and he may well be forced to take ever more violent means to get his vision across to this hostile audience. . . . [Y]ou have to make your vision apparent by shock — to the hard of hearing you shout, and for the almost-blind you draw large and startling figures. (MM, 33-34)

I believe that the church, altogether as much as the secular world, requires the awakening jolt of O'Connor's fiction.[6] Most Christian communities have failed to embody, in both worship and witness, their own saving alternative to our "terrible world." They have lost what is repeatedly found in O'Connor's fiction: the glad news that God's goodness is even more shocking than our violations of it. The God of Abraham and Sarah, of Isaac and Rebekah, of Jacob and Rachel, of Jesus Christ and the Virgin Mary — this stubborn, relentlessly pursuing Hound of Heaven — is determined to deny

---

5. Walker Percy, "The State of the Novel: Dying Art or New Science?" in *Signposts in a Strange Land*, ed. Patrick Samway (New York: Farrar, Straus & Giroux, 1991), p. 141.

6. In *Contending for the Faith: The Church's Engagement with Culture* (Waco, TX: Baylor University Press, 2003), I have sought to offer an overt theological critique of contemporary American Christianity, especially its evangelical expression.

all our denials of his mercy. Though she owned only one of Karl Barth's books,[7] O'Connor shared his ultimately comic understanding of the gospel as undeserved mercy rather than much-deserved wrath. O'Connor and Barth both hear the Word of God as first and finally an affirmation rather than a negation. It is the one message that opens out to eternal life rather than closing down to eternal death:

> [The Word of God] does not proclaim in the same breath both good and evil, both help and destruction, both life and death. It does, of course, throw a shadow. We cannot overlook or ignore this aspect of the matter. In itself, however, it is light and not darkness. We cannot, therefore, speak of the latter aspect in the same breath. In any case, even under this aspect, the final word is never that of warning, of judgment, of punishment, of a barrier erected, of a grave opened. We cannot speak of it without mentioning all these things. The Yes cannot be heard unless the No is also heard. But the No is said for the sake of the Yes and not for its own sake. In substance, therefore, the first and last word is Yes and not No.[8]

This is the Word which, whether for good or ill, almost all Southerners have heard. O'Connor repeatedly declared her high regard for the South as a Bible-reading region. "When the poor hold sacred history in common," she wrote, "they have concrete ties to the universal and the holy which allow the meaning of their every action to be heightened and seen under the aspect of eternity" (CW, 858). To have a biblical cast of mind is to value concrete stories over abstract propositions, for Scripture is the story-borne account of God's mercy and judgment as they have become incarnate in Israel and Christ. The biblical accounts of these ancient Jews and their Messiah and his Jewish-Gentile church are meant redemptively to shape history more than they are

---

7. The list of her library books contains only *Evangelical Theology*, the lectures Barth gave on his single visit to America in 1962. O'Connor annotated it heavily and reviewed it favorably in her diocesan newspaper, declaring that "There is little or nothing in this book that the Catholic cannot recognize as his own" (*"The Presence of Grace,"* p. 165). In a 1963 letter to Brainerd Cheney, O'Connor again affirmed her crusty kinship with Barth: "I distrust folks who have ugly things to say about Karl Barth. I like old Barth. He throws the furniture around" (*The Correspondence of Flannery O'Connor and the Brainerd Cheneys,* ed. C. Ralph Stephens [Jackson, MS: University Press of Mississippi, 1986], pp. 180-81). And in an unpublished letter to Maryat Lee in 1962, O'Connor praised Barth for giving Protestantism a swift boot away from the subjective and experience-centered theology of Friedrich Schleiermacher. His theology is real theology, O'Connor declared, and not social science or history or culture.

8. Karl Barth, *Church Dogmatics,* 4 vols., trans. G. W. Bromiley (Edinburgh: T&T Clark, 1934-69), II/3, Part 2, p. 13.

meant scientifically to record it. Quoting St. Gregory of Nyssa, O'Connor declared that "every time the sacred text describes a fact, it reveals a mystery" (MM, 184). Scripture impinges wonderfully and horribly on the way we now live, while empirically verifiable events from the distant past spark largely antiquarian interest. "Our response to life is different if we have been taught only a definition of faith," O'Connor observed, "than it is if we have trembled with Abraham as he held the knife over Isaac" (CW, 859). Even if their treatment of blacks did not shake Southerners with Abraham's life-shattering fear, they have known that, like him, we shall all be brought to the ultimate test.

The central premise of this book is that the contemporary church faces a similar test: whether it is willing to slay certain things that seem to be good — the seemingly necessary modifications of the gospel that would make it fit modern needs and thus ensure its success. As with Abraham's understandably fond regard for young Isaac, so with our apparently worthy by-paths around the Cross: they block obedience to and trust in the one true God. Yet O'Connor's fiction does not constitute a stern summons for the church to rescue itself from its malaise any more than Abraham was required to provide a ram to be sacrificed in Isaac's stead. Divine hope always arrives when it is least expected, when God's people have learned to hope against hope (Romans 4:18). Hence the hopeful irony of Southern history and the hopeful subject of this book. The South lost the Civil War in defense of an indefensible and evil institution. Yet it proved to be a blessed defeat. As we shall see, the South won the spiritual war by retaining its truest legacy, not the heritage of slavery and segregation and discrimination, but the Bible-centered and Christ-haunted faith that it still bequeaths to the churches and the nations as their last, best, and only true hope.

ONE ❧ *A Roman Catholic at Home*
*in the Fundamentalist South*

Speaking magisterially for her fellow Catholics in the American South, Flannery O'Connor offered a startling prophecy at the close of a 1959 book review: "It is an embarrassment to our fundamentalist neighbors," she wrote, "to realize that they are doctrinally nearer their traditional enemy, the Church of Rome, than they are to modern Protestantism. The day may come when Catholics will be the ones who maintain the spiritual traditions of the South."[1] It has become commonplace to note O'Connor's affinity with her Southern backwoods prophets and preachers, though her early critics assumed, quite wrongly, that she was making literary sport of them. Yet no one has explored the real depth of this kinship. Robert Brinkmeyer has argued that, while O'Connor's narrators assume a fundamentalist tone, she herself maintains a serene Catholic stance above them.[2] It is not difficult to understand Brinkmeyer's embarrassment, his unwillingness to admit that O'Connor's tough narrative voice is really hers.

Brinkmeyer is not alone in finding it difficult to grant cultural standing to fundamentalism. The liberal Protestant theologian H. Richard Niebuhr, in his 1929 analysis of American Christianity, devoted only three pages to fundamentalists. In standard Weberian fashion, he attributed the primitive quality of their faith to their agrarian existence:

> In recent times the conflict between urban and rural religion took on dramatic form in the theological battles of Modernism and Fundamentalism. . . . [T]he religion of the primitive agriculturalist is inclined to

1. *"The Presence of Grace" and Other Book Reviews by Flannery O'Connor,* compiled by Leo J. Zuber (Athens, GA: University of Georgia Press, 1983), p. 77.

2. Robert Brinkmeyer, "Asceticism and the Imaginative Vision of Flannery O'Connor," in *Flannery O'Connor: New Perspectives,* ed. Sura P. Rath and Mary Neff Shaw (Athens, GA: University of Georgia Press, 1996).

magic, to the compulsive spell upon the powers of nature on which the rural worker is so dependent for his whole economic existence. . . . Hence the faith of the rural community centers more in the appropriation of the grace of God that men may live in harmony with Him, while urban religion is more concerned with the gain of that same grace that men may live at peace with one another.[3]

George Marsden has shown that American fundamentalism is, in fact, an urban rather than a rural phenomenon, that its conflict with modernism arose in the North rather than the South, and that it was birthed by legitimate concerns over scientific and historical challenges to the main claims of Christian faith.[4] This is not to deny that most revivalistic Methodists and Baptists and Pentecostals living in the rural South during the publishing years of O'Connor's life (1948-64) were also fundamentalists. They, too, held that the Bible is God's verbally inspired, inerrant, infallible book — not only in matters of faith and morals, but of history and science as well. Yet their biblical literalism was taken for granted rather than pitted against an alleged enemy. Marsden wittily notes, therefore, that to speak of most Southern Christians as fundamentalists was to indulge in redundancy. There was no need to give them the name, since the South remained largely immune to the angry battles that racked the Northern churches.[5]

Once the warfare ended with an overwhelming modernist triumph, fundamentalism came to be regarded as the worst of abominations. In high academic and ecclesial places, whether Catholic or Protestant, its adherents have been dismissed as rigid and narrow, as mean-spirited and closed-minded folks who bludgeon their enemies with their Bible. Most scholars and critics see themselves, by contrast, as enlightened and compassionate, as inclusive and diversity-desiring people. We thus give thanks that we are not like the fundamentalists, the one group whom everyone can despise without guilt. Many liberal Protestants, by contrast, regard the Bible as a classic work of religious literature, one sacred text among other kindred books, the West-

---

3. H. Richard Niebuhr, *The Social Sources of Denominationalism* (New York: Living Age, 1957; first published in 1929), pp. 184-85.

4. George M. Marsden, *Fundamentalism and American Culture: The Shaping of Twentieth-Century Evangelicalism, 1870-1925* (New York: Oxford University Press, 1980).

5. It is extremely ironic that the fundamentalist strategy was (and remains) a product of the Enlightenment. Over against the closed, miracle-denying cosmos of modernist science, fundamentalists attempt to create a hermetically sealed world of Scripture. They seek empirical proofs for doctrines and miracles that are not meant for scientific or historical validation, precisely because they are God's unique provision for the life of Christian faith.

ern equivalent of the Muslim's Koran or the Hindu's Gita. Why, then, would O'Connor cast her allegiance with the old-line Southern fundamentalists rather than the up-to-date liberals?

## The American Way of Life: Materialist Individualism

The answer lies, at least in part, in the 1950s cultural circumstance of O'Connor's work. Jon Lance Bacon has shown that O'Connor's faith and art were not solely fixed on transtemporal truths, but that she was deeply concerned about the homogenizing ethos of the Eisenhower era. It was a time rife with anti-Communism and pro-Americanism. "The American Way of Life" became the talismanic phrase for hailing all that was virtuous about our system of government and for damning all competing systems. It was the first American age to witness the triumph of the automobile and advertising, of consumerism and suburbanism. The chief demand of this new era was for individual conformity and "adjustment" to fit the demands of the emerging consensus in both politics and religion. O'Connor was openly allied with other critics of this consumer-centered call for conformity and homogeneity: C. Wright Mills and Marshall McLuhan, David Riesman and Vance Packard, William H. Whyte and Reinhold Niebuhr. They all saw that the rampant new commercialism and commodification of American life obliterated "the possibility of some other reality than the material."[6]

O'Connor protested against the postwar attempt to baptize individualist self-sufficiency and materialist well-being in the name of sentimental uplift. In a 1957 essay she declared that "there is some ugly correlation between our unparalleled prosperity and the stridency of these demands for a literature that shows us the joys of life." She also asked whether "these screams for joy would be quite so piercing if joy were really more abundant in our prosperous society" (MM, 30). Raising her voice as a bullhorn against the trumpetings of middle-class contentedness, O'Connor insisted that "Catholicism is opposed to the bourgeois mind," while also praising her own favorite art form, the grotesque, as the "true anti-bourgeois style" (CW, 862). In her very first novel, *Wise Blood* (1952), her protagonist is a hayseed rather than a suburbanite, but he announces the new American gospel with consummate complacency: "Nobody with a good car," declares Hazel Motes, "needs to be justified" by Jesus (CW, 64). Motes's broken-down Essex is indeed his deity:

6. Jon Lance Bacon, *Flannery O'Connor and Cold War Culture* (New York: Cambridge University Press, 1993), p. 125.

he sleeps in it, preaches from it, and relies on it to escape from all obligations that are not of his own choosing.[7]

Among O'Connor's many satiric portraits of the bitch-goddess — as D. H. Lawrence called the deity of bourgeois success — none is more acute than the figure of a copper flue salesman named Meeks in her second novel, *The Violent Bear It Away*. Meeks is an apostle of hard work, extolling it not as an intrinsic good but as the way to get ahead:

> He said this was the law of life and it was no way to get around it because it was inscribed on the human heart like love thy neighbor. He said these two laws were the team that worked together to make the world go round and that any individual who wanted to be a success and win the pursuit of happiness, that was all he needed to know. (CW, 365)

Meeks has also mastered the art of salesmanship by way of feigned concern for his customers. In his cornpone espousal of the utilitarian creed, Meeks also reveals the nihilism lurking beneath it:

> He said love was the only policy that worked 95% of the time. He said when he went to sell a man a flue, he asked first about that man's wife's health and how his children were. He said he had a book that he kept the names of his customers' families in and what was wrong with them. A man's wife had cancer, he put her name down in the book and wrote *cancer* after it and inquired about her every time he went to that man's hardware store until she died; then he scratched out the word *cancer* and wrote *dead* there. "And I say thank God when they're dead," the salesman said; "that's one less to remember." (CW, 362)

While O'Connor joined the 1950s liberal critique of American materialism, she was not deluded about the genuine threat posed by Communism. Yet she was hardly a McCarthyite, confessing that the death camps could have been constructed in her own native Georgia as readily as in far-off Poland. In her story "The Displaced Person," a Polish refugee is in fact slain by the same sort of "good country people" who operated Hitler's ovens. Yet O'Connor refused to sell her work to Czech and Polish publishers in 1956, vowing to keep it

7. In a similar way, Walker Percy regards the automobile, even more than the movies, as the great American Dream Machine. In his novel entitled *Love in the Ruins*, Percy likens the mobile home to the Conestoga wagon; it enables latter-day Americans to remain perpetually unrooted and displaced and on the move, ever able to light out for the territories like Huck Finn.

out of "Russian-occupied territory" for fear that it might be used for propaganda purposes, as had the fiction of Jack London. She was also a close friend of Granville Hicks, the anti-Communist editor of *Saturday Review*, and she joined with Robert Lowell and Elizabeth Hardwick in seeking to oust an alleged Communist, Agnes Smedly, as director of the writer's retreat at Yaddo in upstate New York. More revealing still is O'Connor's high regard for Reinhold Niebuhr, the American theologian whose understanding of human evil made him a fierce critic of Communism. O'Connor joined Niebuhr, not only in his critique of American economic and intellectual smugness, but also in his denunciation of Stalin's desire to remake the whole of humanity into *homo Sovieticus*, a creature whose abject political conformities made bourgeois Americanism seem, by comparison, to be liberating indeed.

## The American Way of Faith: Civil Religion

O'Connor's critical independence — her unwillingness to equate Christianity with any scheme or program — led her to reject another consensus that she regarded as far more noxious than bourgeois prosperity and anti-Communist hysteria: the newly emerging American civil religion. Its intentions were no doubt good. As the sociologist Will Herberg argued in his influential 1955 book *Protestant-Catholic-Jew*, various representatives from the nation's historic faiths joined in an effort to combat ethnic and racial discrimination. United in their opposition to bigotry in all its forms, they agreed to ignore their fundamental theological differences for the sake of a common need. The cause of social justice came to be defined, however, as a larger good than the historic traditions themselves. Thus was the old civil religion of Washington and Jefferson and the other Founding Fathers reshaped into a new Americanism that could suffice quite well without any confessional particularities at all.

> The assumption underlying the view shared by most Americans, at least at moments when they think in "non-sectarian" terms, is not so much that the three religious communities possess an underlying theological unity, which of course they do, but rather that they are three diverse representations of the same "spiritual values," the "spiritual values" American democracy is presumed to stand for (the fatherhood of God and brotherhood of man, the dignity of the individual human being, etc.). That is, at bottom, why no one is expected to change his religion as he becomes American; since each of the religions is equally and authentically

American, the American is expected to express his religious affirmation in that form which has come to him with his family and ethnic heritage. Particular denominational affiliations and loyalties within each of the communities . . . are not necessarily denied, or even depreciated, but they are held to be distinctly secondary.[8]

"Each of the religions is equally and authentically American" — there could hardly be a clearer articulation of American civil religion: we are first of all Americans, and only secondarily are we Jews or Muslims, Protestants or Catholics or Orthodox. O'Connor discerned that something deadly had occurred when national identity had been made to trump religious faith. She proved to be recalcitrantly unpluralistic, therefore, at a gathering of eminent scholars, theologians, and writers at Sweet Briar College in 1963, which included Franz Boas, Stanley Romaine Hopper, and John Ciardi. "The Devil had his day" at this conference, O'Connor lamented, because the participants all sought to reduce specific religious doctrines to general human possibilities. "I waded in," O'Connor wrote to Sally and Robert Fitzgerald, "and gave them a nasty dose of orthodoxy. . . . I told them that when Emerson decided in 1832 that he could no longer celebrate the Lord's supper unless the bread and wine were removed that an important step in the vaporization of religion in America had taken place" (CW, 1180).[9]

O'Connor's objection to a blithe indifferentism concerning truth and error, to an all-tolerant notion that one church or synagogue or mosque is as good as another, to a reduction of doctrinal and communal faith to uncritical moral earnestness, was also voiced by the Jesuit Gustave Weigel in a debate with the liberal Protestant Robert McAfee Brown: "The average Protestant seems to think it makes little difference what you believe so long as you are decent and virtuous. About the only faith he seems to demand is the one implied in the sincere effort to do the right thing."[10] Whenever the choice lay be-

8. Will Herberg, *Protestant-Catholic-Jew: An Essay in American Religious Sociology* (Garden City, NY: Doubleday Anchor, 1960; first published in 1955), pp. 38-39. It is noteworthy that Herberg had no cause, in that now-distant age, to consider either Islam or Orthodoxy as significant American faiths.

9. O'Connor parodies the Heideggerianism of Hopper, who at the time was dean of the Divinity School at Drew University: "He was a Methodist-Universalist. I gather this means that you don't drink but about theology you are as vague as possible and talk a lot about how the symbology has played out in Christianity and it's up to artists to make up a new symbology. At these things you are considered great in direct proportion to how often you can repeat the word symbology" (CW, 1179-80).

10. Robert McAfee Brown and Gustave Weigel, S.J., *An American Dialogue: A Protestant Looks at Catholicism and a Catholic Looks at Protestantism* (Garden City, NY: Doubleday Anchor,

tween vaporized liberalism and hidebound fundamentalism, O'Connor chose fundamentalism, as we shall see. She heartily agreed with the Presbyterian theologian Hugh T. Kerr, who once said that it is easier to cool down zealots than to warm up corpses.

Not only did the civil religion of the 1950s melt particularized historic faiths into a thin religious gruel; it also made even the most secular Americans into allegedly religious people. As President Dwight D. Eisenhower once declared, "Our government makes no sense . . . unless it is founded in a deeply felt religious faith — and I don't care what it is."[11] Once the substance of "faith" no longer needs to be specified, as long as it is "deeply felt," then the public atheist has no more function and virtually vanishes from the American scene. In 1954, the phrase "under God" was added to the pledge of allegiance to the American flag, making atheists such as Robert Ingersoll and Clarence Darrow and H. L. Mencken seem like irrelevant figures from the remote past. Flannery O'Connor was not alone in sensing that something had gone profoundly wrong; so did her fellow Catholic and fellow novelist Walker Percy. Writing amidst the mushrooming American religiosity of the 1950s, Percy has his narrator and protagonist Binx Bolling confess his vexation that his own groping quest for God is out of kilter with the boosterish religiosity animating the great preponderance of Americans:

> As everyone knows [declares Bolling], the polls report that 98% of Americans believe in God and the remaining 2% are atheists and agnostics — which leaves not a single percentage point for a seeker. . . . Am I, in my search, a hundred miles ahead of my fellow Americans or a hundred miles behind them? That is to say: Have 98% of Americans already found what I seek or are they so sunk in everydayness that not even the possibility of a search has occurred to them?[12]

---

1961), p. 197. Weigel's charge is reminiscent of the allegation made by the fallen Episcopal priest Thomas Marshfield, who is the narrator of John Updike's *A Month of Sundays*. Marshfield complains that Jane, his Unitarian wife, "doesn't believe in God, she believes in the Right Thing" (New York: Knopf, 1975), p. 154.

11. Herberg, p. 84. The conservative cultural critic Russell Kirk may have caught the religious essence of Eisenhower when Robert Welch, the founder of the John Birch Society, accused the president himself of being a Communist. With wicked bifrontal irony, Kirk responded that Ike was not a Communist but a golfer.

12. Walker Percy, *The Moviegoer* (New York: Farrar, Straus & Giroux, 1967; first published in 1961), p. 14.

## The Sacramental Smile of Success

Herberg makes clear that the 1950s exaltation of the "American way of life" was not a distillation of the deep commonalities lying at the heart of all three faiths.[13] Rather, it was a civil religion that, by subordinating the theological to the political, produced what Herberg calls a "secularized Puritanism, a Puritanism without transcendence, without [a] sense of sin or judgment."

> The American Way of life is individualistic, dynamic, pragmatic. It affirms the supreme value and dignity of the individual; it stresses incessant activity on his part, for he is never to rest but is always to be striving to "get ahead"; it defines an ethic of self-reliance, merit, and character, and judges by achievement: "deeds, not creeds" are what count. The American Way of Life is humanitarian, "forward-looking," optimistic. Americans are easily the most generous and philanthropic people in the world, in terms of their ready and unstinting response to suffering anywhere on the globe. The American believes in progress, in self-improvement, and quite fanatically in education. But above all, the American is idealistic. Americans cannot go on making money or achieving worldly success simply on its own merits; such "materialistic" things must, in the American mind, be justified in "higher" terms, in terms of "service" or "stewardship" or "general welfare." . . . And because they are so idealistic, Americans tend to be moralistic; they are inclined to see all issues as plain and simple, black and white, issues of morality.[14]

13. It needs to be said that the proclivity for civil religion remains alive and well in high places. Richard Rorty is perhaps the most cogent leftist defender of the procedural pluralism that our liberal polity has produced. He holds that we must all choose whatever way of life conduces to our own private happiness, so long as others are not harmed: "The only test for a political proposal is its ability to gain assent from people who retain radically diverse ideas about the point and meaning of human life, about the path to private perfection." For Rorty, we cannot be held to any moral excellence of a public kind, but only to "private perfection." Rorty's individualist civil religion requires that our first loyalty be given to the nation-state, not to what he regards as our merely private religious convictions: "The Founding Fathers . . . asked people to think of themselves not so much as Pennsylvania Quakers or Catholic Marylanders but as citizens of a tolerant, pluralistic, federal republic" (Rorty, *Philosophy and Social Hope* [New York: Penguin, 1999], pp. 173, 88).

14. Herberg, p. 79. Though the degradations of the Clinton presidency put a permanent end to old-fashioned idealistic moralism, American civil religion still has its defenders. Sixties-style liberals such as Martin Marty and Bill Moyers, Peter Berger and Arthur Schlesinger, Jr., often lament its decline. For them, the victim-group tribalism of the left and the unbridled consumerism of the right could still be remedied by a return to the humanitarian and progressive virtues that Herberg rather ironically hymns.

The first half of Herberg's statement still holds true nearly half a century after he first formulated it. American civil religion was displayed in remarkable ways in the national outpouring of care and concern for the victims of the terrorist strikes of September 11, 2001. Yet Herberg's latter claims have been severely if not completely undermined. In the consumerist ethos now engrossing American life, materialism no longer needs to be justified in high-sounding terms.[15] Old vices have become new virtues, as conspicuous extravagance and 'round-the-clock entertainment have become the rule rather than the exception. Religion itself, as James C. Edwards once put it, has become another consumer choice at the smorgasbord of the American emporium:

> In air-conditioned comfort one can stroll from life to life, from world to world, complete with appropriate sound effects (beeping computers; roaring lions). Laid out before one are whole lives that one can, if one has the necessary credit line, freely choose to inhabit: devout Christian; high-tech yuppie; Down East guide; great white hunter. This striking transformation of life into lifestyle, the way in which the tools, garments, and attitudes specific to particular times and places become commodities to be marketed to anonymous and rootless consumers: they are the natural (if also banal) expressions of our normal nihilism.[16]

The Catholic sociologist John Murray Cuddihy is perhaps our fiercest critic of what he calls this "religion of civility" that seeks to baptize the Amer-

15. Yet among certain corporate executives, the old unction is still lathered thick. Kenneth Lay, the chairman of the failed Enron Corporation — whose various malfeasances cost both the jobs and the retirement funds of 20,000 employees — offered pious justifications of his ill-gotten wealth only a few months before the collapse of his economic empire: "Excellence is one of our core values, along with respect, integrity and communication. We try to achieve excellence in everything we do. The Bible is very clear that we each need to be the best that we can be to realize our God-given potential. I use those words quite freely within Enron. I basically try to create an environment at Enron where everybody has the opportunity to realize his or her God-given potential" (Robert Darden, "Interview with Kenneth L. Lay," *The Door Magazine* 181 [May-June 2002], 7).

16. James C. Edwards, *The Plain Sense of Things: The Fate of Religion in an Age of Normal Nihilism*, quoted in Stanley Hauerwas, "Preaching as Though We Had Enemies," *First Things* 53 (May 1995): 47. The life of autonomous self-construction, it should be added, produces an anybody, a creature having either anything or nothing at its onion-like center. And as Charles Taylor makes clear, an anybody is a nobody: "This democratized self which has no necessary social identity can then be anything, can assume any role or take any point of view, because it is in and for itself nothing" (Charles Taylor, *Sources of the Self: The Making of Modern Identity* [Cambridge, MA: Harvard University Press, 1989], p. 32).

ican way of life. In the name of a saccharine tolerance, our religious civility elides real dogmatic differences, agreeing benignly to disagree about crucial matters, thus covering a multitude of incompatibilities with an oleaginous ecumenicity. Cuddihy notes that even Catholics and Jews have been suborned to "the Protestant Etiquette," as he wittily names it. This code of civility denies all radical and exclusive claims to religious finality, turning authoritative revelation and tradition into pluralist and individualist "choices." Religious belief becomes essentially a private matter that should give no public offense. Cuddihy cites Philip Rieff on the chief social effect of our regnant civil religion: it freezes American faces in the smile of sociability and success. "In that wide, ever-ready smile," Cuddihy quotes Rieff, "the abundance of America may be said to be transubstantiated into the personality of the American."[17] Yet this sacramental smile turns out to be oddly aggressive: it demands a smile in return.

Flannery O'Connor was not often pictured smiling. In her famous self-portrait, she stares out at the world with the sternness of a prophet. She saw that, once the American virtues of self-reliance and hard-work and self-discipline are abstracted from their particular historical communities, their particular narrative traditions, their particular religious practices, they do worse than fail: they succeed as the false god of civil religion, the deity to which the churches must bow down in obeisance. The laudable call for religious cooperation in stanching bigotry had dangerous if largely undetected implications. It meant that God's act in Israel and Christ and the church was no longer understood as the unique and decisive provision for the world's salvation, but rather as but one among several religious buttresses for "democratic spiritual values." What matters is that we must all dwell together (as Herberg notes) "in a pluralistic harmony that is felt to be somehow the texture of American life."[18]

## Dogma as the Penetration of Mystery

O'Connor was as impatient with the glib sophistication of the elite as with the slick purveyors of American civil religion. That she would not conform to the new secular Puritanism at work in high literary circles became evident at a New York party hosted by the poet Robert Lowell and his future wife

17. John Murray Cuddihy, *No Offense: Civil Religion and Protestant Taste* (New York: Seabury, 1978), p. 5.
18. Herberg, p. 86.

Elizabeth Hardwick. It was a dinner at which the novelist Mary McCarthy, who would later proclaim her emancipation from the church in *Memories of a Catholic Girlhood*,[19] opined that she still found the symbolism of the Eucharist to be useful for her fiction, though of course she didn't believe a word of its hocus-pocus. The ordinarily quiet and unassertive O'Connor — who rarely spoke to strangers unless first addressed, and then only with a shy hesitance — made a notoriously acid reply: "Well, if it's a symbol, to hell with it" (CW, 977). The response by the other dinner guests must have been similar to what William F. Buckley described many years later. If you mention God at a New York dinner party, said Buckley, you get stared at; but if you mention God twice, you're not invited back. There is little doubt that these New York literati regarded O'Connor as a fundamentalist Catholic, and they had considerable cause.

For O'Connor, unlike advocates of the civil religion that was aborning in the 1950s and that would triumph by the end of the century, dogma was a salutary rather than a pejorative term. Thus did she make her upper-case confession: "My stories have been watered and fed by Dogma" (CW, 930). She rejected the common view that dogmas divide while ethics unite ("deeds, not creeds"), since doctrines are supposedly focused on esoteric matters, and thus are not amenable to practical use. O'Connor declared, quite to the contrary, that they are compressed narrative summaries of God's self-identification in Israel and Christ; they are vehicles "of freedom and not of restriction" (CW, 943). "Dogma is an instrument for penetrating reality," O'Connor insisted. On another occasion she added that "Christian dogma is about the only thing left in the world that surely guards and respects mystery" (MM, 178).

O'Connor did not make mystery a synonym for puzzle or riddle or conundrum, those things that balk the mind and stifle understanding. Nor was it a convenient locution for vaguely spiritual concerns. "To St. Paul and to the

19. McCarthy is thankful for little else about her native Catholicism than that it offered her a sense of beauty: "Our ugly church and parochial school provided me with my only aesthetic outlet, in the words of the Mass and the litanies and the old Latin hymns, in the Easter lilies around the altar, rosaries, ornamented prayer books, votive lamps, holy cards stamped in gold and decorated with flower wreaths and a saint's picture." But she laments the moral complacency that lured so splendid a sinner as herself: "From what I have seen, I am driven to the conclusion that religion is only good for good people. . . . Only good people can afford to be religious. For others, it is too great a temptation — a temptation to the deadly sins of pride and anger, chiefly, but one might also add sloth. . . . The Catholic religion, I believe, is the most dangerous of all, morally . . . because, with its claim to be the only true religion, it fosters . . . the notion that not everyone is lucky enough to be a Catholic" (*Memories of a Catholic Girlhood* [Harmondsworth, UK: Penguin, 1963], pp. 20, 24).

early Christian thinkers," writes one of her favorite Old Testament scholars, Claude Tresmontant, mystery is on the contrary "the particular object of intelligence, its fullest nourishment. The *mysterion* is something so rich in intelligible content, so inexhaustibly full of delectation for the mind that no contemplation can ever reach its end. It is an eternal delectation of the mind."[20] The more deeply we penetrate mystery, the greater our ignorance grows. "Mystery isn't something that is gradually evaporating," O'Connor wrote to Alfred Corn. "It grows along with knowledge" (HB, 489). Kallistos Ware, a bishop in the Greek Orthodox Church, elaborates this same Christian understanding of dogma and mystery as the ultimate means of knowledge:

> In the proper religious sense of the term, "mystery" signifies not only hiddenness but disclosure. The Greek noun *mysterion* [which can also be translated "sacrament"] is linked with the verb *myein*, meaning "to close the eyes or mouth." The candidate for initiation into certain of the pagan mystery religions was first blindfolded and led through a maze of passages; then suddenly his eyes were uncovered and he saw, displayed all round him, the secret emblems of the cult. So, in the Christian context, we do not mean by a "mystery" merely that which is baffling and mysterious, an enigma or insoluble problem. A mystery is, on the contrary, something that is revealed for our understanding, but which we never understand exhaustively because it leads into the depth or the darkness of God. The eyes are closed — but they are also opened.[21]

## The Life of Drastic Religious Discipline

O'Connor's open-eyed praise for Protestant fundamentalists entailed no slackening of her taut Catholicism. On the contrary, her fidelity to Catholic dogma also nourished her Catholic determination to live a disciplined religious life. It was no sacrifice of her intellect to honor the Vatican's Index of Forbidden Books, for she believed obedience to be a virtue not meant only

20. Quoted by John Desmond, *Risen Sons: Flannery O'Connor's Vision of History* (Athens, GA: University of Georgia Press, 1987), p. 9.

21. Bishop Kallistos Ware, *The Orthodox Way*, rev. ed. (Crestwood, NY: St. Vladimir's Seminary Press, 1995), p. 15. Hans Urs von Balthasar constantly recurs to the formula of the Fourth Lateran Council (1215) concerning the mystery of likeness and unlikeness of earthly things to God: "the ever-greater dissimilarity to God no matter how great the similarity" (quoted in Francesca Murphy, *Christ the Form of Beauty: A Study of Theology and Literature* [Edinburgh: T&T Clark, 1995], p. 133).

for monks.[22] Yet she did ask her confessor for a special dispensation to read Camus and Sartre, fearing that the Protestant members of her monthly book club would regard her Catholic faith as too frail to withstand atheist opposition. O'Connor was also diligent about observing meatless Fridays in reverence for the Crucifixion. Her days began with early mass when it was available and she was mobile. Even after she was largely confined to the farmhouse outside her rural Georgia home, O'Connor often attended the service of Benediction of the Blessed Sacrament at her parish church. Her days ended with prayers from her bedside missal, as she made her confessions and petitions in consort with the church universal, guarding against any sentimental focus on her own selfish needs, exigent though they were. Her deeply communal faith prompted her practice of private prayer. Though O'Connor admitted that her orisons often seemed to rise no higher than the ceiling, she wasn't deterred from praying them. They were not matters of religious feeling but of Christian discipline.

O'Connor's disciplined life included an immersion in the chief works of Catholic tradition. To have an uninformed Christian mind was, to her, an oxymoronic sin that no intelligent believer should commit. Her library was a virtual compendium of pre-Vatican II theologians and writers: Romano Guardini and Jacques Maritain, Etienne Gilson and Teilhard de Chardin, Gabriel Marcel and Leon Bloy and Charles Peguy, Martin D'Arcy and Christopher Dawson and Eric Voegelin. O'Connor was also an enthusiast for the burgeoning Catholic biblical scholarship of the 1950s. She carefully read and favorably reviewed the work of such biblical pioneers as Bruce Vawter, John McKenzie, and Claude Tresmontant. She was also a shrewd critic of fiction produced by modern Catholic writers: Georges Bernanos and François Mauriac, Graham Greene and Evelyn Waugh, J. F. Powers and Caroline Gordon.[23] Yet O'Connor hardly confined her reading to works by fellow Catholics, determined as she was to encounter modernity on its own terms. With both care and insight, therefore, she attended to such non-Catholic

---

22. She drolly added, however, that there should be a reverse Index of Required Books (*"The Presence of Grace,"* p. 146).

23. Far from being uncritical of fellow Catholic writers, O'Connor objected to *The Diary of a Country Priest* as "only a slight framework of [a] novel to hang Bernanos' religious reflections on" (HB, 304). She also anticipated the turn Graham Greene would later take toward his self-confessed "Catholic atheism." She scored his play *The Potting Shed* for juxtaposing outrageous decadence with equally outrageous saintliness, as if the union of total opposites somehow constituted truthfulness: "What [Greene] does, I think, is try to make religion respectable to the modern unbeliever by making it seedy. He succeeds so well in making it seedy that then he has to save it by the miracle" (HB, 201).

theologians and scholars as Martin Buber and Mircea Eliade, Reinhold Niebuhr and Carl Jung, Paul Tillich and Karl Barth. She lamented the sorry state of Catholic theology in America, confessing that "we have very few thinkers to equal Barth and Tillich, perhaps none" (HB, 306).[24] Among modern literary masters whom O'Connor herself mastered — none of them being Christian in any orthodox sense — the most prominent were Hawthorne and Poe, Conrad and James, Faulkner and Joyce. She was also drawn to the experimental fiction of such atheists as Nathanael West and John Hawkes rather than the conventionally Catholic novels of Paul Horgan.

Though O'Connor was determined to cultivate a tough-minded faith by engaging the most rigorous secular minds no less than thoughtful fellow Christians, she learned most from the visionary writers and saints of her own tradition. She delved deeply into the masters of the mystical tradition, especially Anthony and the Desert Fathers, Teresa of Avila and John of the Cross, the two Catherines — of Genoa and Siena — as well as her own contemporary, Thomas Merton.[25] The saints whom she admired most were Thérèse of Lisieux and Francis de Sales, the former for her simplicity, the latter for his practicality. She also read the chief interpreters of Christian mysticism, especially Evelyn Underhill and Baron von Hügel. During the fourteen years of her illness, as she moved ever more consciously toward death, O'Connor formed the habit of reading Thomas Aquinas twenty minutes before bed each night.

She found St. Thomas's definition of art as "reason in making" (MM, 82) to be especially astringent and bracing. To link imagination with reason is to free the artist from merely personal and subjective concerns. A faith centered on the confession and redemption of sin serves as a restraint on self-indulgent art. "Self-knowledge," she declared, "is a great curb to irresponsible self-expression, for to know oneself is, above all, to know what one lacks."[26] O'Connor also found that the Christian life of self-denial reinforced her artistic self-discipline. "There seem to be other conditions in life," she confessed, "that demand celibacy besides the priesthood" (HB, 176). Just as the celibate

---

24. Walter Ong and William Lynch, who focused their theological work largely on literary matters, were two American Catholic thinkers whose work she praised.

25. Merton wrote a memorable tribute to O'Connor upon her death: "When I read Flannery O'Connor, I do not think of Hemingway, or Katherine Anne Porter, or Sartre, but rather of someone like Sophocles. What more can you say of a writer? I write her name with honor, for all the truth and all the craft with which she shows man's fall and his dishonor" (*Raids on the Unspeakable* [New York: The Abbey of Gethsemani, 1966], p. 42).

26. Quoted in Henry T. Edmonson III, *Return to Good and Evil: Flannery O'Connor's Response to Nihilism* (Lanham, MD: Lexington Books, 2002), p. 169.

surrenders married love for nonexclusive friendships — having many spiritual spouses and producing many spiritual progeny — so did O'Connor find a wondrous congruity between rigorous belief and rigorous art: "I never completely forget myself except when I am writing and I am never more completely myself than when I am writing" (HB, 458).

## Art and Faith: Congruent Ways of Seeing

Rather than turning inward in indulgent self-exploration, O'Connor believed that the writer is called to cultivate a Conradian vision focused on everything that is radically other:

> The artist uses his reason to discover an answering reason in everything he sees. For him, to be reasonable is to find, in the object, in the situation, in the sequence, the spirit which makes it itself. This is not an easy or simple thing to do. It is to intrude upon the timeless, and that is done only by the violence of a single-minded respect for the truth. (MM, 82-83)

Long before the postmodernists vanquished the Enlightenment chimera of unlensed seeing and ungrounded truth, O'Connor knew her faith to be the basis of her vision. "It is popular," she observed, "to believe that in order to see clearly one must believe nothing." The true order, as she discerned, is the other way around: "For the fiction writer, to believe nothing is to see nothing."[27] "If I were not a Catholic," O'Connor confessed, "I would have no reason to write, no reason to see, no reason ever to feel horrified or even to enjoy anything." Her prophetic angle of vision enabled her to see in modern life those grotesque distortions of truth that pass as normal and acceptable. She became our great satiric master of the grotesque, not in order to flee from the truth but to limn it more precisely.

That O'Connor saw more than she was able either to say in her fiction or to demonstrate in her life was sometimes troubling to her. She was encouraged, therefore, by St. Thomas's claim that the making of art does not require total rectitude of the appetites. It was no contradiction, Thomas demonstrated, to produce artistic work that was morally superior to one's own life. Jacques Maritain gave O'Connor almost comic relief in his interpretation of Aquinas on art as a virtue of the practical intellect:

27. Quoted in Edmonson, p. 19.

In contradistinction to prudence, which is also a perfection of the practical intellect, art is concerned with the good of the work, not with the good of man. The ancients took pleasure in laying stress on this difference, in their thorough-going comparison of art and prudence. If only he contrives a good piece of woodwork or jewelwork, the fact of a craftsman's being spiteful or debauched is immaterial, just as it is immaterial for a geometer to be a jealous or wicked man, if only his demonstrations provide us with geometrical truth. . . . Oscar Wilde was but a good Thomist when he wrote: "The fact of a man being a poisoner is nothing against his prose."[28]

The function of art is to move its beholders not to moral action but to a sense of wonder and mystery at the excellence of the artifact. Such visionary beauty may in fact produce moral and religious insight — for the good of a literary artifact must include its truthfulness concerning the human condition — and such wisdom may indeed issue in praiseworthy acts. But this is its ancillary, not its primary, purpose. The medievals thus distinguished between the craftsmanship that goes into the making of a thing (*ars artefaciens*) and the result the crafted thing produces (*ars artefacta*). Etienne Gilson puts the matter clearly:

> The perfect artist is not he who puts the highest art at the service of the highest truth [which is the first principle, being itself], but he who puts the highest truth at the service of the most perfect art. It simply follows from this that art is not the highest of the activities of man. Still it is one of them, and no other can take its place. If art is the making of beauty for beauty's own sake, there is no imaginable substitute for it.[29]

The conviction that art is hugely but not absolutely important freed Flannery O'Connor from an overseriousness about her own craft. It enabled her to be playful even about St. Thomas himself. She called herself "a hillbilly Thomist" (HB, 81), perhaps because she thoroughly approved Thomas's use of a red-hot poker to rout a prostitute whom his brothers had sent to his

28. Jacques Maritain, *Creative Intuition in Art and Poetry* (New York: Meridian, 1961; first published in 1953), p. 36.

29. Etienne Gilson, *The Arts of the Beautiful* (Chicago: Dalkey Archive Press, 2000; first published in 1965), pp. 15-16. A less abstract defense of the blessed "uselessness" of art is to be found in W. H. Auden's *The Dyer's Hand and Other Essays* (New York: Random House, 1962). For an elevation of craftsmanship over the moral life of the craftsman, see Dorothy L. Sayers's fine chancel-drama *The Zeal of Thy House.*

room in the hope that her charms might dissuade him from becoming a Dominican. Thomas's *sed contra* method of answering his opponents also provided O'Connor a means for dealing with her sometimes domineering mother, Regina Cline O'Connor. If she had insisted that her daughter turn off the light because the night was growing late, Flannery imagined her ideal response: "I with lifted finger and broad bland beatific expression, would reply, 'On the contrary, I answer that the light, being eternal and limitless, cannot be turned off. Shut your eyes,' or some such thing." O'Connor's affection for the medieval doctor was as fond as it was deep: "I feel I can personally guarantee that St. Thomas loved God because for the life of me I cannot help loving St. Thomas" (CW, 945).

Like Aquinas, O'Connor was a virtual mystic of the mass. In "A Temple of the Holy Ghost," she has two pubescent Catholic school girls sing St. Thomas's sublime Eucharistic hymn in order to mock the saccharine gospel songs sung by two preacher-boys named Cory and Wendell Wilkens. When Wendell dismisses the *Tantum ergo Sacramentum* as "Jew singing," the proud little girl who is the story's protagonist finds herself terribly unamused: "You big dumb ox!" she shouted. "You big dumb Church of God ox" (CW, 202). Unbeknownst to the girl, this is also the epithet thrown at the ungainly and slow-speaking Aquinas — the dumb ox. His teacher, Albertus Magnus, said of his allegedly bovine student, "When this ox roars, the whole world will listen." Listening carefully seven hundred years later, O'Connor was not moved by the aesthetic appeal of the mass — by its musical rendering or its architectural setting — but by its sheer objective truth. "Mass could be said out of a suitcase in a furnace room," she declared, "and the same sacrifice would take place" (CW, 1085). The mass was no means of escape, for O'Connor, into some longed-for future bliss; it was the heavenly banquet that irrupts into earthly life, overturning the false sovereignties of this world and reordering them truly to the love of God. She was reacting not from pride but humility, therefore, when she sternly reminded the cultured ex-Catholic Mary McCarthy that the Eucharist is not a convenient literary symbol but the one indestructible reality: "That was all the defense I was capable of but I realize now that this is all I will ever be able to say about it, outside of a story, except that it is the center of existence for me; all the rest of life is expendable" (CW, 977).

## A Roman Catholic Not Like a Baptist or Methodist but Like an Atheist

"Wherever virtue observes the mean, it is possible to sin by excess as well as by deficiency. But there is no sinning by excess against God, Who is the object of theological virtue . . . so that never can we love God as much as He ought to be loved, nor believe and hope in Him as much as we should." So writes Aquinas toward the end of his *Summa Theologica*. Peter Kreeft offers a comment on this passage that applies equally well to Flannery O'Connor: "Here St. Thomas breaks out of the Greek, classical, finite mold to a Christian 'extremism.'"[30] That there can be no excessive love of God might well serve as the motto for O'Connor's life and work. The love of both God and neighbor — the second commandment always being inseparable from the first — is by necessity drastic, radical, immoderate. Her fiction is fierce and violent because it seeks to show what it is like for her characters, if only at the last minute, to love God absolutely. Her work also demonstrates what it is like to ignore or scorn God absolutely, seeking substitutes in various Laodicean moderations. Total faith and total unbelief: these were for her the only alternatives.

O'Connor had little patience with "mass" Catholics who receive the weekly sacrament without its making any discernible difference in their lives. "The Church for them," she wrote, "is not the body of Christ but the poor man's insurance system."[31] When once asked what kind of Christian she would become if she were not a Roman Catholic, she replied, far from jestingly, that she would join a Pentecostal Holiness church. Belief for Flannery O'Connor must be radical or it is not belief at all. Faith is not another item in the laundry list of one's loyalties: it is all or nothing at all. Thus did she confess that she was "a Catholic (not because it's advantageous to my writing but because I was born and brought up one) and at some point in my life I realized that not only was I a Catholic but that this was all I was, that I was a Catholic not like someone else would be a Baptist or a Methodist but like someone else would be an atheist" (CW, 930).[32] O'Connor had no patience for a merely

30. The sentences are from I-II, 64.4, and the comment is found in Peter Kreeft, ed., *A Summa of the "Summa"* (San Francisco: Ignatius, 1990), pp. 472-73, n. 214.

31. Quoted by William Sessions, "'Then I discovered the Germans': O'Connor's Encounter with Guardini and German Thinkers," unpublished essay.

32. Here, as in so many other things, O'Connor stands near to Walker Percy. Anyone living in an age as morally and religiously intolerable as ours, said Percy, has the right to demand "a gift commensurate with the offense": "This life is much too much trouble, far too strange, to arrive at the end of it and then be asked what you make of it and have to answer, 'Scientific humanism.' That won't do. A poor show. Life is a mystery, love is a delight. Therefore, I take it as

polite piety. She admired Camus and Sartre and Nietzsche because they took God seriously enough to deny his reality. O'Connor's God-botherers resemble an atheist in a Peter De Vries novel who cannot forgive God for not existing. Yet O'Connor's atheists, whether Christian or secular, are usually unable to elude the divine Pursuer. They blessedly fail to escape the etymological paradox wittily voiced by Chesterton: "If there were no God, there would be no atheists." Without the *Theos,* those who are *a-theos* would have nothing to set over against themselves, nothing to reject and deny.

Though she was a convinced rather than a conventional believer, there was never anything triumphalist about O'Connor's Catholicism. As we have seen, she lamented the suffering that the church inflicts on those who are most committed to its faith. O'Connor often took umbrage at the Catholic piety of her day — a complaint no less legitimately aimed at contemporary Protestant piety — because of its smarmy sentimentality and its close-minded scorn for the intellect. Since for O'Connor the church is the one universal community of God, she objected to the insularity that ethnic celebrations encourage. She derided diocesan newspaper accounts of St. Patrick's Day parades, for example, calling them "the kind of literature I approve of burning" (HB, 150). She lashed out at her own priest when he festooned the altar with green carnations in honor of Ireland's patron saint. She also ridiculed the pastor's sermons for being "full of such locutions as, 'as the Irishman said.'" Neither did O'Connor find herself at ease with such traditional spiritual practices as novenas, rosaries, and prayers of the saints: "I hate to say most of these prayers written by saints-in-an-emotional-state. You feel you are wearing somebody else's finery and I can never describe my heart as 'burning' to the Lord (who knows better) without snickering" (HB, 145). Far from having hearts aflame with holiness, O'Connor's characters remain so adamant and recalcitrant that the work of the Spirit must first of all be incendiary, as the girl-evangelist proclaims in *The Violent Bear It Away:* "The Word of God is a burning Word to burn you clean, burns man and child, man and child the same, you people! Be saved in the Lord's fire or perish in your own!" (CW, 415). O'Connor found such a purging fire in the one service and the one book that contain not an iota of false sentiment: "The only places you can really avoid the Pious Style are in the liturgy and in the Bible; and these are the places where the Church herself speaks" (HB, 370).

---

axiomatic that one should settle for nothing less than the infinite mystery and the infinite delight; i.e., God. In fact, I demand it. I refuse to settle for anything less. I don't see why anyone should settle for anything less than Jacob, who actually grabbed aholt of God and wouldn't let go until God identified himself and blessed him" ("Questions They Never Asked Me," in *Signposts in a Strange Land,* ed. Patrick Samway [New York: Farrar, Straus & Giroux, 1991], p. 417).

Because saccharine piety produces dry-rot minds, O'Connor had a short fuse for Catholic anti-intellectualism. When the editors of the Catholic journal *Cross Currents* suggested that it be used for small-group discussions, O'Connor replied tartly that "the use of the mind is seldom encouraged in parish activities."[33] She was also concerned about Catholics who would not read novels that depict the harsh realities of modern life: "Not enough Catholics read good fiction. To write for a Catholic audience would mean that the writer would either 1) have to write down, or 2) starve to death. Neither is advisable."[34] O'Connor was appalled that several of her friends had left the church because of its intellectual dishonesty: "I wish we would hear more preaching about the harm we do from the things we do not face and from all the questions that we give Instant Answers to. None of these poor children want Instant Answers and they are right" (HB, 309). "We [Catholics] judge," she confessed to Sister Mariella Gable, "before we experience and never trust our faith to be subjected to reality, because it is not strong enough. And maybe in this we are wise" (CW, 1183).

Yet O'Connor did not expect Catholic bishops to become eminent literary men. When Caroline Gordon and Allen Tate criticized Cardinal Spellman of New York for publishing such maudlin works as *The Foundling*, O'Connor wittily replied, "If he wrote good novels, I'd be worried about the Church" (HB, 588).[35] O'Connor's many complaints about the unfaithfulness of the church were finely expressed by the French Catholic writer Georges Bernanos: "The Church is something alive, a force at work; but many pious people seem to believe, or pretend to believe, that she is simply a shelter, a place of refuge, a sort of spiritual hotel by the roadside from which they can have the pleasure of watching the passers-by."[36] She offered her own summary complaint to Betty Hester: "Smugness is the Great Catholic Sin." Lest she herself seem to be dwelling in a rock fortress of righteousness, casting stones at the glass houses of those who were less faithful, O'Connor quickly added: "I find it in myself and don't dislike it any less" (HB, 131).

---

33. *"The Presence of Grace,"* p. 113.

34. Rosemary M. Magee, ed., *Conversations with Flannery O'Connor* (Jackson, MS: University Press of Mississippi, 1987), p. 14.

35. Yet O'Connor was hardly cheered to learn that, when the eminent French Catholic writer François Mauriac was seated next to Cardinal Spellman on some official occasion, Mauriac "felt that he would have had more spiritual kinship with the Dalai Lama" (HB, 357).

36. Quoted by Jane Hannon, "The Wide World Her Parish: O'Connor's All-Embracing Vision of Church," *Flannery O'Connor Bulletin* 24 (1995-96): 13. I have used Hannon's fine essay as my guide to O'Connor's criticisms of American Catholicism.

## The Christ-Haunted South

O'Connor turned to the fundamentalists of her own place and time as the chief subject of her fiction, offering them as a corrective to the smugness of Catholic ecclesialism and the blandness of Protestant liberalism.[37] She risked gross misunderstanding, of course, in allying herself with these retrograde believers from a retrograde region. In fact, the early reviewers of her work, secular and Catholic alike, read her fictional portraits of religious fanatics as a satirical attack on fundamentalism. They saw her as a modern-day Mencken, deriding Southern religion for its foolish and over-heated religiosity.[38] For O'Connor, on the contrary, the South was to be admired for the same reason that Mencken despised it: for its branch-head proclaimers and wool-hat testifiers to the Truth, for its apocalyptic signs abjuring all and sundry to "GET RIGHT WITH GOD," and asking, "DOES SATAN HAVE YOU IN HIS POWER? REPENT OR BURN IN HELL. JESUS SAVES."[39] O'Connor admired these uncouth markers of an unapologetic Christianity. She knew, of course, that the fundamentalists did not return her regard. They had long since dismissed her Catholicism as the popish and monkish anti-Christ, the enemy and persecutor of the true church. Because Catholics venerate the Vir-

37. O'Connor admired old-fashioned Southern fundamentalists, the kind who were poor and marginalized, derided and passed-over, not the new-fangled kind who have grown materially prosperous and politically powerful, who influence the outcome of presidential elections, and who dominate the nation's largest Protestant body, the Southern Baptist Convention. These latter-day fundamentalists lost their authenticity, as Stanley Hauerwas observes, when Texas preachers became indistinguishable from Texas politicians. O'Connor's attitude toward fundamentalists was voiced, at least in part, by Donald Davidson, an Agrarian who was not in fact a Christian — though of course she would have rejected his condescending adjective "poetic":

> Fundamentalism, in one aspect, is blind and belligerent ignorance; in another, it represents a fierce clinging to poetic supernaturalism against the encroachments of cold logic; it stands for moral seriousness. The Southerner should hesitate to scorn these qualities, for, however much they may now be perverted to bigoted and unfruitful uses, they belong to the bone and sinew of his nature as they once belonged to Milton, who was both Puritan and Cavalier. To obscure them by a show of sophistication is to play the coward; to give them a positive transmutation is the highest function of art.

Quoted in Peter A. Huff, *Allen Tate and the Catholic Revival: Trace of the Fugitive Gods* (Mahwah, NJ: Paulist, 1996), 40.

38. The *Time* reviewer of *The Violent Bear It Away* interpreted "her handling of God-drunk backwoodsmen" as "the secure believer poking bitter fun at the confused and bedeviled" ("God-Intoxicated Hillbillies," *Time* LXXV [February 29, 1960]: 121).

39. The latter admonition actually appears in O'Connor's story "The Lame Shall Enter First" (CW, 600-601).

gin Mary, it is easy for fundamentalists to regard the Roman church as the whore of Rome described in the book of Revelation, the strumpet astride a scarlet beast, upon whose "forehead was written a name, MYSTERY, BABYLON THE GREAT, THE MOTHER OF HARLOTS AND ABOMINATIONS OF THE EARTH" (Rev. 17:5).[40]

Such spite mattered little to Flannery O'Connor. She saw that Southern fundamentalists held fast to twin realities often abandoned by Christians and secularists alike: an unembarrassed supernaturalism on the one hand, and a deep veneration of Holy Scripture on the other. After the debacle of the Scopes trial in 1925, it became fashionable to dismiss fundamentalists as Southern rubes and obscurantists, even though the origins of fundamentalism had been Northern, urban, and intellectual, not Southern, rural, and revivalist.[41] Yet O'Connor shrewdly discerned the deep religious concerns that lay hidden beneath the vulgar kind of anti-evolutionism to which fundamentalists often descended, as when William Jennings Bryan famously said that "it is better to trust the Rock of Ages than to know the age of rocks." Fundamentalists of a more thoughtful stripe than Bryan discerned that evolutionary theory presents a threat not only to a literal reading of Genesis but also to an affirmation of the purpose and order of the cosmos itself. Hence the valid question put by Charles Hodge, an Old School Presbyterian, in his 1874 book *What Is Darwinism?*: "Is [evolutionary] development an intellectual process guided by God, or is it a blind process of unintelligible, unconscious force, which knows no end and adopts no means?"[42]

Protestant liberals, following the lead of Friedrich Schleiermacher and Albrecht Ritschl, sought to avoid the tension between the natural and the supernatural by declaring a truce between biology and theology. They came to regard faith and science not as opposed but as autonomous, nonintersecting realms. George Marsden explains their mediating position: "Religion would

40. All Bible quotations are from the King James Version, since it is the only translation that O'Connor's characters would have accepted as authoritative, especially after the "heretical" Revised Standard Version was published in 1952.

41. James Moore demonstrates that many nineteenth-century Christian critics of Darwinism offered objections that were more scientific than biblical. They were not worried about Adam and Eve's having descended from apes so much as about Darwin's abandonment of the Baconian method of induction, which insisted on complete factual certainty about all scientific hypotheses. To Louis Agassiz and John William Dawson and Charles Hodge, Darwin was a mere probabilist who failed to account factually for the gaps between the species and thus for the ascending forms that culminate in humankind. (See James R. Moore, *The Post-Darwinian Controversies: A Study of the Protestant Struggle to Come to Terms with Darwin in Great Britain and America, 1870-1900* [New York: Cambridge University Press, 1979], pp. 213-16.)

42. Quoted in Marsden, *Fundamentalism and American Culture*, p. 19.

no longer be seen as dependent on historical or scientific fact susceptible of objective inquiry; religion had to do with the spiritual, with the heart, with religious experience, and with moral sense or moral action."[43] Fundamentalists steadfastly refused this inward retreat into the realm of the experiencing subject, and so did Flannery O'Connor. At one time, in fact, she became enamored of Teilhard de Chardin's attempt to unite evolutionary naturalism with Christian faith, but she developed grave misgivings about it and finally rejected it.[44]

Though she agreed with St. Thomas that faith and science cannot ultimately conflict, O'Connor also wanted to integrate the two spheres in ways that do not cancel the miracle of God's self-identification in Israel and Jesus Christ and the church. And because she suffered from the wasting illness lupus, she sought to understand providence in ways that could account for her disease in terms other than divine intention or biological chance. The issue at stake is not only the primal origin of the cosmos but also its final direction and purpose — its teleology. Alvin Plantinga makes clear the antiteleological assumptions undergirding evolutionary naturalism:

> There is no such person as God (no all-powerful, all-knowing, and wholly good person who has created the world and has created human beings in his image), nor anything at all like God. . . . The living world with all its beauty and wonder, all of its marvelous and ingenious design, was . . . produced by blind, unconscious, mechanical, algorithmic processes. . . . Mind, intelligence, foresight, planning, design are all latecomers in the universe, themselves created by the mindless process of natural selection.[45]

## A Bible-Rooted Faith

In O'Connor's *The Violent Bear It Away*, the fundamentalist prophet Mason Tarwater gives his grandnephew an antinaturalist and thoroughly teleological education, though of course he wouldn't have recognized such ponderous adjectives: "His uncle had taught him Figures, Reading, Writ-

43. Marsden, p. 20.

44. I have recounted the story of her gradually altered regard for Teilhard in "The Heterodoxy of Flannery O'Connor's Book Reviews," *Flannery O'Connor Bulletin* 5 (1976): 3-29.

45. Alvin Plantinga, "Dennett's Dangerous Idea," *Books & Culture* (May-June 1996): 16.

ing, and History beginning with Adam expelled from the Garden and going on down through the presidents to Herbert Hoover and on in speculation toward the Second Coming and the Day of Judgment. . . . [T]he companions of his spirit [were] Abel and Enoch and Noah and Job, Abraham and Moses, King David and Solomon, and all the prophets, from Elijah who escaped death, to John whose severed head struck terror from a dish" (CW, 331, 340). Young Tarwater has been given biblical lenses that, no matter how furiously he seeks to smash them, enable him to descry the universe aright. His education forms him both morally and teleologically, for he can discern both the origin and aim not only of his own life but of the entire cosmos.

As Tarwater's primitive version of home-schooling indicates, O'Connor honored the fundamentalists' high regard for the Bible. "Scratch an Episcopalian," O'Connor tartly remarked, "and you're liable to find most anything" (HB, 259).[46] That fundamentalists have scorned all historical criticism of Scripture was of no great moment to her. After all, none of the central Christian claims — Virgin Birth and Incarnation, Atonement and Resurrection, Ascension and Second Coming — can be scientifically or historically verified.[47] That Southern fundamentalists care more for biblical doctrines than empirical evidence placed them, in her view, nearer to her own Catholicism than to liberal Protestantism. She was not alone in this estimate. Abraham Kuyper and J. Gresham Machen, two eminent Calvinists, also discerned the odd kinship between Roman Catholicism and Reformed Protestantism. In his Stone Lectures at Princeton University in 1898, Kuyper declared that Dutch Calvinists like himself "have in common with Rome

46. Suzanne Britt Jordan suggests a nice corollary to O'Connor's saying: "Scratch a Baptist, and you will find the inerrant word of God, or worse" (*Show and Tell* [Raleigh, NC: Morning Owl, 1983], p. 10).

47. Once again, O'Connor was far in advance of her times. Recent biblical scholarship has begun to question the crippling effect of historical criticism on the life of the church. Scripture scholars are admitting that there is a cribbed circularity confining traditional higher criticism: it can verify only the empirically verifiable. From at least Augustine forward, the church's chief biblical interpreters have insisted, on the contrary, that to discern the significance of an event is not to establish its factual occurrence so much as to determine its religious meaning. This task requires, in turn, a metaphysics that can detect the subtle but deep junctures of the divine and the human. Three recent books that take this latter approach are Roy A. Harrisville and Walter Sundberg, *The Bible in Modern Culture: Baruch Spinoza to Brevard Childs*, rev. ed. (Grand Rapids, MI: Eerdmans, 2002); Paul S. Minear, *The Bible and the Historian: Breaking the Silence About God in Biblical Studies* (Nashville: Abingdon 2002); and Luke Timothy Johnson and William S. Kurz, S.J., *The Future of Catholic Biblical Scholarship: A Constructive Conversation* (Grand Rapids, MI: Eerdmans, 2002).

precisely those fundamentals of the Christian creed now most fiercely assaulted by the modern spirit." Machen, who in 1929 helped found Westminster Theological Seminary in protest against the liberalism of his colleagues at Princeton, confessed his admiration of the Roman church's "maintenance of the authority of Holy Scripture" and "its acceptance of the great early creeds."[48]

O'Connor honored the Bible-centered faith of fundamentalists because, as we have seen, it gave them a storytelling cast of mind. Stories were not for her mere devices for entertainment; they were vehicles of moral and religious truth. Whereas Catholics have the teachings of the church to guide their behavior, Southern Protestants have the biblical narratives as the mirror wherewith to measure themselves and their world. These character-laden stories were greatly superior, in her view, to propositional abstractions. When O'Connor heard the old canard that Northerners discuss ideas while Southerners merely tell stories, she replied starchily that this narrative habit of discourse proves the innate superiority of the Southern mind. It was also the basis, she felt, for the flowering of Southern literature during the twentieth century:

> It takes a story to make a story. It takes a story of mythic dimensions; one which belongs to everybody; one in which everybody is able to recognize the hand of God and imagine its descent upon himself. In the Protestant South the Scriptures fill this role. The ancient Hebrew genius for making the absolute concrete has conditioned the Southerner's way of looking at things. That is one of the big reasons why the South is a story-telling section at all. (CW, 858-59)

A sweated, Bible-rooted faith that takes the God of the gospel with utmost seriousness was, for O'Connor, ever so much more desirable than the standard kinds of unbelief — a suave secularity or a smug religiosity. Hence her justifiably celebrated praise of the South as a region that, while hardly Christ-centered, "is most certainly Christ-haunted" (CW, 861). This is far from a comforting claim. It fills denizens of the region with fear and trembling: "The Southerner . . . is very much afraid," she added, "that he may have been formed in the image and likeness of God" (CW, 818). O'Connor also worried that the South was exorcising this figure of the ragged Nazarene who swings from limb to limb in the back of the Southern

---

48. Quoted by J. Daryl Charles, "Heroes or Heretics?" *Regeneration Quarterly* 1.1 (Winter 1995): 26-27.

mind.[49] Yet she remained confident that he cannot be banished: "Ghosts can be very fierce and instructive. They cast strange shadows, particularly in our literature, for it is the business of the artist to reveal what haunts us" (CW, 861). There is no denying that the large and startling figures that lurk in O'Connor's fiction have fundamentalist origins:

> The Catholic novelist in the South is forced to follow the spirit into strange places and to recognize it in many forms not totally congenial to him. His interests and sympathies may very well go, as I find my own do, directly to those aspects of Southern life where the religious feeling is most intense and where its outward forms are farthest from the Catholic and most revealing of a need that only the Church can fill. The Catholic novelist in the South will see many distorted images of Christ, but he will certainly feel that a distorted image of Christ is better than no image at all. I think he will feel a good deal more kinship with backwoods prophets and shouting fundamentalists than he will with those politer elements for whom the supernatural is an embarrassment and for whom religion has become a department of sociology or culture or personality development. (CW, 859)

## The Misfit: Fundamentalist and Nihilist

In her most memorable character, The Misfit from "A Good Man Is Hard to Find," O'Connor creates an ex-fundamentalist who is not embarrassed but scandalized by the supernatural. Having felt the Abrahamic knife at his own throat, he has become a mass murderer. He is appalled that Jesus raised the dead. This bringer of death is profoundly offended that the Giver of Life cannot be dismissed as a mere holy man or eminent ethical figure but must be adjudged as either the incarnate God or else a wholesale fraud. Unlike the psychopathic Misfit, the Grandmother is a proper lady who would gladly reduce Christian faith to sociology or culture or personality development if, in so doing, she could save her own life. She proves to be a good Christian atheist in the sense memorably specified by John Wesley,

49. While the South is still regarded as the Bible Belt, a recent poll reveals that the largest per capita percentage of Americans who regard themselves as practicing Christians are now concentrated in the upper Midwest — North and South Dakota, Minnesota, and Nebraska. That several large black denominations declined to participate in this poll may have skewed the results. Even so, O'Connor's fears about the South were justified ("Study: Conservative faith groups see big growth," *Waco Tribune-Herald* [September 22, 2002]: 13A).

who said that we are practical atheists whenever we live as if God does not matter. The Grandmother's self-assurance is so complete that she believes she can manage not only her own life but her family's as well. She also believes that she can convince even this serial killer to spare them all. In a crescendo of desperate defenses, she assures The Misfit that he is a good man, that he is not mediocre, that he should pray for Jesus to help him. In a last maniacal attempt to save herself, even at the cost of her own soul, the Grandmother denies her own Laodicean faith, declaring that perhaps Jesus did not raise the dead. Undeterred by these frenetic acts of self-protection, The Misfit kills her in cold blood and with cynical clarity: "She would of been a good woman," he observes with redneck grammatical truthfulness, "if it had been somebody there to shoot her every minute of her life" (CW, 153).

O'Connor offered a witty clue to the comedy implicit in this seemingly gruesome story, which also entails the heartless execution of the Grandmother's son and daughter-in-law and three grandchildren, one of them an infant: she observed that, while a lot of folks get killed in her work, nobody gets hurt. No one is made to cringe while anticipating a horrible death, or to suffer abominable tortures. The Grandmother's otherwise nondescript son and daughter-in-law muster a surprising dignity as they face their own and their children's deaths. The Grandmother is brutally slaughtered, therefore, but not spiritually injured. The Misfit murders her in a horrified recoil from her confession of their deep kinship. He is prompted to pump bullets into her chest when she touches him on the shoulder in an outrageous act of mutual identification: "Why you're one of my babies," she cries. "You're one of my own children" (CW, 152). In this single saving gesture that costs her her life, the Grandmother at last drops all of her fearful self-justifications, all of her vain attempts to stay alive at whatever price. Finally she tells the truth: she is not a good woman; he is not a good man; they both are in terrible trouble, and they both need radical help.

When The Misfit first confronts the Grandmother, she confesses her essential kinship with this calloused killer: "His face was as familiar to her as if she had known him all her life but she could not recall who he was" (CW, 146). The Misfit is her *Doppelgänger,* her shadow, her second and secret self. This is not to say that the Grandmother is a monster of malevolence. Like nearly everyone else, she is a well-meaning but self-serving person. Her life rests on nothing more solid than her desire for respectability. She wears a hat and gloves when traveling so that, if found dead beside the road, she will be recognized as a lady. She fantasizes about taking her family to see a plantation mansion with white columns and a secret panel. She sees a naked Negro child standing in the door of a shack, not as a child living in abject poverty, but as "a cute little pickaninny." Convinced that her own way is always best, she manages to prevail in all family disputes.

Yet her conscience is sufficiently pained at having lied about the antebellum mansion that, in a sudden upsurge of emotional guilt, she indirectly causes their car wreck. Yet the Grandmother has no deeply ingrained moral and religious character; she is a practical atheist. When faced with the threat of death, therefore, she is willing to deny her faith in an attempt to save her life. The Grandmother is a woman who lives by her own lights, though they provide little illumination of her sinful condition. She is Flannery O'Connor's portrait, not of *l'homme moyen sensuel*, but of the average Christian soul living amidst the compromises and deceits of ordinary life. Hence her capitalized generic name: she is not one of our grandmothers; she is one of us.

The Misfit perhaps once found himself in her place: a man seeking the easiest path, avoiding all trouble, staying out of harm's way. But at some indiscernible point, his good intentions ceased to suffice. He began to cut corners and to trim edges, until he gradually came to commit and to justify evil deeds. The Misfit is thus a mirror of the Grandmother, a man who might well have the face of her own child. Seeing at last the desperate place he has come to, she can also see how much it is like her own. Such shared sinfulness is what The Misfit dare not confess, and so he guns down the old lady with three quick shots.

Though the Grandmother enunciates no overt faith, she seems to make what ancient Christian tradition called "a good death." She dissolves a lifetime of complacency and conceit in a brief acknowledgment of her Adamic solidarity with her killer. Her divinely happy ending is perhaps figured in her final posture. Sinking down to death in her puddling blood, she is not wrought with anguish or regret; instead, her legs are "crossed under her like a child's and her face [is] smiling up at the cloudless sky" (CW, 152). O'Connor leaves her ending open to conflicting interpretations: the Grandmother can also be construed as having remained as spiritually childish in death as in life. Yet the cruciform legs and the beatific expression and the inviting heavens suggest that she has died in a state of grace.

It must be confessed that few readers have discerned the Grandmother's saving gesture of grace without O'Connor's later explanation: "Her head clears for an instant and she realizes, even in her limited way, that she is responsible for the man before her and joined to him by ties of kinship which have their roots deep in the mystery she has been merely prattling about so far. And at this point, she does the right thing, she makes the right gesture"

(MM, 111-12).[50] As a still maturing writer, O'Connor would not again make the moment of self-awakening so obscure, even though her endings would remain no less disturbing. They leave us with a chilling sense of our own complicity in the evils that her characters often commit.

If the Grandmother's final state is ambiguous, The Misfit's is not. He is a confessed nihilist who, unlike her, has wrestled hard with the God of the gospel. His unbelief is as thoughtful as her piety is unreflective. We learn, from his reported confession to a prison psychiatrist, that he has been reared as a Bible-believing Baptist. Having never heard of Sigmund Freud, The Misfit responds with a wondrous literalism to the psychiatrist's suggestion that his homicidal acts were products of an unconfessed Oedipal desire to slay his father. The Misfit will have nothing of such reductionist psychology. In his brilliantly cornpone way, he denies that he is a victim of his unconscious drives, insisting that he is the agent of his own self-will:

> It was a head-doctor at the penitentiary said what I done was kill my daddy but I known that for a lie. My daddy died in nineteen ought nineteen [an unusual year, to say the least] of the epidemic flu and I never had a thing to do with it. He was buried in the Mount Hopewell Baptist churchyard and you can go there and see for yourself. (CW, 150)

The Misfit rejects the faith of his fathers because he's a good historicist, though he's far from knowing it: he will not credit ancient events that he cannot empirically verify. Since he was not present to witness Jesus' miraculous acts, for example, he will not believe them. Yet his literalism also has its merits: it will not permit him to make the typical modernist disjunction between Jesus' message and his miracles — as if one could keep the former as moral truth while discarding the latter as crass superstition. The Misfit refuses this convenient dichotomy between the human and the divine. Jesus' power over physical death, he knows, is the mark of his power over spiritual death. Christ's raising of the dead constitutes a command for The Misfit also to be transformed: to surrender his proud sufficiency for the love of God and neighbor. From the fundamentalist sermons of his Baptist boyhood, The Misfit knows that he must either gladly embrace or bitterly reject Jesus' invitation. There is no safe middle way, no accommodating alternative to the drastic extremes of belief and unbelief, no bland neutrality between Jesus Christ and absolute nothingness.

---

50. O'Connor explains in a letter why The Misfit shrinks from the old lady's touch: "Grace is never received warmly. Always a recoil . . ." (CW, 1150).

"Jesus was the only One that ever raised the dead," The Misfit continued, "and He shouldn't have done it. He thown everything off balance. If He did what He said, then it's nothing for you to do but thow away everything and follow Him, and if He didn't, then it's nothing for you to do but enjoy the few minutes you got left the best way you can — by killing somebody or burning down his house or doing some other meanness to him. No pleasure but meanness," he said, and his voice had become almost a snarl. (CW, 152)

The Misfit has pushed the logic of his unbelief to its dreadful conclusion. He sees, as O'Connor often observed, that ours is not a culture of moral progress and evolutionary development but the culture of death. The final alternatives, The Misfit discerns, are not religion and science but the gospel and nihilism. Like Ivan Karamazov, he wants to return his ticket to the arena of life. But The Misfit has chosen nothingness, unlike Ivan, as a practical reality rather than a theoretical possibility. He is determined to offer scandalous signs of his spiritual offenses. In practicing his nihilism, The Misfit is not tempted by anything so small as theft. He is a murderer rather than a robber because, as he confesses, "Nobody had nothing I wanted" (CW, 150). To steal a desirable object would be to acknowledge the reality of a good other than his own sovereign self-will. The Misfit relishes, instead, the deeds of annihilation: murder and arson and cruelty. They alone are able to display his naked will to power.

Yet The Misfit is a civilized Nietzschean, a courteous killer whose manners match those of the Grandmother. He is embarrassed, for example, that he has no shirt to wear in the presence of women, having shed his prison uniform in making his escape. The Misfit always addresses the Grandmother as "Lady," and he always uses a proper "Yes'm" and "Nome" in responding to her. O'Connor was a stout defender of such outward politeness, but not when it serves to obscure the canker of soft-centered sentimentality. The Misfit's misery lies, he believes, in his failure to meet the expectations of society. He has failed to conform to the world's standards, and thus to "fit in," to live the balanced and well-adjusted life that perhaps the prison psychiatrist had urged upon him. For all the brilliance of his fundamentalist nihilism, The Misfit fails to see that it is not Nietzschean nonconformity but Christian eccentricity that he needs: to acquire another Center than the world's hub, to become a fool for Christ's sake, to be re-formed in the image of the Cross. Gradually, therefore, he slides into whining self-justification. At first he admits that he is not a good man but a guilty convict, but finally alleges that he cannot even remember his evil acts and thus that he does not deserve to be punished for them. "I call myself The Misfit," he says, "because I can't make what all I done wrong fit what all I gone through in punishment" (CW, 151). Nietzschean will to power ends in solipsistic victimology. If only he had been present at Jesus' miracles, he explains, "I would have known and I wouldn't be like I am now" (CW, 152). The Misfit's voice is choking with self-pity when the Grandmother extends him her surprising gesture of solidarity. And as soon as he kills her, the red-eyed homicide wipes his glasses, since they are fogged with a terrible tenderness toward himself. O'Connor discerns that The Misfit's alternative to the hard realism of the gospel is not an equally hard nihilism but a squishy self-pity.

## O. E. Parker: The Scandal of the Incarnate Word Made Tattooed Flesh

Even so, O'Connor retained such high regard for The Misfit that she augured him well. She predicted that a man so God-obsessed would finally be unable to elude his divine pursuer. "I don't want to equate the Misfit with the devil," she wrote. "I prefer to think that, however unlikely this may seem, the old lady's gesture, like the mustard-seed, will grow to be a great crow-filled tree in the Misfit's heart, and will be enough of a Pain to him there to turn him into the prophet he was meant to become" (MM, 112-13). O'Connor gave full vent to her sympathy with God-inebriated fundamentalists such as The Misfit in a revealing letter to Sister Mariella Gable:

> [T]o a lot of the monks and nuns I know, my Protestant prophets are fa-
> natics. For my part, I think the only difference between them [and mo-
> nastics] is that if you are a Catholic and have this intensity of belief you
> join the convent and are heard from no more; whereas if you are a
> Protestant and have it, there is no convent for you to join and you go
> about in the world, getting into all sorts of trouble and drawing the wrath
> of people who don't believe anything much at all down on your head....
>
> I am more and more impressed with the amount of Catholicism that
> fundamentalist Protestants have been able to retain. Theologically our
> differences with them are on the nature of the Church, not on the nature
> of God or our obligation to him. (CW, 1183, 1184)

O'Connor's declaration of the ecclesial difference is by no means negli-
gible, as becomes evident in her last published story, "Parker's Back." It features a Southern fundamentalist named Sarah Ruth Parker; this woman,

Parker's wife, is an emblem of a larger suspicion of sacraments that has characterized American culture at least since the day in 1832 when Emerson refused to celebrate the Lord's Supper at the Second Church of Boston.

O. E. Parker, the story's protagonist, is an early-day tattoo enthusiast. He became a convert to the needled figuration of his body when, at age fourteen, he experienced something akin to a mystical vision upon seeing a man whose entire body was "a single intricate design" of brilliantly colored tattoos:

> The man, who was small and sturdy, moved about on the platform, flexing his muscles so that the arabesque of men and beasts and flowers on his skin appeared to have a subtle motion of its own. Parker was filled with emotion, lifted up as some people are when the flag passes. . . .
>
> Parker had never before felt the least motion of wonder in himself. Until he saw the man at the fair, it did not enter his head that there was anything out of the ordinary about the fact that he existed. Even then it did not enter his head, but a peculiar unease settled in him. It was as if a blind boy had been turned so gently in a different direction that he did not know his destination had been changed. (CW, 657-58)

Like Enoch Emery in O'Connor's first novel, young Parker has "wise blood," a natural instinct for discerning the outward and visible sign of an inward and invisible grace. Despite this recognition of the holiness that suffuses the world, Parker has been living virtually as an unconscious animal, never noticing the splendor and uniqueness of his own existence. Yet he remains inwardly uneasy and dissatisfied, as if there were an Augustinian ache at the core of his unquiet soul, a restlessness seeking the rest that only God can grant. O'Connor's narrator takes us inside Parker's aching conscience: "Long views depressed Parker. You look out into space like that and you begin to feel as if someone were after you, the navy or the government or religion" (CW, 661).

Upon seeing how art had made an ordinary man's body beautiful, Parker wants such transformation for himself. He seeks the new life that The Misfit denied. Yet Parker seeks it on his own terms, refusing to let his artistic impulse liberate him from his own small and self-centered world. He gradually becomes obsessed, instead, with the power that his tattoos give him, especially the power to dominate women. Covering his body with images of predatory violence — a tiger, a panther, a cobra, and hawks on both thighs — Parker comes to think of himself as the all-conquering Don Juan. Hence the peculiarity of his attraction to an emaciated and unappealing woman named Sarah Ruth Cates. She is also obsessively religious, caustically critical of his tattoos, and a puritan to boot. She is always "sniffing up sin." Yet Parker is doubly attracted to Sarah Ruth: he wants to prove that no woman, no matter how ugly, can resist the lure of his tattooed body; but he also wants to fathom Sarah Ruth's strange spiritual power, the better to conquer her.

The story seems to set up the quintessential O'Connor situation: a cocksure atheist about to be undone by an even shrewder fundamentalist. Yet O'Connor turns the tables on our expectations. And in so doing, she also gives frightening fictional life to her worry that the same fundamentalists whose Jesus-obsession she admired were dangerously gnostic in their denial of the sacramental presence of God in the natural order, whether in artistic creation or in the created cosmos itself. In a letter to the atheist novelist John Hawkes, O'Connor explained that, for Catholics, divine grace is always mediated through some human or natural agency, rather than being experienced directly. "In the Protestant view," she added, "I think Grace and nature don't have much to do with each other" (CW, 1125). She thus urges an aspiring Protestant novelist, Ted Spivey, to stop writing out of his head and to enter the concrete world. She warns him that he is too much "in line with the Protestant temper — approaching the spiritual directly instead of through matter" (CW, 1080).

Having made her conquest of Parker, Sarah Ruth Cates insists on a civil wedding. She refuses to be married in a church: such mediations of grace are "idolatrous." Like Mrs. Shortley in "The Displaced Person," Sarah Ruth is a Bible-memorizer who can readily quote Scripture in order to condemn and reject, rather than to succor and save. She denounces the images covering Parker's body, calling them "vanity of vanities" and demeaning the lordly eagle tattooed on Parker's arm as a mere "chicken." She also forces Parker to reveal his biblical name, which he hates: Obadiah Elihue.[51] These Old Testament prophets are, for her, not figures of reverence but means of humiliation. She requires Parker to wear a long-sleeved shirt, and only in the dark will she let him undress. She is a gnostic believer who is scandalized by all forms of human embodiment, whether in erotic nakedness or in alluring tattoos: "At the judgement seat of God, Jesus is going to say to you, 'What you

---

51. Obadiah means "servant of the Lord," and Elihue means "God is He." O. E. Parker will come to live out the meaning of both names. His wife, however, contradicts her own names: Sarah is the mother of Israel, while Ruth, whose name means "mercy," is the woman who follows her mother-in-law Naomi into a foreign country, declaring "thy people shall be my people, and thy God my God" (Ruth 1:16). Though pregnant, this Sarah Ruth is ruthless in her scorn for life, and her progeny is not likely to bear spiritual fruit.

been doing all your life besides have pictures drawn all over you?'" (CW, 663-64). When Parker suggests having a Bible verse tattooed on his skin, she answers in scorn: "Ain't I already got a real Bible? What you think I want to read the same verse over and over for when I can read it all?" (CW, 664). Not even John 3:16 would have satisfied Sarah Ruth; for all such inscriptions, even of the Bible's most oft-quoted verse, are empty and useless materializations of her disembodied Word.[52]

Parker is as thoroughly sacramental in his imagination as Sarah Ruth is gnostic in hers. He becomes so preoccupied with dreaming up a tattoo that will bring his wife to heel that, one day while plowing with a tractor, he smashes into the lone tree in the field. As the tractor explodes, knocking him free but burning the tree as well as his shoes, Parker has a Moses-like response: "GOD ABOVE!" He also scrambles backward, "his eyes cavernous, and if he had known how to cross himself he would have done it" (CW, 665). Sensing in an inchoate way that he has received a revelation, Parker makes his way immediately from the farm to the city, there to have incised on his back the Christ-identifying tattoo that he believes Sarah Ruth will be unable to resist. At first, he pages through sample images revealing the sentimental religiosity that, four decades after O'Connor wrote her story, still dominate the religious market: "The Good Shepherd, Forbid Them Not, The Smiling Jesus, Jesus the Physicians' Friend." In his hurry, Parker flips past the one page that contained eyes so arresting they eventually command him to "GO BACK." Almost against his will, Parker returns to this drastically different sort of Savior: this one has "the haloed head of a flat stern Byzantine Christ with all-demanding eyes" (CW, 667).[53]

This is the Pantocrator, the Orthodox icon of the Lord of the universe, the Master of all things visible and invisible, He Who Is. Its effect on Parker is precisely what iconic art seeks to accomplish: it commands his response. Icons are unlike anything in the Western artistic tradition. They deliberately reject all concern with proportion and perspective, all realistic imitation of the created order. Icons are deliberately flat and disproportionate in order that divine reality might emanate from them. Western paintings situate the vanishing point behind the picture, enabling the beholder to comprehend if

---

52. Sarah Ruth's contempt for all things earthly is evident even in her cooking: she "just threw food in the pot and let it boil." The result is that Parker himself is becoming an ever less carnal creature, as he is "already losing his flesh" (CW, 664).

53. Parker's own eyes, in contrast, are extraordinarily absorptive, as we learn from his life as a sailor: "He stayed in the navy five years and seemed a natural part of the grey mechanical ship, except for his eyes, which were the same pale slate-color as the ocean and reflected the immense spaces around him as if they were a microcosm of the mysterious sea" (CW, 658-59).

not master the subject of the work; Eastern icons situate the vanishing point in front of the icon. The focus thus moves out and away, as the iconic figure emerges to meet the viewer. "The result is an opening," writes Michel Quenot, "a radiating forth, while the vanishing point in ordinary [Western] painting results in a convergence that closes up."[54] The energy radiating from the eyes of this Pantocrator lays hold of Parker unforgettably: "[E]ven though he could not summon up the exact look of those eyes, he could still feel their penetration. He felt as though, under their gaze, he was as transparent as the wing of a fly" (CW, 669).

Like St. Peter, Parker thrice denies the Savior who is now figured permanently on his body. When the tattooist asks whether he wants Christ incised on his skin because he is one of the "saved," Parker offers a tough-guy response: "Naw," he said, "I ain't got any use for none of that. A man can't save his self from whatever it is he don't deserve none of my sympathy" (CW, 669). Parker claims, instead, that the image of the incarnate God is meant merely to subdue his recalcitrant Sarah Ruth. Yet this Petrine denial, like the two others that follow, carries little conviction. Nor does the liquor he has gulped down serve to silence the unease that rages within Parker. When his pool-hall buddies make wicked fun of Parker's new tattoo, he claims that it is just a joke. In the fisticuffs that ensue, they throw Parker into an alley as if he were a latter-day Jonah cast into the sea. There Parker sits, bereft and destitute, until he receives a final revelation akin to the one Jonah receives in the belly of the fish. It prompts this man who has stitched his epidermis with a patchwork of images to examine at last not his skin but his soul, as the divine eyes now incarnate on his back penetrate the secret places of his being. They reveal his life to be "a spider web of facts and lies." Yet Parker's sinful past, though egregious, cannot compare to the cure he is offered — a lifetime of discipleship to Christ: "The eyes that were now forever on his back were eyes to be obeyed" (CW, 672).

O'Connor seems to move her story toward a hopeful climax, for Parker has at last found the new life he had secretly desired but publicly denied ever since seeing the tattooed man at the fair: "It was as if he were himself but a stranger to himself, driving into a new country though everything he saw was familiar to him, even at night" (CW, 672). As a newly born Christian, Parker no longer desires to dominate Sarah Ruth. He returns home to please her, hoping to find real communion with his new sister in Christ. Parker is willing even to confess to her his prophetic name. No longer ashamed of it,

54. Michel Quenot, *The Icon: Window on the Kingdom* (Crestwood, NY: St. Vladimir's Seminary Press, 1991), p. 106.

he knows that prophecy is the true legacy of all Christians, called as they are to announce the Good News. The name thus suffuses Parker with a transforming light. It turns "his spider web soul into a perfect arabesque of colors, a garden of trees and birds and beasts" (CW, 673). His life is not the botched crazy quilt of self-serving desires it once was, for he has literally put on Christ.

Sarah Ruth will have none of this husband who is now "a new creature" in Christ (2 Cor. 5:17). When Parker finally forces her to behold the Christ on his back, she confesses the terrible truth: "It ain't anybody I know." This Christ-denying Christian continues her barrage of gnostic rejections when Parker identifies the Christ image that she cannot recognize: "God don't look like that!" she insists. "He don't look. . . . He's a spirit. No man shall see his face," Sarah Ruth screams: "Idolatry! Enflaming yourself with idols under every green tree! I can put up with lies and vanity but I don't want no idolator in this house!" As if scourging Christ himself, she beats Parker with a broom, "until she had nearly knocked him senseless and large welts had formed on the face of the tattooed Christ" (CW, 674). The story ends as Parker staggers out of his house and into the yard. Sarah Ruth still glares at him with her hard eyes, as her husband leans "against the tree, crying like a baby" (CW, 675).

It is difficult to construe "Parker's Back" as a comic story, even in the sense earlier specified, that is, as opening out to lasting life rather than closing down to final death. Parker has been gruesomely defeated in his very first effort as a Christian witness. Yet this failure, sad though it is, does not cancel his new birth. Parker is learning the truth that a cheering kind of Christianity seeks to deny: the fact that the *via dolorosa* is the path all Christians must sooner or later travel. The Byzantine Christ will keep summoning him down the road to suffering and, given the fierceness of Parker's character, he will no doubt follow his call.

Parker will have to learn — as O'Connor believed contemporary Protestants must learn — to reject the discarnate religion of his wife. Though Sarah Ruth quotes the Old and New Testaments, she misconstrues them both. The God who declares to Moses, "Thou canst not see my face: for there shall no man see me and live" (Exodus 33:20), is neither unimaged nor unplaced. He reveals himself in the burning bush, in pillars of cloud and fire, in the Ark of the Covenant. He also speaks to Moses in the smoke atop Sinai. The prohibition against graven images given in the Decalogue was not meant to deny all icons of God. Rather, it prohibited Israel from imitating her pagan neighbors, who selfishly imaged their deities. Hence the Bible's repeated denunciations of pagan fertility cults set on hilltops and amid groves and "under every green tree" (Deuteronomy 12:2, et al.).

There are to be no images of Yahweh, not because he is abstract spirit but because he is thoroughly involved in the world's life, creating his own image of himself through Israel as his chosen people, through Israel's messiah called Jesus, and through the church as the Second Israel. When Christ insists that "they that worship him must worship him in spirit and in truth" (John 4:24), he speaks not as the disembodied but as the incarnate Lord, the Savior who resorts repeatedly to images and metaphors in identifying his true nature. He is the bread of truth, the light of the world, the shepherd of the flock — indeed, "the way, the truth, and the life: no man cometh unto the Father, but by me" (14:6). The Bible-citing Sarah Ruth has not come to the Father because she has refused to come to his enfleshed Son. She wants to separate the spirit and the body into hermetically sealed spheres.

It is not surprising that this gnostic believer denies all communion with Parker, who should, in fact, be her new companion in Christ. Unlike her, he has a sacramental faith; the Pantocrator now incised on his back is not so much a means of declaring Parker's faith as it is an efficacious icon enabling it. The antisacramental Sarah Ruth seeks the impossible: she wants to be a solitary Christian, alone with her Bible and her God, independent of all other believers. She is committing the sin of the eighth-century iconoclasts whom John of Damascus denounced. They in effect deny, said the Damascene, "the doctrine of the communion of saints, because if *proskinesis* (veneration) is forbidden to painted images of God incarnate it must be denied to other images of Christ as well: the Mother of God, the apostles, and all the saints who because they have been revealed as faithful members of Christ's body command the reverence of all believers."[55]

## Conclusion

Flannery O'Connor's high estimate of Southern fundamentalism remains salutary and instructive. She honors the uncompromising atheism of The Misfit because he so clearly articulates the gospel that he opposes, even as he provokes such a vacuous and complacent Christian as the Grandmother to true belief. O'Connor's fiction thus offers a numerically successful and economically prosperous church — a church "at ease in Zion" (Amos 6:1) — a startling summons to intense belief through the immoderate love of God. Yet

---

55. David Anderson, "Introduction" to *St. John of Damascus, On the Divine Images* (Crestwood, NY: St. Vladimir's Seminary Press, 1980), pp. 9-10. I owe this quotation to my former student Elizabeth Newman.

intensity of conviction can never produce superabundance of faithfulness if it refuses all material mediations of the gospel. Sarah Ruth Parker abjures Christ's bodily being and, in so doing, she rejects much more than crucifixes and shrines and rosaries and novenas. She rejects the church. Roman Catholics regard the church as nothing less than the extension of the Incarnation. While Protestants cannot make this claim, because it denies the final fallibility of the church, they can certainly affirm the ancient adage *extra ecclesiam non salus* (there is no salvation outside the church). This is a universally Christian claim because there is no solitary salvation, no salvation accomplished alone, by and for ourselves — no salvation outside Christ's body. To ensure that the Christ whom we follow is not a creature made in our own self-serving image, the sweet Jesus with a blinding smile whom Parker is commanded to pass over, we must behold the "flat stern Byzantine Christ with all-demanding eyes."[56]

56. "In Defense of Disbelief" is my critique of the sentimentally obscene spirituality that pervades much of contemporary evangelicalism (*First Things* 86 [October 1998]: 28-33).

TWO ❧ *The Burden of Southern History
and the Presence of Eternity within Time*

"Virginia is the best of the south to-day, and Georgia is perhaps the worst.
The one is simply senile; the other is crass, gross, vulgar and obnoxious. Between lies a vast plain of mediocrity, stupidity, lethargy, almost of dead silence. . . . The north, in its way, is also stupid and obnoxious. But nowhere in
the north is there such complete sterility, so depressing a lack of all civilized
gesture and aspiration." Thus spoke H. L. Mencken in his notorious 1917 condemnation of the South as "the Sahara of the Bozart."[1] Soon after Mencken's
attack, a group of writers and thinkers calling themselves the Southern
Agrarians rose up to defend Southern civilization, together with its rural and
religious virtues, against Mencken and other Northern critics. John Crowe
Ransom, Robert Penn Warren, Andrew Nelson Lytle, and Donald Davidson
were among this new cadre of Southern intellectuals determined to vindicate
their region; but surely the leader of this movement was Allen Tate. In an essay published in 1935, Tate offered his own celebrated defense of Southern
culture:

> The South was settled by the same European strains as originally settled
> the North. Yet, in spite of war, reconstruction, and industrialism, the
> South to this day finds its most perfect contrast in the North. In religious
> and social feeling I should stake everything on the greater resemblance to
> France. The South clings blindly to forms of European feeling and con-
> duct that were crushed by the French Revolution and that, in England at
> any rate, are barely memories. How many Englishmen have told us that
> we still have the eighteenth-century amiability and consideration of
> manners, supplanted in their country by middle-class reticence and sus-

1. H. L. Mencken, *Prejudices: A Selection*, ed. James T. Farrell (New York: Random House,
1958), pp. 73-74.

picion? And where, outside the South, is there a society that believes even covertly in the Code of Honor? . . . Where else in the modern world is the patriarchal family still innocent of the rise and power of other forms of society? . . . Where else does so much of the reality of the ancient land society endure, along with the infatuated avowal of beliefs that are hostile to it? . . . The anomalous structure of the South is, I think, finally witnessed by its religion. . . . [O]nly in the South does one find a convinced supernaturalism: it is nearer to Aquinas than to Calvin, Wesley, or Knox. Nor do we doubt that the conflict between modernism and fundamentalism is chiefly the impact of the new middle-class civilization upon the rural society; nor, moreover, should we allow ourselves to forget that philosophers of the State, from Sir Thomas More to John C. Calhoun, were political defenders of the older religious community.[2]

As if to confirm Tate's defense, Flannery O'Connor responded vigorously to Mencken's condemnation of the South as a region whose devotion to a primitive book left it too culturally bereft even to spell beaux arts: "It was about 1919 that Mencken called the South the Bible Belt and the Sahara of the Bozart" (MM, 201). It was only a few years, she added with gratified irony, "before the emergence in the South of a literature to be reckoned with" (CW, 857-58). This statement and others like it would seem to make O'Connor the natural ally of Allen Tate and the natural enemy of H. L. Mencken. In fact, O'Connor was a personal friend of Tate and his sometime wife, Caroline Gordon. From them she gratefully derived her basic aesthetic principles, even as she also shared their Catholic faith. But in a curious and surprising way, O'Connor also had deep affinities with H. L. Mencken. There was something suspect about the Agrarian idealization of the Old South, as Eugene Genovese will help us discern. O'Connor herself spotted the fly in the Agrarian ointment: they ignored what Mencken rightly saw as the heart of Southern culture — its fundamentalist Christianity. Though the great satirist regarded that religion as ludicrously false, O'Connor admired his obsession with its falsity. At least he did not have a functionalist and utilitarian regard for Christian faith. It was not for him a system of ideas or a cultural way of life that could be employed for extrinsic purposes. The brittle secularist joined the crusty Catholic in seeing, as the Agrarians did not, that the real quandary for both the region and the nation — indeed, for the entirety of modernity — concerns the gospel.

2. Allen Tate, "The Profession of Letters in the South," *Essays of Four Decades* (Chicago: Swallow, 1968), pp. 520-21.

## H. L. Mencken and the Sahara of the Bozart

If Henry Louis Mencken had not existed, it would have been necessary for Southerners to invent him. The sage of Baltimore was the ideal nemesis of all things Southern. "The religious thought of the South," he declared in his famous essay condemning the backwardness of the region, "is almost precisely identical with the religious thought of Wales. There is the same naïve belief in an anthropomorphic Creator but little removed, in manner and desire, from an evangelical bishop; there is the same submission to an ignorant and impudent sacerdotal tyranny, and there is the same sharp contrast between doctrinal orthodoxy and private ethics."[3] It wasn't only the religion of the South that Mencken found woefully wanting; it was also the artistic impoverishment of the South:

> Down there a poet is now almost as rare as an oboe player, a dry-point etcher or a metaphysician. It is, indeed, amazing to contemplate so vast a vacuity.... Nearly the whole of Europe could be lost in that stupendous region of fat farms, shoddy cities and paralyzed cerebrums.... And yet, for all its size and all its wealth and all the "progress" it babbles of, it is almost as sterile, artistically, intellectually, culturally, as the Sahara Desert. There are single acres in Europe that house more first-rate men than all the states south of the Potomac; there are probably single squares miles in America. If the whole of the late Confederacy were to be engulfed by a tidal wave tomorrow, the effect upon the civilized minority of men in the world would be but little greater than that of a flood on the Yang-tse-kiang. It would be impossible in history to match so complete a drying-up of a civilization.[4]

We have heard O'Connor declaring that she was a Catholic not as someone else would be a Baptist or a Methodist but as someone else would be an atheist. Mencken was such an atheist. Once American civil religion had made faith a matter of mere personal preference and private practice, a sort of higher hobby, there was no longer any need for public infidels such as Mencken. It is all the more important, therefore, to hear his voice.

> Today no really civilized man or woman believes in the cosmogony of Genesis, nor in the reality of Hell, nor in any of the other ancient imbecilities.... What survives under the name of Christianity ... is no more than

---

3. Mencken, p. 76.
4. Ibid., pp. 69-70.

a sort of Humanism, with hardly more supernaturalism in it than you will find in mathematics or political economy.

In other words, civilized man has become his own god. When difficulties confront him he no longer blames them upon the inscrutable enmity of remote and ineffable powers; he blames them on his own ignorance and incompetence. And when he sets out to remedy that ignorance and to remove that incompetence he does not look to any such powers for light and leading; he puts his whole trust in his own enterprise and ingenuity.[5]

For a Christian such as Flannery O'Connor, Mencken's credo is a virtual astringent. Ruby Turpin and Mrs. May and Mrs. McIntyre and Mrs. Hopewell are all "good Christian women" who mouth moralistic pieties in the absence of authentic faith. Until they are made painfully aware of their unconscious atheism, they act as if they were their own gods. Yet Mencken was no easy atheist: he discerned the human contradictions that vex believers and nonbelievers alike. He, too, knew how hard it is to find a truly good man. As if prophesying the coming of such disfigured do-gooders as Rayber in *The Violent Bear It Away,* Sheppard in "The Lame Shall Enter First," and Julian in "Everything That Rises Must Converge," Mencken penned this acidic description of "The Good Man" in a 1923 issue of *The Smart Set:*

> Man, at his best, remains a sort of one-lunged animal, never completely rounded and perfect, as a cockroach, say, is perfect. If he shows one valuable quality, it is almost unheard of for him to show any other. Give him a head, and he lacks a heart. Give him a heart of a gallon capacity, and his head holds scarcely a pint. The artist, nine times out of ten, is a dead-beat and given to the debauching of virgins, so-called. The patriot is a bigot, and, more often than not, a bounder and a poltroon. The man of physical bravery is often on a level, intellectually, with a Baptist clergyman. The intellectual giant has bad kidneys and cannot thread a needle. In all of my years of search in this world, from the Golden Gate in the West to the Vistula in the East, and from the Orkney Islands in the North to the Spanish Main in the South, I have never met a thoroughly moral man who was honorable.[6]

This troubling human paradox was compounded, in Mencken's view, by religion. Everywhere in his work, therefore, he hacked away at the barnacles of be-

---

5. H. L. Mencken, *Treatise on the Gods* (New York: Knopf, 1965; originally published in 1930), pp. 252-53.
6. H. L. Mencken, "The Good Man," *The Smart Set* (1923).

lief. The human frigate was burdened down by what he contemptuously called "Puritanism," which he famously defined as the fear that somewhere, somehow, somebody might be having a good time. Mencken was no less scornful of Catholics and other kinds of Christians. To him, they were all adherents of an irrational faith; it appallingly subjected human life to the control of a malevolent God who does not even bother to exist. The ideal standing over against Puritanism was enshrined for Mencken in the eighteenth century, the age of Enlightenment. It was a time, Mencken believed, when man stopped fearing hell and hoping for heaven, when man began to live for the glories of this world alone, when the arts and sciences, at last unfettered from the shackles of biblical faith, were allowed to celebrate beauty and practicality for the benefit of humanity. "At no time in history, either before or since," said Mencken, "have men and women lived more delightfully, or better deserved to be called civilized."[7]

Mencken was convinced, moreover, that the civilized world of Voltaire and Rousseau, of Gibbon and Kant, of Franklin and Jefferson and Paine, had been enshrined in the Old South.[8] Following the Civil War, with the advent of the redneck and his religion, this enlightened Southern culture was lost. The benighted South of the 1920s lacked orchestras and operas, theaters and museums, philosophers and poets and scientists, said Mencken, because of its Neanderthal devotion to the rude deity of Israel:

> [The Jews] imagined Him as a sort of glorified desert *sheik*, a veritable father of His tribe, full of very human whims and caprices, eager for flattery, sociable in His more amiable moments, but quick to punish contumacy, or even mere impoliteness. . . . This primitive Yahweh survives as one of the many forms of the Christian God, and has always been a favorite among the more simple varieties of Christians. It is easy for them to understand Him, for his childlike moods are their own, and they can smell His sweat. He it is that bucolic Methodists and Baptists think of when their thoughts turn to the Most High.[9]

Mencken proved wrong about so many things that it has become difficult to credit him when he was right. His racist scorn for blacks and Jews, his maniacal hatred of Franklin D. Roosevelt, his uncritical regard for Adolf Hitler and German culture, his contempt for lintheads and rednecks no less than the

---

7. *Treatise on the Gods*, pp. 248-49.

8. Allen Tate will arrive at exactly the opposite estimate of the Old South, as a region rooted not in the Enlightenment but the Middle Ages.

9. *Treatise on the Gods*, pp. 195-96.

"booboisie" — such vaunted "prejudices," as Mencken proudly called them, have not worn well. The misanthropic venom uncapped with the publication of Mencken's diaries created such a stink of resentment that John Kenneth Galbraith was prompted to defend the tart-tongued curmudgeon. He praised Mencken for his precision with words, for putting "the way of saying a thing above the thing said." Galbraith's curiously aesthetic endorsement of Mencken — ignoring the moral quality of his work — is virtually unbounded:

> What those of us who . . . read him long ago remember was his wonderfully explosive, some have said liberating, attack on an otherwise conventional, even stuffy world. Perhaps what he said was somctimes wrong, but he was our example in taking on the reputable view, saying what we believed was right and needed. . . .
>
> Three other qualities endeared Mencken to my generation. There was, of course, his mastery of the American idiom, something to which he devoted a lifetime of prideful study. And there was his ability to compress great and enduring truth in a phrase or two. . . . And there was the friendship and support he gave to the best writers of his generation, [including Sinclair Lewis, Faulkner, and Fitzgerald] as well as Dreiser, Sherwood Anderson, and Eugene O'Neill.[10]

Donald Davidson, along with the other Agrarians, reviled Mencken for his failure to comprehend the South, but Flannery O'Connor did not. She saw that he had laid his pen on the very quality of Southern life — its sweated, Bible-centered, Christ-haunted religion — that gave it a distinctive and potentially redemptive character.

## The Tragic Irony of Southern History

Mencken was not alone in his lament over the literary and intellectual stuntedness of the South. In *The American Scene,* Henry James called Southern culture a "great melancholy void."[11] Nor were Yankee readers of *The Smart Set* and *The American Mercury* the only critics who discerned the need for more ironic and self-critical spirit in Southern letters. Fred Hobson has shown that a whole generation of Southern writers answered Mencken's challenge to in-

---

10. John Kenneth Galbraith, "Viva Mencken!," *New York Review of Books* (28 June 1990): 41.

11. Quoted in Lewis P. Simpson, *The Brazen Face of History: Studies in the Literary Consciousness in America* (Athens, GA: University of Georgia Press, 1997; originally published 1980), p. 237.

dict their native land for its sundry failures.[12] By the 1930s, Thomas Wolfe and James Branch Cabell, Gerald Johnson and W. J. Cash, were all engaged in a severe regional self-critique. They had cause, as Hobson observes:

> The dramatic rise in lynchings in 1919 and 1920, the Scopes evolution trial of 1925, the anti-Catholicism engendered by the Al Smith campaign of 1928, the textile mill violence of Gastonia and Marion and Elizabethton in 1929: in all these the South called attention to its ignorance, violence, and religious bigotry.[13]

At the vanguard of the new school of Southern cultural criticism stood Howard Odum and his fellow sociologists at the University of North Carolina in Chapel Hill. Mencken was eager to endorse what he called their "dynamitical" attempt "to upset all the assumptions upon which the thinking of North Carolina, and indeed of the whole South, [had] been grounded since the Civil War, and to set up a new theory of the true, the good, and the beautiful upon a foundation of known and provable facts."[14] By means of careful sociological analysis, Odum and his colleagues measured "Southern per capita income, agricultural production, industrial output, welfare expenditures, highway construction, and some six hundred other categories and found the South deficient in nearly every one — except homicide."[15] During the Roosevelt administrations of the 1930s, the heads of various national agencies began to refer to "the Southern problem," as if the South were the nation's only region needing to be rescued from its retrograde condition and thus to be brought into the American mainstream. Odum's school was convinced that, with massive federal aid in support of agricultural, industrial, and cultural planning, the South could overcome its inveterate ills: poverty and disease, malnutrition and illiteracy, bigotry and racial brutality.

Yet the Agrarians joined William Faulkner in his conviction that Odum's sociological cure was worse than the Southern disease. Tate, Warren, Ransom, Davidson and the other contributors to the 1930 Manifesto entitled *I'll Take My Stand* were steadfastly opposed to the abstract scientism and humanitarianism of Mencken and his Chapel Hill advocates. The juggernaut of Northern progress, they warned, would crush the South's evils only by

12. Fred Hobson, *Serpent in Eden: H. L. Mencken and the South* (Chapel Hill, NC: University of North Carolina Press, 1974), p. 78.

13. Fred Hobson, *Tell About the South: The Southern Rage to Explain* (Baton Rouge: Louisiana State University Press, 1983), p. 185.

14. Quoted in ibid., p. 191.

15. Ibid., p. 196.

stamping out its virtues: the elaborate code of manners shared by both high and low strata of Southern society; the importance of blood kinship and familial ties; the lasting reverence for locality fostered by rural life; the tragic sense of history engendered by defeat in the Civil War; the narrative gift for telling stories rather than generating ideas; the deep supernaturalist faith common to blacks and whites alike. Donald Davidson asked, with arch sarcasm, "Can sociology explain why William Faulkner, or some other novelist of comparable stature, did not appear, during this period [1920-50], somewhere north of the Ohio — say, in Massachusetts or Wisconsin?"[16]

Flannery O'Connor largely agreed with the Agrarians in opposing the various "isms" they accused Odum and the Menckenites of supporting: rationalism, determinism, naturalism, cosmopolitanism, and the like. And, along with the Agrarians, she feared that the South would be homogenized into another bland, secular region — a country-wide Levittown, as Walker Percy called it, indistinguishable from all the others. In 1957, the editors of *Life* magazine made their own summons to success, calling for America's novelists to reflect more of the nation's unparalleled prosperity and to mirror "the joy of life itself." They also suggested, in concert with earlier laments, that the South was a troubled region because it was culturally isolated from the remainder of the nation. O'Connor's stark reply stood very much in line with the Agrarians:

> The anguish that most of us have observed for some time now has been caused not by the fact that the South is alienated from the rest of the country, but by the fact that it is not alienated enough, that every day we are getting more and more like the rest of the country, that we are being forced out not only of our many sins but of our few virtues. This may be unholy anguish but it is anguish nevertheless. (CW, 802-3)

Walker Percy largely shared O'Connor's defense of the South, though not on the matter of race, as we shall see. Percy praised the South because it exalted what other American regions have degraded: "a grace and a gift for human intercourse."[17] It has also possessed an elaborate set of manners,

16. Quoted in ibid., p. 238.

17. Walker Percy, *Signposts in a Strange Land*, ed. Patrick Samway (New York: Farrar, Straus & Giroux, 1991), p. 51. Though Percy loathed what he called "the monstrous mythologizing" of the Southern Way of Life, he lauded the region's authentic virtues: "the conservative tradition of a predominantly agrarian society, a tradition which at its best enshrined the humane aspects of living for rich and poor, black and white. It gave first place to a stable family life, sensitivity and good manners between men, chivalry toward women, an honor code, and individual integrity" (ibid., p. 91).

Percy noted. When united imaginatively, these Southern virtues have produced some of the most remarkable literature of the previous century, especially in the work of William Faulkner and Eudora Welty, Robert Penn Warren and Allen Tate, Flannery O'Connor and Percy himself. This renascence of Southern literature did not occur, Percy observed, during the leisured antebellum period, but only with the experience of defeat and humiliation. When *The Moviegoer* won the National Book Award in 1962, Percy was asked to explain the prominence of Southern literature in twentieth-century America. "It's because we lost the War," he said. After quoting Percy's quip, O'Connor added her distinctively religious interpretation of it:

> He didn't mean . . . simply that a lost war makes good subject matter. What he was saying was that we have had our Fall. We have gone into the modern world with an inburnt knowledge of human limitations and with a sense of mystery which could not have developed in our first state of innocence — as it has not sufficiently developed in the rest of our country. (MM, 59)

With its humiliating defeat in defense of an indefensible cause, the South acquired an ineradicable sense of the tragic: the awareness that even the best of cultures can go profoundly wrong, that seeming good can be built on massive evil, that many things broken cannot be mended, and that much evil must patiently be endured.

Henry James registered much the same sentiment about certain Southern cities, declaring that if he were to return to America from England, he would choose to live in a place such as Charleston, since it retained a sharp sense of the tragic past, as Northern cities did not. For the same reason, perhaps, Hawthorne set *The Marble Faun* in Italy, since it was haunted by reminders of the permanent intractability of evil, as his native New England was not. R. W. B. Lewis argued, in *The American Adam*, that Melville and James joined Hawthorne's protest against the dangerous complacency endemic to American moral innocence.[18] It leads to a reformist understanding of human nature as so malleable that it can be reshaped into a veritable mechanism of righteousness. O'Connor often cited James and Hawthorne no less than Edgar Allan Poe as three nineteenth-century writers who understood evil and tragedy as most other Americans do not. She also gave her assent to the Protestant theologian Reinhold Niebuhr in his sustained critique of our American obliviousness to

---

18. R. W. B. Lewis, *The American Adam: Innocence, Tragedy, and Tradition in the Nineteenth Century* (Chicago: University of Chicago Press, 1955).

the perennial effects of Original Sin (CW, 897-98). Robert Penn Warren also came to lament the Northern belief in its own "Treasury of Virtue," the fund of moral righteousness that Northerners credited to themselves for having put a stop to slavery.[19] The war gave the victors a shining new millennial sense of destiny for the secular American republic. Southerners demurred. In unpublished lecture notes for a course on the modern novel, Walker Percy referred to Faulkner and other Southern writers as having created "the great literary secession," a refusal to endorse the new moral and religious triumphalism.[20]

C. Vann Woodward offers the similar observation that, prior to Vietnam, Southerners were the only Americans who ever experienced defeat in battle, a defeat made all the more grueling for being fought largely on Southern territory and in defense of an unworthy cause. It gave the citizens of Dixie, Woodward argues, a tragic sense of life, a unique ability to spurn the profound American delusion that besets their fellow countrymen, namely, "that there is nothing whatever that is beyond their power to accomplish."[21] The terrorist horrors of September 11, 2001, have only partially qualified Woodward's judgment. From a larger perspective, Woodward wrote in 1960,

> it is not the South but America that is unique among the peoples of the world. This peculiarity arises out of the American legend of success and victory, a legend that is not shared by any other people of the civilized world. The collective will of this country has simply never known what it means to be confronted by complete frustration. Whether by luck, by abundant resources, by ingenuity, by technology, by organizing cleverness, or by sheer force of arms America has been able to overcome every major historic crisis — economic, political, or foreign — with which it has had to cope. This remarkable record . . . explains in large part the national faith in unlimited progress, in the efficacy of material means, in the importance of mass and speed, the worship of success, and the belief in the invincibility of American arms.[22]

19. Warren was no less vehement in his denunciation of the South's "Great Alibi," the convenient excuse that defeat and occupation gave Southerners for doing little or nothing about their region's inveterate poverty and illiteracy, its racism and violence and political corruption (Robert Penn Warren, *The Legacy of the Civil War: Meditations on the Centennial* [New York: Random House, 1961]).

20. Quoted in Benjamin B. Alexander, "Good Things Out of Nazareth: The Unpublished Letters of Flannery O'Connor" (unpublished essay).

21. C. Vann Woodward, *The Burden of Southern History*, rev. ed. (New York: New American Library, 1969), p. 27.

22. Ibid., pp. 134-35. Woodward cites, as a telling case of Yankee naivete about the nature

## Allen Tate: Idealizer of Southern Culture

Allen Tate often echoes these vigorous defenses of Southern culture, for he also believed that the South had religious instincts that the rest of the nation lacked. Yet he began as an early supporter of Mencken, believing that Mencken's attack on Southern sentimentality and romanticism was justified. Gradually, however, Tate came to discern that, while Mencken was right about much of modern Southern culture — the moonlight and magnolias and mint-julep myth spawned by postbellum Southern writers such as Thomas Nelson Page — he was wrong about the true culture of the Old South. Its traditionalist culture, we have heard Tate declaring, offers a still-powerful witness against the depredations inflicted by modern industrialism and capitalism on the once-coherent civilization of the West. It is important to note that Tate and the other Agrarians were as vehement in their denunciations of wage labor and the market economy as was Karl Marx himself, and that they are not therefore to be confused with contemporary Southern conservatism. Marx prophesied that the self-destructive character of capitalism would usher in a new age of socialism, while Tate and his friends lamented the capitalist destruction of the old order of Christendom.

In a 1929 letter to Donald Davidson (which Lewis Simpson has shown to be seminal for the whole of the Southern literary renascence), Allen Tate made the case for a revolutionary attempt to overthrow the community-destroying evils of modern individualism by recourse to the virtues of Southern agrarian culture. He proposed a symposium of essays defending the South's rural way of life against the North's materialism and industrialism. It would show that the South recognized the profound limits inherent in human existence that Yankee rationalism and scientism had ignored for the sake of a self-righteous and moralistic way of life. For the fueling of this bonfire, Tate was not interested in historical accuracy, he admitted, so

---

of evil, the virtual deification of John Brown, the mass murderer of Harper's Ferry, by nearly all the luminaries of nineteenth-century New England: Emerson, Thoreau, Channing, Longfellow, Bryant, Lowell, the Alcotts, Theodore Parker, Henry Ward Beecher. Thoreau likened Brown's execution to Christ's crucifixion, calling Brown "the bravest and humanest man in the country," "a Transcendentalist above all." "When a noble deed is done, who is likely to appreciate it?" asked Thoreau. "They who are noble themselves," he replied to his own question. "I was not surprised that certain of my neighbors spoke of John Brown as an ordinary felon, for who are they? They have either much flesh, or much office, or much coarseness of some kind. They are not ethereal [i.e., Transcendentalist] natures in any sense. The dark qualities predominate in them. . . . For the children of light to contend with them is as if there should be a contest between eagles and owls" (quoted in ibid., pp. 48-49).

much as in metaphysical ideals: "Philosophically, we must go the whole hog of reaction, and base our movement less upon the actual Old South than upon its prototype — the historical social and religious scheme of Europe. We must be the last Europeans — there being no Europeans in Europe at present."[23]

Just as slavery was inessential to medieval Europe, so Tate came to believe that slavery was an actual detriment to the feudal society that Southerners had originally sought to erect. The real heroes of the Old South, argued Tate, were not the plantation and slave owners but the yeoman farmers and modest landowners who cultivated small plots of land for their own and their neighbors' benefit, who created a close-knit culture of kinship connections, and who thus made humble obeisance before the perennial vicissitudes of human existence. Like all societies, it was inevitably stratified; yet the division between the Southern equivalents of lords and serfs was not meant to be vicious but virtuous. They were bound together in a profoundly communal and interdependent enterprise. The Civil War was not fought against the North in the defense of slavery, Tate argued, but for the sake of an entirely antithetical way of life — for a Southern culture that honored such traditional virtues as "hierarchy, duty, chivalry, reverence, piety, and faith."[24] Though the South had been defeated in war, Tate and the Agrarians maintained that the ideals of traditional Southern culture could be resurrected "to save the rudiments of Christian civilization in the West. They defined the nature of that civilization as the continual struggle for discipline, self-control, and order against latitude, excess, and chaos."[25]

Yet Tate was saddled with the task of explaining how a venerable Southern civilization could have fallen to so callow an enemy culture as Northern capitalism. He came to his answer, at least in part, through the influence of T. S. Eliot, especially Eliot's critique of Irving Babbitt and Paul Elmer More. They had made their literary humanism, Eliot argued, into a sorry substitute for religion. In a 1929 essay that Eliot published in *Criterion* and hailed for its brilliance, Tate attacked these new humanists for advocating a morality that had no ultimate source of support. "The religious unity of intellect and emotion, of reason and instinct," he explained in a

23. Quoted in Mark G. Malvasi, *The Unregenerate South: The Agrarian Thought of John Crowe Ransom, Allen Tate, and Donald Davidson* (Baton Rouge: Louisiana State University Press, 1997), p. 115. For a scathing critique of the Agrarian notion that the South possessed a coherent culture, see Michael Kreyling, *Inventing Southern Literature* (Jackson, MS: University Press of Mississippi, 1998).

24. Malvasi, p. 6.

25. Ibid., p. 22.

sentence that would be prophetic of his later work, "is the sole technique for the realization of values."[26] Tate had found his answer to his quandary about the South's failure, and it was a matter of religion: religion understood as the groundwork of order and the buttress of civilization, rather than anything confessionally and communally borne. The Agrarian Manifesto's introductory statement on religion, for example, contains nothing explicitly theological or specifically ecclesial, even though the postbellum South had been a region characterized by a thoroughly church-centered and doctrinal Christianity:

> Religion can hardly expect to flourish in an industrial society. Religion is our submission to the general intention of a nature that is fairly inscrutable; it is the sense of our rôle as creatures within it. But nature industrialized, transformed into cities and artificial habitations, manufactured into commodities, is no longer nature but a highly simplified picture of nature. We receive the illusion of having power over nature, and lose the sense of nature as something mysterious and contingent. The God of nature under these [illusory] conditions is merely an amiable expression, a superfluity, and the philosophical understanding ordinarily carried in the religious experience is not there for us to have.[27]

In his own contribution to *I'll Take My Stand*, Tate baldly states his reason for the Southern failure: the "remarkable society of the old South . . . was a feudal society without a feudal religion."[28] Southerners were prevented from developing a proper culture-forming religion, Tate argues, because their religious inheritance was Protestant. Unlike the Catholicism of the Middle Ages, Tate claims, the Reformation produced what is "hardly a religion at all, but rather a disguised secular ambition." The real motive of the Reformers, he adds, was mercantile and materialist, and their religion was inevitably fissiparous: "The South's religious mind was inarticulate, dissenting, and schismatical. She had a non-agrarian and trading religion that had been invented in the sixteenth century by a young finance-capitalist economy."[29] As the editor of *Criterion*, Eliot refused Tate's request to publish this remark-

26. Allen Tate, "Humanism and Naturalism," *Reactionary Essays on Poetry and Ideas* (New York: Charles Scribner's Sons, 1936), pp. 139, 143.

27. *I'll Take My Stand: The South and the Agrarian Tradition. By Twelve Southerners* (New York: Harper Torchbooks, 1962; first published in 1930), pp. xxiv-xxv.

28. Allen Tate, "Remarks on the Southern Religion," in *I'll Take My Stand*, p. 166.

29. These phrases are found in Tate's slightly revised 1936 version of his 1930 essay, retitled "Religion and the Old South," *Essays of Four Decades*, p. 570.

ably unhistorical reading of history.[30] Eliot may have not noticed — since he shared Tate's vision in this regard — that his friend had not only misread the antebellum South as having no essential dependence on slavery, and that he had made a crude misprision of the magisterial Reformers as mere capitalists, but that he had also adopted a largely functionalist understanding of religion.

For Tate, it becomes ever so evident that religion is the main unifying force of society because it alone has the power to "realize values." Rather than seeing medieval Catholicism as having its own unique purposes, often overlapping but never being identical with the purposes of the medieval state, Tate regards true Christianity as a bulwark for morality and civilization. It does not exist first and last for the kingdom of God but for the rightful rule of man. Thus does Tate contend that medieval society developed dogma, not as something intrinsic to Christian faith and as coeval with both the church and Scripture, but rather as a way to uphold tradition by giving rational structure to the irrational supernaturalism of religion: "The Western Church established a system of quantity [i.e., ordered ideas] for the protection of quality [i.e., mystical experience]." The special feature of Western dogma, Tate declares — in astonishing indifference to all the councils and creeds and confessions of the church — is "an ineradicable belief in the fundamental evil of nature."[31]

Tate feared that modern materialism has reduced human existence to total continuity with nature understood as a mechanical process. The resulting science has made man little more than an anthropoid. Tate and his fellow Agrarians rightly predicted that the triumph of such scientism would produce a rampant secularism, a degradation of the environment, and the collapse of communal civility. For Tate, the reduction of the human to the natural is exemplified in the American "religion concerning how things work,"[32] that is, in the Yankee devotion to the secular law of cause and effect, and thus in the almighty efficiency of machine production. The South resisted Northern industrialism and materialism, Tate argues, but it failed to create a religion that would fit its social and economic structure. "The South would not

30. Thomas A. Underwood, *Allen Tate: Orphan of the South* (Princeton, NJ: Princeton University Press, 2000), p. 163.

31. *Essays of Four Decades*, p. 567. Ross Labrie observes that Tate regarded "its unblinking consciousness of evil . . . as the most valuable contribution of Catholicism to the modern age, where he witnessed evil being explained out of existence by scientist and neoscientist alike" (*The Catholic Imagination in American Literature* [Columbia, MO: University of Missouri Press, 1997], p. 54).

32. *Essays of Four Decades*, p. 560.

have been defeated," he concludes, "had she possessed a sufficient faith in her own kind of God. She would not have been defeated, in other words, had she been able to bring out a body of doctrine setting forth her true conviction that the ends of man require more for their realization than politics."[33]

## Tate's Catholic Defense of Western Civilization

The important question for understanding Allen Tate's relationship to Flannery O'Connor, and thus for assessing the larger issue of the church in the South, is whether Tate altered his old exaltation of the feudal South when he entered the Roman Catholic Church in 1950.[34] Mark Malvasi contends that Tate did not change his mind substantially. It is true that Tate later repented of the heresy inherent in the Agrarians' attempt to divinize Southern history. Yet his repentance is curiously qualified: "We were trying to find a religion in the secular, historical experience as such, particularly in the Old South. I would now go further . . . and say we were idolaters. But it is better to be an idolater than to worship nothing, and as far as our old religion went I still believe it."[35] Southern Christianity, because it was Protestant, could not go very far toward making the church the basis of a hierarchical and agricultural civilization. In his essay on Southern religion in *I'll Take My Stand*, Tate all but calls for the Agrarians to look to Catholicism as their means for correcting the Southern error. Yet his entrance into the Church of Rome was another two decades in coming. In 1929, Tate still called himself "an enforced atheist," though one with a religious sensibility. He was an unbeliever who craved not eternal salvation, he confessed, but "some ultimate discipline of the soul" to order his daily affairs.[36] The kind of convert Tate would make was already evident in this important letter of 1929 written to Donald Davidson:

> I am more and more heading towards Catholicism. We have reached a condition of the spirit where no further compromise is possible. . . . There is no dualism without religion, and there is no religion without a

---

33. Ibid., p. 575. The final phrase refers to what Tate regards as Thomas Jefferson's regrettably secularized and politicized conception of human existence.

34. Jacques and Raïssa Maritain served as godparents. Though Tate took the name Augustine at his confirmation, he was baptized — perhaps more revealingly — on December 22, the feast day of St. Thomas the Doubter (Peter A. Huff, *Allen Tate and the Catholic Revival: Trace of the Fugitive Gods* [Mahwah, NJ: Paulist, 1996], p. 82).

35. Quoted in Malvasi, p. 142.

36. Quoted in Underwood, p. 154.

Church, nor can there be a Church without dogma. Protestantism is virtually naturalism; when morality lacks the authority of dogma, it becomes private, irresponsible, and from this it is only a step to naturalism. . . . Without the external authority good conduct cannot last, it becomes . . . merely "gentlemanly feeling" which is not enough to keep control of those who lack it.[37]

It would be churlish to suggest that Allen Tate converted to Roman Catholicism as a convenient way of justifying the absolutist kind of traditionalism that he had long held.[38] Yet it is not unfair to suggest that his entrance into the church has the whiff of the nostalgic search for refuge that Ronald Knox, a fellow convert, praised in 1927:

> More and more, I think, as the changing conditions of modern society cut us off from the memory of old things; as customs die out, and property changes hands, and our language loses its virility, and even (perhaps) the power of the Empire we live in sinks in the scale of political values, men will look towards the Catholic Church, if only as the repository of long traditions, the undying, unmoved spectator of the thousand phases and fashions that have passed over our restless world.[39]

Even as a Christian, Tate retained his pre-Christian concerns. Fearing that the Western cultural tradition was collapsing, he believed that its morality could not be renewed without religion, that religion must be specific rather than generic, that dogma guaranteed such specificity, that Catholicism had the most fully developed dogmatic system, and that it thus remained the best means for preserving what he repeatedly called "the permanent values of Western society."[40] Tate extols neither the gospel nor the church so much

37. Quoted in Malvasi, p. 94. For Tate, "dualism" preserves the connection between the visible and invisible realms, while "naturalism" reduces everything to the material and the mundane.

38. This is precisely the charge brought against Tate by John M. Bradbury in *The Fugitives: A Critical Account* (Chapel Hill, NC: University of North Carolina Press, 1958) and by John L. Stewart in *The Burden of Time: The Fugitives and Agrarians* (Princeton, NJ: Princeton University Press, 1965).

39. Ronald Knox, *The Belief of Catholics* (San Francisco: Ignatius, 2000; first published in 1927), p. 23.

40. Quoted in Michael Millgate, "An Interview with Allen Tate," *Shenandoah* 12 (Spring 1961): 32. I have found only one exception to Tate's instrumental regard for Christianity; it appears in a 1954 letter to Andrew Lytle: "I have come to the view that no society is worth 'saving' as such: what we must save is the truth of God and Man, and the right society follows" (quoted in

as the power of "classical-Christian culture." By uniting the virtues of the biblical and Greco-Roman traditions, this ideal hybrid civilization provided "for the highest development of man's potentialities as man. Man belonged to his village, valley, mountain, or seacoast; but wherever he was he was a Christian whose Hebraic discipline had tempered his tribal savagery and whose classical humanism had moderated the literal imperative of his Christianity to suicidal other-worldliness."[41]

For Tate, religion is the ultimate stay against chaos, and Christianity is the best means the West has developed for establishing civilized order. Barbarism is Tate's deepest dread, especially the late modern barbarism of "[t]echnology without Christianity . . . refined, violent, and decadent, not the vigorous barbarism of the forest and the soil."[42] Thus Tate joined critics ranging from Oswald Spengler to Alasdair MacIntyre in warning that a new Dark Age was already descending upon the West. "There is perhaps no anodyne for the pains of civilization," he glumly confessed, "but savagery."[43]

Tate's cultural project came perhaps to its clearest focus in his 1952 Phi Beta Kappa address delivered at the University of Minnesota and employed as the lead item in *Essays of Four Decades:* "The Man of Letters in the Modern World." Speaking to a postwar generation beginning to batten on American economic prosperity and to worship at the altar of burgeoning technology, Tate pled with men and women of letters not to withdraw from the world of politics but to join the battle being waged "between the dehumanized society of secularism . . . and the eternal society of the communion of the human spirit."[44] Tate warned against the rise of the new technological science of mass communication. He urged his audience to return to the root meaning of the word: "Communication that is not also communion is incomplete. We use communication; we participate in communion." "Neither the artist nor the statesman," he added, "will fully communicate again until the rule of love, added to the rule of law, has liberated them." Tate alluded to St. Augustine's *credo ut intelligam* in setting forth his guid-

---

Huff, *Allen Tate and the Catholic Revival,* p. 98). Even here, however, it is not clear whether Tate regards the church as essential for such a task. Nowhere have I been able to locate in Tate's prose any distinctive claim made for the Body of Christ akin to the affirmations made by his friend Jacques Maritain, who straightforwardly extolled "the supernatural society whose life is the communicated life of God — the Church herself" (*The Person and the Common Good,* trans. John J. Fitzgerald from the 1946 original [Notre Dame, IN: University of Notre Dame Press, 1966], p. 84).

41. "The New Provincialism," *Essays of Four Decades,* p. 542.

42. Ibid., p. 539.

43. "The Man of Letters in the Modern World," ibid., p. 6.

44. Tate did not define secularism as something so obvious as the denial of God but as something far subtler and more sinister: the substitution of means for ends.

ing principle: "Man is a creature that in the long run has got to believe in order to know, and to know in order to do. For doing without knowing is machine behavior, illiberal and servile routine...." He also quoted Scripture to assert that it is impossible to love one's neighbor without loving God. Invoking Jacques Maritain on "the supratemporal destiny of man," Tate ended with an eschatological claim: "The end of social man is communion in time through love, which is beyond time."[45]

The winsomeness of Tate's Phi Beta Kappa address, like much else in his enormously influential work, cannot be denied. For all of the enormous differences between him and the liberal Protestant theologian Paul Tillich, Tate resembles Tillich in this one regard: they appealed to secular audiences by recasting Christian claims into largely nontheological terms. Yet Tate sacrificed something essential to Christian faith by repeatedly refusing to employ the church's own particularistic language. "The communion of the human spirit," whatever might be implied by so woolly a phrase, is not the same thing as "the communion of saints." Tate also withholds any sacramental or ecclesial referent from his defense of "communion." His use of Augustine is also skewed: for the bishop of Hippo, the City of God is no abstract eschatological ideal but rather a living reality present in the church's witness to the Christ, who alone enables the knowledge that rightly orders our loves.[46] Nor does Augustine call for love to be "added" to law, but rather for the incarnate *caritas* to inform — and thus both to guide and restrain — secular law. Tate's avoidance of theological specificity for the sake of transcendent generality makes the church and its gospel serve as buttresses for moral ends that he has reached largely by other means.[47] In a private letter written only two years before his death, Tate made a deeply revealing confession about his ultimate concerns: "I am not moved by the Negro's demand for social justice and equality (worthy as those may be); I am interested in order and civilization, which in a crisis take precedence over all other aims."[48]

45. *Essays of Four Decades*, pp. 7, 9, 16.

46. The subtheological generality of Tate's idea of love is manifest in his appeal to a controverted line from Auden's poem "September 1, 1939": "We must love one another or die." In 1952 Tate could not have known that Auden would repudiate this line because of its inane vagueness but, by 1968, when Tate republished his essay, the disclaimer was well known.

47. In an essay on Russell Kirk, I have argued that a similarly functionalist understanding of Christian faith undermines the witness of another cultural conservative whose outlook was closely akin to Tate's. See *Contending for the Faith: Essays on the Church's Engagement with Culture* (Waco, TX: Baylor University Press, 2003), pp. 29-42.

48. Quoted in Fred Hobson, "The Cosmopolitan Provincial," *Atlantic* (December 2000): 121.

While Flannery O'Connor did not devote her work to the salvaging of Western culture, she no doubt honored the worthiness of Tate's endeavor. We are inheritors of goods created by our occidental ancestors that are both too numerous in their variety to list and too extraordinary in their benefits to measure. In an essay on this subject, William F. Buckley names but three products of Western civilization that are of specific value to him as a sailor and writer and lover of music: the astrolabe, the *Oxford English Dictionary*, and Bach's *St. Matthew's Passion*. They are the creations of enormous human ingenuity and prolonged communal cooperation no less than individual genius. Buckley illustrates the preciousness of our cultural legacy by noting that, in the thirteenth century, the one-room library at the University of Salamanca contained all the known literature of the West, and that Pope Gregory IX signed a bull of excommunication against anyone who stole one of its treasures. Rather than honoring and furthering such a legacy, Buckley notes, "the disposition of modern man [is] to take for granted everything he enjoys, without any sense of incurring an obligation, either to pay the old woman [the Statue of Liberty] from whose larder he has helped himself, or even to share with others what the larder contained."[49]

Despite their common desire to conserve the treasures of our common cultural heritage, O'Connor and Tate remained divided about the most fundamental thing. She was devoted to the fundamentalist South because she believed that its Christianity proffered a divine remedy for the perennial human malaise, while Tate exalted the antebellum South because he believed its civilization provided an answer to modern barbarity. Yet the nervousness of Tate's ultimate conviction is poignantly revealed in a confession made by Lacy Buchan in Tate's novel *The Fathers:* "Excessively refined persons have a communion with the abyss; but is not civilization the agreement, slowly arrived at, to let the abyss alone?"[50] If by "the abyss" Tate means the demonic, he is right to warn against a hyper-sophistication that toys with the Void.[51]

---

49. William F. Buckley, Jr., *Gratitude: Reflections on What We Owe to Our Country* (New York: Random House, 1990), p. 16.

50. Quoted in Dennis Donoghue, "Second Thoughts," *New York Review of Books* (May 22, 1969): 44. Not long before his baptism in 1950, Tate made a similar confession: "As I look back upon my own verse, written over more than twenty-five years, I see plainly that its main theme is man suffering from unbelief; and I cannot for a moment suppose that this man is some other than myself" (quoted in Huff, *Allen Tate and the Catholic Revival,* p. 118).

51. In a letter to Betty Hester, O'Connor lamented the sorry state of Allen Tate and Caroline Gordon's marriage, attributing their difficulty not to his philandering alone but also to their "sophisticated" attitude toward alcohol. Since O'Connor was hardly a teetotaler herself, she was not indulging in a hectoring self-righteousness. She was perhaps recalling St. Augus-

Christians are enjoined to avoid all commerce with the satanic "principalities and powers" (Eph. 3:10). Even so, the church finds no refuge from the abyss in the safeties of civilization. The central teaching of *The City of God* is that evil corrupts not chiefly individuals but rather civilizations. The wondrous ideal of *Romanitas* was ruined not only by the invading Visigoths, nor by Rome's own governmental and economic failures, but also by its moral and religious pretense. Romans believed their civilization to be eternal, a realm where "it was possible to attain a goal of permanent security, peace and freedom through political action, especially through submission to the 'virtue and fortune' of a political leader."[52] Even if Tate meant to be calling for a Christian civilization that would correct the errors of both Greece and Rome, he never clarifies its relationship to the church.

Neither does Tate seem to recognize the fallibility of Western civilization itself, a matter that G. K. Chesterton clarified with his usual pungency and precision. The latter argues that, just as poetry precedes prose in the order of literature, so does democracy precede civilization in the order of politics. It's when democracies can no longer depend on simple majorities that they must rely on the received traditions and inherited wisdom of civilization. Against the naive notion that the human species has risen progressively out of barbarity, Chesterton maintains that civilizations always dwell alongside barbarism, "the civilisation sometimes spreading to absorb the barbarians, sometimes decaying into relative barbarism, and in almost all cases possessing in a more finished form certain ideas and institutions which the barbarians possess in a ruder form."[53] Despotism is not the result of barbaric self-assertion, Chesterton insists, but rather of civilized exhaustion. Because they are temporal and fallen creations — the thousand-year rule of Romanitas to the contrary — civilizations are subject not only to decay but also to corruption. Just as Jews had to survive both Egyptian and Babylonian corruption and decay, so have Christians had to face the failure of both Greek and Roman civilizations. Now that we are witnessing the collapse of our own

---

tine's celebrated saying that God is nearer to us than we are to ourselves: "I guess they just don't see anything wrong with drinking (both of them) as much as they do, but the Lord knows it creates a terrible waste, waste of time, waste of talent, waste of spiritual energy, waste of existence. It must come from some misunderstanding about the nearness of God. You get drunk when you aren't conscious that God is immediately present. I mean that is the only time it would seem possible to get drunk" (CW, 1012).

52. Charles Norris Cochrane, *Christianity and Classical Culture: A Study of Thought and Action from Augustus to Augustine* (New York: Oxford University Press, 1957; first published in 1940), p. vi.

53. G. K. Chesterton, *The Everlasting Man* (New York: Image, 1955; first published in 1925), p. 64.

Western civilization, the chief task of the church is to differentiate itself from the moribund Christendom with which it was once so fully allied and even identified.[54]

Flannery O'Connor understood, as Allen Tate and the Agrarians did not, that there can be no identification of Christian faith and Western civilization. "It's in the nature of the Church," she wrote, "to survive all crises — in however battered a fashion. The Church can't be identified with Western culture and I suppose the wreck of it doesn't cause her much of a sense of crisis" (HB, 299). This remarkable confession may explain O'Connor's surprising confession to Elizabeth Hester, made less than six months before her death, that she was reading *I'll Take My Stand* "for the first time." Perhaps she waited so long because she feared what she might find. Given her friendship with Allen Tate and Caroline Gordon, as well as their shared cultural conservatism, one would have assumed that O'Connor had read this book eagerly and early in her career. She calls the anthology "a very interesting document" and praises it as "the only time real minds have got together to talk about the South" (HB, 566). Yet one can hardly imagine O'Connor's having perused Tate's "Remarks on the Southern Religion" with anything other than shock and perhaps even anger. For her, the religion of the South was never something to be created for the sake of a faith in its "own kind of God." O'Connor believed, on the contrary, that the triune God has uniquely disclosed himself in Israel and Christ, and that he has instituted the very existence of the one holy, catholic, and apostolic church. From her careful observation of Southern fundamentalists, she could have told Tate that their "convinced supernaturalism" derives not from St. Thomas Aquinas but, however distantly, from John Calvin and John Wesley and John Knox. For her, the Christ-haunted quality of Southern life made it admirable even if it remained alien to the rest of the nation. For Tate, by contrast, a narrow-minded Protestantism was the chief religious failing of the South. Never

---

54. Søren Kierkegaard was the first modern prophet of this necessary differentiation, though many others have followed in his train. In our final chapter, we shall discuss Karl Barth's express call for a deliberate Christian divorce from Christendom. It must be confessed that Chesterton — living almost a century ago and not yet faced with the full barbarity of the twentieth century — was only partially aware of Christendom's radical fallibility. Even so, he could never make the complete identification of Christianity and Western civilization offered by his friend Hilaire Belloc: "The Faith is Europe, Europe is the Faith." What Belloc meant, Michael Novak insists, is that "Europe is the child of Christianity, and Christianity shows its incarnate flesh in Europe, as one day it will also [embody itself] in all cultures that will accept the yeast of its joyous, suffering-tempted vision" ("July's Child," an introduction to Belloc's *The Path to Rome* (Washington, DC: Henry Regnery, 1987; first published 1915), p. xviii.

could he see the link between fundamentalism and Catholicism that was so central to O'Connor's vision and work. It was not aesthetic contempt alone that prompted Tate's response. He knew that its angular and obstreperous kind of faith could never be used for his urbane program to revive the cultural unity of the West. She, by contrast, was convinced that thorny Christianity of the Southern kind, despite its many failings, preserved the scandal and offense of the gospel as a radical corrective to the best no less than the worst of cultures and civilizations.

## Eugene Genovese on the Conflicted Character of Southern Culture

Eugene Genovese, a former Marxist now returned to his native Catholicism, is a much better guide to antebellum Southern culture than is Allen Tate. Although Genovese's work postdates O'Connor's, her regard for the South is much closer to Genovese's than to Tate's. Genovese sees slavery as absolutely essential to the Southern civilization, not (as Tate argued) an unfortunate excrescence, a disfiguring barnacle on the Southern ship of state. Genovese's work can best be read, I believe, against the complaint that Lionel Trilling, himself a venerable liberal, made in the 1950s. Trilling complained that America has had no other cultural tradition than liberalism: "In the United States at this time liberalism is not only the dominant but even the sole intellectual tradition. For it is a plain fact that nowadays there are no conservative or reactionary ideas in general circulation." Trilling offered his magisterial judgment not boastfully but regretfully. He complained that, in its prosaic desire to enlarge human freedom through a rational organization of life, liberalism neglects the poetic "imagination of variousness and possibility, which implies the awareness of complexity and difficulty." Liberals often forget, Trilling warned, that "the world is a complex and unexpected and terrible place which is not always to be understood by the mind as we use it in our everyday tasks."[55] Trilling feared that our monolithic optimism about human nature and destiny has robbed many Americans of any acute sense of self-criticism, leaving us inattentive to the complexity and tragedy of our mortal existence.

Eugene Genovese has spent much of his career both describing and defending what Lionel Trilling overlooked, namely, the lively Southern alterna-

55. Lionel Trilling, *The Liberal Imagination* (Garden City, NY: Doubleday Anchor, 1950), pp. vii, xii.

tive to standard American liberalism. In an age that values "difference" and "otherness" above nearly all other qualities, Genovese has sought to vindicate, albeit critically, the highly discomfiting kind of difference and otherness that has thrived below the Mason-Dixon line. Against Dixie-haters both genteel and crude, he insists that the South possesses an estimable antiliberal tradition. For more than two centuries, he argues, it has produced intellectuals

> ... whose work ranked with the best the North had to offer and in some cases overmatched it: George Tucker and Jacob N. Cardozo in political economy; John Randolph of Roanoke, John C. Calhoun, and Albert T. Bledsoe in political theory; James Henley Thornwell, Robert Breckenridge, and Robert L. Dabney in theology and ecclesiology; Thomas Roderick Dew and William H. Trescot in the interpretation of history; George Frederick Holmes and Hugh S. Legare in social and cultural criticism. ...
>
> [M]uch of their thought has passed into some of twentieth-century America's most penetrating social and literary criticism at the hands of southerners who, alas, are largely ignored in Academia: Allen Tate, John Crowe Ransom, Donald Davidson, John Gould Fletcher, Richard Weaver, and, more recently, M. E. Bradford, John Shelton Reed, Thomas Fleming, and Clyde Wilson.[56]

Genovese's work is at once corrective and restorative. He wants to rescue these emarginated Southern thinkers and writers from the oblivion to which academic correctness would condemn them. He demonstrates that, far from being merely racist and reactionary, the intellectuals of the antebellum South sought to undergird their culture with the virtues displayed in "the organic communities of pre-modern Europe." "They struggled," says Genovese, "to create a culture that would stand as a worthy heir to the best in the Western Christian tradition and [thus] prove a bulwark against the disintegrating tendencies of the modern world." They sought, in short, to create "a plantation on a hill."[57] This allusion to John Winthrop's celebrated call for the Puritans to create "a city set upon a hill" is more astute than clever. Genovese contends that the early Southern aristocrats set themselves deliberately in opposition to the Emersonian ideal of the sovereign autonomous self, the individual set over against all confining institutions, even against so-

---

56. Eugene Genovese, *The Southern Front: History and Politics in the Cultural War* (Columbia, MO: University of Missouri Press, 1995), p. 108.

57. Ibid., p. 57.

ciety itself. The chief founders and sustainers of the Southern tradition sought, by contrast, to create an integral society that would offer a morally superior and more socially cohesive way of life than embodied in the rampant individualism of the North. They also opposed the unrestrained capitalism undergirding the economic life of their northern counterparts. When they spoke of "the infidel North," they did not decry abolitionism and unbelief alone, but also "the marketplace society that promoted competitive individualism and worshipped Mammon."[58]

The South's racial legacy has led, Genovese argues, to the obscuring of its salutary critique of bourgeois liberalism. As a result, the North is commonly seen as having racial virtue almost entirely on its side, while the South has been regarded as racist and reactionary at its core. George Washington Cable appeared manifestly correct, therefore, in calling Southerners to shuffle off their race-based alienation from the rest of the country and to be folded into the generic American mix. Hence his summons to an audience of fellow Southerners gathered at the University of Mississippi in 1882.

> When the whole intellectual energy of the Southern states flew to the defense of that one institution which made us the South, we broke with human progress. We broke with the world's thought. We have not entirely in all things joined hands with it again. When we have done so we shall know it by this — there will be no South. We shall be Virginians, Texians, Louisianians, Mississippians, and we shall at the same time and over and above all be Americans. . . . Let us hasten to be no longer a unique people.[59]

Genovese dissents from this standard liberal reading of both national and regional history. What he discovered in the South's ablest thinkers is an argument that he first learned from Vilfredo Pareto and that his Marxism would never refute: human society is unavoidably hierarchical. Like the Marx whom they never knew, the slaveholding aristocrats and divines argued, with considerable cogency, that every society is inevitably stratified, that the laboring classes (whether white or black) will always be subordinated to the master classes, and yet that the masters are themselves accountable to God in their responsibility for the householders and servants and workers in their

---

58. Eugene Genovese, *A Consuming Fire: The Fall of the Confederacy in the Mind of the White Christian South* (Athens, GA: University of Georgia Press, 1998), p. 102.

59. George W. Cable, *The Negro Question: A Selection of Writings on Civil Rights in the South*, ed. Arlin Turner (New York: Doubleday Anchor, 1958), p. 43.

care. Here people are related to each other personally and not by the cash-nexus.

To these tradition-loving Southerners, elitism was not a bad but a good thing. They acknowledged the superiority of some kinds of talent and effort and education over others. They believed in the ideal of noblesse oblige. They held that the weak must be protected by the strong, the poor by the wealthy, rather than leaving them at the mercy of the market forces that would surely devour them. Thus did the slaveholders see themselves not as oppressors but as protectors and guardians of their slaves. They spoke of their chattels as members of "our family, white and black." "They described their ownership of slaves as a 'duty' and a 'burden,'" Genovese notes, "and were convinced that without the protection they offered the blacks would, literally, be exterminated in a marketplace in which they could not compete."[60] David Hundley of Alabama was at once crystal clear and acidly ironic in putting the slaveholders' case:

> It may be that the older order of things, the old relationship between landowner and villein, protected the latter from many hardships to which the nominal freemen of the nineteenth century are subjected by the blessed influences of free competition and the practical workings of the good old charitable and praiseworthy English maxim: "Every man for himself, and the devil take the hindmost."[61]

Genovese argues that it was not only Southern vices but also Southern virtues that enabled the region to practice compulsory bondage. The slave-sanctioning theologians — in fact, most of the slaveholders themselves — were not monsters of self-interest but men of good will. It is not their gross sins, Genovese reveals, but their subtle self-contradictions that remain most significant. Setting out to be a traditionalist and humane society, the South became, unwittingly, a modernist and inhuman culture. For the South gradually embraced the most fundamental modern premise: the notion that everything can be commodified, even human life itself. To offset the ruthless capitalist urge that animated its life, the Southern conservative tradition proposed an allegedly benign paternalism. The aristocrat theologians of the South called on slaveholders to treat their slaves humanely, lest God be pro-

60. Eugene Genovese, *"Slavery Ordained of God": The Southern Slaveholders' View of Biblical History and Modern Politics* (Gettysburg, PA: Gettysburg College, 1985), p. 38.

61. Quoted in Eugene Genovese, "The Southern Slaveholders' View of the Middle Ages," in *Medievalism in American Culture*, ed. Bernard Rosenthal and Paul E. Szarmach (Binghamton, NY: Medieval & Renaissance Texts & Studies, 1989), p. 41.

voked to wrath. They urged masters to give their slaves the right to marry and thus to keep their families intact. They even argued that a benevolent Christian slavery was a means of evangelism, offering "the South [its] best hope for the vital work of preparation for the Kingdom."[62] Slaves were held in trust, the theologians insisted. They were not to be brutalized as beasts, but treated as brothers and sisters in the eyes of the Lord, even if not in social and political fact. Richard Fuller, a Baptist minister from South Carolina, sternly warned slaveholders: "The Bible informs us what man is; and among such beings, irresponsible power is a trust too easily and too frequently abused."[63]

Yet abuse was inevitable, and not only because slave owners had inherited the universal human proclivity for inhumane treatment of our own kind. Abuse was sure to come because the desire for a paternalistic protection of slaves could not survive in the new modern setting "of expanding capitalism, industrialization, bourgeois individualism, and Enlightenment liberalism."[64] Southern slaves were not, in fact, sheltered serfs but private property. Despite many firm enjoinders to treat slaves according to the Golden Rule, the slave states removed nearly every humanizing amenity from slave life. As Genovese observes, they passed laws actually prohibiting slave literacy, lest perhaps, in learning to read, slaves might scan Scripture no less than abolitionist tracts. Georgia even prohibited slave ownership of paper and writing instruments.[65] Most of these same Southern states refused also to recognize slave marriages, thus making it easy to break up slave families for the sake of profitable sales. Hence the poignant confession of John S. Wise, writing his postwar account of old Virginia life in *The End of an Era*, a rueful testimony that Genovese sums up succinctly: "The mere sight of [a slave auction] should have told Southerners that slavery was wrong."[66] Abraham Lincoln was far more acerbic, as in this scorching response to Frederick Augustus Ross's *Slavery Ordained of God* (1857): "Nonsense! . . . Wolves devouring lambs, not because it is good for their own greedy maws, but because it is good for the lambs!!!"[67]

The heart of Genovese's accomplishment is to have uncovered the tragic irony underlying the entire Southern slave system. It was a complex

62. Genovese, *A Consuming Fire*, p. xiv.
63. Quoted in ibid, p. 9.
64. Genovese, "The Southern Slaveholders' View of the Middle Ages," p. 32.
65. Genovese, *A Consuming Fire*, p. 24.
66. Ibid., p. 20.
67. Quoted in Allen C. Guelzo, *Abraham Lincoln: Redeemer President* (Grand Rapids, MI: Eerdmans, 1999), p. 314.

three-pronged business. The aristocratic slaveholders sought to build a Christian republic that would retrieve the finest ideals not only of ancient Greece and Rome but also of medieval Europe. At least in this first regard, Allen Tate read them aright. Their cultural vision enabled them acutely to foresee, in the second place, that a triumphant market economy would eventually consume modern society itself, subjecting all spiritual traditions and moral values to commercial forces. As an alternative to such heartless Enlightenment economic individualism, Southern aristocrats sought to create an organic society built on radical mutual dependence, a high sense of personal and familial honor, and a chivalric code of manners — the entire enterprise being undergirded by the allegedly benign paternalism of master-slave relations. Tate made accurate judgments on this second score as well. Yet he misread the third and fatal quality of the Old South: its high cultural aims clashed with the economic means of achieving them. However much the South's aristocratic thinkers sought to liken their kind of slavery to medieval serfdom, the fact remained that the slave-plantations were the creation of the modern market system, the "young finance-capitalist economy" that we have heard Tate mistakenly attributing to the Reformation. This system was not driven by the much-touted mutuality of slave and master relations, Genovese demonstrates, but by the ruthless capitalist law of supply and demand, especially the demand "for human labor and the commodities which it produced."[68] Thus was the South's venerable cultural ideal of a humane society tragically undermined by an economic system that was itself the product of the modern capitalist culture that the Southern gentry abominated.

## Lewis P. Simpson, Lionel Trilling, and the Burden of the Southern Past

More than any other critic, Lewis P. Simpson has discerned the disagreement between Flannery O'Connor and the Agrarians. He affirms Genovese's contention that the so-called feudal South was almost wholly a myth invented by Allen Tate. No matter how noble its attempt to establish a traditionalist culture, the slave society of the Old South was driven by economic motives that could not be isolated from the world marketplace. This brave new world was democratic as well as capitalist, since it was animated by the modernist impulse to make "the sovereignty of the people the center of . . . political

68. Genovese, *"Slavery Ordained of God,"* p. 35.

life."[69] Simpson praises Tate and his fellow Agrarians for joining William Faulkner, Eudora Welty, and others in rescuing Southern literature from its futile attempt to justify slavery and segregation. They sought, instead, to assimilate their work to the high culture of the modern West that springs from Proust, Joyce, and Mann and their successors. The leaders of the Southern literary renascence rightly discerned that the medieval communal world had been steadily dissolving for centuries, not only in the South but also throughout the whole of Europe and America.

Beginning with the sixteenth-century recovery of classical culture, perhaps even with the late Middle Ages, the literary imagination of the West became gradually dispossessed of its singular metanarrative concerning human nature and destiny: its calamitous Fall, its costly Restoration, its hoped-for Consummation. At the same time, the West also lost the ethical and philosophical tradition that had become the legacy of this grand Christian narrative. Once this taken-for-granted metaphysical and moral order collapsed, Simpson observes, modern Western culture was left with the terror of history. He quotes Wilhelm Dilthey, the nineteenth-century German philosopher who summarized the modern pathos succinctly: "We are open to the possibility that meaning and significance arise only in man and in his history."[70] No longer is history understood as the dramatization of the one Story, but rather an ineluctable process or series of processes, an inexorable succession of events, the forward-rushing river of time. History is all we have. It can be understood either rationally, as having its own internal *telos* (in Hegel and his followers), or else irrationally, as having neither sponsorship nor direction (in Nietzsche and his legatees). This world is the only locus of meaning, and man is its only maker. The sea of faith, once at full tide and brimming with confidence, has left only its "melancholy, long, withdrawing roar," as Matthew Arnold called it. The rise of industrial and commercial civilization has produced what Simpson identifies as yet another emptiness: the disappearance of the organic community "of kinship and custom, of tradition and myth."[71] The upshot is that modern literary culture lacks any bardic or epic expression of a common and collective good, any communal world built on shared beliefs and virtues.

Following the lead of Mann, Proust, and Joyce, modern Southern writers have sought to replace the lost Story of transcendent meaning with

---

69. Lewis P. Simpson, *The Brazen Face of History: Studies in the Literary Consciousness in America* (Athens, GA: University of Georgia Press, 1980), p. 76.

70. Simpson, p. 125.

71. Ibid., p. 241.

what Simpson calls "an aesthetic of memory."[72] They have been determined to remember the rich social history of the South, especially the tragedy of the Civil War, by transfiguring it into enduring art. But lacking the confidence that this history belongs to any grand pattern of divine order, they have been compelled to assimilate history to memory by sifting it through the sieve of their own consciousness. The "turn to the subject" that has been the hallmark of modern philosophy and theology finds its natural counterpart in modern Southern literature. While offering nothing akin to salvation, either individual or communal, this literary remembrance of things past does provide an aesthetic island of refuge amidst the historicist floods of modernity.

Robert Penn Warren illustrates this turn toward the remembering subject, this reduction of history to personal and individual construction, perhaps more clearly than any other Agrarian. Unlike Tate, who sought to retrieve the heroism and dignity allegedly inherent in Southern social life, Warren discerned that the past exists only in the consciousness of individuals — individuals who are able to do with history as they want, ascribing as little or as much meaning to it as they will:

> Warren . . . understood history as provisional, relative, and contingent. Knowledge of history, like knowledge of the self, was a human construct that offered no innate value or meaning. If modern men wanted history to mean something, if they wanted to locate themselves in time and mold their identities, they would have to do so themselves. Yet Warren insisted that, whatever the disabilities under which they labored, modern men were obliged to create values and meaning if they hoped to transcend the essential chaos of the modern world. It was simply that society, history, tradition, and faith tendered little help or solace in this endeavor. Modern men lived without certainty, subject to, and striving against, anxiety, anomie, rootlessness, subjectivity, and loneliness.[73]

---

72. Ibid., p. 233.

73. Malvasi, p. 12. For Warren, even the Civil War failed to display the virtues of heroic men who were bound together by the pieties of blood and kin, who were joined by region and cause, and thus who were fighting a battle of good against evil. As the war of a nation divided against itself, its main interest for Warren derives from the conflicted and tormented souls of its chief agonists — Lincoln and Grant, Lee and Davis: "These were modern men. . . . In their efforts to overcome strife and division, to establish a clear purpose, and to fashion an identity amid the riot of events, the men who fought the war mirrored the aspirations, disappointments, and fears of Americans in the late twentieth century" (ibid., p. 15).

Simpson stands in full accord with Mark Malvasi's assessment of Warren and the other Agrarians. Yet he admits that there are exceptions to this Southern recourse to an "aesthetic of memory": Walker Percy and Flannery O'Connor. As Christians writing against the historicizing grain of their age, they unabashedly deny, though in radically different ways, that history is the sole and final reality. They assume, instead, "a transcendent referent for human existence" and thus "a divine authorization" for both art and life. But Simpson complains that, unlike Percy, O'Connor purchased her prophetic literary vision — her "aesthetic of revelation" — at a fearful price that the Agrarians and other modernists were unwilling to pay. She declined the troublous exigencies of modern history. The result, in Simpson's view, is that her characters lack the requisite

> . . . sophistication to grapple inwardly with the subtleties of the self as a creature of modern secular history. She lacks, perhaps refuses, an intimacy with history. . . . Her vision is directed toward timeless order and the ultimate beatitude of the soul. . . . The result is that, in spite of their detailed portrayal of the manners of her region, [her stories] divest it of a tension toward historical reality.[74]

Simpson reaches his negative verdict on O'Connor because he assumes that "historical reality" displays itself primarily in large public events and among the established institutions of society.[75] Lionel Trilling points out, on the contrary, that American history has been either too thin or else too dreadful to command the artist's interest. Apart from the Civil War, modern Americans have experienced no political struggles large enough to engage the literary imagination. The terrors of the previous century's unprecedented blood-letting, together with the ideologies that spawned it, have given most imaginative writers a virtual contempt for society and the state and history. The incommunicable atrocities of modern life have prompted in artists what

74. Simpson, p. 248.

75. Yet Simpson is right to regard the problem of historicism as a uniquely modern problem. Karl Löwith observes, for example, that atheism as we know it is a paradoxically Christian phenomenon. It was not a problem for our ancient pagan forebears since, for them, the world was both eternal and divine. The world becomes godless and godforsaken, says Karl Löwith, only with the collapse of Christian "belief in a transcendent Creator-God who . . . is as distinct from the world as a creator is from his creatures and yet is the source of every being. . . ." Nothing is then left but what Löwith calls "the sheer contingency of [the universe's] mere 'existence'" (*Meaning in History: The Theological Implications of the Philosophy of History* [Chicago: University of Chicago Press, 1949], p. 201).

Ortega y Gasset called "a real loathing of living forms and living beings," a disgust with the "rounded and soft forms of living bodies." That Ortega has in mind the art of his countryman Pablo Picasso seems evident. Trilling also notices that even our advertising, which pretends to celebrate human life, can scarcely disguise its scorn for the human form it exploits. Amidst such a terribly dehumanized world as ours, the function of art, says Trilling, is to rehumanize us. What we least need, says Trilling, is the anonymous and silenced voice of many modern novelists. Their disappearing narrators "have but reinforced the faceless hostility of the world and have tended to teach us that we ourselves are not creative agents and that we have no voice, no tone, no style, no significant existence." Hence Trilling's call for novelists whose voice is not banished from their books: "Surely what we need is . . . the opportunity to identify ourselves with a mind that willingly admits that it is a mind and does not pretend that it is History or Events or the World but only a mind thinking and planning — possibly planning our escape."[76]

Flannery O'Connor has won a large audience, despite the smallness of her oeuvre, because she is such a voice and such a mind. The narrative voice that speaks in her work is akin to the Old Testament in its unapologetic directness of approach to the reader. She is also a writer who, in speaking as one intelligence to another, helps spring our escape into the reality of a larger history than that of the Civil War. Perhaps sensing the dead end that the Agrarians had already reached in their attempt to create a new aesthetic of memory from the resources of Southern history, she expressed her own boredom with the "late unpleasantness," as some Southerners persist in calling the Civil War. In her only story devoted to the topic, "A Late Encounter with the Enemy," she makes merciless fun of the annual Confederate Day celebration that was still being held in her own town of Milledgeville. O'Connor agreed with Trilling that ours is a time when even the most ordinary person is engaged with ideas:

> Every person we meet in the course of our daily life, no matter how unlettered he may be, is groping with sentences toward a sense of his life and his position in it; and he has what almost always goes with the impulse to ideology, a good deal of animus and anger. What would have so much pleased the social philosopher of an earlier time [i.e., Karl Marx!] has come to pass — ideological organization has cut across class organization, generating loyalties and animosities which are perhaps even more intense than those of class. The increase of conscious formulation,

76. Lionel Trilling, "Art and Fortune," in *The Liberal Imagination*, pp. 257, 261.

the increase of a certain kind of consciousness by formulation, makes a fact of modern life which is never sufficiently estimated.[77]

In ages when faith could be taken for granted — when one could be a Catholic just as someone else would be a Baptist or Methodist — there was no occasion for vehement loyalty or bitter animosity. O'Connor discerned that such an age is forever past, that we live in what has been called "a tournament of narratives," a contest of storied ideas, a clash of faiths which unite and divide people along class-transcending lines. Tate's attempt to repristinate a feudal version of Southern history, even if it had existed, would have been an otiose exercise to O'Connor. Nor would she have engaged in the culture wars that have riven American life at the turn of the millennium. Both endeavors are picayune when compared to the question that Simpson rightly poses. The central quandary for our time is whether secular history constitutes the beginning and end and sum of human existence, or whether there is another history, a history that the elites of literary and academic culture have ignored because it has been enacted by poor white and poor black Christians.

Against Simpson's claim that O'Connor refused the burden of history by failing to encase it in the web of the self, I maintain that she assumed it heroically by giving voice to those whom official history has left almost unnoticed. O'Connor believed that there is another history, that it has been lived out by obscure fundamentalist Protestants, and that, when rendered into art, it answers Lionel Trilling's call for a literature of ideas. Dennis Covington maintains, in this same vein, that Southern poor whites have been "the only ethnic group in America not permitted to have a history." Nor have we noticed the vigor of their religious protest against the vacuity of modern American culture:

> The peculiarity of Southern experience didn't end when the boll weevil ate up the cotton crop. We didn't cease to be a separate country when Burger King came to Meridian. We're as peculiar a people now as we ever were, and the fact that our culture is under assault has forced us to become even more peculiar than we were before. Snake handling, for instance, didn't originate back in the hills somewhere. It started when people came down from the hills to discover they were surrounded by a hostile and spiritually dead culture. All along their border with the modern world — in places like Newport, Tennessee, and Sand Mountain, Ala-

---

77. Ibid., p. 266.

bama — they recoiled. They threw up defenses. When their own resources failed, they called down the Holy Ghost. They put their hands
through fire. They drank poison. They took up serpents.[78]

In his remarkable account of Appalachian snake-handlers, Covington
reveals the profound humanity of these people whom our official histories
dismiss as bizarre if not certifiably insane. He also demonstrates the splendid
Blakean literalism of their imagination. Inspired by their central biblical text,
one group of serpent-handlers named themselves "The Church of Jesus with
Signs Following": "And these signs shall follow them that believe: In my name
they shall cast out devils; they shall speak with new tongues; they shall take
up serpents; and if they drink any deadly thing, it shall not hurt them; they
shall lay hands on the sick, and they shall recover" (Mark 16:17-18). Facing
constant ridicule and scorn, these foot-washing Pentecostals remain undaunted in their determination to be "a separated people," followers of the
Christ who commanded them to be "in the world but not of the world." As a
sophisticate reporting for the *New York Times,* Covington came only to observe. But he became so convinced of the divine power at work in these ne-
glected and despised people that he joined in their sacraments. At first he was
stirred to participate in their biblical practice of washing each other's feet. "I
was moved by something I could not name. It was like desire, and not like desire, a longing for something that could not be possessed."[79] Finally,
Covington was sufficiently anointed by the Spirit to handle the same serpent
that had bitten and killed other members:

> I turned to face the congregation and lifted the rattlesnake up toward the
> light. It was moving like it wanted to get up even higher, to climb out of
> that church and into the air. And it was exactly as the handlers had told
> me. I felt no fear. The snake seemed to be an extension of myself. And
> suddenly there seemed to be nothing in the room but me and the snake.
> Everything else had disappeared . . . all gone, all faded to white. And I
> could not hear the earsplitting music. The air was silent and still and
> filled with that strong, even light. And I realized that I, too, was fading
> into the white. I was losing myself by degrees, like the incredible shrink-
> ing man. The snake would be the last to go, and all I could see was the
> way its scales shimmered one last time in the light, and the way its head

78. Dennis Covington, *Salvation on Sand Mountain: Snake-Handling and Redemption in Southern Appalachia* (New York: Penguin, 1995), pp. xvii-xviii.
79. Ibid., p. 120.

moved from side to side, searching for a way out. I knew then why the handlers took up serpents. There is power in the act of disappearing; there is victory in the loss of self. It must be close to our conception of paradise, what it's like before you're born or after you die.[80]

Not many will be moved to follow Covington's example.[81] Yet only the most blinkered and blinded will deny the truthfulness of his claim that these Appalachian Pentecostals have laid hold, in admittedly extreme ways, of the transcendent Story that breaks the closed circle of secular history. Far from being irrelevant to such secularity, these backcountry Christians live in a community that leaves them at least partially immune from the market-driven materialism that has destroyed much of Western religion and culture. James Peacock and Ruel Tyson, an ethnographer and a historian respectively, attest to the similarly stringent testimony that the Primitive Baptists of southern Virginia offer to secular history. They refuse the sundry blandishments of modernity to spiritualize the secular, as Hegel called it. "Primitive Baptist churches do not recognize Memorial Day, Fourth of July, town or county commemorations, or Father's Day and Mother's Day. To wed ritual to [civic] community, family, or state is to lose the transcendence of the sacred. Hence, in neither theory nor practice do Primitive Baptists support any semblance of American civil religion."[82] These unabashed literalists and fundamentalists and supernaturalists, in their very resistance to the corrosives of modernity, interest Flannery O'Connor — not as quaint relics from a bygone era but as powerful witnesses to our own age.

## The Scopes Trial, Writhing Pentecostals, and Eternity within Time

The turning point for many things Southern occurred in 1925 with the trial of John T. Scopes for teaching evolution in the public schools of Dayton, Tennessee. William Jennings Bryan, a native Nebraskan and three-time Democratic nominee for the presidency, as well as Secretary of State under Wood-

---

80. Ibid., pp. 169-70.

81. I asked Covington what he would have done if he had been bitten. "I would have screamed for someone to call 911!" It's one thing to take up serpents, another to rely on faith-healers.

82. James L. Peacock and Ruel W. Tyson, Jr., *Pilgrims of Paradox: Calvinism and Experience among the Primitive Baptists of the Blue Ridge* (Washington, DC: Smithsonian Institution, 1989), p. 194.

row Wilson, was the chief attorney chosen by the World's Christian Fundamentals Association to prosecute the case against Scopes. Yet Bryan was not a fundamentalist of the Southern stripe at all. In fact, the Southern Baptist Convention (at its annual meeting, which happened to be held in Memphis just prior to the trial) refused to pass a resolution calling for anti-evolution laws. Nor did Bryan himself oppose the teaching of evolution on the grounds that it contradicted a literal reading of Genesis. He argued, on the contrary, that it lacked scientific proof and that it undermined the religious faith and the moral values of the students. Bryan had seen that, in the hands of a thinker such as Herbert Spencer, evolution could be put to dreadful social uses — eliminating the weak members of society, for example, for the sake of the "fittest" who survive and prosper. Bryan was committed, above all else, to the proposition that local schools should be controlled by their own citizens, not by an oligarchy of scientists and educationists.[83] And though Bryan mouthed the standard affirmations about the inerrant inspiration of Scripture and the deity of Christ, his abiding interest lay with the preservation of Christian civilization. In a speech entitled "The Old-Time Religion" he had given in 1911 at the Winona Bible Conference, Bryan had set forth his conviction that "Christian civilization is the greatest that the world has ever known because it rests on a conception of life that makes life one unending progress toward higher things, with no limit to human advancement or development."[84] Far from being akin to anything resembling a Southern fundamentalist, Bryan shared the basic Northern and liberal assumptions concerning human nature and destiny.

As always, the ironies of history are remarkable. Mencken's dark Spenglerian cynicism about the future of civilization gave him far greater kinship with an Agrarian pessimist such as Allen Tate than with a Christian optimist such as Bryan. But it was Mencken who helped persuade Clarence Darrow to defend Scopes after H. G. Wells had declined; and it was Mencken himself who served as a reporter for the notorious event. The onslaught of anti-Southern criticism that the Scopes trial prompted in the pages of many Northern newspapers and journals, especially *The New Republic,* helped to inspire the Agrarians' defense of the South.[85] Though Mencken failed to discern authentic Southern virtues, he was right about the terrible link between Southern biblicism and Southern racism: "The most booming sort of piety,

83. Edward J. Larson, *Summer for the Gods: The Scopes Trial and America's Continuing Debate over Science and Religion* (Cambridge, MA: Harvard University Press, 1997), pp. 98-99.

84. Quoted in George M. Marsden, *Fundamentalism and American Culture: The Shaping of Twentieth-Century Evangelicalism, 1870-1925* (New York: Oxford University Press, 1980), p. 134.

85. See Hobson, *Tell About the South*, pp. 183-243.

in the south, is not incompatible with the theory that lynching is a benign institution."[86] In a letter to Mencken, Howard Odum confirmed the veteran South-hater's view that religious revivals "often joined hands with the Ku Klux Klan. . . . The revivals came also to be a fanning breeze for the fires of bigotry and intolerance, and the revivalists used a powerful mob psychology to warp the minds and souls of thousands of children and youth who were never to recover."[87]

While covering the Scopes trial, Mencken attended a brush-arbor revival in a nearby Tennessee community. He was horrified by what he saw. When the Pentecostal believers gathered at the front to make intercession for one especially distraught sinner, Mencken described the scene as an incredible "barbaric grotesquerie":

> At a signal all the faithful crowded up to the bench and began to pray — not in unison but each for himself. At another [gesture] they all fell on their knees, their arms over the penitent. The leader kneeled, facing us, his head alternately thrown back dramatically or buried in his hands. Words spouted from his mouth like bullets from a machine gun — appeals to pull the penitent back out of hell, defiance of the powers and principalities of the air, a vast impassioned jargon of apocalyptic texts. Suddenly he rose to his feet, threw back his head and began to speak in tongues — blub-blub-blub, gurgle-gurgle-gurgle. His voice rose to a higher register. The climax was a shrill, inarticulate squawk, like that of a man throttled. He fell headlong across the pyramid of supplicants.
>
> A comic scene? Somehow no. The poor half-wits were too horribly in earnest. It was like peeping through a knot-hole at the writhings of a people in pain.[88]

Despite his unbridled contempt for these "poor half-wits," Mencken was too honest to deny that, because they were grappling with something painfully real, they were not to be idly mocked. Neither could he laugh at the Maryland Baptist whose execution he witnessed. The convict had slain his unfaithful wife, thus breaking the sixth commandment, Mencken snidely observed, while enforcing the seventh. The condemned man mounted the gallows while quoting Psalm 23. As he came to the final phrase ("And I shall

---

86. *Prejudices*, p. 77.

87. Quoted in Hobson, *Serpent in Eden*, p. 96.

88. Quoted in Carl Bode, *Mencken* (Carbondale, IL: Southern Illinois University Press, 1973), p. 267.

dwell in the house of — "), the floor dropped from beneath him and he was hanged. Mencken's response to this scene serves as the final words to his *Treatise on the Gods:* "As an American, I naturally spend most of my time laughing, but that time I did not laugh."[89] The power of retrograde religion to shackle the simple-minded was, for Mencken, far too grievous an evil to justify a comic response. Yet Mencken's identification of himself as an always-laughing American indicates at least a residual unease. Mencken hints that, like many of his amused countrymen, he may not have formulated what Trilling calls a satisfying "sense of his life and his position in it." For Flannery O'Connor, a Baptist murderer quoting Psalm 23 may have made considerable advance over a joshing nihilist who has nothing to say in the face of death. Alistair Cooke, a Mencken disciple, once observed that the Depression shredded Mencken's sails, as his smirking cynicism proved both irrelevant and insulting to a suffering people.

A writhing Pentecostal of Mencken's "barbaric grotesquerie" appears in O'Connor's story called "Greenleaf," perhaps as a reminder that the people whom Mencken mocked and Tate condemned had access to history-transcending Truth. Despite its title, the story chiefly concerns Mrs. May, the widowed owner of a large dairy farm. Vexed with many woes, failed by many so-called helpers, and wronged by alleged friends, she sees herself as a victim of everybody and everything. Her one comfort is that, for all the injustices she suffers, her land remains her own. Mrs. May is enormously pleased that the piercing Southern sun cannot break through the trees that line the boundary of her farm. The great yellow disc must get off her property at nightfall. The chief irritant to her sense of supreme ownership is the neighbor's scrub bull. As she tosses in fitful sleep, Mrs. May can hear this taurine intruder chewing the hedge outside her window. He is the emblem of all her grievances, and she meditates on him obsessively, both night and day.

> She has been aware that whatever it was had been eating as long as she had had the place and had eaten everything from the beginning of her fence line up to the house and now was eating the house and calmly and with the same steady rhythm would continue through the house, eating her and her boys, and then on, eating everything but the Greenleafs, on and on, eating everything until nothing was left but the Greenleafs on a little island all their own in the middle of what had been her place. (CW, 501-2)

---

89. *Treatise on the Gods*, p. 293.

The Greenleafs are the neighboring "white-trash" family who, much to Mrs. May's disgust, have come up in the world. It galls her that the twin Greenleaf sons, E.T. and O.T., have prospered despite their uncouth names and their general lack of class and culture.[90] Mrs. May's own pampered sons, by contrast, have turned out to be sorry, no 'count souls. Scofield is a "policy man" who sells overpriced insurance to Negroes, and Wesley is a weakling professor who became an academic because he had rheumatic fever when he was seven. Though unable to judge herself with any acuity, Mrs. May is devastatingly accurate about her son: she observes that "being an intellectual was a terrible strain on [Wesley's] disposition" (CW, 509). By far the worst offense to Mrs. May's Southern sense of propriety comes from Mrs. Greenleaf herself. This redneck woman practices what she calls "prayer healing." She collects clippings of "all the morbid stories out of the newspaper — the accounts of women who had been raped and criminals who had escaped and children who had been burned and of train wrecks and plane crashes and divorces of movie stars" (CW, 505). Mrs. Greenleaf takes these cuttings into the woods and buries them, flings her huge body over the mound of dirt, and then cries aloud for Jesus to heal these sundry cases of human misery and bondage.

One day as she is walking in her woods, Mrs. May happens upon Mrs. Greenleaf writhing in the dirt — not unlike the Tennessee Pentecostals Mencken observed. Mrs. Greenleaf's eyes are swollen with tears, her piercing voice is shouting for Jesus to salve the world's sufferers, and "her legs and arms [are] spread out as if she were trying to wrap them around the earth." Like Mencken, Mrs. May is scandalized by such "barbaric grotesquerie."

> Mrs. May winced. She thought the word, Jesus, should be kept inside the church building like other words inside the bedroom. She was a good Christian woman with a large respect for religion, though she did not, of course, believe any of it was true. . . . Mrs. May felt as furious and helpless as if she had been insulted by a child. "Jesus," she said, drawing herself back, "would be ashamed of you. He would tell you to get up from there this instant and go wash your children's clothes!" (CW, 506-7).

Mrs. May is no Smart Set sophisticate, and she has never heard of *The American Mercury*, the other magazine Mencken edited. Yet she is engaged in

---

90. O'Connor's deft touch for class distinctions is evident in the names of the Greenleaf sons. Their letters are not abbreviations but actual names — the gift of parents with exceedingly limited nominative powers. One of my friends has suggested, however, that an inside joke may also be at work. Since Milledgeville is the home of Georgia's largest mental hospital, the Greenleaf names may suggest Educational Therapy and Occupational Therapy.

the struggle that Trilling sees as endemic to every modern person. She is a solid citizen of her community and an ethical person in every regard. She no doubt attends the church of her choice and perhaps even reads her Bible daily. For one of its verses is locked in her head, the saying of St. Paul that "we shall all stand before the judgment seat of Christ" (Rom. 14:10). This phrase haunts Mrs. May's day-time reveries no less than her nighttime visions: "She decided she was tired because she had been working continuously for fifteen years. She decided she had every right to be tired, and to rest a few minutes before she began working again. Before any kind of judgement seat, she would be able to say: I've worked, I have not wallowed" (CW, 522).

Mrs. May's life of unrelenting labor, even if we acknowledge her claims to be highly exaggerated, has been twisted into a proud denial of divine grace. The terrible paradox of the moral law is that it can be perversely fulfilled as well as sinfully transgressed. Righteousness can become the occasion for the most egregious of evils, says the Apostle, if by the doing of good we seek to establish our worth before God (Rom. 10:3). Divine condemnation falls far harder, therefore, on church-going atheists such as Mrs. May than on irreverent God-botherers such as H. L. Mencken. In his impassioned unbelief, Mencken takes God seriously, whereas Mrs. May does not. Religion is but her civic duty, and church is a place where she hopes her sons will meet "nice" girls. Jesus is a figure of such public embarrassment that his name, like the words for sex, should be kept private. Cleanliness is not only next to godliness but actually superior to it. Holiness of life is commendable, according to Mrs. May, only if it contributes to a well-rounded personality. "'I'm afraid your wife has let religion warp her,' [Mrs. May] said once tactfully to Mr. Greenleaf. 'Everything in moderation, you know'" (CW, 522).

We have earlier heard Aquinas condemning moderation in the love of God as a vice. O'Connor's narrators are Thomists in their unabashed and immoderate willingness to join the reader in subjecting her characters to withering irony. Mrs. May is "a good Christian woman," we learn, exactly because she is a practical atheist. That she "tactfully" tells Mr. Greenleaf about his wife's warped condition reveals her comic blindness to her own Laodicean condition. The primitive Pentecostal woman knows that trust in Jesus Christ requires either all or nothing at all, there being no safe middle way between. Unlike the cultured Mrs. May, she practices no pious neglect of God, no benign neutrality toward the One with whom, as the book of Hebrews declares, we are required to deal (4:13). Instead, she pours out her soul and life in the conviction that God desires none to be lost. Mrs. Greenleaf seeks not only figuratively but literally to wrap herself around the world in Christian concern. That this gesture is sexual no less than spiritual is undeniable. Mrs.

Greenleaf's faith opens her to the world both generously and sensuously, just as Mrs. May remains clamped rigidly shut to everything but her own interest.

Sexual overtones are discernible from the beginning of the story, and its openness to Freudian interpretation accounts, no doubt, for its frequent appearance in anthologies. Secular exegetes — unlike their medieval counterparts, discerning only two levels of meaning rather than four — often read the story as an account of Mrs. May's sexual awakening as it is allegorized through the myth of Zeus and Europa. Wearing only her nightgown, Mrs. May first hears the bull munching outside her bedroom window like a hedge-wreathed god "come down to woo her," like "an uncouth country suitor" (CW, 501-2). She repeatedly imagines the bull making a charge on her until, with dread Chekovian inevitability, he buries his head in her lap. This bestial thrust, though undeniably sexual in its implication, is also a moral and anagogical penetration. It is not the orgasmically writhing Mrs. Greenleaf but the prim Mrs. May who is pierced with the force of "a wild tormented lover" (CW, 523). Though initially terrified at the bull's approaching rush, Mrs. May at last discerns that he is her rightful judge, the savior whom she has sought to deny, the ardent suitor of her soul. She dies while seeming to whisper "some last discovery into the animal's ear" (CW, 524).

The narrator hints at the nature of Mrs. May's newfound knowledge by describing the bull as not only having impaled the widowed farm woman, but also as having turned her upside down, enabling her to see the world from a wondrously new perspective: "[T]he tree line was a dark wound in a world that was nothing but sky — and she had the look of a person whose sight has been suddenly restored but who finds the light unbearable" (CW, 523). If only for a single saving moment, Mrs. May has learned that her life is not her own. It is not akin to a piece of property whose boundaries she can fix with good deeds and hard work. The tree line along the edge of her estate is no longer a border inviolable even by the sun. It is a dark wound, perhaps the sign of her own sinful spear-thrust into Christ's side. As if this moral truth were not sufficient, O'Connor grants Mrs. May an eschatological vision as well. Having been stood literally on her head, she discovers that the world is bounded by the infinite sky belonging to the infinite God. To have been opened to such saving truth, even in the violent stab of death, is a consummation ever so much better than to have lived a closed and contented life in damning self-ownership.

Thus has O'Connor woven pagan myth, Freudian psychology, moral realism, and Christian revelation into a seamless fictional fabric. And she has dealt with an utterly real slice of Southern history as well, not by internalizing the memory of the Civil War or even the Civil Rights movement, but by limning the outward and visible life of a Pentecostal woman whose concern for the victims of history encompasses the whole globe, and also of a thoroughly conventional Christian lady who discovers that eternity has entered time and given history its significance.

THREE ❧ *The Problem of the Color Line:*
*Race and Religion in*
*Flannery O'Connor's South*

The idea of race is largely a product of the Enlightenment. Many previous ages had known racial distinction, of course, but the notion that a privileged entitlement inheres in being white is a relatively recent thing. "Before the eighteenth century," writes Thomas F. Gossett, "physical differences among peoples were so rarely referred to as a matter of great importance that something of a case can be made for the proposition that race consciousness is largely a modern phenomenon."[1] Why this late development, when something as obvious as skin color seems undeniable? "The Western sense of immutable racial superiority," explains Shawn Kelley, "coincided with chattel slavery and with the colonial conquests of Africa, the Middle East, and the Far East, with the Holocaust, and with Hitler's brutal war in the East." Kelley quotes G. W. F. Hegel as an altogether typical modern thinker about race: "What we properly understand by Africa is the Unhistorical, Undeveloped Spirit, still involved in the conditions of mere nature, and which had to be presented here [in his Philosophy of History] only as on the threshold of the World's History."[2] Despite their modern vogue, racial distinctions seem all the more futile when we consider that no one is really black or really white — dermatological differences being spread along a spectrum that seems to prove the anthropologists' claim that everyone is at least the forty-fifth cousin of everyone else.

Yet there is no denying the enormous power and horror of racial difference as it has been played out in American history, especially in the history of the American South. W. E. B. DuBois prophesied in 1903 that the chief prob-

1. Thomas F. Gossett, *Race: The History of an Idea in America* (New York: Schocken, 1965), p. 3.

2. Shawn Kelley, "Race," in *Handbook of Postmodern Biblical Interpretation*, ed. A. K. M. Adam (St. Louis: Chalice, 2000), p. 213.

lem for twentieth-century America would be "the problem of the color line." It has also been observed that the word "Mississippi" is the most emotionally charged proper noun in the American language. The race question, like religion and the middle classes, refuses to wither away. "It seems to me," wrote the humanist poet Vachel Lindsay in 1922, that "Mason Dixon's line runs around every country, around France, Japan, Canada, or Mexico, or any other sovereignty. It is the terrible line, that should be the line of love and goodwill, and witty conversation, but may be the bloody line of misunderstanding." The argument of this chapter is that Flannery O'Connor's art gives enduring testimony to the one Source of love and good will, as Lindsay called them, that might overcome this dread line of misunderstanding.

"Racist" and "racism" often become code words for silencing genuine debate about the most important moral question in American history. It is easy to damn and dismiss opponents by spraying them with the epithet "racist." Yet the term has quite specifiable moral meaning: racists deny the dignity and worth of other human beings because of their skin color; they assert the inherent superiority of their own race over others; and they deny all decency and respect to members of the so-called inferior races. Politically, racism means refusing the justice and the equality of opportunity that are due every citizen. Theologically, racism rejects the doctrine that all people are created in the image of God, that all races have sinned and fallen short of God's glory, that we are therefore brothers and sisters who are redeemed by neither our race nor our righteousness but by the death and resurrection of Jesus Christ. Flannery O'Connor was not a racist, either politically or theologically. I maintain, on the contrary, that she was a writer who — though not without temptation and struggle — offered the one lasting antidote to racism.

To make such a case, we must first examine O'Connor's relationship to Eudora Welty and Maryat Lee, two fellow Southerners who made overt denunciations of racism in their work.[3] Next we examine O'Connor's understanding of the important difference between the charity that stems from fellow-feeling and the charity that is enacted as a divine command, especially when such charity concerns race relations. Because biblical faith is centered on the command to live in charity with both God and neighbor, and because

---

3. Public knowledge of private correspondence, especially the letters of artists and thinkers, remains an enormously thorny problem. On the one hand, writers are likely to reveal their deepest sentiments in unguarded confessions to friends. On the other hand, letters may reflect superficial opinions that have been tossed off in a trice and thus never meant for conclusion-drawing scrutiny. O'Connor's letters to Elizabeth Hester were of the former kind, I suspect, while her correspondence with Maryat Lee was of the latter.

the Bible has played a dominant role in shaping the religious and imaginative life of the South, we will consider Eugene Genovese's thesis that Southerners have made a successful scriptural defense of slavery and segregation. Finally, we will seek to fathom the considerable moral and artistic courage that O'Connor displayed in offering acute criticism of white self-righteousness in two of her later stories, "Everything That Rises Must Converge" and "The Enduring Chill."[4]

## Eudora Welty, Maryat Lee, and Flannery O'Connor on Race

There is no better place to begin a study of Flannery O'Connor's racial attitudes than by comparing them with Eudora Welty's. On June 12, 1963, a thirty-nine-year-old Negro dentist and field secretary for the NAACP, Medgar Evers, was shot in the back and killed in the driveway of his home in Jackson, Mississippi. Less than a month later, Eudora Welty published a story in *The New Yorker* entitled "Where Is the Voice Coming From?" It was an angry work written "overnight," Welty confessed, in "straight fury." Though Welty's work is noted chiefly for its boisterous inventiveness, not for its crusading righteousness, the story offers artistic protest against the racist savagery of her own city and state and region. It is Welty's imaginative attempt to impersonate the mind and thus to denounce the act of the racist killer who murdered Medgar Evers. Welty shows him to be a paranoid fanatic, a self-justifying coward, a ne'er-do-well redneck who resents black prosperity, a man of such small soul that he cannot discern the link between his guilty conscience and the hot weather that bears down upon him. The story also implies that the legal recalcitrance of elected officials such as Governor Ross Barnett had encouraged the brutality of racists such as Evers's murderer, Byron de la Beckwith.[5]

---

4. I want to express my immense gratitude to W. A. Sessions for his help in sorting out this most difficult of all questions concerning the life and work of Flannery O'Connor. Professor Sessions is an excellent guide in these matters, since he was a friend of Flannery O'Connor for almost a decade, remained a companion to Regina O'Connor until her death in 1995, and knew Elizabeth Hester quite well. In fact, he is Hester's literary executor, and his authorized biographies of O'Connor and Hester will illuminate much that has seemed obscure about both figures.

5. Welty's remarks on "Where Is the Voice Coming From?" are recorded in the introduction to her *Collected Stories* and in a *Paris Review* interview collected by George Plimpton, ed., *Writers at Work* (4th series, 1977). They are both quoted and interpreted in Charles Clerc, "Anatomy of Welty's 'Where Is the Voice Coming From?'" *Studies in Short Fiction* 23 (1986): 389-400.

Only because she feared that her story might prejudice a jury trial and perhaps entangle *The New Yorker* in a lawsuit did Welty omit a direct and scathing reference to Barnett from her story. "I might even ask old Ross to be my lawyer," the murderer declares in an early draft. Barnett's law firm did, in fact, eventually serve as Beckwith's counsel. Welty later confessed that she had fictionally misconstrued Beckwith only in one way: she had depicted Evers's killer as a descendant of the Snopeses, Faulkner's paradigmatic redneck family, when he turned out to be a Compson, Faulkner's typically aristocratic family. According to Reed Massengill, however, Welty may have been right to think of Evers's murderer as more Snopes than Compson.[6] Although the de la Beckwiths had once belonged to Mississippi gentility, and though Byron himself remained a devout Episcopalian until middle age, his childhood in Greenwood was far from genteel. As an adult he joined the White Citizens Council and began to preach racial purity. Like the narrator of "Where Is the Voice Coming From?" de la Beckwith also made racism a refuge from his personal failings, especially his poor schooling and his ruined marriages, both of which thrust him even deeper into lower-class life. That de la Beckwith was not convicted of his crime for more than thirty years seems to validate Welty's contention that he acted with the approval, if not on the order, of state authorities.[7]

Yet O'Connor had no sympathy for Welty's attempt to turn her anti-racist convictions into propagandistic art. She complained to Elizabeth Hester that "Where Is the Voice Coming From?" is "the kind of story that the more you think about it the less satisfactory it gets. What I hate most is its being in the *New Yorker* and all the stupid Yankee liberals smacking their lips over typical life in the dear old dirty Southland. The topical is poison.... I say a plague on everybody's house as far as the race business goes" (HB, 537). O'Connor did not mean that the integrationists and the segregationists stood on equal footing, nor that she refused to choose between them, but that they had both arrogated to themselves a righteousness that she found deeply dis-

---

6. Reed Massengill, *Portrait of a Racist: The Man Who Killed Medgar Evers* (New York: St. Martin's, 1994).

7. That the genteel no less than the barbaric South recoiled in contempt against court-ordered desegregation of the public schools was also a perplexity to a Southerner such as William Faulkner, whose stance on the race question was often ambivalent. Speaking to the Southern Historical Association in Memphis, Faulkner declared sardonically that "to live anywhere in the world of A.D. 1955 and be against equality because of race or color is like living in Alaska and being against snow" (William Faulkner, "American Segregation and the World Crisis," *Three Views of the Segregation Decisions: William Faulkner, Benjamin E. Mays, Cecil Sims* [Atlanta: Southern Regional Council, 1956], p. 9).

turbing, especially when the racists were made to seem the sole evildoers. And when current events were made the subject of serious art, as Welty had done, the results were usually dreadful.[8]

O'Connor's short fuse for the racially righteous may derive from her indebtedness to Reinhold Niebuhr, whose work she knew well. Niebuhr helped her affirm, I suspect, the difficult Christian conviction that all people are equally sinful, even though their sin is unequal in its effects and thus in its guilt. Niebuhr describes guilt as "the objective consequence of sin, the actual corruption of the plan of creation and providence in the historical world." He cites broken homes, tyrannical parents, grinding poverty, and internecine wars as typical evils that result from our equal fallenness, while producing our unequal guilt. Yet Niebuhr never deviates from the conviction concerning the peril of moral superiority: "The Christian doctrine of the sinfulness of all men is thus a constant challenge to re-examine superficial moral judgments, particularly those which self-righteously give the moral advantage to the one who makes the judgment."[9] O'Connor believed that, in addition to having written an awful story, Welty had indulged in the moral advantage-taking that Niebuhr rightly deplores.

Three weeks after Welty's story appeared in *The New Yorker*, and six weeks after Evers's death, O'Connor reported on Southern race relations in a letter to the Chicago writer Richard Stern. Adopting her typically antic stance toward all "innerluckchuls," as she called them, and thus using white-trash grammar and redneck spelling, she makes joshing reference to Mississippi Governor Ross Barnett: "It's just like Cudden Ross says all us niggers and white folks over here are just getting along grand — at least in Georgia and Mississippi. I hear things are not so good in Chicago and Brooklyn but you wouldn't expect them to know what to do with theirself there."[10] In dealing with scholars and writers, O'Connor almost always adopts this self-mocking tone. It was her prophylactic against any easy

8. With heavy irony, Welty has the murderer's wife repeat a Kennedy joke that she had learned at work: "Heard what Caroline said? Caroline said, 'Daddy, I just can't wait to grow up big, so I can marry James Meredith.'" (Meredith was the first black student to attend the University of Mississippi at Oxford, and his entrance to the university in 1962 occasioned a bloody riot in which several students were killed.) About this matter, O'Connor indulged in a heavy-handed japery of her own. Soon after the 1960 presidential election, O'Connor reported to Lee that her friend George Haslam had written to say there was "no truth in the rumor that the Kennedys were going to name their baby Martin Luther Kennedy" (HB, 418).

9. Reinhold Niebuhr, *The Nature and Destiny of Man: A Christian Interpretation, I. Human Nature* (New York: Charles Scribner's Sons, 1949), p. 222.

10. Richard Stern, "Flannery O'Connor: A Remembrance and Some Letters," *Shenandoah* 16 (1965): 10.

contempt for the unenlightened, any easy self-congratulation for her own kind.

Nowhere is O'Connor's joshing self-ridicule concerning the race question made more evident than in her correspondence with Maryat Lee.[11] As the Kentucky-born sister of the local college president, as a bisexual and Wellesley graduate, as a New York playwright and self-styled intellectual, Lee formed the perfect antithesis to O'Connor. That their many antagonisms served to attract rather than repel is the real miracle of their relationship. Each defined herself in response to the other, thus revealing the aptness of William Blake's aphorism: "In opposition is true friendship." Yet O'Connor and Lee did not have their long exchange of letters merely to trump each other's arguments. Their playful spoofing and witty parody were means of real engagement. Lee thus appears as the pluperfect bleeding-heart Yankee liberal, while O'Connor assumes the role of the starchily unreconstructed Southern racist. Lee confessed to Sally Fitzgerald that satirical banter lay at the heart of their relation: "Flannery permanently became the devil's advocate with me in matters of race, as I was to do with her in matters of religion. Underneath the ugly caricatures of herself . . . I could only believe that she shared with me the same sense of frustration and betrayal and impotency over the dilemma of the white South" (HB, 193).

Lee's willingness to believe the best about her Milledgeville friend must have sometimes been strained. In a 1962 letter, for instance, O'Connor addresses Lee as a white New Yorker who loves "niggers." At the end of the same letter, O'Connor proclaims her own neutrality toward "niggers." Even if one were to construe this confession as the wildest burlesque, the letters to Lee contain occasional expressions of malice, especially toward black activists who angrily agitated for racial justice. O'Connor likens the suffering of jailed black demonstrators, for example, to a grasshopper that Lee had left at the O'Connor farm. Feeling sorry for the caged creature, O'Connor tells Lee that she released it, only to see it promptly gobbled up by a duck. In what is perhaps the most troubling of all her letters to Lee, O'Connor admits that she is an integrationist in the legal but not the aesthetic sense. With remarkable candor, she confesses her distaste for Negroes. The greater her dealings with them, especially with the new liberated blacks, the less her regard for them.[12]

11. All references to the unpublished letters between Lee and O'Connor (housed in the O'Connor Collection at the Georgia College and State University Library in Milledgeville) will be paraphrased rather than quoted.

12. O'Connor also mocked the racial utopia that many liberals thought the Kennedy presidency would bring. After her visit to East Texas State College in November 1962, O'Connor reported to Lee and other correspondents a joke that she heard there: "Somebody from Texas

Though Flannery O'Connor was no racist, her frequent recourse to the demeaning term "nigger" is troubling. Southern whites of her social class and Christian conviction did not regularly resort to the word.[13] The problem lies not so much with the frequency of the slur in O'Connor's letters — any more than if she had blacks refer to whites as "honkies" — but with the way she uses it. Racial epithets can be employed by insiders both to vilify and to compliment. The black rap group NWA (Niggers Wit' Attitude) turns the offending word into ironic praise. Yet a liberal use of the term can disclose an illiberal numbness to the evils that blacks suffered in the segregated South. The lynchings and castrations and murders are the obvious horrors that O'Connor never mentions. Nor do we hear about the lesser evils of racial discrimination — in schooling and voting, in employment and medical care, in restaurants and hotels, in housing and loans and almost everything else. We do hear a good deal of complaint, by contrast, about Northern journalists who regarded court-ordered desegregation as the only interesting Southern question. In her less testy moments, O'Connor replied that blacks and whites have always "milled around" in the South, and that integration would serve only to increase the number of places where the races would "mill around" together.[14] O'Connor was convinced that time and history would resolve the race question as instant solutions would not. Yet her own impatient response to the integration crisis — she confessed to Maryat Lee that only the Lord kept her from making it public — was to urge that the "niggers" be sent back to Africa.[15] O'Connor also ridiculed the effort of an Oklahoma City group to foster interracial understanding through shared meals. She suggested to Lee

---

calls up the White House, says, 'Is President Kennedy there?' Voice says, 'Nawsuh, he ain't here.' 'Well is Miss Jackie there?' 'She ain't here neither.' 'Well where is Mr. Lyndon?' 'He done gone too.' 'Well who's running things up there?' 'We is'" (Stern, p. 10).

13. As a youth coming of age in the segregated South of the 1950s, I never heard my own parents, who were Baptists and public school teachers, use the word; in fact, they explicitly forbade me to use it in the presence of blacks, knowing that it would deeply wound them.

14. Rosemary Magee, *Conversations with Flannery O'Connor* (Jackson, MS: University Press of Mississippi, 1987), p. 102.

15. The late James Wm. McClendon offered a telling response to those who read O'Connor's letters to Lee as evidence of her alleged racism: "She was saying, 'We're all sinners, and I'm such a sinner that I here commit the sin you regard as most gauche — racism. So much for your sinless liberalism!' . . . O'Connor — as one more original sinner — could make the caricature of herself work because . . . racial ill will was part of the fabric of her life. It was there . . . as a habit, a side of herself, felt rather than thought out, sensed rather than adopted. . . . So the real dolts (like those banning Huckleberry Finn from library shelves) are [those] so invincibly once-born as to have no sense of the complexity of selfhood" (letter to the author, April 14, 1994).

an ugly little jingle that might serve as the white liberals' motto: Take a colored out to supper. The real rhyme-words are not difficult to imagine. Such unsavory opinions must not be sanitized. O'Connor's ugly racial sentiments, while never leading her to commit racist actions, remain nonetheless vexing.

## Charity as Fellow-Feeling vs. Divine Command

Flannery O'Connor admitted that she was not natively drawn to humanity in the aggregate. Perhaps remembering the character in Dostoevsky who professes to love humankind but cannot abide individual human beings, she confessed to Elizabeth Hester her own "lack of love for the race of man." But then O'Connor immediately added that her lovelessness toward the human species "is only a sentiment and a sentiment falls before a command." She cites Aquinas as her authority in making this important distinction: "According to St. Thomas an act can be derived from charity in one of two ways. The first way the act is elicited by charity and requires no other virtue — as in the case of loving the Good, rejoicing in it, etc. In the second way, an act proceeds from charity in the sense of being commanded by it" (HB, 335). Whatever her likes or dislikes about black people as a race, therefore, O'Connor acted on the dominical directive that Christians are to treat every single person with the utmost charity; her Christian faith trumped her deficiency in fellow-feeling. In one of her last letters to Maryat Lee, for instance, O'Connor urged her old friend and antagonist to endow a scholarship for Negro girls at the newly integrated Wesleyan College in Macon. It also is noteworthy that she assigned the crudest of her racial opinions to an unsavory character in "Revelation": "They ought to send all them niggers back to Africa," the white-trash woman said. "That's wher they come from in the first place" (CW, 640).

That O'Connor sometimes made uncharitable remarks about blacks in private, while treating them with unfailing charity in her essays and fiction, does not make her an oleaginous hypocrite. In all public matters, she was an unfailing advocate of racial reconciliation. That O'Connor never gave public voice to her racial opinions also indicates that she doubted them even if she did not completely silence them in her letters. Opinions are often quickly formed and just as quickly abandoned, since they do not constitute the fundament of our lives. We often keep our opinions to ourselves, lest they give needless offense, and lest we be made ashamed at their disclosure. Convictions, by contrast, are slowly acquired and firmly maintained. We do not surrender our convictions readily nor keep them private, no matter whom they may offend. They are the public verities upon which we stand, the truths by which we live and die.[16] O'Connor's racial convictions were so firmly Christian that she never asked her friend and confessor, Father James McCown, S.J., to pull back from his uncompromising insistence on racial justice, nor did she utter any complaints about his scaring confessions of white Southern guilt:

> [W]e southerners showered our black domestics with shallow affection, then exploited them shamelessly. We claimed really to know blacks, but lived with our own self-serving image of them. We paid them starvation wages, then feigned disappointment when they turned out to be "ungrateful," or "shiftless," or "thieving." We paid them not enough to rent a decent home, [nor] to buy clothes or soap, then complained about their odor. We kept them from getting a good education, then complained of their ignorance. We read happiness and contentment in their comedy and obsequiousness, then were outraged if they expressed their human dignity. For our own use we stereotyped them and their language and habits. We never really accepted the Emancipation Proclamation, which took away our human chattels. And we begrudged them most of the amenities we so generously bestowed on ourselves.[17]

Over and again, in both her letters and her stories, O'Connor stresses the necessity of slow sanctification in Christ, the perennial struggle for a holiness that will issue in the beatific vision of the triune God, and thus the arduous task of daily conversion to the Cross. More than once she declared her strong belief in Purgatory, as if to admit how incompletely her life had been transformed by the gospel: "I already have a berth there reserved for myself" (HB, 965). Not one of O'Connor's close friends — including Maryat Lee, who surely had cause for suspicion — has ever accused O'Connor of being a racist. Her friend Tom Gossett reports, on the contrary, that O'Connor reacted angrily to the story of a black woman who was almost cheated out of a new automobile she had won in a Milledgeville lottery. Upon discovering that the winner's address was located in the town's black section, the judge sought to have the name discarded. Only at the insistence of local whites was the black woman given her prize. "When Flannery O'Connor was told of this incident," Gossett writes, "she was naturally indignant that a black could . . . have been dishon-

16. I owe this distinction between opinions and convictions to John Sykes, my very first student.

17. James Hart McCown, *With Crooked Lines: Early Years of an Alabama Jesuit* (Mobile, AL: Spring Hill College Press, 1990), p. 91.

estly deprived of what was legitimately hers."[18] And when Gossett himself was dismissed from his teaching post at Georgia Wesleyan College in Macon for openly advocating racial justice, O'Connor staunchly supported him, lamenting that he had been treated in a "low-down fashion."[19]

O'Connor reported to Hester that she once heard a white driver ridicule blacks by ordering them to the rear of the bus and calling them "stovepipe blonds." At that moment, O'Connor declared, "I became an integrationist" (HB, 253). O'Connor also lampooned the segregationists who had protested a joint meeting of black and white educators at her alma mater, Georgia State College for Women in Milledgeville. "Everything was as separate and equal as possible," O'Connor joked, "even down to two Coca-Cola machines, white and colored." O'Connor had nothing less than contempt for the racist acts of terrorism that followed: "The people who burned the cross [on the president's lawn] couldn't have gone past the fourth grade but, for the time, they were mighty interested in education" (HB, 195). And when a small Georgia college inaugurated a new literary series by inviting Donald Davidson, the most unreconstructed segregationist among the original twelve contributors to *I'll Take My Stand,* O'Connor complained, "How far to the right can you get?"[20]

W. A. Sessions reports that the young Flannery O'Connor became close friends with a black woman who was a fellow graduate student at the University of Iowa. When Mrs. O'Connor warned her daughter that such interracial contacts were dangerous, Flannery replied heatedly that her friendships would not be fettered by racial considerations. Neither was O'Connor restrained in her regard for Martin Luther King, Jr. With uncanny prescience of King's moral failings, she denied that he was "the ages [sic] great saint"; but she also affirmed that "at least he's doing what he can do & has to do" (CW, 1208). It is not clear whether O'Connor ever read King's celebrated 1963 letter from the Birmingham jail. There King chose not to denounce the rank white racists so much as the "peaceful" white moderates who upheld "order" at all costs, who condemned the bus boycotts and lunch-counter sit-ins, and who

---

18. Thomas F. Gossett, "Flannery O'Connor's Attitude to Blacks," unpublished essay, p. 3.

19. Benjamin B. Alexander, "Good Things Out of Nazareth: The Unpublished Letters of Flannery O'Connor" (unpublished essay).

20. Ibid. O'Connor was proud to have, at last, a Catholic occupant of the White House, and she declared her pleasure with the way President Kennedy was running the country. But she was less happy about the twin opponents of Lyndon Johnson in 1964: "Dont [sic] know which is worse, CORE [Congress of Racial Equality] or Young Republicans for Goldwater" (CW, 1196).

quietly refused to summon their churches and communities to racial justice and reconciliation. "Shallow understanding from people of goodwill," King wrote, "is more frustrating than absolute misunderstanding from people of ill will. Lukewarm acceptance is much more bewildering than outright rejection." In a remarkable letter of her own, also written in 1963, O'Connor expressed strong support for the civil rights movement, eagerly embracing the gains in black-white relations that had been made in her own native state. In full refutation of the mocking claims made in her letters to Maryat Lee, O'Connor states her real racial convictions: "I feel very good about those changes in the South that have been long overdue — the whole racial picture. I think it is improving by the minute, particularly in Georgia, and I don't see how anybody could feel otherwise than good about that."[21]

Flannery O'Connor died four years prior to the assassination of Martin Luther King in 1968, an event that shocked several Southern writers into making public statements about the race question. One can only suppose that O'Connor would have joined them in the breaking of their silence. Walker Percy, for example, offered this plangent lament about their Christ-haunted country in 1965:

> The failure of the Christian in the South has been both calamitous and un-remarkable. And perhaps that is the worst of it: that no one finds the failure remarkable, not we who ought to know better, not the victims of our indifference who confess the same Christ, and not even the world who witnessed our failure. No one was surprised. The world which said many years ago, "See how the Christians love one another," would presumably have been surprised if these earlier Christians had violated each other or turned their backs upon the violation. Now as then, the children of the world are wiser than the children of light: they witnessed the failure we concealed from ourselves and found it not in the least remarkable.[22]

21. I am immensely grateful to Professor Sessions for sharing this previously unpublished letter and to the O'Connor estate for permission to quote from it.

22. Walker Percy, *Signposts in a Strange Land*, ed. Patrick Samway (New York: Farrar, Straus & Giroux, 1991), pp. 326-27. Percy was equally vehement in a 1970 letter: "I have never once seen the white Christian community do anything for the Negro that it didn't have to do. I am not speaking of course of personal acts of kindness and generosity with which we are all familiar. But if it had been left to the white Christian community, the Negro would still be without the vote, without decent schools. . . . I once heard a black Baptist preacher say something that chilled my blood that I have never forgotten. He said the white Christian Southerner, the good decent moderate, will be remembered in eternity — for his silence" (quoted by Alexander, "Good Things Out of Nazareth").

Like O'Connor, Percy knew that racial justice was a far more complicated matter than many integrationists allowed. Southern colleges and
schools, Percy observed, served as social as well as educational institutions.
They were not impersonal public spaces akin to grocery stores where, despite physical intimacy, people do not feel they are sharing the same living
space. The social body and the student body virtually coincided in the South,
Percy argues, far more than in the North. This meant that federally mandated
school desegregation was no simple matter of public justice and equal rights;
it was an act of aggression against a quasi-tribal society. As Percy wryly observed in 1965, "The whole of the Delta, indeed of white Mississippi, is one big
kinship lodge." When James Meredith integrated the social club called Ole
Miss, the students vilified him. Yet Percy noticed that they "also wept with
genuine grief. It was as if he had been quartered in their living room."[23]

As both North and South continued to be wracked by racial violence
during the 1960s, Percy called for a national renewal that, in order to preserve
their own distinctive merits, would enable both regions to extol each other's
virtues rather than lamenting their faults. Percy urged his fellow Americans
not to make their nation into "a countrywide Levittown in which everyone is
a good liberal ashamed of his past, but [to achieve] a pluralistic society, rich
in regional memories and usages." "Surely it would be better," Percy added,
"to cherish rather than destroy the cultural cleavage between the North and
the South, a cleavage which accounts for the South's pre-eminence in creative literature and the North's in technics, social propaganda, and objective
scholarship. The difference has been traced to a Southern preoccupation
with the concrete, the historical, the particular, the immediate; and the
Northern passion for the technical, the abstract, the general, the ideological. I
see no reason why either tradition should not be enriched rather than reviled
by the other."[24]

In the unpublished letter previously quoted, where O'Connor lauds the
accomplishments of the civil rights movement, she expressed convictions
similar to Percy's, hoping that the salutary racial changes made in the South
would not lead the region to abandon its lasting virtues: "Those changes I dislike . . . have more to do with industrial living, men working for machines,
etc., the breakdown of the country community, cities all turning into Nowhere or Anywhere, and most of all the watering down of belief, the so-
called Enlightenment." O'Connor believed that her region's narrative and historical rootedness in Scripture, together with the tragic vision enabled by the

23. Ibid., pp. 48-49.
24. Ibid., pp. 92-93.

Civil War, had protected it from this dilution of religious conviction. It has also yielded Southern fruit that neither the most fully developed ideas nor the most advanced technology can produce: "[W]hat has given the South her identity are those beliefs and qualities which she has absorbed from the Scriptures and from her own history of defeat and violation: a distrust of the abstract, a sense of human dependence on the grace of God, and a knowledge that evil is not simply a problem to be solved, but a mystery to be endured" (MM, 209).[25]

## The Bible and Slavery

Eugene Genovese argues that the seemingly unbreakable link between Southern religion and Southern racial injustice derives not only from slavery itself but also from the Southern antebellum preachers and theologians who gave it biblical justification. He maintains that these Southern vindicators of slavery were more biblically astute than their Yankee counterparts. Most of the abolitionist divines made easy targets: they argued on broadly humanist — rather than strictly theological — grounds that injustice should not be tolerated, that personal aspiration should not be thwarted, that legitimate government should not be overthrown, that freedom of conscience should not be violated. While contradicting nothing Christian, such claims required no distinctively Christian warrants. Southern ministers answered these sub-biblical arguments by supplying a theology that justified slaveholding on abundant biblical grounds: that the Old Testament patriarchs owned slaves, that Jesus nowhere condemns slavery, that Paul and other New Testament writers quite clearly sanction it. Paul even urged the runaway slave Onesimus to return to his master, Philemon.

Repeatedly, Genovese commends the Southern theologians for besting their Northern abolitionist opponents in biblical argument. In my view, they compounded the Southern tragedy by supplying theological sanction for a pitiless enterprise.[26] While biblically consistent, the Southern slave-justifying

25. The scriptural depth of O'Connor's work led Percy to laud both her and Faulkner as the two novelists "who lived during this period of the long Southern obsession [with race] and who were great enough to transcend it." O'Connor's art succeeds, Percy added, "largely by steering clear of [the race question]. . . . Mainly she stuck to whites, figuring, I guess, that whites had enough troubles with themselves without dragging in white-black troubles" (ibid., p. 31).

26. I have offered a full critique of Genovese's attempt to vindicate the slavery-defending theologians in "Eugene Genovese and the Biblical Tragedy of the South," *Perspectives in Religious Studies* 28, no. 1 (Spring 2001): 99-113.

theologians ignored a host of subtleties and counter-arguments. Perhaps their most notable omission is that Jesus' acceptance of slavery is much like that of Paul and the other New Testament writers, who enjoin slaves to obey their masters "as unto the Lord," even as he abjures masters to treat their slaves with the same compassion that they have themselves been shown in Jesus Christ (Eph. 6:5-9; Col. 4:1). The author of 1 Timothy urges Christian slaves not to despise their Christian masters but to recognize that they, too, are brothers in Christ. Henry Breckenridge of Kentucky (1800-1871) added a further interpretive stipulation that had long been a mainstay of Protestant exegesis: Biblical norms cannot be applied to contemporary existence *tout court* without considering the differences between ancient and modern contexts. Breckenridge maintained that the slavery practiced in the Roman world was grossly unlike the chattel bondage practiced in the South. Modern historical research has vindicated Breckenridge. Nowhere does the Bible sanction the enslavement of one race only. Nor was slavery a contested institution in the ancient Mediterranean world. There was no northern and southern Rome divided by their attitudes toward slavery. Even in the slave-sanctioning Old Testament, bondsmen were not distinguished by their race. Some of them were indeed purchased as chattels; but others were either prisoners of war who had been put to work on large state construction projects, or else household servants who had indentured themselves to satisfy debts. Job thus declares (31:13-15) that he must not reject the complaints of his slaves, for they are human beings as he is.[27]

Similar conditions prevailed among slaves in the Greco-Roman world of the New Testament. Though as many as a third of all urban dwellers were slaves, and though another third may have once been enslaved, they were distinguished from free persons not in racial but only in legal terms: they were the property of another. Their suffering was often great, especially when they served as galley-drudges, mineworkers, and toilers on estates. Yet they were not set apart by their race or class, by their clothing, or even by their work.[28] Paul's plangent confession that he is "sold under sin," and thus that he does not do what he wants "but what I hate, that I do" (Rom. 7:14-15), may derive from metaphors drawn from the auction block as well as the life of servitude to menial tasks. John Nordling also argues that the New Testament exhortations for slave-Christians to be obedient to their masters assume that they

27. Edd Rowell, "Slavery in the Old Testament," *Mercer Dictionary of the Bible*, ed. Watson Mills (Macon, GA: Mercer University Press, 1990), pp. 831-32.

28. David Garland, *NIV Application Commentary on Colossians and Philemon* (Grand Rapids, MI: Zondervan, 1998), pp. 342-51.

were "responsible moral agents — not chattel property which must be whipped and beaten to perform necessary tasks."[29]

More telling still is the fact that the ancient Romans knew nothing akin to modern racism. Though they originally formulated the notion of chattels, the Romans were xenophobic toward the white barbarians of the north, not toward the black Ethiopians of the south, whom they tended to associate with the cultured Egyptians.[30] It is also noteworthy that a favorite biblical verse among American slaves was Psalm 68:31: "Princes shall come out of Egypt; Ethiopia shall soon stretch out her hands unto God."[31] Roman slaves were often better educated, in fact, than their masters. They were put to work keeping records, therefore, or even educating their master's children. The former slave Epictetus, for example, became an important Stoic philosopher. Nordling lists four categories of urban and domestic slaves who were not subjected to violent labor conditions but who could probably have expected manumission by age thirty: "highly educated slaves — akin to our own college/university professors; slaves who carried out highly technical financial transactions on behalf of their masters — akin to a modern C.P.A., or to a 'bonded' employee; slaves who could own their own property (*peculium*); slaves who enjoyed pretty much the same rights as freeborn citizens, such as the right of public assembly to worship the god or goddess of one's own choice."[32] No such dignities and privileges were available to the slaves of the American South, though their general human rights were never questioned by the slave-defenders. There is no doubt that many Southern masters treated their slaves humanely. Even so, they remained chattels — commodities to be bought, bartered, and sold like all other property. Their servile and commercial identity was determined, moreover, by one thing above all else: their race.

Northern abolitionists hammered away at this historical contradiction. In response, Southern advocates of slavery gradually softened their biblical argument in favor of a different tack altogether: slavery, they insisted, is an unavoidable condition of human existence. The Southern theologians and economists thus came to exalt slavery over wage labor as a much-preferred means for managing an inevitably stratified economic world. "Free wage labor," they argued, "spells misery for the masses and therefore disorder, revo-

29. John Nordling, "Christ Leavens Culture: St. Paul on Slavery," *Concordia Journal* 24, no. 1 (January 1998): 49, 51.

30. Ibid., p. 51.

31. Mark A. Noll, "The Bible and Slavery," in *Religion and the American Civil War*, ed. Randall Miller, Harry S. Stout, and Charles Reagan Wilson (New York: Oxford University Press, 1998), p. 54.

32. Nordling, p. 47.

lution, and anarchy for society. Stable societies require strict relations of superordination and subordination in which capital assumes full responsibility for labor, whether through outright ownership of human beings or through less direct methods of command."[33] The ethos of ancient Greece and Rome was consonant, Genovese contends, with the Southern conviction that involuntary servitude, in whatever form it may take, constitutes the proper condition of all labor, regardless of race.[34]

James Henley Thornwell, one of the chief theological defenders of slavery, articulated the new case ever so clearly: "What rational man ever thought that it is immoral to hold in involuntary servitude any one who is, by his own mental state, unfit for freedom?"[35] Yet this appeal to cultural precedent marks a decided Southern shift away from biblical — and even further from theological — argument. If precedent were indeed the Christian norm, Thornwell would have done better to notice that neither Jesus nor any of his New Testament disciples owned slaves. It is virtually impossible, moreover, to credit the notion that, if Christian slaves had prayed for God to release them from their bondage — even as Yahweh had once freed Israel from its Egyptian vassalage — they could have expected the Lord to reply: "But remember that Father Abraham owned slaves." Nor is it possible to imagine Jesus visiting a Southern slave auction — where husbands and wives, parents and children, were torn permanently asunder — only to hear him observe, "Forget that I proclaimed release to the captives and liberty to the oppressed (Luke 4:18). Recall only that Paul urged the runaway slave Onesimus to submit to his master Philemon."

This, I believe, is the tragedy of the Southern defense of slavery on scriptural grounds. Having learned to give biblical sanction to slavery understood as a warm brotherly guardianship, Christians closed their eyes to the horrors of slavery understood as a cold commercial enterprise. Charles Hodge (1798-1879), the conservative Princeton theologian, showed his Southern friends a more excellent way. Even when slaves were objects of paternal care more than monetary investment — and surely this was the exception more often than the rule — Hodge did not believe that Christians could hold fellow believers in perpetual vassalage. He contended, on the contrary, that

---

33. Eugene Genovese, *"Slavery Ordained of God": The Southern Slaveholders' View of Biblical History and Modern Politics* (Gettysburg, PA: Gettysburg College, 1985), p. 12.

34. Genovese, "The Southern Slaveholders' View of the Middle Ages," in *Medievalism in American Culture*, ed. Bernard Rosenthal and Paul E. Szarmach (Binghampton, NY: Medieval & Renaissance Texts & Studies, 1987), p. 40.

35. Quoted in John W. Stewart, "Mediating the Center: Charles Hodge on American Science, Language, Literature, and Politics," *Studies in Reformed Theology and History* 3, no. 1 (Winter 1995): 95-96n.273.

the call to slave-submission found in Philemon is always trumped by the call to Christian mutuality found nearly everywhere in the New Testament, but most notably in Galatians 3:28: "There is neither Jew nor Greek, there is neither bond nor free, there is neither male nor female: for ye are all one in Christ Jesus." Hodge was not nearly so forceful as the Apostle Paul, but already in 1836 he was sharply to the point: "The South, therefore, has to choose between emancipation by the silent and holy influence of the gospel, securing the elevation of slaves to the stature and character of freemen, or to abide the issue of a long continued conflict against the laws of God. That the issue will be disastrous there can be no doubt."[36]

Like Lincoln, Hodge was no immediatist. He knew that the elevation of slaves to true freedom would be a slow and gradual process. He also knew that the emergence of Christian truth is gradual, as the historical development of doctrine demonstrates. Genovese is only partially correct, therefore, to insist that, prior to the nineteenth century, no one had interpreted Paul's Galatians summons to total mutuality in Christ as a call for the outright overthrow of slavery. Neither, it should be observed, had eighteen hundred years of Christian history ever witnessed any practice of slavery such as the Southern kind. Once the gospel became the means for unshackling bodies no less than souls, the results have been remarkable, though they are far from being fully realized. Even as a former Marxist, Genovese gladly acknowledges the point. "The dominant religions everywhere," he writes, have "accepted slavery as part of the social order. Only in the West did a great movement arise to assert everyman's right to freedom, and it arose primarily on Christian foundations."[37]

The essential tragedy of the South has lain in its slowness to discern the tie, if not the identity, between the two kinds of freedom — Christian and political. Prominent Southern voices once used the Christian scriptures to vindicate and preserve an often vicious kind of slavery. The North, by contrast, once ignored the Bible because it passively acquiesced to a considerably milder sort of slavery. Thus did a humanist culture arise in the North that would have an ever smaller regard for the Bible. Victory in battle led Northerners to false assumptions concerning their moral superiority. Southerners lost the military war in defense of an unbiblical cause, but they won the spiritual war by giving the South its truest legacy. And as a Bible-centered, Christ-haunted region, it has bequeathed the one race-transcending, race-reconciling gospel to both the nation and the world.

36. Quoted in ibid., 60.
37. Genovese, *The Southern Front: History and Politics in the Cultural War* (Columbia, MO: University of Missouri Press, 1995), p. 31.

## O'Connor's Satire of the Self-Righteous

Flannery O'Connor believed that, when H. L. Mencken sought to insult the South by calling it the Bible Belt, he paid it the highest of tributes. For all its terrible faults, the South's biblicism provided a necessary corrective to the assorted naïvetes of the North.[38] O'Connor feared that a friend such as Maryat Lee, imbued as she was with the Yankee reformist spirit, had come to misconstrue human nature in the most fundamental way. She had ignored the perduring reality of original sin, especially its power to infect the racially righteous no less than the racially sinful. O'Connor was also impatient with her fellow Southerners — especially with her fellow Christians — who regarded racism as the essence of Southern evil, and who thus believed that integration was its magical cure. She did not think highly of Clarence Jordan, for example, an outcast Baptist preacher who led an interracial endeavor in communal living outside Americus, Georgia. Jordan was a Greek scholar who translated various New Testament gospels and epistles into vernacular "Cotton Patch" versions, and who thus called his agricultural community Koinonia (Greek for "fellowship"). Jordan's venture in racial reconciliation was met with fierce verbal intimidation and physical assault, including gunshots fired into his home.[39] Tom and Louise Gossett, O'Connor's professorial friends from Macon, often sought to aid Jordan's efforts. They once asked O'Connor to join them on a trip to Koinonia Farms. In a letter to Elizabeth Hester, O'Connor confesses that she found this invitation to be "inconvenient in more ways than one." She detected an odor of moral adventurism in Jordan's effort. Far from admiring its supporters, she feared that they were having ethical "fun" (HB, 223). As O'Connor iterated endlessly, interracial progress in the South would require the slow and careful development of a new set of racial manners; it would not result from well-meant racial experiments.[40]

38. To my knowledge, O'Connor had no embittering experience with blacks while living in Iowa and New York and Connecticut, though she does report (in an unpublished letter to Maryat Lee) one unhappy racial incident that occurred while she sat waiting for a train in the Dearborn Street Station in Chicago. O'Connor had sat down beside a black woman who, in an overture of comradeship, had offered to share her lunch. But when the woman discovered that her seatmate was from Georgia, she harrumphed and stalked off.

39. O'Connor's conviction that lasting interracial life could not be created by goodwill alone was perhaps justified. The whites at Koinonia could afford to live in poverty, since they had banked their savings in advance. Already poor when they arrived, many of the blacks wanted out once they began to flourish. Monetary prosperity trumped racial amity.

40. The failure to develop such manners — rather than any overt racism — may account for the continued segregation of many Southern institutions, especially Protestant congregations. Catholic churches, working on the parish system, have done much better.

O'Connor felt that the brash young boxer who later renamed himself Muhammad Ali understood this complex matter as many others did not. In a televised interview with Eric Sevareid, Cassius Clay (as he was then called) had lamented the hatred of whites that the civil rights movement had spawned. A convert to the Nation of Islam, Clay forecast the contemporary resurgence of black separatism, arguing that Negroes should demand fair treatment from whites without denying the social distance that would remain between the races. O'Connor obviously relished the colorful language of Clay, whom she quotes: "'If a tiger move into the room with you,' says Cassius, 'and you leave, that dont [sic] mean you hate the tiger. Just means you know you and him can't make out'" (CW, 1208-9). O'Connor suspected that the uneducated ring-fighter from Louisville struck deeper truth than the cultured integrationists who had no real understanding of Southern blacks.

In contrast to her amused regard for the future Muhammed Ali, O'Connor had little patience with John Howard Griffin, her fellow Catholic. She remained unconvinced by Griffin's celebrated attempt — recorded in *Black Like Me* — to expose racial prejudice and to foster racial understanding by darkening his skin and living with blacks as he traveled incognito across the South. "If I had been one of them ladies Griffin sat down by on the bus," O'Connor observed acerbically to Maryat Lee, "I would have got up PDQ preferring to sit by a genuine Negro." "An interesting man," O'Connor concludes, "but I wouldn't have liked him" (HB, 580).[41] One can only speculate about the nature of O'Connor's scorn for Griffin's life-endangering effort. Perhaps she feared that Griffin had acted in moral pretense, prompted more by sentimental fellow-feeling than by obedience to divine charity, and thus that he had condescended to blacks by seeking their acceptance according to his newly adopted skin color rather than his long-established character.

There is little doubt that Griffin's endeavor was based on conflicting premises. On the one hand, he extols an abstract kind of "love" that could be learned if Southern whites would sympathetically experience, as he did, the constant degradation suffered by Southern blacks. Griffin subscribes, moreover, to a sociological understanding of human nature as being "born blank" and thus as capable of being made humane "by the great civilizing influences of art, history, literature and philosophy."[42] Racial bigotry can be overcome, according to Griffin, simply by offering blacks their full-fledged American

41. O'Connor also felt that Griffin's ethical sentimentality had leaked into his imaginative work. Hence her description of his novel *The Devil Rides Outside* as emotionally out of control: "I don't mean hysterical ha ha but hystericaleeeek" (HB, 580).

42. John Howard Griffin, *Black Like Me* (New York: Signet, 1962), pp. 90-91.

citizenship: "We must return to them their lawful rights, assure equality of justice — and then everybody leave everybody else to hell alone."[43] Such oxymoronically cynical idealism and individualism are contradicted, on the other hand, by Griffin's theological convictions. He discovered, to his great surprise, that many black people experienced profound happiness even in their poverty and misery, a familial and religious joy that the prosperous and the well-educated often miss. Theirs was not a sentimental freedom grounded in theoretical rights, Griffin saw, but a moral liberty that was ordered to the love of God. This transcendent and transforming love was best expressed to Griffin by a Bible-quoting black preacher:

> We spoke of the whites. "They're God's children, just like us," he said. "Even if they don't act very godlike any more. God tells us straight — we've got to love them, no ifs, ands, and buts about it. Why, if we hated them, we'd be sunk down to their level. There's plenty of us doing just that, too."
>
> "A lot of the people I've talked to think we've turned the other cheek too long," I [Griffin] said.
>
> "You can't get around what's right, though," he said. "When we stop loving them, that's when they win."[44]

O'Connor's fiction gives artistic embodiment to this black minister's voice, as we shall see in the following chapter.

It was the presence of charity that O'Connor failed to detect in James Baldwin — for all of his justified rage. His pseudo-prophecies would not be tolerated, she said, if he were white. "Baldwin can tell us what it feels like to be a Negro in Harlem," she wrote to Maryat Lee, "but he tries to tell us everything else too." O'Connor brusquely refused Lee's offer to meet with Baldwin on one of his trips southward: "Might as well expect a mule to fly as me to see James Baldwin in Georgia. I observe the traditions of the society I feed on — it's only fair" (CW, 1095).[45] In an unpublished exchange with Lee, O'Connor made a similarly sharp response to Lee's suggestion that she write a public letter on the race question. Southerners do not use the newspapers for social protest, O'Connor fulminated, and such a statement would thus have no effect.

43. Ibid., p. 125.
44. Ibid., p. 96.
45. It needs to be remembered, yet again, that O'Connor always cast herself in the most antagonistic terms when writing to Lee. W. A. Sessions reports that O'Connor expressed considerable anguish at not being able to receive Baldwin in her home.

O'Connor had deep respect for the local and the particular. Location provides limits, she said, and "like all limitations, is a gateway to reality." The artist's "true audience, the audience he checks himself by," she added, "is at home" (MM, 54). She also decried the romantic notion of the artist as the anguished victim of cultural prejudice. Even so, her own social location as a Catholic intellectual who was sympathetic to the civil rights movement made her doubly out of place in the Protestant and segregated South.[46] The denial of our fundamental human rootedness, especially as it reveals a far deeper theological dependence, made O'Connor suspicious of Northern reformers who, leaving behind their own segregated cities that were seething with racial discord, inundated the rural South to aid the cause of black voter registration. The ethical energy of the civil rights workers increased, O'Connor caustically observed, in direct proportion to their distance from home (MM, 200). Thus would she have found herself in sympathy, I believe, with the black woman who, fifteen years after the fact, recalled the Mississippi Summer Project of 1964. Her testimony, recorded by Robert Coles, reveals the religious chasm that often lay between religious blacks and their secular liberators:

> You'd tell your faith to the civil rights folks, and they'd look down at the ground, and they'd wait you out, with a bad, bad look in their eyes, and their mouths turned down, and they'd be scratching the back of their necks, until you've stopped talking, so they could start talking. And boy, did they talk! I told one white boy from up there in Massachusetts that he's going to be a minister of Christ the Lord one of these days, when he sees the light. But he didn't like what I said, no he didn't. He just went on, telling me what I should be, and telling me about the heaven we're going to have here in this country, if we'd only turn everything around.
>
> Well, there's no heaven but in Heaven. And if you don't know that, you don't know much. That's what I believe. Of course, you can't tell some people much. They want to tell you everything. That's how it goes: they come here to help us, but oh, if we don't bow and scrape to their every idea, then they lose patience with us, and I declare, you see them looking at you no different than the sheriff, and the people at the post office, and

46. Professor Sessions also recalls an episode that graphically reveals the complexity of Flannery O'Connor's religious and racial ethos. Once when Sessions was visiting the O'Connor family at Thanksgiving, O'Connor's Uncle Louis Cline angrily slammed down a copy of *Life* magazine after discovering that it depicted Cardinal Cushing of New York washing the feet of a black man in a Maundy Thursday service. It may have been tolerable to dwell as a disliked minority in the South, but it was intolerable to be identified with a far more despised minority.

like that. Scratch some of the white civil rights people and you have the plantation owners. Scratch some of the black civil rights people, and you have the white talkers. . . .

Some of these people who came down here, they believed in men, not angels; and sure enough, they didn't believe in God. It's their choice; but it might have been nice if they'd said to me: it's your choice. Instead, they felt sorry for us. Jesus Christ didn't feel sorry for the people He went and attended to. He loved them. He healed them out of love. He wanted them on their feet and the equal of other people. . . . He wanted them to thank God. On your knees to Him; "yes, sir," and "yes, ma'm" to the white folks, and hello to your colored brethren, but to God Almighty, it's a prayer, and it's please, dear Lord, please, and I've failed again. There's a big difference between Him and us, that's for sure. And if you follow Him, if you really do, then there's a big difference between yourself and your neighbor, that's for sure, too.[47]

Flannery O'Connor's work centers on this huge chasm between human and divine righteousness. She turned her satirical eye on the enlightened rather than the benighted. She would have agreed with David Solomon's observation that white liberals who cut their teeth on the easiest moral issue of the twentieth century stand in peculiar moral danger, tempted as they are to regard all ethical issues as matters of simple injustice that can be corrected by the application of simple justice. The Eudora Weltys of this world, O'Connor believed, were sufficient critics of the Bull Connors and the Byron de la Beckwiths. She cast her own stone of accusation not at the Snopeses, who were her moral inferiors, but at the Maryat Lees, who were sinners of her own kind. It may have taken more courage for O'Connor to resist the moralistic tendency of high literary culture, therefore, than for Welty to publish a single story in *The New Yorker*, where she could be assured of an approving audience.[48]

One of O'Connor's most hilarious sallies against the racially righteous occurs in "The Enduring Chill." There two black farmhands named Randall and Morgan play a wicked trick on Asbury Fox, the white intellectual who wants to liberate them from his mother's seemingly repressive rules for operating her dairy. Asbury regards his mother as a rabid racist for refusing to let

47. Robert Coles, *Flannery O'Connor's South* (Baton Rouge: Louisiana State University Press, 1980), pp. 100-101.

48. It should also be noted that, while Flannery O'Connor has been censured for refusing to entertain James Baldwin at her home in Milledgeville, Eudora Welty also refused to be interviewed by the distinguished black novelist Ralph Ellison, lest her mother be offended.

her black laborers have their fill of the farm's abundant and nutritious milk. But the uneducated Randall and Morgan prove far smarter than the cultured Asbury. They know that to drink unpasteurized milk is to court serious if not deadly disease. They also see that Asbury's professed solidarity with them is a form of moral preening. So little has Asbury come to know Randall and Morgan that he cannot tell them apart. Yet he wants them to imbibe the forbidden milk in a sort of secular communion, as they will be united in common defiance of his mother's racist restrictions. After encouraging the gullible Asbury to drink deeply from this sickening font, the two blacks offer their own devastating commentary:

> "Howcome you let him drink all that milk every day?" [asked Morgan].
> "What he do is him," Randall said. "What I do is me."
> "Howcome he talks so ugly about his ma?" [Morgan again asked.]
> "Because she ain't whup him enough when he was little," Randall said. (CW, 560)

Asbury earns the wages of his sinful righteousness when he contracts undulant fever from having drunk the bacteria-laden milk. Because he hopes to die as a martyr to his mother's alleged ruination of his natural talent, Asbury calls for a sophisticated priest such as the Jesuit he had met in New York City, perhaps one who can talk to him about the cultured agnosticism of James Joyce. He wants nothing to do with the Methodist preacher who is his mother's minister. Mrs. Fox does the best she can by summoning the local Catholic priest, a deaf and unreconstructed Roman Catholic named Father Finn. He cuts to the heart of Asbury's pretense by asking uncultured but comically apt questions:

> "What do you think of Joyce?" Asbury said louder.
> "Joyce? Joyce who?" asked the priest.
> "James Joyce," Asbury said and laughed.
> The priest brushed his huge hand in the air as if he were bothered by gnats. "I haven't met him," he said. "Now. Do you say your morning and night prayers?"
> Asbury appeared confused. "Joyce was a great writer," he murmured, forgetting to shout.
> "You don't, eh?" said the priest. "Well you will never learn to be good unless you pray regularly. You cannot love Jesus unless you speak to Him."

"The myth of the dying god has always fascinated me," Asbury shouted, but the priest did not appear to catch it.

"Do you have trouble with purity?" he demanded, and as Asbury paled, he went on without waiting for an answer. "We all do but you must pray to the Holy Ghost for it. Mind, heart and body." (CW, 565-66)

Asbury's body will not be purified by the nonfatal illness he is so disappointed to have contracted, thus being deprived of the death that would mark "his greatest triumph" over his smothering mother. Instead, his enduring chills and fevers will require him to live in lasting dependence on her. Nor is it likely that Asbury's mind will be disinfected from worshiping at the altar of Kafka and Joyce and the other modern masters whom he so greatly admires. But there is at least a chance that he will find the purity of heart that beholds God himself. For at the end of the story, Asbury enters the purgatorial life that has the power to cleanse all his unrighteousness, whether racial or filial, as the Holy Ghost descends on him — not as a dove carrying the olive branch of peace but as a fierce bird bearing the icicle of judgment in its beak.

O'Connor feared that such racial liberators as Asbury Fox could become as complacent as the most bigoted racists. Julian, the protagonist in "Everything That Rises Must Converge," is another white liberal who turns a rightful demand for racial justice into a wrongful demand for moral congratulation. As Sarah Gordon has shown, this story arises directly out of O'Connor's correspondence with Maryat Lee concerning a bus ride that Lee made from Georgia back to New York. In an attempted gesture of human solidarity with a victim of racial injustice, Lee had sat beside a black woman who was wearing a purple hat and who was burdened with a fussy child. Perhaps sensing what was self-seeking in such white "charity," the black woman removed herself to a distant seat, Lee reports, as soon as she could.[49] So it is with Julian, who, in order to prove his own liberation, deliberately takes a seat next to a black man on the bus. The Negro instantly penetrates his new "friend's" pretense, seeing that Julian wants to use him as a means for practicing his own moral hygiene. Julian is so obsessed with casting out the racist mote in his mother's eye that he remains blind to the beam-like presumption and ingratitude that afflict his own vision. Julian can "love" the anonymous Negro whom he does not know, but not the mother whom he does know and who also knows him (cf. 1 John 4:20).

49. Gordon notes that the limits of Lee's own liberality become evident when, exasperated by the black woman's refusal to honor her act of good will, Lee calls her a "bitch" (Sarah Gordon, "Maryat and Julian and the 'not so bloodless revolution,'" *Flannery O'Connor Bulletin* 21 (1992): 32.

As often happens in O'Connor's stories, the liberated offspring proves to be a far worse sinner than the unprogressive parent. Though conventionally prejudiced, Julian's mother is capable of the love that matters most: she cares deeply about her uncaring son. And despite her verbal scorn for blacks, she is not a vicious racist. On the contrary, she humorously accepts the hard lesson in economic equality that she is forced to learn. Across the aisle there is a black woman whose purple hat is identical to one that Julian's mother had recently purchased in the assurance that only her class of people could afford it. Julian's friendly and outgoing mother is not soured by this harsh revelation, even though he seeks to humiliate her with it. On the contrary, she plays peek-a-boo with the little black boy whose mother wears the matching hat, and the child in turn is drawn to the white lady's jovial affection. In her innocent glad-heartedness, Julian's mother gives the boy a shiny copper as she leaves the bus. The child's mother is infuriated. Blinded by a racial rage that is unable to distinguish a kindly from a condescending gesture, the black woman strikes Julian's mother to the ground, giving her a fatal stroke. Yet the addled white woman remains gracious rather than resentful, even as she dies. She calls out for Caroline, the black nurse from her childhood, perhaps remembering her as one who gave her the unqualified love that her own son had refused to grant.

Some readers have seen the penny-giving gesture as the ultimately racist act, and they have thus justified the black woman's splenetic response.[50] Wanting their ethical categories absolutely pure, these interpreters cannot countenance the moral complexity that O'Connor knew to be the stuff of truth and thus of fiction. Rather like Regina Cline O'Connor, Julian's mother holds to conventional racial attitudes.[51] But while she can speak with scorn for blacks in general, this kindly woman never mistreats any particular black person whom she happens to encounter. Hence her instinctive act of affec-

---

50. See Alice Walker, *In Search of Our Mothers' Gardens* (New York: Harcourt, 1983), pp. 53-56.

51. O'Connor would warn some of her guests not to bring up the race question in the presence of her mother, lest it propel her attitudinizing locomotive onto a track that had no end (Gossett, "Flannery O'Connor's Attitude to Blacks"). At the same time, Mrs. O'Connor's regard for individual blacks was quite remarkable. When one of her black farmworkers suffered a back injury, Mrs. O'Connor not only visited the house where this black man lived but also gave him a liniment rubdown. This stunningly intimate gesture proves the truth of a tart black aphorism: "Down South, they don't care how close we get, as long as we don't rise too high. Up North, they don't care how high we rise, as long as we don't get too close." This adage, reported to me by the Southern historian David Smiley, explains yet another black maxim — that in the North blacks are often honored as a race but not as individuals, while in the South they are often honored as individuals but not as a race.

tion toward the black child. To view the gift of the pretty penny as anything other than blameless is to indulge in the same vicious moralizing that Julian pours on his mother as she lies fatally stricken by the black *furiosa*:

> "Don't think that was just an uppity Negro woman," [Julian] said. "That was the whole colored race which will no longer take your condescending pennies. . . . What all this means," he said, "is that the old world is gone. The old manners are obsolete and your graciousness is not worth a damn." . . .
>
> "You needn't act as if the world has come to an end," he said, "because it hasn't. From now on you've got to live in a new world and face a few realities for a change. Buck up," he said, "it won't kill you." (CW, 499-500)

Julian's mother does in fact die, but her death is not due to any unpurged racism, nor is it due entirely to the blow struck by the violent black woman. She also dies from the racial righteousness of her own son. In the name of an abstract justice meant for people he does not really know or care about, he has denied the most fundamental of all loves: the filial love for the mother who has not only given him birth and nourished his youth, but who has also sustained his feckless adult life at considerable sacrifice.[52]

Flannery O'Connor's critique of morally presumptuous reformers is her fictional answer to Eudora Welty's question about the origin of Southern anger in "Where Is the Voice Coming From?" The voice that cries with hatred and the hand that strikes with death spring not only from the seething envy of white trash; they also burst from the unredeemed rage of the righteous, whether black or white. At a depth as yet unplumbed, O'Connor understood the truth voiced by the slave Ishmael in Herman Melville's novel of 1851, *Moby-Dick*:

> What of it, if some old hunk of a sea-captain orders me to get a broom and sweep down the decks? What does that indignity amount to, weighed, I mean, in the scales of the New Testament? . . . Who ain't a slave? Tell me that. Well, then, however the old sea-captains may order me about — however they may thump and punch me about, I have the

---

52. This is not to suggest that "Everything That Rises" is a story without faults of its own. As with Asbury Fox in "The Enduring Chill," so with Julian here: O'Connor turns him into a virtual demon of self-righteousness, peering out of a mental bubble that is hard to credit. His total opacity to his own moral failings makes him slightly unreal, as I have argued elsewhere (*The Comedy of Redemption: Christian Faith and Comic Vision in Four American Novelists* [Notre Dame, IN: University of Notre Dame Press, 1988], p. 121).

satisfaction of knowing that it is all right: that everybody else is one way or other served in much the same way — either in a physical or metaphysical point of view, that is: and so the universal thump is passed round, and all hands should rub each other's shoulder-blades, and be content.[53]

O'Connor agreed that we are all slaves to evil, that we all suffer considerable indignities from the unavoidable fact of our mortality, that the blows of fortune strike all and sundry alike, and that, above all, the scales of the New Testament find both the righteous and the unrighteous woefully wanting. Yet she also knew that something other than either shoulder-rubbing solidarity or legally enforced integration was needed for healing the racial wounds that continue to suppurate at the core of both the nation and the church. She was not resigned, therefore, to the perpetual division of black and white into separate, even if equal, spheres. In her two most important stories with racial themes, "Judgment Day" and "The Artificial Nigger," O'Connor gestures at a more excellent way, the way of reconciliation between brothers and sisters of the same Lord.

53. Herman Melville, *Moby-Dick; or, The Whale* (New York: Modern Library, 1950; first published in 1851), pp. 4-5. I owe my emphasis on this splendid saying to Frank Leavell.

FOUR ❧ *The South as a Mannered and*
*Mysteriously Redemptive Region*

"A candid history of the South and its people would be unendurable for a Southerner to read. We could not face it. Shorn of its myths and legends we would repudiate it as not our own." So wrote Carlyle Marney, a renegade Southerner and a Baptist preacher who knew both the horror and wonder of his region. Chief among Southern myths and legends is the one W. J. Cash described as the "moonlight-magnolias-and-mint juleps" vision of the South as the realm where happy darkies toiled in the cotton fields as their masters sat on the veranda discussing Plato:

> It was a sort of stage piece out of the eighteenth century, wherein gesturing gentlemen moved soft-spokenly against a background of rose gardens and dueling grounds, through always gallant deeds, and lovely ladies, in farthingales, never for a moment lost that exquisite remoteness which has been the dream of all men and the possession of none. Its social pattern was manorial, its civilization that of the Cavalier, its ruling class coextensive with the planter group. . . .
>
> They dwelt in large and stately mansions, preferably white and with columns and with Greek entablature. Their estates were feudal baronies, their slaves quite too numerous ever to be counted, and their social life a thing of Old World splendor and delicacy. What had really happened here, indeed, was that the gentlemanly idea, driven from England by Cromwell, had taken refuge in the South and fashioned for itself a world to its heart's desire: a world singularly polished and mellow and poised, wholly dominated by ideals of honor and chivalry and noblesse. . . .[1]

1. W. J. Cash, *The Mind of the South* (New York: Vintage, 1962, first published 1941), p. ix.

121

As we have seen, there is more than an iota of truth in such derisive irony; but there is also a subtle complexity about the Southern picture that Cash misses. The region in its prime produced men and women of such eminent character and conduct that it has sometimes left their modern legatees paralyzed, incapable of defining who they are or what they are supposed to do. The protagonist of Walker Percy's *The Last Gentleman*, Williston ("Bibb") Barrett, is a notable example of the befuddlement that the scions of this grandiose Southern tradition often face:

> Over the years his family had turned ironical and lost its gift for action. It was an honorable and violent family, but gradually the violence had been deflected and turned inward. The great grandfather knew what was what and said so and acted accordingly and did not care what anyone thought. He even wore a pistol in a holster like a Western hero and once met the Grand Wizard of the Ku Klux Klan in a barbershop and invited him then and there to shoot it out in the street. The next generation, the grandfather, seemed to know what was what but he was not really so sure. He was brave but he gave much thought to the business of being brave. He too would have shot it out with the Grand Wizard if only he could have made certain it was the right thing to do. The father was a brave man too and he said he didn't care what others thought, but he did care. More than anything else he wished to act with honor and to be thought well of by other men. So living for him was a strain. . . . As for the present young man, the last of the line, he did not know what to think. So he became a watcher and a listener and a wanderer.[2]

If a native Southerner such as Carlyle Marney regarded the evils of his region too egregious to confront, and if Walker Percy's autobiographical character found that his inherited Southern virtues left him both confused and paralyzed, the South has seemed even more perplexing to outsiders. In *Absalom, Absalom!* William Faulkner registers the response of Shreve McCannon, a sympathetic but exasperated Canadian, after he has listened to his Harvard roommate, the Southerner named Quentin Compson, "tell of the South," giving account of his own "unendurable history." "The South," McCannon exclaims, "Jesus. No wonder you folks outlive yourselves by years and years and years." Southerners outlive themselves because they are haunted by their past. Another Faulkner character, Gavin Stevens in *Requiem*

2. Walker Percy, *The Last Gentleman* (New York: Farrar, Straus & Giroux, 1966), pp. 9-10.

*for a Nun,* articulates the nature of the Southern historical sense ever so memorably: "The past is never dead. It's not even past."

The thesis of this book is that the South, while bearing the greatest historical guilt of any American region, offers the nation its largest religious hope. We have already heard Flannery O'Connor explain why this is so: because the Christ-haunted South has been possessed by the one past that can never be merely past, the eschatological history of the risen Lord and his living embodiment in the church. "As belief in the divinity of Christ decreases," she wrote, "there seems to be a preoccupation with Christ-figures in our fiction. What is pushed to the back of the mind makes its way forward somehow. Ghosts can be very fierce and instructive. They cast strange shadows . . ." (CW, 861). Though a non-Christian writer himself — perhaps even an anti-Christian writer — William Faulkner could not exorcise the ghost of Golgotha. Toward the end of his writing career, Faulkner returned to the Christian myth, as he called it, for his novel entitled *A Fable.* Faulkner remained deeply akin to such Southerners as Hazel Motes, the hero of O'Connor's novel *Wise Blood.* As the narrator says of him, Motes is blessedly unable to elude the pursuing Nazarene, who moves "from tree to tree in the back of his mind, a wild ragged figure motioning him to turn around and come off into the dark where he was not sure of his footing, where he might be walking on the water and not know it and then suddenly know it and drown" (CW, 11).

The redemptive quality of Southern life lies in its Bible-centeredness and its Christ-hauntedness. The secular reflections and echoes of Christianity at work in Southern culture are to be found in its elaborate set of manners. In this chapter we will turn first to the redemptive quality of Southern manners as they are displayed in "Judgment Day," the story O'Connor was still working on when she died. Even at their best, manners are a secondary substitute for the gospel itself, especially when we are faced with the inveterate Southern problem of race and its twisted rootage in human pride. This chapter will conclude, therefore, by examining the redemptive powers of the gospel at work in O'Connor's most controverted story, "The Artificial Nigger." She called it her personal favorite — "and probably the best thing I'll ever write" (CW, 1027).

## Manners, Civility, and Courtesy

Flannery O'Connor sometimes complained that the South of her era was being purged not only of its many social vices but also of its few social virtues.

The chief of these virtues, she declared, is to be found in our "fierce but fading manners" (MM, 29). The best of Southern manners deal not with mere politeness, O'Connor understood, but with the formal gestures that both bind and separate people in deeply informal ways. Manners provide the constraints necessary for social intercourse. Emerson put the matter in his characteristically moralizing way: "Your manners are always under examination, and by committees little expected . . . but are awarding or denying you very high prizes when you least think of it." The sage of Concord meant that, in the broadest sense, manners constitute a code of conduct that summons us to treat others with dignity and respect.[3] Henry Grunwald offers a similar definition of manners as "a surface sign of an underlying order — or at least the wish for it. They are an indication that certain standards exist. We may be fortunate in having largely eliminated social hierarchies, but we still need, more than ever, a hierarchy of values."[4]

All faiths and cultures — even secular and academic cultures — have their conventional distinctions between clean and unclean, holy and profane. These codes carefully demarcate the proper and improper ways for eating and dressing, for bathing and having sex, no less than for performing the more obviously ritualized practices of praying and offering sacrifice. Without such mannerly codes, we would not be able to inhabit and enact the communal roles that are indispensable for both private and social life. Manners give order and significance to a world that would otherwise be chaotic and anarchic. That civilization is based on such artifice does not make it false. The anthropologist Mary Douglas warns those who would banish all cultural codes that on "the day when everyone can see exactly what is on the end

---

3. Emerson's own manners were notoriously staid. One of Emerson's early biographers complained that, at his center, the seraphic sage contained a bloodless heart, "an inner diaphanous core." "If an inhabitant of another planet should visit the earth, he would receive, on the whole, a truer notion of human life by attending Italian opera than he would by reading Emerson's volumes. He would learn from Italian opera that there were two sexes . . ." (John Jay Chapman, *Emerson, and Other Essays* [New York: AMS Press, 1969; reprint of 1899 edition], pp. 71, 83). Louisa May Alcott was even more acerbic: "How should I dare to interfere with the proper grayness of old Concord? The dear old town has never known a startling hue since the redcoats were there. Far be it from me to inject inharmonious color into the neutral tint. And my favorite characters! Suppose they went to cavorting at their own sweet will, to the infinite horror of dear Mr. Emerson, who never imagined a Concord person as walking off a plumb line stretched between two pearly clouds in the empyrean. To have had Mr. Emerson for an intellectual god all one's life is to be invested with a chain armor of propriety" (quoted in LaSalle Corbell Pickett, *Across My Path: Memories of People I Have Known* [New York: Brentano's, 1916], pp. 107-8.

4. Henry Grunwald, "Jane Austen's Civil Society," *Wall Street Journal* (2 Oct. 1996).

of everyone's fork, on that day there is no pollution and no purity and nothing edible and inedible, credible or incredible, because the classifications of social life are gone. There is no more meaning."[5] O'Connor's sentiments were almost identical: "Traditional manners, however unbalanced, are better than no manners at all" (MM, 200).

The collapse of manners has long been an American danger. Fearing that recourse to refined comportment would reinstate the static and oppressive hierarchies they had fled, nineteenth-century American settlers often made crudity into a new kind of virtue rather than a vice. Frances Trollope was properly appalled by the domestic manners of frontier Americans. She lamented their habit of picking teeth with a knife after meals, and she was outraged at their propensity for spitting. Oscar Wilde was more jauntily appalled, calling America "one long expectoration." Alexis de Tocqueville, by contrast, regarded the loss of civility as intrinsic to American politics. "The effect of democracy," Tocqueville wrote, "is not . . . to give men any particular manners but to prevent them from having manners at all." He saw that Americans would be governed by public opinion rather than by received manners or traditions.

The question of manners was also the chief division between Edmund Burke and Jean-Jacques Rousseau. Rousseau argued that civilizing restraints keep humanity in misery and chains, and so he sought to strip human nature naked in order to expose all the conventions that had disfigured human innocence and thus ruined "man as nature had made him." Burke, on the other hand, decried this attempt to deprive humanity of what he called "the decent drapery of life," as it is furnished from the wardrobe of social custom and tradition. He believed that our "naked shivering nature," as Shakespeare describes it in *King Lear,* requires the clothing of manners and civilization, of aristocracy and the established church. Russell Kirk sums up Burke's case sharply, and in a way O'Connor would surely have approved: "Man is not fully man . . . until he is fully civilized; he acquires his higher nature as a member of a culture, of a civil social order. Man's true nature is only latent in the savage."[6] In a similar vein, O'Connor declared: "Anybody who sets out to be an individual is intolerable." They become what she called professional Californians.[7]

This is not to say that all manners must be preserved at all costs. Ritual-

5. Quoted in Cynthia Clossen, "Know Thy Father," *Wall Street Journal* (1997).

6. Russell Kirk, *Edmund Burke: A Genius Reconsidered* (Wilmington, DE: Intercollegiate Studies Institute, 1997), p. 18.

7. Quoted in Rosemary Magee, *Conversations with Flannery O'Connor* (Jackson, MS: University Press of Mississippi, 1987), p. 31.

ized codes of conduct often mask vicious evils.[8] Hypocrisy, snobbery, and even cruelty often underlie the most refined manners. Hideous crimes can be committed with the utmost politeness. One can show a gelid scorn for others with an extravagant niceness — killing, as it were, with kindness. Marriages based entirely on social considerations find their political equivalent in elegant entertainments conducted within earshot of the utmost misery and poverty. Manners can thus become the instruments of deceit, and their dismantling can be a necessary act of good faith. G. K. Chesterton sought, therefore, to dismantle the moralistic manners that were often the legacy of Victorian Christianity. He lamented the reduction of the gospel to mere respectability: "This alarming growth of good habits really means too great an emphasis on those virtues which mere custom can ensure, it means too little emphasis on those virtues which custom can never quite ensure, [those] sudden and splendid virtues of inspired pity or inspired candour."

Flannery O'Connor often sought to deconstruct the allegedly Christian manners of her own time. As we have seen, she satirizes Mrs. May, the protagonist of "Greenleaf," as a Christian who wanted to keep certain words in the church as others are kept in the bedroom. Such mannerly churchgoers find Christ in the conversation as embarrassing as their forebears blushed at the subject of sex. O'Connor elected the grotesque as her own literary medium because she sought a rough artistic manner that would convey the unmannerly matter of her faith. She also grew exceedingly weary of the small-minded politeness that characterized proper Milledgeville "society." Book clubs were her special bane: there she encountered pretentious ladies trying to outdo each other by naming the authors who had most influenced their childhood imagination — one citing Shakespeare, another Milton, and so forth. O'Connor waited until the end, and then candidly cited the primary inspiration of her youth: the Sears and Roebuck catalogue. After giving a talk at a book club luncheon, O'Connor wrote this sardonic report to Betty Hester:

8. It is also exceedingly difficult to translate manners from one culture to another. The French, for example, do not believe it either uncivil or impolite for people to refuse even an obligatory nod to others whom they are squeezing past in a narrow lane, for clerks utterly to ignore customers in shops, nor for those who have been given a request to respond always with the word *non*. "But you should never take *non* for an answer," writes Alice Furlaud. "You're expected to repeat your request again, and after you're told *non* a number of times, the answer will usually be changed to *oui*. . . . [I]f the requester turns away, accepting the *non* as the final word, the *non*-sayer may well be disappointed. The effect is rather like that when one side in a tug-of-war suddenly lets go of the rope, causing the opponents to fall down in a heap" ("Civility vs. *Civilité*," *Atlantic* [October 2001]: 107).

When it was over, one lady said to me, "That was such a nice dispensation you gave us, honey." Another said, "What's wrong with your leg, sugar?" I will be powerful glad when they leave off sugaring me. The lady who officiates at these things does it in a sweet dying voice as if over the casket of a late beloved. They pray, then eat, then introduce everybody but the waiters and the cat, then get round to the speaker. (CW, 974)

Yet while O'Connor scorned a merely civil religion, she had the greatest regard for civility itself. She knew that a democracy, perhaps more than any other polity, requires manners. Exactly to the extent that ancient inequalities have been overcome, there is an even greater demand for social restraint, for privacy, for the individual space one grants to others because one knows one's own need for it. Without such encoded self-limitations, the personal and the public realms become dreadfully conflated. The result of such conflation, as Jean Elshtain makes clear, is a political absolutism that forbids all privacy: "Nothing is exempt from political definition, direction and manipulation — not sexual intimacy, not love, not passion, not raising children, not friendship. Those who think there ought to be places to hide are deemed to have something to hide and thus are not to be trusted."[9] The exhortation to make the personal into the political denies the truth of original sin, which holds that we cannot overcome our ineluctable propensity for self-interest without the aid of divine grace. Perhaps O'Connor was referring to this deadly incurvature of the will when she declared that "the basic [human] experience . . . is the experience of human limitation" (MM, 131). Such finitude and fallenness require a code of self-restraint, a set of manners, a mask. Without such limits, we radically fallen creatures would devour each other, like so many monsters of the deep, in a cynical war of all against all, as Thomas Hobbes called it.

It is less obvious but perhaps more important for our own unmannerly age to remember that manners help prevent the crimes of sentimental self-revelation; they check the uninhibited desire to tell all. Against the burgeoning culture of therapy, where we no longer confess to priests or pastors but unmask our souls to virtual strangers, O'Connor warned that there is a secret link between sentimentality and pornography.[10] The former undermines

9. Jean Elshtain, "Bad publicity," *New Republic* (August 12, 1996): 25.

10. Rochelle Gurstein has recently shown that, contrary to popular opinion, the legal category of obscenity was not the invention of Puritans and Victorians, who had no need for it. It is an early twentieth-century construction, however clumsy and unworkable, devised as a defense against those who would demand the end of all constraints (*The Repeal of Reticence: A History of America's Cultural and Legal Struggles over Free Speech, Obscenity, Sexual Liberation, and Modern Art* [New York: Hill and Wang, 1996]).

faith as the latter destroys art. They are both shortcuts to emotional fulfill-ment, bypassing the hard moral and spiritual obstacles scattered along the road to truth (MM, 147-48). O'Connor opposed the notion that Christians should be glad-handing and well-met folks, declaring acidly that such gentil-ity would be an artistic liability: "A golden heart would be a positive interfer-ence in the writing of fiction" (MM, 192). Tough-minded charity discerns the worth of human beings through the aperture of God's own costly sacrifice, while soft-core pity sees them through the lens of easy and all-sanctioning emotions. Elshtain discerns the odd connection between pity and terror, even as she also links it to manners. Drawing on a distinction made by the political philosopher Hannah Arendt, Elshtain explains that

> [t]he French Revolutionary reign of pity was abstract and limitless, turn-ing on an ideology of victimization rather than on a response to the con-crete claims of victims, and it ended in terror. . . . One feels compassion, or comprehends it, only if sufficient distance between people is main-tained; only when human distinctiveness is preserved as we recognize and respond to the claims of another.[11]

Manners have the power to preserve this salutary distance between the public and the private by enabling us to recognize the distinctive and legiti-mate claims that others make on us. The codes of charitable behavior require lessons in wearing the right kinds of masks. Against the contemporary urge to dispense with masks and to "let it all hang out," as the crude metaphor has it, W. H. Auden insists:

> Only animals who are below civilization and the angels who are beyond it can be sincere. Human beings are, necessarily, actors who cannot be-come something before they have first pretended to be it; and they can be divided, not into the hypocritical and the sincere, but into the sane who know they are acting and the insane who do not.

The ancient Greeks understood this necessity of wearing a face, the require-ment to project a certain image of oneself in order to exist as any self at all. We become the things we perform, as the outward life largely shapes the in-ward, despite modern notions to the contrary. In fact, the Greek word *persona* means "mask." The question is never whether we shall wear masks, therefore, but what kind of masks we shall wear.

11. Jean Elshtain, "Sense and sensibility," *New Republic* (September 30, 1996): 29.

Auden further elaborates the nature of manners: "To be well-bred means to have respect for the solitude of others, whether they be mere acquaintances or, and this is much more difficult, persons we love; to be ill-bred is to importune attention and intimacy, to come too close, to ask indiscreet questions and make indiscreet revelations, to lecture, to bore."[12] Good breeding and gracious manners cannot serve, of course, as a surrogate for grace itself. Yet in a culture at least nominally Christian — as O'Connor's Christ-haunted South most surely was — the two orders of grace should not be wholly alien. There is something profoundly courteous in the call of the gospel to count others better than oneself: "Let each of you look not only to his own interests, but also to the interests of others" (Philippians 2:4). O'Connor believed that the social manners of the South, despite their many deceptions and hypocrisies, could sometimes serve as a far-off reflection of God's own incarnate love.

## Obedience to the Unenforceable

It cannot be denied that even the best Southern manners kept black people in a state of subjection. Among Southerners of wealth and rank, the codes and customs served to oil the machinery of daily life, exacting sure and often severe penalties for those who violated them. But when Southern social etiquette crossed the lines of race and class, it often worked to preserve the hierarchy of position and privilege: the hegemony of rich over poor, of whites over blacks — even of the unworthiest of whites over the worthiest of blacks. The ideal of noblesse oblige called for these privileged ones at the top to treat the hapless ones at the bottom with both courtesy and charity. Yet there could be no fundamental breach of the system itself, even among whites. "Despite the many provocations and depredations [that] rich white Southern men inflicted on poor whites," asks John Mayfield, "how often did the latter lynch the former?"[13]

At its worst, the Southern social code led not to mere benign condescension toward blacks but also to malign oppression. And when black men were erotically embraced by white women, it meant their death.[14]

12. W. H. Auden, *Forewords and Afterwords*, selected by Edward Mendelson (New York: Random House, 1973), p. 394.

13. Mayfield asks this question in correspondence with the author.

14. Bertram Wyatt-Brown shows that Southern moral dissonance was even more pronounced during the nineteenth century, when "manners" were still closely linked to "honor": "The interior contradictions of [Southern] honor held men in shackles of prejudice, pride, and

Lynchings and castrations were the most brutal way of upholding "the Southern way of life"; yet the verbal means for supporting the vicious side of Southern tradition were no less powerful. Taylor Branch reports that the violence that greeted James Meredith's enrollment at the University of Mississippi was fomented, in no small part, by Governor Ross Barnett's defense of Southern traditions and manners. Students attending the 1962 Kentucky-Mississippi football game in Jackson chanted, "We want Ross," until the governor finally came to the 50-yard line and shouted the litany they wanted to hear: "I love Mississippi. . . . I love her people. . . . I love our customs."[15]

At about the same time that Ross Barnett was defending racial segregation and injustice in the name of "our customs," Flannery O'Connor was making a radically different kind of plea: "It requires considerable grace for two races to live together, particularly when the population is divided about fifty-fifty between them and when they have our particular history. It can't be done without a code of manners based on mutual charity."[16] O'Connor feared that the mannered charity of the South was in danger of being lost throughout the entire American republic, not only in Dixie. Hence her sharp retort to the charge that the South had become estranged from mainstream America; on the contrary, she complained, "it is not alienated enough." O'Connor expressed her fear, in fact, that the South is "getting more and more like the rest of the country" (MM, 28-29).

O'Connor wanted the South to preserve its own special character by developing a new set of regional manners. "For the rest of the country," she declared, "the race problem is settled when the Negro has his rights, but for the Southerner, whether he's white or colored, that's only the beginning."[17] It was not to be an easy task, for the desegregation of Southern society would complicate interracial closeness with interracial competition. Blacks making their way up from slavery and segregation would begin to compete economi-

---

superficiality. It often existed not in authenticity of the self but in symbols, expletives, ritual speeches, gestures, half-understood impulses, titles, and physical appearances. All these might conform with rational, innovative thought and action, but often enough they were diametrically opposed. Thus holding men in bondage could not have worried too many Southerners so long as they were committed to the age-old morality. Honor, not conscience, shame, not guilt, were the psychological and social underpinnings of Southern culture" (*Southern Honor: Ethics and Behavior in the Old South* [New York: Oxford University Press, 1982], p. 22).

15. Taylor Branch, *Parting the Waters: America in the King Years, 1954-63* (New York: Simon and Schuster, 1988), p. 659.

16. Quoted in Magee, p. 103.

17. Ibid., p. 104.

cally with whites, especially poor whites. O'Connor correctly predicted that the triumph of business and industry over agriculture would change the culture of the South far more than court-ordered integration of the public schools: "I think as [the region] gets to be more and more city and less country — as . . . everything . . . is reduced to the same flat level — we'll be writing about men in gray flannel suits. That's about all there'll be to write about, I think, as we lose our individuality."[18]

The intervening decades have revealed, alas, that the race problem has not been solved by granting black people their rights; on the contrary, the removal of old oppressions has made the remaining inequities even more egregious. Many people, black and white alike, believe that the project of integration has been a massive failure. It has produced an official equality but a practical inequality, and thus a de facto resegregation. On college and university campuses, black and white students rarely intermingle. One can sometimes hear blacks turning the old segregationist code on its head: "Equal," they say, "but separate." Black impatience with the slowness of racial justice, combined with white resentment toward racial quotas and set-asides, confirms the need for what O'Connor called a new "code of manners based on mutual charity." The development of such a charitable code requires great patience, as she noted: "You don't form a committee or pass a resolution; both races have to work it out the hard way." For O'Connor, the better way would be genuine forgiveness and reconciliation; but, failing that, there is always the hope of manners: "Manners are the next best thing to Christian charity. I don't know how much pure unadulterated Christian charity can be mustered in the South, but I have confidence that the manners of both races will show through in the long run." She elaborated her defense of manners in a crucial statement:

> [A]fter the Civil War, formality became a condition of survival [for Southern interracial life]. This doesn't seem to me any less true today. Formality preserves that individual privacy which everybody needs and, in these times, is always in danger of losing. It's particularly necessary to have in order to protect the rights of both races. When you have a code of manners based on charity, then when the charity fails — as it is going to do constantly — you've got those manners there to preserve each race from small intrusions upon the other. . . . The South has survived in the past because its manners, however lopsided or inadequate they may have been, provided enough social discipline to hold us together and give us

18. Ibid., p. 30.

an identity. Now those old manners are obsolete, but the new manners will have to be based on what was best in the old ones — in their real basis of charity and necessity.[19]

In a speech given at the outbreak of World War I, John Fletcher Moulton dealt with what O'Connor calls the social discipline that must be rooted in manners by distinguishing between the obligatory and the voluntary spheres of human life. He argued that the domain of "Positive Law" prescribes the things we are required to do and to refrain from doing in order for society to exist at all. Here our masks are effaced, as it were, in the act of becoming public citizens. At its opposite extreme lies the domain of "Absolute Choice": there we are at liberty to follow the bent of our own wills, without prohibitions or commands of any kind — thus wearing whatever masks we choose. In that realm of utter freedom are born all "spontaneity, originality, and energy." But between these two rather restricted realms lies the vast uncharted region that Lord Moulton calls "manners." Here we impose limits on ourselves; here we do what we ought to do even though we are not obliged to do it; here we refuse to turn our liberty into license, honoring instead "the sway of duty, fairness, sympathy, taste." The task of manners, therefore, is to find the right mask, the projected image that enables uncoerced charity. Hence Moulton's description of manners as "Obedience to the Unenforceable":

> To my mind the real greatness of a nation, its true civilization, is measured by the extent of this land of Obedience to the Unenforceable. It measures the extent to which the nation trusts its citizens, and its existence and area testify to the way they behave in response to that trust. Mere obedience to Law does not measure the greatness of a Nation. It can easily be obtained by a strong executive, and most easily of all from a timorous people. Nor is the license of behavior which so often accompanies the absence of Law, and which is miscalled Liberty, a proof of greatness. The true test is the extent to which individuals composing the nation can be trusted to obey self-imposed law.[20]

19. Ibid., pp. 102, 104.
20. John Fletcher Moulton, "Law and Manners," *Atlantic Monthly* (July 1924): 4, 10, 6. I am indebted to Brian Frizell for putting me on to this essay.

## The Lensless Spectacles of Vision and Charity

Flannery O'Connor discerned that the manners of art are related to manners in the social sense, and that, when properly linked, they impinge on ultimate realities. She protested, therefore, against all attempts to "separate mystery from manners and judgment from vision" (MM, 80). Much like Eliot and Joyce and the other high modernists, O'Connor sought to create an art that would have its meaning in its manner. Over and over she stressed that she was not a thesis-writer, not a novelist of ideas or doctrines, much less a fictional apologist for Roman Catholicism. When asked where a Catholic writer would find the best subject matter, O'Connor answered acutely: "This depends on what he knows and where he comes from. Subject matter has more to do with region than religion, at least in fiction."[21] For a Southerner such as O'Connor, region is not a geographical so much as a cultural and linguistic matter: "We carry our history and our beliefs and customs and vices and virtues around in our idiom."[22] "An idiom characterizes a society," she wrote, "and when you ignore the idiom, you are very likely ignoring the whole social fabric that could make a meaningful character" (MM, 104).[23]

Though patterns of speech lay at the heart of O'Connor's native Georgia idiom, many other particularities of behavior and belief shaped this idiom. Hence her immense regard for human rootedness in time and place. Commenting on the artificiality of New York literary parties, O'Connor asked and answered her own question: "You know what's the matter with all that kind of folks? They ain't frum anywhere."[24] She also advised the Birmingham writer Cecil Dawkins to return to her native state if she wanted to give her fiction the heft and grit of reality: "You'd be better off in any town population under 5,000 in south Alabama than you would be in New York City. That's where reality goes out the window. That is, when it ain't your reality. I don't mean by this that you should come home and write 'Southern,' but only that you should be where you belong for a while, a part of a society that has some real extension outside of the mind" (HB, 493).

---

21. Quoted in Magee, p. 16. "You don't begin a story with a [theological] system," O'Connor added. "You can forget about the system. These are things that you believe; they may affect your writing unconsciously. I don't think theology should be a scaffolding" (ibid., 29).

22. Ibid., p. 40.

23. Speech sounds, O'Connor noted, "build up a life of their own in your senses" (ibid., p. 64). "A great deal of the Southern writer's work is done for him before he begins, because our history lives in our talk" (MM, 105).

24. Quoted by Robert Drake, *Flannery O'Connor: A Critical Essay* (Grand Rapids, MI: Eerdmans, 1966), p. 11.

"Judgment Day" is the story in which O'Connor probes most deeply the mystery of Southern manners and masks, especially as they reveal their rare capacity to produce charity. What makes this last story all the more remarkable is that it is a complete recasting of her first published story, "The Geranium." That initial story is, surprisingly, a callow critique of Southern racial attitudes. O'Connor's protagonist, Old Dudley, is appalled by the freedom that blacks enjoy in the integrated North. They inhabit the same New York apartment building where Dudley has come — mistakenly, he believes — to live with his daughter in an all-white environment. Dudley regrets losing the naturally advantageous relationship he once enjoyed with the Negro orderlies who worked at his boarding house down South. He had not objected to their stealing as long as they accepted his own superior "wisdom" about fishing and hunting and guns. In the North, the Southern racial codes do not obtain. Dudley is incensed that blacks have moved into an adjacent apartment, and that his daughter has made no protest. Her one concern is that Dudley tend to his own business and leave black people alone. Dudley is enraged: "'You ain't been raised that way!' he said thundery like. 'You ain't been raised to live tight with niggers that think they're just as good as you, and you think I'd go messin' around with one er that kind. If you think I want anything to do with them, you're crazy'" (CW, 707).

While Dudley is predictably vicious in his racist attitudes, his black counterpart is predictably virtuous in his patience and charity. He calls Dudley by the endearing name of "old timer." He helps the crippled and failing Dudley descend the stairs of the apartment building, waiting patiently for him to take one step at a time. This generous black neighbor also eschews all forms of violence. He thus parries Dudley's asinine suggestion that they go hunting, not by pointing out that New York is hardly a hunting ground for raccoons or possums, but by declaring that he "never was much at killing anything." The ending of O'Connor's first story enforces its rather heavy-handed moral: just as the potted geraniums finally crash to the ground below Dudley's window, so must the bigotry of the old man's generation be shattered on the hard fact of racial equality.

Why, at the very end of her life, did Flannery O'Connor spend her waning energies reworking this story that had launched her career? I suspect that it had less to do with her changing racial views than with the false idiom that both the black and white characters use, with the fake manners that characterize their actions, and thus with the deep untruthfulness of the story.[25] She

25. Alice Walker is right to complain about O'Connor's portrait of the "passive, self-effacing" blacks in "The Geranium" as an example of her "ignorant and insulting racial stereo-

had failed to enmesh the moral matter of the story with its literary and social manners. By the end of her outrageously and providentially brief life, O'Connor had deepened and toughened both her faith and her art. "Judgment Day" is thus as complicated in scene and imagery, in plot and character, as "The Geranium" is simplistic.

In this last work, as in the original story, a white man comes to live in New York with his daughter, only to be horrified by the way people live way up there in the "Deep North." He urgently desires to get back home to his native Georgia. But beyond these superficial resemblances, everything else in the story is changed. T. C. Tanner is neither an unrepentant racist nor a saintly humanist. He is a strange amalgam of pride and humility, the first having to be confessed painfully before the latter can be embraced graciously. O'Connor's complex narrative method also echoes the story's complex moral insight. As in *The Violent Bear It Away*, the opening scene is only a short remove from the story's ending. A series of five interwoven remembrances enables Tanner to burrow ever more deeply into his past, there to discern both the horror of his guilt and the hope of his salvation. It all has to do with what Lord Moulton called "Obedience to the Unenforceable": how Tanner learned this charitable code long ago, how he sinfully came to repudiate it, how he recovers it at the price of his own murder, and how it leads to his comic vindication, both in this life and the next.

Kenneth Greenberg, following the lead of Bertram Wyatt-Brown, argues that Southern obsession with honor made the antebellum South "essentially a masquerade culture." Southern gentlemen maintained their honor by assuming elaborate masks and displaying "a crafted version of themselves through their voices, faces, noses, and a thousand other projections into the world."[26] Though T. C. Tanner lives an entire century after the Civil War, he is no less obsessed with his honor, especially his racial honor. He has moved to the metropolitan North because the farm containing his backwoods shack has been purchased by a black dentist named Dr. Foley. Tanner could have stayed put, since his black landlord has asked only that Tanner share the profits of his whiskey still; but Tanner refuses this mutually convenient arrangement. He insists on maintaining his racial superiority, knowing that, in the still-segregated South, color distinction brings honor that neither money nor property can purchase.

---

typing" (*In Search of Our Mothers' Gardens* [New York: Harcourt, 1983], p. 53). It was a mistake she would not make in her mature fiction.

26. Kenneth S. Greenberg, *Honor & Slavery* (Princeton, NJ: Princeton University Press, 1996), p. 25.

Tanner's racial honor is strange and complex. While he refuses to live on a black man's property, he has spent his past thirty years — in total violation of the Southern racial code — living with a black man named Coleman Parrum on the land that now belongs to Dr. Foley. The story centers on Tanner's retrospective explanation of this odd ménage. As the white master of a remote Georgia logging operation, Tanner had established symbolic authority over his black workers by constantly carving figurines with his penknife. These crude objects became virtual fetishes to the Negro laborers at his mill. But the knife was Tanner's emblem of physical power as well. More than once, he recalls, he had warned his lazy and laggard helpers that he would bury his blade in their innards if they did not work more diligently.

Into this scene of conventional racial domination had entered a "stranger," a drunken black named Coleman Parrum. In his loitering and no-'count condition, Parrum threatened to disrupt the labor of the other blacks at the sawmill. There seemed no way for Tanner to get rid of Parrum except with his familiar threat of violence: "Nigger, this knife is in my hand now but if you ain't out of my sight . . ." (CW, 682). Though addled by alcohol, Parrum knew that this sickly white man would be no match for him, and that in these remote piney woods he could perhaps kill him without being caught. Yet both men were oddly checked in their violent desire to dominate, perhaps even to murder, each other. Their unaccountable self-restraint is the moral and dramatic high point of the story; and it is figured in nothing artificial, such as a bursting pot of flowers, but in something intrinsic to Tanner's talent as a whittler: a pair of mock spectacles that Tanner mysteriously found himself fashioning and that Coleman no less mysteriously found himself wearing.

These glasses that are no glasses become the means, in fact, of their mutual Obedience to the Unenforceable. Tanner remembers this life-turning event of thirty years past as if it were yesterday, so formative did it become for everything that followed. He recalls that his own refusal to wield his knife had been matched by a similar restraint in the drunken Coleman.[27] The black man watched, with mesmerized attention, as Tanner carved the mysterious lensless glasses. When the white man commanded him to wear them, as if to confirm that he was yet another Negro clown — a "pantaloon in black," to use the title of Faulkner's story — Coleman strangely complied. Yet it was not a frightened and cringing subservience that prompted Coleman's obedience. Another power was at work in him no less than in Tanner, a willingness to play the fool for something unfoolish. Tanner "saw the exact instant in the

27. Throughout the story, Parrum is addressed as Coleman, since rarely in the segregated South did whites ever grant blacks the honor of being called by their surname.

muddy liquor-swollen eyes when the pleasure of having a knife in this white man's gut was balanced against something else, he could not tell what" (CW, 683). Coleman proceeded not only to wear the crude glasses but also to perform his own mask-wearing minstrelsy:

> The negro reached for the glasses. He attached the bows carefully behind his ears and looked forth. He peered this way and that with exaggerated solemnity. And then he looked directly at Tanner and grinned, or grimaced, Tanner could not tell which, but he had an instant's sensation of seeing before him a negative image of himself, as if clownishness and captivity had been their common lot. The vision failed him before he could decipher it. (CW, 683)

This masquerade of thirty years past haunts the aged Tanner like a crow-filled tree in the back of his mind, as he recalls even its minute particulars. Coleman had done the unthinkable. Not only had he maintained his own honor by refusing to be unmasked by this white man, who was his supposed superior; he also unmasked Tanner, exposing his presumption.[28] It was no ordinary clownishness that Coleman mimed. By putting on and looking through these glasses that had no glass, he offered his own comic Obedience to the Unenforceable: he stayed his murderous hand for the sake of an uncompelled charity. The drunken Coleman could not kill Tanner because, in a moment of transcendent vision, he saw the white man as a pathetic, even a ludicrous creature, not the domineering figure of power that Tanner's racist mask sought to project.

Yet Tanner could not long retain Coleman's miming of their mutually foolish and sinful humanity. His moment of clarity was fleeting perhaps because it revealed only the negative obedience of restraint, not the positive obedience of reconciliation. Whereas Coleman used the glasses to see another man fundamentally akin to himself, Tanner insisted that Coleman must see him as a white man who could still command his servitude. Tanner quickly resumed his old mask of racial entitlement, abandoning his high vision of Coleman's fellow humanity for a low and sentimental regard for him as his monkey, his factotum, a "no-good scoundrel" who is "paroled" to him.

28. The bravery of Coleman's liberating masquerade is made all the more remarkable when we recall that, in personal relations with whites, Southern blacks had but little more freedom than their ancestors: "Slaves did not have the power to prevent themselves from being unmasked. Sometimes, kindly men of honor might indulge the masks of their slaves, especially if they were masks of subservience. But a mask worn at the indulgence of a master could never be a mask of honor" (Greenberg, p. 33).

Thus had they lived together for thirty years. Not until he is forced to relinquish this delusory vision of himself — the mask of the "nigger-handler" — can Tanner come to recognize Coleman as his one true companion, as the man who has acted out the masquerade of their quintessentially human mutuality.[29]

   We discover gradually that it is not Coleman alone who has the capacity to assume another mask, a version of himself that surrenders rather than asserts power. Tanner is also capable of a liberating masquerade, for he also believes in the eternal consequences of his earthly deeds. He confesses, for example, that the fear of hell has deterred him from killing Dr. Foley.[30] He also cites Jesus' saying about the final division of the sheep and the goats in order to warn his daughter that she will fry in Hades if she reneges on her promise to have him buried, not in alien and hateful New York, but in his own dear Georgia. As a convert to Yankee secularism, she dismisses her father's belief in the Last Things as "a lot of hardshell Baptist hooey" (CW, 678). The daughter's scornful reference to the foot-washing, double-predestinarian Calvinism of the Primitive Baptists reveals her ignorance of her father's true character. He is a man whose hat-wearing distinctiveness reveals a spiritual resilience that her cap-wearing husband lacks.[31]

29. Nor was Coleman able to sustain the brief freedom won in his masquerade, perhaps because there was no liberating *persona* that black men could occupy in the segregated South that would enable them to maintain their honor. He reassumes the mask of racial deference that requires him to *be* no more than he *seems* — a monkey who dances to the grinding of Tanner's organ. Yet there is a hint of their original freeing clownishness when Coleman writes a note to Tanner in New York: "This is Coleman — X — howyou boss." Guilty at having given up their long life together, Tanner replies grimly: "This place is alrite if you like it" (CW, 686-87).

30. O'Connor knew the need for such religious restraint, since it was possible, until very recently, for Southern whites to commit capital crimes against blacks with virtual impunity. Prior to the bombing of the Sixteenth Street Baptist Church in September 1963, killing four young black girls, the homes of prominent Birmingham blacks suffered such repeated incendiary attacks that one section of the city became known as Dynamite Hill. Robert Chambliss, one of the men eventually convicted of the church killings, was a well-known Birmingham bomber. His acts of destruction had so regularly gone unpunished that he feared no prosecution. Thanks to the courage and persistence of the Alabama Attorney General Bill Baxley, as well as the willingness of Chambliss's niece Elizabeth Cobbs to testify against him, Chambliss was finally prosecuted. At the trial, Cobbs named dozens of potential suspects and informers, including her own relatives. Chambliss was finally convicted and sentenced in 1977. A lesbian who underwent sex-change surgery, Cobbs became known as Pete Smith and published a book entitled *Long Time Coming* in 1994.

31. This is a fine point of Southern manners that is likely to go unnoticed. Southern men once wore hats as a matter of style and distinction. Caps, by contrast, served the mere utility of keeping one's head warm and dry, and were thus worn mainly for hunting or working out of

In the New York pigeon-hutch, as he calls his daughter's apartment building, Tanner encounters a different kind of black man than Coleman, one who professes to wear no mask — except as a condition of his mask-wearing profession. He is an actor who, together with his live-in girlfriend, inhabits the flat next door. Still clinging to the Southern delusion of black-white commonality, Tanner mistakenly identifies this New York black as a fellow exile longing to be back home in the South, and thus as a potential black companion like Coleman. Tanner suggests, all too inanely, that they find themselves a fishing hole where they could perhaps bait a hook and while away an afternoon. The black thespian is outraged at such false familiarity and racial condescension; but his racial righteousness blinds him to what is innocent in the repentant Tanner's desire to find comradeship with a black man. The actor is so infuriated when Tanner calls him "preacher" that he loses control both of his temper and his grammar:[32]

> "I don't take no crap," he whispered, "off no wool-hat red-neck son-of-a-bitch peckerwood old bastard like you." He caught his breath. And then his voice came out in the sound of an exasperation so profound that it rocked on the verge of a laugh. It was high and piercing and weak. "And I'm not a preacher! I'm not a Christian. I don't believe in that crap. There ain't no Jesus and there ain't no God."
>
> The old man felt his heart inside him hard and tough as an oak knot. "And you ain't black," he said. "And I ain't white!" (CW, 690)

Had Tanner been schooled in the gospel of mere civility, with its prohibition against giving religious offense, he would have politely remained silent before the black actor's confession of an "alternate belief system," as it might now be called. Yet Tanner refuses to don such a faithless mask: he will not blandly acquiesce to the New Yorker's profession of atheism, as if all viewpoints were equally valid. He insists, instead, on offering his unapologetic witness. Anything less would make a travesty of the truth. Tanner answers

---

doors. That Tanner wears his hat while sitting all day inside his daughter's New York apartment is a double act of defiance and distinction. Gentlemen never wear hats indoors — except in this instance, as Tanner is determined to remind his daughter that he is *somebody "frum" somewhere.*

32. In the South of the pre–civil rights era, whites would often address blacks, especially educated or otherwise accomplished blacks, as "preacher" or "professor." Though these locutions offered homage, they also served to deny blacks the dignity of such ordinary terms as "mister" and "mistress." Yet the black actor perhaps resents being called "preacher" for a different reason: he does not want to be reminded that the vast majority of American blacks are Christians, and thus that Christian faith is his essential heritage as a black man.

the actor's brazen unbelief with his own unashamed testimony that the God of Jesus Christ is as real as skin color. Outraged at such unfrightened faith, and restrained neither by fear of perdition nor hope of redemption, the black actor slams Tanner against the wall, yanks his hat over his eyes, and knocks him backward into his daughter's apartment, precipitating the old man's first cerebral hemorrhage.

Tanner knows, as a result of this appalling encounter, that his time is shortened, and so he determines to return home, whether alive or dead. In the meantime, he has overheard his daughter declare that she won't bother keeping her promise to bury her father back in Corinth. Tanner's desire to be laid to rest in his native Georgia clay is more than nostalgia for the warm Southern womb he has mistakenly left for the cold Northern city. It is also a confession that his notion of "nigger-handling" was a sinful delusion, and that the mercy that Coleman had mimed thirty years ago is the real truth. Now cut off from the only companion he has ever known, Tanner imagines taking Coleman on a tour of New York, showing him that this city is "no kind of place." It is not humanely habitable because there are no self-imposed deterrents, no manners. In this Yankee Babylon, Tanner complains, people run over each other in their unrestrained and hell-bent rush. He wants to return, whether living or dead, to his Dixie homeland. There, he knows, people live in a mutuality whose manners are marked by humorous charades. Hence Tanner's dream of arriving home in a pine coffin, only to jump out and startle Coleman with a joke: "Judgment Day! Judgment Day!" he would cry. "Don't you . . . know it's Judgment Day?" (CW, 692). Tanner has finally learned that he is truly free only in play-acting and mask-wearing of the right kind. He fears neither bodily evil nor the shadow of the death that shall soon fall upon him. Judgment Day is a welcome prospect because he has both confessed the gargantuan sin of his false racist mask and identified the far larger liberty of his true identity as a witness to the truth.

As Tanner tries to make his way to the train station, he barely emerges from the apartment before collapsing from another stroke. Yet he dreams not of a dreadful *dies irae* but of the casket charade, and so he mutters his jaunty punch line about Judgment Day. The black actor, having heard the commotion in the hall, comes to the door. As a mannerless man, he believes that there is no law enforcing mercy to the dying Tanner. Utterly at liberty to do his own unrestrained will, he taunts the old man, declaring that there is no such thing as an eternal court of judgment. There is nothing beyond this present day, Tanner's dying day, the day of his extinction. Though muddled by his rupturing brain vessels, Tanner remains undaunted. Again he calls the black entertainer a "preacher," the same word that had excited the man's murderous wrath once before. That the black man viciously kills the white man, stuffing his head and arms and legs through the banisters, is nothing to the point.[33] Tanner's grisly death is yet another validation of O'Connor's witty analysis of her work: while a lot of folks get killed, nobody gets hurt. Tanner is physically brutalized but remains spiritually unscathed. He cannot be deterred by something so small as death, for he is headed home — in the ultimate if not in the immediate sense. He is bound not for Corinth, Georgia, but for the Promised Land, the region whose silence is broken only with shouts of hallelujah, the Eternal City of transparent masks where everyone is joined in glad Obedience to the Unenforceable in the precise sense that W. H. Auden described:

> We must never attempt to throw our mirrors away. We may only pray that God shall one day see fit to take them away from us. Perhaps they are never taken away, even from the saints, but in Paradise all mirrors become transparent and so cease to reflect.[34]

O'Connor's ending is so triumphant that she dared not add anything preachy or pontifical to it. No sooner has Tanner's daughter broken her promise and buried her father in New York than she is conscience-stricken by her act of bad faith. In a small show of penitence, she orders that his body be disinterred and sent back for its final ease in Georgia soil. "Now," the narrator blithely explains, "she rests well at night and her good looks have mostly returned" (CW, 695). Tanner's daughter has recovered, no doubt, the self-enforced smile of the happy American. Tanner's own triumph, by contrast, partakes of a comedy that is at once human and divine: he has learned to wear his true mask, projecting a self that is better by far than his regional

---

33. O'Connor rightly protested overzealous hunters of Christ-images in her fiction, but the dead Tanner resembles the crucified clowns of Rouault's paintings, as well as the Christ who is killed as a cruelly manipulated marionette in the film entitled *The Clown*.

34. W. H. Auden, "Lecture Notes," *Commonweal* (September 6, 1942): 22. Auden also argues that Carnival is the one public occasion when everyone is equal because it allows everyone to play the role of one's own choosing. Prayer is the only other place where one finds a similar equality. There, in utter transparency before God, one wears no mask at all. "The only occasion upon which both forms of equality are simultaneously asserted is during Mass, at which we both pray and eat. As biological organisms we must all assimilate other lives in order to live. As conscious beings the same holds good on the intellectual level: all learning is assimilation. As children of God, made in His image, we are required in turn voluntarily to surrender ourselves to being assimilated by our neighbors according to their needs. One might define the difference between Hell and Heaven," Auden concludes, "by saying that the slogan of the former is Eat *or* be eaten, of the latter, Eat *and* be eaten" (W. H. Auden, "Laughter and Carnival," *The Episcopalian* [May 1974]: 22).

and racist self. In her final story, unlike her first, O'Connor succeeds in making theological mystery cohere ever so finely with both manners and masks. She shows that Southern manners, at their worst, undergird an evil system of race and class domination. Yet she also demonstrates that, at their best, these same manners enable her protagonist to wear the gracious mask of Obedience to the Unenforceable. It is not the old mask of the will to power but the new mask that surrenders such power for a greater one — the power of radical mutuality.

## The Black Statuary of Both Mockery and Redemption

In "Judgment Day," O'Connor fictionally demonstrates that manners can be the means not only to restrain human evil but to transform it into human good, reconciling those who have sinned against each other in thought, word, and deed. As both the narrative voice and the plot make clear, the revolution wrought in Tanner is not only due to the elaborate charade that he and Coleman had enacted but also to the mysterious grace of God at work in Tanner's remembrance of it. That we do not see Coleman's own similar redemption is not the result of O'Connor's racist oversight. She confessed — and even Alice Walker has honored this confession — that, having no real capacity to enter a black person's mind, she never tried to do so. And while in her letters O'Connor sometimes used the word "nigger" in contempt, in her fiction she used it strictly to disclose habits of speech and temperament. The ugly word never appears except in the mouths of characters whose idiom and morals require it. O'Connor's narrators always use the old and dignity-granting — though now discarded — word "Negro."

It is noteworthy that not a single black character is treated as an object of mockery or contempt anywhere in O'Connor's fiction. Only four blacks come under O'Connor's authorial censure, whereas virtually all of her white characters receive severe condemnation for their sins. Astor and Sulk, the good-for-nothing farmhands in "The Displaced Person," are so scandalized by the excellence that Mr. Guizac brings to Mrs. McIntyre's farm that they conspire with her and her white-trash tenants to get rid of him. They keep silent when they could have saved him, as murderous self-interest proves to have no racial boundaries.[35] The purse-wielding black furiosa in "Everything

35. Even so, Astor still speaks the truth about the condition of blacks under racial segregation when he tells the younger and more resentful Sulk that "your place is too low for anybody to dispute with you for it" (CW, 297).

That Rises Must Converge" and the murderous black actor in "Judgment Day" are also filled, as we have seen, with a racial rage that causes them to commit deadly violence against guileless if not guiltless whites. On the other side of the ledger, O'Connor has created black characters who become vehicles of salvation for whites. Coleman Parrum is the most obvious example, but Buford Munson also serves as the instrument of young Tarwater's religious rescue in *The Violent Bear It Away*. By giving old Mason Tarwater a reverent Christian burial after the boy had sought to incinerate him, Buford spares young Tarwater the guilt that surely would have consumed him had he succeeded in his blasphemous act.

Despite O'Connor's clear demonstration of her redemptive convictions about race in her fiction, her work has nonetheless come under severe censure. In secular and religiously affiliated colleges and universities alike, the title "The Artificial Nigger" is so offensive to most people that the story is rarely taught. Since the odious word appears in nearly all of O'Connor's work, her fiction in general is often censured and censored. In the diocese of Lafayette, Louisiana, the Roman Catholic bishop actually banned O'Connor's story as a required text in Opelousas Catholic High School. It had been assigned as summer reading by Orsenio Arteza, a young English teacher of mixed race who, far from being a reactionary, had written for such left-of-center publications as the *Village Voice* and *The Door*. But several black parents protested against the requirement that their sons and daughters read "The Artificial Nigger." The high school principal agreed to remove the book from the obligatory reading list. She was supported by the local Catholic priest, and finally by the bishop himself — though not one of them had read the story.

There can be no doubt that an insulting word such as "nigger" gains power merely by appearing in print, and that it increases in authority when used in an official text. Yet Bishop O'Donnell's justification for banning O'Connor's story is altogether typical of our time: "[N]o one can tell another whether or not he or she should be offended. That is simply a matter of fact and should be respected in so far as possible." The bishop also urged all parties to find the "sensitivity to see matters through the eyes of others."[36] Though crucial questions of pedagogy are at stake here, especially for high school teaching, there is also a worrisome return to what John Murray

36. Unpublished but widely circulated letter of August 17, 2000, from Bishop Edward J. O'Donnell to Father Malcolm O'Leary, the black priest of Holy Ghost Catholic Church in Opelousas. It should be added that, ironically, Bishop O'Donnell is a veteran of the struggle for black civil rights, having joined the historic Freedom March from Selma to Montgomery in 1965.

Cuddihy has called "the religion of civility." Orteza ruefully concludes that the banning of O'Connor's story will have a dreadful counter-effect, that it will "further racism among black people, because black people will never know there was a white author who wrote with passionate disapproval about the very sins they suffered from the most."[37]

"The Artificial Nigger" is O'Connor's most convincing fictional rendering of the charity that alone has the power to reconcile men and women, rich and poor, urban and rural, young and old, black and white. She repeatedly singled out this story as her favorite work, without explaining the nature of her fondness. Perhaps the reason lies in her description of "the action of mercy" that pours down on Nelson and Mr. Head at the end of the story. There, she confessed, something akin to sacred inspiration had overtaken her craft: she had voiced truths deeper than she herself could fathom. I suspect that there is another reason for O'Connor's fond regard for "The Artificial Nigger": it is the work that reveals how fully she had purified the moral and religious source from which her fiction flowed.

"The Artificial Nigger" was a title so likely to seem racist that John Crowe Ransom, the editor of the *Kenyon Review*, asked O'Connor to change it before it was to appear in a 1955 issue of his journal. She refused.[38] To have sanitized the title would have robbed the story of its real power, the power to invert racist intention into antiracist redemption. Yet the story is not a study in black-white relations. The characters who stand most drastically in the need of reconciliation are divided not by race but by will. A grandfather named Mr. Head and his grandson Nelson dwell alone in the remote reaches of rural Georgia, and thus they should be bound by the most blessed ties of familial interdependence. Instead, they are bitterly determined to dominate each other. Though these two rustics have never heard of Nietzsche, their ruthless will to power lies at the dark core of their sinfulness.

37. Quoted by Bret Schulte, "Diocese misses the moral point of Flannery O'Connor," *Arkansas Democrat-Gazette* (December 17, 2000): 8J.

38. "[W]hen I sent the story to Mr. Ransom, he said, 'Well, we'd better not use this title. You know, it's a tense situation. We don't want to hurt anybody's feelings.' I stood out for my title" (Magee, 21). One wonders whether the transcription of a taped interview has not been garbled, and thus whether O'Connor said, instead, that she stood *up* for her title. In any case, O'Connor also objected to tampering with other literary titles, as she confessed to her Danish-born friend Erik Langkjaer, who was a Harcourt, Brace textbook representative: "The State of Georgia recently banned two text books for sale in the schools here, one that said Negroes learned as fast as white folks and another, a song book, that changed the word "darkies" to the word "brothers," in one of Steven Forster's [sic] songs. With the latter I am wholly in sympathy (with the banning that is) as I am afraid the next thing to go will be 'Ol Black Joe.' 'Old Neutral-colored Joe'" (CW, 936-37).

At the three chief turning points of the story — and in utterly unsentimental ways — Nelson and Mr. Head are offered redemption by black people. The first occasion for deliverance occurs on the train to Atlanta.[39] Knowing that his grandson Nelson has never seen a black person in the hills of northern Georgia, Mr. Head determines to take him to the city in order to teach him that it is an alien place, not least of all because it is full of "niggers" — a blackened and unsavory race. Once Nelson learns to scorn the loathsome city, Mr. Head hopes he will want to return to the farm forever, taking care of the old man in the years of his decrepitude. No sooner have grandfather and grandson boarded the train than a large light-skinned black man strides majestically past them, followed by two young women of similar hue, as if in a grand procession. With one hand resting on his ample stomach, the "coffee-colored" man uses his other hand to pick up and set down his cane in a slow, stately gait. With his neat mustache and his light-colored suit, with his yellow satin tie, his ruby stickpin, and his sapphire ring, this "tremendous man" is clearly prosperous: he has risen well above his assigned place in the segregated South. But having climbed so high, the black man cannot be allowed to come too close. Hence his movement from the carriage for blacks at the back of the train to the segregated dining car at the front. Yet there are no marks of resentment in this man who has every right to rage and chafe at his fate. In spite of the injustice done to him, he maintains his quiet but proud dignity.

Once the entourage has passed, Mr. Head does not tell Nelson that this was a "nigger." Instead, hoping to trap the boy in his ignorance, he asks Nelson what he has seen. "A man," Nelson replies. As often happens in O'Connor's fiction, children have an instinctive discernment of the truth. The boy knows what he cannot articulate: he has seen a regal instance of our common humanity. Sinfully opaque to such obvious truth, Mr. Head publicly humiliates Nelson for failing to detect "his first nigger." Nelson is furious at his grandfather for tricking him ("You said they were black. . . . You never said they were tan"); but he is also furious at the chocolate-colored man for

39. We know that the story occurs well below the Mason-Dixon Line when Mr. Head shouts the names of the buildings they are passing as they enter the city. Rarely does such regional pride find its equivalent in the North: "The Dixie Chemical Corp!" he announced. "Southern Maid Flour! Dixie Doors! Southern Belle Cotton Products! Patty's Peanut Butter! Southern Mammy Cane Syrup!" We also know that they are approaching Atlanta when the conductor snarls the name of the train station at the edge of the city, "Firstopppppmry" (CW, 218). Locals who were familiar with the region would have deciphered the conductor's elisions as declaring the first stop to be Emory, the university community located in the northeastern Atlanta suburb of Decatur.

failing to be recognizably black ("He felt that the Negro had deliberately walked down the aisle in order to make a fool of him and he hated him with a fierce raw fresh hate" [CW, 216]). Moralists are likely to read this episode as revealing the true nature of racism: it shows how ethnic distinctions are socially constructed, how racial hatred must be willfully inculcated, how we might overcome the petty barriers of race, class, and gender by taking our indiscriminate place in the universal human family. While all of these ethical claims are true, they are too obvious to animate a serious work of art. They do not plumb the depths of the real human difficulty. Nelson and Mr. Head are bound in the Adamic sinfulness that is the real root of racism: they share a spiritually fallen nature, not an innocent, Rousseauian humanity corrupted only by artificial social distinctions.

Nelson and Mr. Head remain oblivious to the first revelation they have witnessed. They are too busy putting each other down. In their sinful struggle for power, grandfather and grandson continue their journey once they are off the train, circling leftward until they eventually lose themselves in the hellish maze of Atlanta's streets. Mr. Head proves a poor Vergil to his unwilling Dante.[40] Finally they stumble into a black ghetto. Nelson wants to cry out for help, since he feels homeless and parentless and hopeless for the first time in his life. Gladly would he cast himself in abject reliance upon anyone who could deliver him and his grandfather from their lostness. Yet it is not physical direction alone that the frightened boy desires. Nelson wants the giant black woman they see leaning in her doorway to draw him to her huge bosom, to hold him tightly in her arms, to breathe warmly on his face, letting him look "down and down into her eyes" (CW, 223). Unembarrassed to manifest sacramental grace through ordinary human means, O'Connor reveals Nelson's longings to be erotic and filial no less than religious. This white boy would happily collapse in supplication at the feet of this black Madonna.[41] Yet Nelson does not dare confess his desires either to the black woman or to

---

40. There are several references to Dante's hell in addition to the fact that they are always moving to the left, the "sinister" direction. Mr. Head explains to Nelson how the sewer system "underlined" the entire city, "how it contained all the drainage and was full of rats, and how a man could slide into it and be sucked down along endless pitchblack tunnels. At any minute any man in the city might be sucked into the sewer and never heard from again. He described it so well that Nelson was for some seconds shaken. He connected the sewer passages with the entrance to hell and understood for the first time how the world was put together in its lower parts" (CW, 220).

41. O'Connor wrote to Ben Griffith that she meant the black woman to suggest "in an almost physical way . . . the mystery of existence to [Nelson] — he not only has never seen a nigger but he didn't know any women and I felt that such a black mountain of maternity would give him the required shock to start those black forms moving up from his unconscious" (CW, 931).

Mr. Head, for such admission would violate the racial code he has so recently and painfully learned. Even worse, it would put him at a fearful disadvantage in his contest of wills with his grandfather. The luxury of their alienation is far too rich for either of them to discern in this black redemptrix an embodiment of their salvation.

Soon Mr. Head commits a further and crueler act of alienation when, with the exhausted Nelson having fallen asleep on a sidewalk, he hides from the boy. The grandfather knows that when his grandson awakes, he will eagerly — even desperately — seek his solace, collapsing gratefully into the old man's arms when he steps from the shadows to rescue him. Instead, Nelson is so frightened when he awakens alone that he begins to run wildly down the street, flattening an old white woman who is carrying bags of groceries. She shouts threats of legal action and then screams for the police, just as Mr. Head walks slowly and hesitantly onto the scene. In clear repetition of Peter's denial of Jesus, as well as in crass self-interest, the grandfather denies any connection with the boy. Nelson is devastated by such treachery and abandonment. This is a betrayal beyond all human bounds.

No sooner has Mr. Head subjected Nelson to this awful denial than he recognizes the horror of it. Offering to get them "a Co'Cola somewheres" and later to fetch water from a hose, the grandfather all but begs for the boy's forgiveness. If Nelson would only grant it, they could at least meet on the common ground of their confessed sin and need. Nelson spurns such summons to reconciliation: "His mind had frozen around his grandfather's treachery as if he were trying to preserve it intact to present at the final judgment" (CW, 228). The boy refuses to pardon the old man because he has now acquired ultimate power over him. From having first been horrified at his grandfather's betrayal, he now revels in it. This, O'Connor suggests, is the vicious cycle of hellish evil: every violation of charity begets yet another and worse one, until the warring parties are caught in sin's unbreakable grip. Nelson turns the awful wrong he has suffered into a worse wrong of his own, paradoxically treasuring his grandfather's treachery as the final means of dominating him. Such involuted distrust and vengeance, such proud self-sufficiency — denying all communal dependence and mutuality — is the primordial root of all evil, whether personal or ethnic, social or political.

So tightly have Nelson and Mr. Head entangled themselves in the knot of recrimination and justification that they seem beyond saving. The circle of self-perpetuating sin, O'Connor reveals, can be broken only by transcendent goodness. It is granted when, hopelessly lost, bewildered, and estranged, the grandfather and grandson wander into a white suburb. There they discover a cast cement Negro statue in front of an elegant house. But this degraded lawn jockey is neither carrying a lantern nor grasping a horse's reins, two of the more benign statuary images of black servitude; instead, he is holding a piece of watermelon, as if blacks were capable of nothing more than the cheap gratification of their appetites. He is supposed to be a smiling and carefree "darky," but he has a chipped eye, he lurches forward at an awkward angle, and the watermelon he is supposedly eating has turned brown. "It was not possible," declares the narrator, "to tell if the artificial Negro were meant to be young or old; he looked too miserable to be either" (CW, 229). There is little doubt that Nelson and Mr. Head have never seen a crucifix, but they would surely know the gospel song "The Old Rugged Cross." Able at last to recognize this third black sign of their redemption, they are both transfixed and transformed by this "emblem of suffering and shame": "They stood gazing at the artificial Negro as if they were faced with some great mystery, some monument to another's victory that brought them together in their common defeat. They could both feel it dissolving their differences like an action of mercy" (CW, 230).[42]

Though meant to signal the proud triumph of whites over blacks,[43] the scornful effigy becomes a sacrament of reconciliation to these mutually sin-

42. O'Connor wrote Father James McCown that she and her mother were cow-buying one day when they were given directions to the home of a cow-owner "because it was the only house in town with an artificial nigger. I was so intrigued with that that I made up my mind to use it. It's not only a wonderful phrase but it's a terrible symbol of what the South has done to itself" (HB, 140). In another letter she declared, "What I had in mind to suggest with the artificial nigger was the redemptive quality of the Negro's suffering for us all" (CW, 931). O'Connor also wrote to Sally and Robert Fitzgerald that "there is nothing that screams out the tragedy of the South like what my uncle calls 'nigger statuary'" (HB, 101).

43. It has often been observed that, while the South lost the military version of the Civil War, it won the long-term cultural war concerning race. C. Vann Woodward argues in *The Strange Career of Jim Crow* (New York: Oxford University Press, 1957) that Southern racism in the twentieth century was spawned less by slavery than by the conditions that prevailed after Reconstruction. Jim Crow laws requiring the segregation of public places were not instituted until the 1890s. The rising prosperity of Negroes had begun to threaten the social superiority of poor whites, thus opening the way to such race-baiting politicians as Pitchfork Ben Tillman of South Carolina and James K. Vardaman of Mississippi. Their mid-twentieth-century legatees were not only Ross Barnett of Mississippi and Lester Maddox of Georgia, but also George Wallace of Alabama. After becoming known as a racial progressive and running a racially neutral campaign, Wallace suffered a humiliating defeat in the gubernatorial race of 1958. He vowed never to be "outniggered" again. The strategy worked and Wallace went on to a notorious political career as a racist governor and even a presidential candidate. Yet he also underwent his own conversion and repentance in 1979, was re-elected as governor in 1982 largely because of the black votes he won, and then distinguished his fourth and final term in office by appointing a record number of black Alabamians to governmental positions.

ful kinsmen. The crimes they have committed against each other begin to melt away in the presence of this inhabited Cross. It possesses transcendent reconciling power because its wretchedness attests not only to the anguish of human injustice but also to the mercy of divine suffering. There is nothing saccharine about the scene. Nelson and Mr. Head do not fall to their knees in tearful embrace. The narrator reminds the reader, on the contrary, that the boulder of the grandfather's pride is far from crushed: "Mr. Head had never known before what mercy felt like because he had been too good to deserve any. . . ." Even while feeling forgiven for the first time, he still wants to remind Nelson of his superiority. He offers a wisecrack about white folks having so few real Negroes under their command that they now need artificial ones. He also refuses Nelson's imploring eyes that call for him "to explain once and for all the mystery of existence" (CW, 230). Neither can the boy long hold on to the revelation they have both received. He lapses, instead, into platitudes about the city's being a place he is glad to have seen once but will never visit again.

Not for a moment does O'Connor suggest that Nelson and Mr. Head have suddenly overcome their sinfulness, that they have adopted a proper regard for blacks, or that they will never again engage in a vicious contest of wills. A long road of renewal and redemption lies before them. Yet they have both been permanently altered by their encounter with the bent and harrowed emblem of the Suffering Servant. Neither of them will be able fully to exorcise this black reminder of the grace that dissolves all personal and racial pride. Nelson speaks more truly than he knows when he cries out, "Let's go home before we get ourselves lost again" (CW, 230). No longer are they lost in the religious sense, and they are returning home in more than the physical sense. As they arrive at their remote station, O'Connor's narrator reminds us that Luciferian evil has been routed: "[T]he train glided past them and disappeared like a frightened serpent into the woods" (CW, 230, 231). Yet only Mr. Head fully comprehends the good that has been born, never again to die:

> Mr. Head stood very still and felt the action of mercy touch him again but this time he knew that there were no words in the world that could name it. He understood that it grew out of agony, which is not denied to any man and which is given in strange ways to children. He understood it was all a man could carry into death to give his Maker and he suddenly burned with shame that he had so little of it to take with him. He stood appalled, judging himself with the thoroughness of God, while the action of mercy covered his pride like a flame and consumed it. He had never thought himself a great sinner before but he saw now that his true de-

pravity had been hidden from him lest it cause him despair. He realized that he was forgiven for sins from the beginning of time, when he had conceived in his own heart the sin of Adam, until the present, when he had denied poor Nelson. He saw that no sin was too monstrous for him to claim as his own, and since God loved in proportion as He forgave, he felt ready at that instant to enter Paradise. (CW, 230-31)

This is one of the most controverted passages in the whole of O'Connor's work; it has encountered both secular and literary opposition. Critics who value "showing" over "telling" complain that O'Connor has condescended to explain what the action of mercy means, when she should have simply dramatized it. Secular readers, from their side, protest the use of overt theological language in a story that, up to this point, has shown no overt religious concern. Both objections are misplaced. While the passage is full of religious language, O'Connor has made clear from the beginning that Nelson and Mr. Head are engaged in a struggle whose proportions are absolute, and that their lostness at the end is metaphysical rather than geographical. Mr. Head has called out, in fact, "Oh Gawd I'm lost! Oh hep me Gawd I'm lost!" (CW, 228). When Nelson continues to scorn his grandfather despite this pleading confession, Mr. Head "felt he knew what time would be like without seasons and what heat would be like without light and what man would be like without salvation" (CW, 229).

For O'Connor at last to make explicit the theological concerns that were heretofore largely implicit is not for her to indulge in literary heavy-handedness but to provide commendable clarification. The author is not required to disappear entirely from her text, standing aloof from it in pure aesthetic neutrality, paring her fingernails. As Wayne Booth demonstrated decades ago, the supposedly impersonal and objective author always remains present in her fiction — whenever she moves inside a character's mind, whenever she gives speech to a reliable character, whenever she resorts to literary allusion or mythic pattern or symbolic reference, whenever she orders the narration of events that have previously occurred, whenever she chooses to recount one incident rather than another, and in many other ways.[44] The question is not whether the author will show or tell, therefore, but how she will do both, and here O'Connor is unapologetic in her telling.

I suspect that critics who complain about the narrative directness of this passage are secretly offended by its theological radicality. The black nov-

---

44. Wayne C. Booth, *The Rhetoric of Fiction* (Chicago: University of Chicago Press, 1961), pp. 16-20.

elist Alice Walker is a happy exception to this sorry pattern, for she has famously said that O'Connor's work is not about race but grace:

> [E]ssential O'Connor is not about race at all, which is why it is so refreshing, coming, as it does, out of such a racial culture. If it can be said to be "about" anything, then it is "about" prophets and prophecy, "about" revelation, and "about" the impact of supernatural grace on human beings who don't have a chance of spiritual growth without it.[45]

Mr. Head's discovery is scandalous because he fathoms the mystery of the gospel in ways that are offensive even to many alleged Christians. He is shown the mercy that is beyond adequate naming because — in ways unknown to Nietzsche — it is beyond good and evil, utterly transcending morality. Here is a mercy that cannot be earned by prior acts of ethical excellence or even by sufficient repentance. Mr. Head sees that mercy is the only gift he can return to God at the end of his life because it is the only gift that can prevent his own sinful presumption. The pattern of forgiveness as preceding and enabling repentance is the pattern everywhere present in Scripture, from Hosea's refusal to divorce his prostitute wife to Christ's words from the Cross. Jesus asks God to forgive those who are crucifying him, not because they have begged his pardon, but because he wants to break the chain of anger and vengeance that has entrapped them. To have given the crowds their due, cursing them in judgment, would have been to seal them in the vicious and unbreakable circle of sin.

Far from achieving anything akin to what Dietrich Bonhoeffer called "cheap grace" — a false reliance on God's forgiveness as an excuse for living a self-indulgent and untransformed life — Mr. Head sees that, precisely to the extent that he has been forgiven, he is also judged and found horribly wanting. He discerns, moreover, that his sin consists not chiefly in the cruel acts he has committed against both Negroes and Nelson; his real transgression lies in the systemic Adamic condition of his utter alienation from God. This aboriginal sin makes him responsible for the most monstrous evils the world has ever known, no less than for his own betrayal of black people and his grandson. Yet God has hidden this worst of all truths from Mr. Head, lest it crush him in damning judgment. Rather than negating divine justice, therefore, divine mercy intensifies it.

The staggering paradox is that God imprisons us, said Karl Barth, by flinging wide our cell door: the gospel "accuses [mankind] by showing that

45. Walker, p. 53.

all the charges against him have been dropped. It threatens him by showing him that he is out of danger."[46] We repent of our sins not in order to be forgiven, according to the odd logic of the gospel, but because we have already been forgiven. Barth liked to tell of a Swiss horseman who became lost in a snowstorm and crossed frozen Lake Konstanz at full gallop before finally making it safely home. When told of the daring deed he had unconsciously done, the man broke down in horror and fright. Only after he was saved did he recognize his dire danger. So it is with Mr. Head; he feels so fully cleansed by God's confession-prompting mercy that he feels "ready at that instant to enter Paradise."

It is precisely Calvary and the Easter event — the Father's gracious rejection of our dreadful rejection, the Son's awful assumption of the world's entire burden of sin, the Holy Spirit's infusion of forgiveness into human lives — that provides the world's precise hope for an utter about-face, for total transformation, for conversion and repentance that will last. John Calvin declared that we woefully misread the Gospels if we misconstrue their report about Jesus' and John the Baptist's calling the crowds to repentance because the kingdom of heaven was at hand. The real theological order is exactly the reverse: because the kingdom of forgiveness was already at hand, said Calvin, Christ and the Baptizer thus summoned everyone to repentance. The gospel would not be cheering news but ill tidings indeed were it anything other than God's gracious, unmerited, and repentance-inducing forgiveness. O'Connor has Mr. Head discern exactly this right ordering of things: the total priority of mercy as the gift that enables repentance.

Like Calvin, Luther employed extravagant metaphors to emphasize the indelibility of divine grace. When confronted by fierce temptation, for example, Luther seized a piece of chalk and scrawled out the words *Baptizatus sum.* Luther's baptism made him the inalienable property of the God who had already done penance for him. It meant that he could not be overtaken by alien and demonic powers, try as they might. Luther also insisted that sin consists not in adultery or theft or even murder — nor, we might add, in mass murder or even genocide — but rather in the unbelief that is their underlying cause: the unbelief that refuses to entrust our lives wholly to the God who has entrusted himself to us. There lies the root of all evils great and small. Yet it is exceedingly difficult, Luther added, to discover this most fundamental of all facts. We cannot learn the true meaning of sin by beholding horrible instances of evil, for example, in our own era, by looking at Auschwitz or

46. Karl Barth, *Church Dogmatics*, 4 vols., trans Geoffrey W. Bromiley (Edinburgh: T&T Clark, 1934-69), III/2, p. 605.

Rwanda or Hiroshima or My Lai. These are the consequences of sin, but not sin itself. Sin is truly discerned, said Luther, only at a single place — at Golgotha. There in the humiliation and crucifixion of Jesus is the one sin that measures all other sins, the sin that reveals the full and total desperation of human existence.

In "The Artificial Nigger," Flannery O'Connor sounds the depths of the abyss that is the love of the triune God. It was her favorite story because it is the work that gives the fullest fictional embodiment to her firmest convictions about both race and religion. Here she instructs herself and her readers in the meaning of the gospel. Perhaps O'Connor knew that her own racial sinfulness had been dissolved in an unbidden gift of artistic liberty. It enabled her to turn a broken lawn jockey into an ironic testament to the mystery of charity — a mystery that, though always hidden, is deeper by far than the mystery of iniquity. Her "artificial nigger" thus becomes the ultimate antiracist emblem. It reveals something far more profound than the evident evils of slavery and discrimination. It discloses the subtle grace inherent in suffering that can be redemptively borne because God in Christ has borne it himself. It becomes the sign of the divine courtesy that, for all our unworthiness, makes us members of the divine court. It reconciles us to both God and each other, and thus offers the one true and radical remedy for our unmannered, unjust, and deeply discourteous society. The narrative of the American South is a story of unspeakable brutality against blacks, but it has been overlaid with another Story that makes it a strangely redemptive region.

## FIVE

ࣱ *Preaching as the Southern
Protestant Sacrament*

Everyone who has read Flannery O'Connor's work has noted the extremity of her imagination. As we have seen, she deliberately cultivated the grotesque as the essential mode of her fiction. In an age of bland mediocrity and conformity, she sought to gain the reader's attention by drastic means: "To the hard of hearing you shout," we have heard her declaring, "and to the almost-blind you draw large and startling figures." But hers was a theological as much as a literary strategy: "Grace," she often observed, "must wound before it can heal." So deep is the spiritual infection of our time that O'Connor turned her fiction into a kind of scalpel for excising, ever so painfully, the undetected cancer eating away at church and culture alike. As a writer seeking to infuse her fiction with the spirit of her own region and its religious ethos, she often had recourse to the Southern preaching tradition as the means of performing such spiritual analysis and prescription — sometimes even surgery. While O'Connor was troubled by the anti-ecclesial quality of Southern Protestantism, she honored its devotion to sermonic exhortation.

An authoritative voice — as well as a powerful counter-voice — speaks in her work, especially in her preachers. It announces the idol-shattering Word of the living God, not the idol-making words of the No-God. To understand both the power and complexity of this sermonic voice, we will first explore the gnostic quality of American religion as it seeks to silence this voice. The answer to such antisacramental gnosticism lies in Karl Barth's thesis that preaching serves as the Protestant sacrament, the singular Word that has authority over everything else. We will then determine how, by contrast, the voice of the No-God can be heard in O'Connor's nihilist preacher Hazel Motes. Finally, we will turn to O'Connor's two Christian preachers, Bevel Summers in "The River" and Lucette Carmody in *The Violent Bear It Away*, in order to hear the Voice that calls both the church and the world to repentance and reconciliation.

## The Gnostic Quality of American Religion

At a time when authentic preaching has become virtually a lost art in our churches — as well as an occasion for dismissal and contempt among secularists — O'Connor's fictional preachers would seem to set her art apart from the modernist tradition in literature.[1] Yet there is a marvelous currency in O'Connor's sermonizers that has gone largely undetected. Her preachers confirm Lionel Trilling's claim, made at the height of the turbulence wracking the 1960s, that the most powerful religious claims are being offered in seeming secular art:

> No literature has ever been so shockingly personal as that of our time — it asks every question that is forbidden in polite society. It asks us if we are content with our marriages, with our family lives, with our professional lives, with our friends. . . . It asks us if we are content with ourselves, if we are saved or damned — more than with anything else our literature is concerned with salvation. No literature has ever been so intensely spiritual as ours. I do not venture to call it actually religious, but certainly it has the special intensity of concern with the spiritual life which Hegel noted when he spoke of the great modern phenomenon of the secularization of spirituality.[2]

Trilling's magisterial judgment reveals why O'Connor's work must be read, at least in part, as belonging to the main modernist tradition that runs from Flaubert and Proust through Joyce and Faulkner on to Frost and Stevens. While they are all non-Christian writers, their work is deeply agitated by the question of salvation and damnation.

Yet for all of O'Connor's commonality with the major modern writers, there is also a huge difference: she does not secularize the spiritual. Salvation and damnation are, for her, more than inward states of subjective consciousness; they are objective states of both our immediate existence and our final destiny. The secularizing of the spiritual — at least from Hegel forward — has been one of the most serious mistakes of modernity. Unlike the literary paragons of high modernism, O'Connor is not concerned with what M. H. Abrams calls a "natural supernaturalism," a kind of immanent divine pres-

---

1. The splendid sermon on hell in *A Portrait of the Artist as a Young Man* is a notable exception; but even there Joyce gives the preacher great rhetorical gifts only in order for Stephen Dedalus to reject his homily all the more completely.

2. Lionel Trilling, "On the Teaching of Modern Literature" in *Beyond Culture: Essays on Literature and Learning* (New York: Viking Compass, 1968), pp. 8-9.

ence suffusing the natural order as this ghostly presence can be perceived through the all-transforming powers of the imagination.[3] Rather does her essential concern lie with palpable signs of both the holy and the satanic as they bear down upon us at every moment of our lives, most notably in death.

That late modern men and women of the West have failed to discern the concrete operations of both the divine and the demonic is largely the church's fault. Christians have failed to embody — in their worship and service, in their art and teaching — a radically alternative way of life that would attest to God's living sacramental presence in the world. We have domesticated the Transcendent.[4] We have worshiped a merely comforting and consoling deity, a god who underwrites our own political and social prejudices, a god who confirms things as they are, the god whom Karl Barth rightly called the No-God:

> We suppose that we know what we are saying when we say 'God'. We assign to Him the highest place in our world: and in so doing we place Him on fundamentally one line with ourselves and with things. We assume that He needs something: and so we assume that we are able to arrange our relation to Him as we arrange our other relationships. We press ourselves into proximity with Him: and so, all unthinking, we make Him nigh unto ourselves. We allow ourselves an ordinary communication with Him, we permit ourselves to reckon with Him as though this were not extraordinary behaviour on our part. We dare to deck ourselves out as his companions, patrons, advisers, and commissioners. We confound time with eternity. . . . We serve the No-God.[5]

When Nietzsche and Marx and Freud all declared God to be dead, they were not asserting their own atheism so much as they were observing the funeral rites of this No-God. "The cry of revolt against such a god," Barth insisted, "is nearer the truth than is the sophistry with which men attempt to justify him."[6]

O'Connor's work makes its own witness against this No-God. Earlier

---

3. See M. H. Abrams, *Natural Supernaturalism: Tradition and Revolution in Romantic Literature* (New York: Norton, 1973).

4. William C. Placher offers a splendid analysis of this problem in *The Domestication of Transcendence: How Modern Thinking about God Went Wrong* (Louisville: Westminster/John Knox, 1996).

5. Karl Barth, *The Epistle to the Romans,* 6th ed., trans. Edwyn C. Hoskyns (New York: Oxford University Press, 1968, first published in 1921), p. 44.

6. Ibid., p. 40.

we heard her argue that, ever since "Emerson decided in 1832 he could no longer celebrate the Lord's supper unless the bread and wine were removed," Christianity in America has been increasingly vaporized. Which is but to say, of course, that it has been thoroughly spiritualized. Harold Bloom contends that the entire American religious project has been so "spiritual" that it is unwittingly gnostic.[7] The empty prairies and endless skies have bred in us a gnostic magnetism to the uncreated, to the as-yet-to-be, to the conviction that we can begin all things innocently anew, escaping not only the burdens of old Europe but the storied past as well. America has thus been the spawning ground for assorted new religions: Christian Scientism and Mormonism, Jehovah's Witnesses and Seventh Day Adventism, Pentecostalism and L. Ron Hubbard's Dianetics. There is also the extravagant revivalism that runs from Cane Ridge, Kentucky, in 1801, to the Toronto Blessing in 1993. These are but the epiphenomena, Bloom argues, for a gnostic religiosity whose real theologian is Ralph Waldo Emerson, the sage of Concord who found God not in doctrine or sacrament or ethical practice but in the possibility of self-creation located within the divinely autonomous self. Hence Emerson's call, in the "Divinity School Address" given at Harvard in 1838, for every man to become his own Jesus: "Alone in all history [Jesus] estimated the greatness of man. One man was true to what is in you and me. He saw that God incarnates himself in man, and evermore goes forth anew to take possession of his World."[8]

The notion of "the absolutely unmediated soul" dominates the spiritual life of a church-going America where, Bloom contends, sacraments and institutions have become increasingly suspect. "Creeds do not suit the American spirit," Bloom argues, because their historical otherness threatens the qualities we most revere: "freedom from mere conscience; reliance upon experiential perception; a sense of power; the presence of the God within; the innocence of one's 'redeemed flesh and blood.'" A triumphant self-awareness enables radical liberty from everything that would shackle the soul — "from nature, time, history, community, other selves." The solitary believer alone with the Bible, interpreting it without the aid of received theological tradition or ethically formed character, often becomes the ideal Christian. We have glimpsed such a gnostic soul in Sarah Ruth Parker, the wife in "Parker's Back," who scorns all incarnate embodiments of Christian faith lest they

7. It should be added that Bloom thoroughly approves of the gnostic spirit pervading American religious life, for he believes that we are creatures engaged in such radical self-construction that we must perpetually invent and re-invent ourselves.

8. Quoted in Harold Bloom, *The American Religion: The Emergence of the Post-Christian Nation* (New York: Simon and Schuster, 1992), p. 23.

crimp her solitary spirit. No wonder, then, that Bloom should declare — ominously, at least for the work of Flannery O'Connor — that America is awash in a sea of gnostic religion[9] that has left Roman Catholicism "a relatively restrained mode of faith."[10]

## Faith Comes by Hearing

Flannery O'Connor's world is profoundly incarnational, sacramental, and thus anti-gnostic. Robert Drake once declared, in fact, that Jesus is the real hero of O'Connor's fiction,[11] and O'Connor herself admitted that "the best of my work [sounds] like the Old Testament would sound if it were being written today" (CW, 963). While O'Connor's pistol-shot sentences do not literally declare, "Thus saith the Lord," their directness has a decidedly biblical quality. Evelyn Waugh infamously and incredulously said of *Wise Blood*, "If this is really the unaided work of a young lady, it is a remarkable product" (CW, 897). He probably was referring to the novel's unladylike violence; but he may also have been referring to the prophetic directness of its narrative technique. The wintry plainness of her prose, its dry and tart matter-of-factness, its spare straightforwardness — none of these traits allow any lazy luxuriation in narrative eloquence. Even continued rereadings of O'Connor's fiction prompt fear and trembling, not only in the foreknowledge that someone will get gored or blinded or shot, but also in the dread that we ourselves will be

9. The metaphor is drawn from Jon Butler's *Awash in a Sea of Faith: Christianizing the American People* (Cambridge, MA: Harvard University Press, 1990). Butler contends that it was not the Puritans who decisively shaped American religious life, but rather the endlessly self-inventive and fissiparous revival movements of the eighteenth and nineteenth centuries.

10. Bloom, pp. 211, 46, 42, 49, and 39 respectively. Bloom is especially devastating in his analysis of American religious gnosticism as it receives Southern Baptist expression. The doctrine of "soul competency," famously formulated by E. Y. Mullins as the one distinctively Baptist principle, refuses all earthly mediations of the Holy. The metaphor of competency is drawn from the Victorian idea of economic self-sufficiency, but it applies to religion as well. "Observe then," wrote Mullins in his hugely influential *The Axioms of Religion* (1908), "that the idea of the competency of the soul in religion excludes at once all human interference, such as episcopacy, and infant baptism, and every form of religion by proxy." Religion is a personal matter between the soul and God. Such privatized faith leaves the solitary believer to intone, even when singing in chorus, a perfectly gnostic hymn: "I come to the Garden alone, while the dew is still on the roses. And the voice I hear, falling on my ear, the Son of God discloses. And He walks with me, and He talks me, and He tells me I am His own. And the joy we share as we tarry there, none other has ever known."

11. Quoted in John Desmond, *Risen Sons: Flannery O'Connor's Vision of History* (Athens, GA: University of Georgia Press, 1987), p. 105.

eviscerated. My former student, the late John Millis, put the matter well when he said that, while no one's salvation depends on getting Faulkner right, we read O'Connor knowing that the stakes are ultimate. Her work is "humorous, yes," Thomas Merton confessed, "but also uncanny, inexplicable, demonic, so you could never laugh at it as if you understood. Because if you pretended to understand, you, too, would find yourself among her demons. . . ."[12]

O'Connor's preachers are scandalous because the gospel, when properly embodied and proclaimed, is also scandalous. It excites vigorous affirmation or equally vigorous negation. It permits no gnostic descent to the No-God within. It demands, instead, that the triune God be acknowledged as the world's true core. Christian faith produces literal eccentrics, people who are off-center because their lives have been made to circle about the real Center. O'Connor is reputed to have altered, with her typical candor, the final word of the dominical saying found in John 8:32: "You shall know the truth, and the truth shall make you odd." Even when rejecting the gospel, we remain irremediably defined and de-centered by it. Hence O'Connor's celebrated reply when asked why Southern fiction contains such a surfeit of freaks: "I say it is because we are still able to recognize one" (CW, 817). In the Bible Belt there is a transcendent norm for measuring anomalies. The biblical plumbline reveals that the real deviant is not the shouting street preacher but the thoroughly well-adjusted man, the completely self-controlled woman, the utterly successful American. In our blithe neutrality and complacent indifference toward the God of the gospel, O'Connor shows, we have become living corpses. Her preachers, by contrast, have been bent out of their sinful shape because they have received an address from beyond themselves. They are grotesque creatures because they are hearers no less than preachers of the Word.

Barry Harvey observes that ancient Israel was unlike its Near Eastern neighbors in one important regard above all others: the Israelites did not worship the chthonic forces of nature so often personified in feminine deities. "Rather than personifying nature (including human nature and history) as deities, in the style of their neighbors in Mesopotamia, Egypt, and Canaan," Harvey declares, "Israel's primal relationship to the world took the form of response to a personal address. Persons, things, and events were interpreted as visible signs of God's activity, created and ordered by the divine utterance."[13] Israel's very identity has an interlocutory character, Harvey

---

12. Merton, *Raids on the Unspeakable* (New York: The Abbey of Gethsemani, 1966), p. 41.
13. Barry A. Harvey, *Another City: An Ecclesiological Primer for a Post-Christian World* (Harrisburg, PA: Trinity Press International, 1999), p. 41.

adds, for Yahweh always dwells in counterpoint with his answer-avoiding yet answer-attempting people:

> Over and over again the word of the LORD comes to claim this people in the entirety of their existence, and their world is turned upside down. God addresses Abraham, calling upon him to give up everything that was safe and familiar and go with his family to a land he had never seen. God addresses Moses, telling him to leave the safety of those with whom he had taken refuge and return to Egypt where his people were oppressed. God addresses David, reminding him that he was but the servant of the LORD. God addresses Elijah, assuring him that there were others who had not bowed down to idols. God addresses the author of the book of Daniel, allowing him to see in dim figures the ultimate fate that awaited the holy ones of the Most High. . . . The story of Israel is that of a people becoming a question to themselves time and again, constantly struggling with the mystery of having been chosen to be God's people. Even Israel's name testifies to the centrality of this interlocutory setting. . . . The eponym Israel, 'he who strives with God,' thus foreshadows the destiny that awaits this community on their pilgrimage through history.[14]

The biblical exaltation of hearing over seeing is no happenstance. We can shutter ourselves to the visible world, for we have eyelids to seal off images and scenes that we do not want to behold. The ear, by contrast, has no flap for silencing unwanted voices. Ear lobes are meant to increase hearing, not to prevent it. The eye is often limited to surfaces, while the ear can penetrate depths. It is an organ for receiving announcements, and thus for either accepting or rejecting commands. "Obedience" derives, tellingly, from the Latin *audire*, "to listen." And since disobedience entails a refusal of the One who can be denied only through a kind of willed irrationality, the word "absurdity" also has an aural etymology: *surdus* is Latin for "deaf." Jesus does not declare, therefore, "He that hath eyes to see, let him see," but rather "He that hath ears to hear, let him hear" (Matt. 11:15). He also warns Thomas the Doubter against the naïve notion that seeing is believing: "Blessed are they that have not seen, and yet have believed" (John 20:29). "We walk by faith and not by sight" (2 Cor. 5:7) is yet another typical scriptural claim. Preaching, it follows, entails bold aural adjurations: "Hear the words of the LORD" (Josh. 3:9). "Hear ye, and give ear; be not proud: for the LORD has spoken" (Jer. 13:15).

14. Ibid., pp. 38, 40.

"Repent ye, and believe the gospel" (Mark 1:15). "Come and follow me" (Matt. 19:21). It comes as no surprise to learn that Luther declared the eyes to be hard of hearing, or that he urged his hearers to stick them in their ears when the Word of God is proclaimed. Preaching is a summons to a new way of seeing — through the hearing of the Word. We learn to look rightly at the world, Luther held, when we learn to hear truly what is announced from the pulpit. "The church is a mouth-house," he declared, "not a pen-house."[15]

## Karl Barth on Preaching as the Protestant Sacrament

The last century's most eminent theologian, Karl Barth, was relentless in his insistence that preaching is the distinctively Protestant sacrament, the equivalent of the Catholic mass:

> From their elevated station [preachers] make statements which demand faith from their hearers — an attitude which is obviously fitting only in relation to God. They make assertions about the final truth not only in [human] existence but above it. They claim to give the profoundest answer to the profoundest human question. They place before the I of the hearers a Thou whom they cannot overlook or dissolve or transcend. . . . Those who speak about God want to set people before God, to claim them for God, to save their souls, to win them.[16]

Contemporary proclamation differs from the original annunciation of the gospel only in degree, not in kind: "If . . . God speaks through our word, then the prophets and apostles are actually there even though it be a simple pastor that speaks."[17] Hence Barth's celebrated insistence that, however apparent its similarity to ordinary discourse, true proclamation of the Word of God must differ radically from all other forms of address: "[O]ne can not speak of God by speaking of man in a loud voice."[18]

---

15. Quoted in Martin E. Marty, *A Cry of Absence: Reflections for the Winter of the Heart* (San Francisco: Harper & Row, 1983), p. 25. Marty also notes that Luther "punned in German that the [W]ord should be 'geschrieen,' shouted, not 'geschrieben,' written — if there was to be the experience of grace in Jesus Christ."

16. Karl Barth, *The Göttingen Dogmatics: Instruction in the Christian Religion*, Vol. I, trans. Geoffrey W. Bromiley, ed. Hannelotte Reiffen (Grand Rapids, MI: Eerdmans, 1991), pp. 46, 50.

17. Karl Barth, *Homiletics* (Grand Rapids, MI: Eerdmans, 1991), pp. 48-49.

18. Karl Barth, *The Word of God and the Word of Man*, trans. Douglas Horton (Gloucester, MA: Peter Smith, 1978), p. 196.

*Fides ex auditu* became the virtual motto of the magisterial Reformers because of the Pauline declaration that "Faith cometh by hearing, and hearing by the word of God" (Rom. 10:17). The gospel is not only a message to be preached, Paul makes clear, but also preaching itself. Authentic proclamation is not simply a word *about* God; it *is* the Word of God. "The preaching of God's Word," the Second Helvetic Confession declares, "is God's Word."[19] "With its preaching," P. T. Forsyth boldly declares, "Christianity stands or falls." "Preaching," he adds, "is the most distinctive institution in Christianity."[20] Like Forsyth, Barth regarded the whole of Scripture as proclamation. In the Bible, he argues, there is an "unusual preponderance of what is said . . . over the word as such."[21] The how of scriptural manner subserves the what of the scriptural Message — form being intrinsic yet subordinate to content. In the jargon of contemporary literary criticism, the *haec dixit Dominus* of Scripture makes the Signified always trump the signifiers. What Barth asserts about the Bible in general must be said also of Flannery O'Connor's preachers: "complete impartiality" toward the Word of God is "merely comical."[22]

Yet to be a proclaimer of the gospel is never an elective affinity: God himself summons preachers to so terrible a privilege and so wondrous a task. Though the church usually ordains its proclaimers of the gospel, their authority derives neither from themselves nor from those who ordain them but only, as Barth insists, from the Author who is the ultimate source and end of all authority. Hence the Apostle Paul's wonderfully and terribly burdened confession: "For though I preach the gospel, I have nothing to glory of: for necessity is laid upon me; yea, woe is unto me, if I preach not the gospel!" (1 Cor. 9:16). Because each age is blinded by the darkness that cannot overcome the Light, and thus because there is no native human inclination to receive the Word, the positive reception of the gospel must always have the character of miracle. As Barth explains, the Word "completes its work in the world in spite of the world."[23] Even when the gospel is heard and transformation results, there is no confident mastery of human words over the holy Word. St. Augustine insisted that any equation of human words with the divine Word is idolatrous. David Jeffrey, interpreting Augustine's claim, ob-

19. Barth, *Göttingen Dogmatics*, p. 32.

20. Peter Taylor Forsyth, *Positive Preaching and the Modern Mind* (the Lyman Beecher Lectures on Preaching delivered at Yale University in 1907) (Grand Rapids, MI: Baker, 1980), p. 3.

21. Karl Barth, *Church Dogmatics*, I/2, p. 468.

22. Ibid., p. 469.

23. Karl Barth, *Witness to the Word: A Commentary on John 1*, trans. Geoffrey W. Bromiley, ed. Walther Fürst (Grand Rapids, MI: Eerdmans, 1986), p. 66.

serves that "Only one 'Word' transcends the mere conventionality and asymptotic liability of all other words, and that word is manifestly not of human utterance. The 'word made flesh' we grasp indeed, but only by imperfect analogy."[24] Only by sheer divine Presence does the fallible and finite discourse of preaching become the means of God's own speech, and God alone can judge its truthfulness and enable its effectiveness.

So unlikely is the preacher's success that Barth describes the task of preaching as the riskiest of all ventures. Faithful preachers must approach their calling in the terror that they will announce something other than the gospel, that they will proclaim a god who is one object among others, a deity who is not the Maker and Redeemer of heaven and earth, but a supreme being who is our own projection and who thus remains at our own disposal.[25] Luther confessed that he preached best when he seemed least in control of his proclamation.[26] The urgency that should characterize all proclamation arises from the sure expectation of its being heard and heeded. The preacher's claim that God in Christ is at work in the midst of the human fray prompts the profoundest of questions:

> The impenetrable muteness of the so-called nature that surrounds us, the chance and shadowy existence of every single thing in time, the ill fortune and ill fate of nations and individuals, the basic evil, death — thoughts of these things come to us, disquiet us, and crowd out all that might assure us God is present. The question will no longer down, but breaks out in flame: is it true? . . . Is it true, this talk of a loving and good God, who is more than one of the friendly idols whose rise is so easy to account for, and whose dominion is so brief? What the people want to find out and thoroughly understand is, Is it true? And so they reach, not knowing what they do, toward the unprecedented possibility of praying, of reading the Bible, of speaking, hearing, and singing of God. So they come to us [preachers], entering into the whole grotesque situation of Sunday morning, which is only the expression of this possibility raised to a high power.[27]

24. David Lyle Jeffrey, *People of the Book: Christian Identity and Literary Culture* (Grand Rapids, MI: Eerdmans, 1996), pp. 6-7.

25. Barth, *Göttingen Dogmatics*, p. 49.

26. Luther also said that there is no other way to become a theologian than by suffering, dying, and being damned. Forsyth offered a similar judgment: "The religious life, that which has religion for a profession, is the most dangerous of all. There are so many temptations to unreality in it — especially in connexion with what is sometimes called the deepening of spiritual life" (Forsyth, p. 190).

27. Barth, *The Word of God and the Word of Man*, pp. 107-8.

Neither is the Word of God a resolution of the world's quandaries; rather, it is the answer that prompts new questions, poses new problems, and requires an entirely new life. It is the grace that brings judgment, the forgiveness that entails condemnation, the eternal life that reveals the abyss of eternal death. In the very gladness of its tidings, it gives offense. "This truth shames the world," Barth adds, "and brings blame upon it and complaint against it."[28]

> Again, those who speak about God must find a need in people that they do not perceive along with all their other needs. . . . [Preachers] must teach them to ask so that they can give them an answer. They must plunge them into the depths so that they can really lead them to the heights. They proclaim to them a peace that the inhabitants of no city or village would call [peace] but which startles them if they have any inkling of what it is all about. To speak about God does not fit in with what they are and do even in their best moments. . . . Those who speak about God, who really speak about him, will have to accept much odium, much responsibility, much conflict of conscience, much temptation to confuse human and divine sorrow [cf. 2 Cor. 7:10] or God's anger at sin with their own anger at others and themselves.[29]

As we shall discover, O'Connor's proclaimers of the Word excite violent opposition. Some of them seem destined for the martyrdom of the prophets and the apostles.

Yet scandalized rejection is immensely preferable to bland indifference. O'Connor constantly reiterates her conviction that spiritual complacency and apathy, whether Christian or secular, are the real mark of our freak-filled era. The massive self-satisfaction of the modern age caused Søren Kierkegaard to declare that God may one day take Christianity away from Europe as the final proof of its truth. Only when church and society alike learn how horrible it is to live in a world devoid of divine mercy and judgment, Kierkegaard prophesied, shall they again thirst for the water of life.[30] Eight centuries before Christ, the prophet Amos warned, in precisely this fashion, of a famine that God himself would send — "not a famine of

---

28. Barth, *Witness to the Word*, p. 66.

29. Barth, *Göttingen Dogmatics*, p. 50.

30. P. D. James, the British detective novelist, envisions such a prospect in her futuristic novel of 1993, *The Children of Men* (New York: Alfred A. Knopf, 1993). She depicts a frightful world in which the last human being has been born. I have discussed the novel's theological implications in "Rapidly Rises the Morning Tide," *Theology Today* 51, no. 2 (July 1994): 277-88.

bread, nor a thirst for water, but of hearing the words of the LORD." The shepherd-prophet from Tekoa warns of a dark future for his people: "And they shall wander from sea to sea, and from the north even to the east, they shall run to and fro to seek the word of the LORD, and shall not find it" (Amos 8:11-12).

Surely this is the most fearful of all prospects, that the Word himself might withdraw and fall silent. Walker Percy envisions such a world in his apocalyptic novel *Love in the Ruins* (1971). There a Catholic priest named Father Rinaldo Smith enters his New Orleans pulpit prepared to deliver his weekly homily, only to discover that he cannot utter a word. "Excuse me," he declares after a long and embarrassing silence, "but the channels are jammed and the word is not getting through." The congregation nervously assumes that there must be a problem with the speaker system. But as Father Smith collapses in the sacristy, he again mutters "something about 'the news being jammed.'" Later, in a psychiatric hospital, as the priest speaks to his attending physician, Dr. Max Gottlieb, he reveals the nature of his aphasia. The principalities and powers, he explains to the uncomprehending Gottlieb, have silenced the Good News. "Their tactic has prevailed," he elaborates. "Death is winning, life is losing." Father Smith refers not only to the massive outward carnage of our culture of death, but also to the terrible inward collapse of those who remain animate. "Do you mean the living are dead?" asks Gottlieb. "Yes," answers Smith. "How can that be, Father? How can the living be dead?" the psychiatrist asks. "I mean their souls," replies the priest. "I am surrounded by the corpses of souls. We live in a city of the dead."[31]

## Hazel Motes as a Scandalized Preacher of Nihilism

Beginning with her very first novel, Flannery O'Connor depicts preachers who seek to awaken the sleeping dead. In *Wise Blood*, first published in 1952 when she was only twenty-seven, her protagonist-antagonist is a preacher named Hazel Motes. He has heard the radical summons of the gospel from his grandfather, an itinerant evangelist. Far from being a church functionary who regarded the *evangelium* as a form of either civil or therapeutic religion, Motes's ancestor was "a waspish old man who had ridden over three counties with Jesus hidden in his head like a stinger" (CW, 20). This uncouth proclaimer of the Word stung his audiences with the awful Truth:

31. Walker Percy, *Love in the Ruins: The Adventures of a Bad Catholic at a Time Near the End of the World* (New York: Farrar, Straus & Giroux, 1971), pp. 184-86.

They were like stones! he would shout. But Jesus had died to redeem them! Jesus was so soul-hungry that He had died, one death for all, but He would have died every soul's death for one! Did they understand that? Did they understand that for each stone soul, He would have died ten million deaths, had His arms and legs stretched on the cross and nailed ten million times for one of them? (The old man would point to his grandson, Haze . . .). Did they know that even for that boy there, for that mean sinful unthinking boy standing there with his dirty hands clenching and unclenching at his sides, Jesus would die ten million deaths before He would let him lose his soul? He would chase him over the waters of sin! Did they doubt Jesus could walk on the waters of sin? That boy had been redeemed and Jesus wasn't going to leave him ever. . . . Jesus would have him in the end! (CW, 10-11)

Hazel Motes is properly scandalized. He spends the rest of his life wrestling with his grandfather's claims, trying desperately to deny them. He knows that the Word he has heard from the old man cries out for total embrace or total rejection. Why, he implicitly asks, would Jesus die massively multiplied deaths to save one boy's soul? What are the waters of sin, and why can Jesus walk on them? Why won't this Jesus simply leave Hazel alone — leaving him free from obligation to anyone or anything but himself, letting him remain content in his present pleasures, permitting him to avoid all considerations of sin, death, and the devil? The youthful Motes had sought such an untrammeled life. He tried to elude his grandfather's summons by living in total self-control: "the way to avoid Jesus was to avoid sin" (CW, 11). The doctrine of humanity's original sinfulness is a profound affront to Hazel. It makes him answerable to evils that he cannot even name, including the transgressions of his primal parents: "If I was in sin I was in it before I ever committed any. There's no change come in me. . . . I don't believe in sin" (CW, 29). Hence his determination to avoid even the notion of sin by remaining morally uncorrupted.

Young Motes has learned that it is no easy task to avoid evil. At a carnival sideshow, he had seen a naked woman squirming in a casket. The mature Motes recalls his father's candid confession of religion's erotic base: "Had one of themther built into ever' casket . . . be a heap ready to go sooner" (CW, 35).[32] No easy hedonist like his father, the boy was overwhelmed by a nameless and placeless guilt, though he knew nothing of the Freudian link be-

---

32. This comic confession may have been inspired by an advertisement O'Connor had seen for "an illustrated sermon" to be preached at a tent revival in Atlanta. It featured an open coffin in front of the pulpit (Mary Barbara Tate, "Flannery O'Connor at home in Milledgeville," *Studies in the Literary Imagination* 20, no. 2 [Fall 1987]: 34).

tween *eros* and *thanatos* that the casket scene suggests. His mother saw the shame inscribed on Hazel's face, and she caned him for it. Yet she also offered the boy a word of hope: "Jesus died to redeem you." Wanting no such reliance on Another, Motes had muttered to himself, "I never ast him." Instead, he walked with stones in his shoes in a penance meant to stanch his conscience: "He thought, that ought to satisfy Him." Much to Hazel's regret, his self-saving act produced no divine response: "Nothing happened" (CW, 36).

Motes's self-punishment fails to satisfy, as O'Connor makes clear, because it is self-referential. If there is no God, there is only the human self, living for little else than its own satisfactions. Still trying to prove that sin is a meaningless word, Motes visits a whorehouse. Yet he finds no pleasure in his prostitute. So little is he present in their coupling that she must remind him to take off his hat! Since carnal indulgence cannot satisfy Motes's Augustinian restlessness, he resorts to blasphemy, denying all promise of transcendent transformation: "I'm member and preacher to that church where the blind don't see and the lame don't walk and what's dead stays that way" (CW, 59). Gradually Hazel comes to see that all denials are parasitic, that his bitter negations register only in relation to positive truth, that he must espouse a gospel of nothingness in his own self-invented "Church Without Christ."

> "I preach there are all kinds of truth, your truth and somebody else's, but behind all of them, there's only one truth and that is that there's no truth," he called. "No truth behind all truths is what I and this church preach! Where you come from is gone, where you thought you were going to never was there, and where you are is no good unless you can get away from it. Where is there a place for you to be? No place.
>
> "Nothing outside you can give you any place," he said. "You needn't to look at the sky because it's not going to open up and show no place behind it. You needn't to search for any hole in the ground to look through into somewhere else. You can't go neither forwards nor backwards into your daddy's time nor your children's if you have them. In yourself right now is all the place you've got. If there was any Fall, look there, if there was any Redemption, look there, and if you expect any Judgment, look there, because they all three will have to be in your time and your body and where in your time and your body can they be?" (CW, 93)

Though Motes seeks converts to his cornpone kind of Sartrean existentialism, he is unsuccessful. His church has only a single member — himself. It is also fitting that Motes the solipsist also has only one true love — his spavined and bleating Essex. This broken-down car serves as the single sacrament of his nihilistic religion, the true *viaticum* for escaping everything that would lay claim on him. O'Connor was an early discerner, together with Walker Percy, that the automobile, even more than the movies and television, is the great American Dream Machine. It fulfills our fantasies of individualist autonomy, enabling us to strike out for the proverbial territories whenever the limits of social existence press in upon us. As Motes's only sacred space, the car serves as both pulpit and residence, enabling him to incarnate his message in a life of perpetual isolation and vagabondage. It's a car, he boasts, that "moved fast, in privacy, to the place you wanted to be" (CW, 105). "Since I've had it," he declares, "I've had a place to be that I can always get away in" (CW, 65). Motes makes no idle boast, therefore, when he offers a fine creedal summary of his modernist faith: "Nobody with a good car needs to be justified" by Jesus (CW, 64). As a countrified Karamazov, Hazel also acts out Ivan's belief that, since God is dead, all things are permitted. He heartlessly runs down a poor derelict who had been paid to impersonate Motes, thus making his car also his weapon of death.

Hazel Motes's life of murderous self-justification ends, appropriately, when a patrolman destroys his automotive idol. Because he has noisily preached an insistent nihilism — deafening himself to the true Word — Motes comes to the truth by means of silence and vision. With his Essex gone, he can at last see that there is a more habitable place than the suffocating confines of his sinful ego. Looking away from himself for the first time, he beholds the infinite space — "depth after depth" (CW, 118) — of the sky. The firmament is not cold and frightening, as Pascal found it at night, but alive with a burning mercy, a purging peace. And having preached the counter-gospel that nothing is true but one's own body and place, Motes must work out his salvation precisely there, by mutilating the flesh that he had once deified: he puts broken bits of glass in his shoes and wraps barbed wire around his chest.

Because he has also sought to cast out the beam of belief in other folks' eyes, Hazel must cleanse the motes from his own offending orbs. Like Oedipus, he learns to see everything by seeing nothing — by blinding himself with quicklime. These drastic acts of *ascesis* are not self-justifying sacrifices meant to earn Motes's salvation; they are deeds of radical penance offered in gratitude for the salvation that has already been won for him at the Place of the Skull.[33] As he approaches death, therefore, Hazel gives testimony

33. When Motes declares that his macabre self-lacerations are his attempt "[t]o pay" (CW, 125), he is not making atonement for his sins so much as he is paying his debt of gratitude for the redemption already wrought for him. Following the example of the Apostle Paul in Rom. 8:13 and Col. 3:5, he is mortifying his flesh, albeit by extreme means, in order to conform his life to the Savior who conformed his own life to the Cross.

to his own little cloud of witnesses: two brutal policemen and his self-seeking landlady. He declares that he is no longer fleeing but rather embarking for his true Country, the place where no car could carry him. "There's no other house," he confesses, "nor no other city" (CW, 129).

## Bevel Summers: River Preacher of the Slow-Healing

O'Connor's positive preachers proclaim a Word that is no less discomfiting than Motes's nihilism. Bevel Summers, a youth still in his late teens, serves as an evangelist of the scandalizing gospel in the story entitled "The River." Having no pulpit of his own, Summers proclaims the Word while standing in the midst of streams, ready to baptize all who hear and heed his preaching. For him, baptism is no mere symbol of the human promise to follow Jesus; it is a sacramental act, even if he would never use such a word to describe it. He makes it ever so clear that baptism is the outward and visible initiation of believers into death and burial with Christ, so that those who are thus called and who thus respond may rise up out of the watery grave of sin into utter newness of life. Summers preaches a clear and discerning Word from the water:

> "If you ain't come for Jesus, you ain't come for me. If you just come to see can you leave your pain in the river, you ain't come for Jesus. You can't leave your pain in the river," he said. "I never told nobody that." . . .
>
> Then he lifted his head and arms and shouted, "Listen to what I got to say, you people! There ain't but one river and that's the River of Life, made out of Jesus' blood. That's the river you have to lay your pain in, in the River of Faith, in the River of Life, in the River of Love, in the rich red river of Jesus' blood, you people!"
>
> His voice grew soft and musical. "All the rivers come from that one River and go back to it like it was the ocean sea and if you believe, you can lay your pain in that River and get rid of it because that's the River that was made to carry sin. It's a River full of pain itself, pain itself, moving toward the Kingdom of Christ, to be washed away, slow, you people, slow as this here old red water river around my feet.
>
> "Listen," he sang, "I read in Mark about an unclean man, I read in Luke about a blind man, I read in John about a dead man! Oh you people hear! The same blood that makes this River red, made that leper clean, made that blind man stare, made that dead man leap! You people with trouble," he cried, "lay it in that River of Blood, lay it in that River of Pain, and watch it move away toward the Kingdom of Christ." (CW, 162)

Bevel Summers's fame as a faith-healer has won him an eager hearing. Crowds gather at the river in the hope that he will perform miracles on the sick and the lame, the blind and the deaf. They are more eager to have their bodily ills cured than to have their spiritual sins redeemed. Yet on this occasion, if not always on others, Summers frustrates their desire. He has come to teach them that there is not one kind of pain but two, even as there are two rivers. There is indeed the terrible physical pain that clamors for cure. As a woman who would die at age thirty-nine of acute lupus erythematosus, Flannery O'Connor knew the terror of such pain. She even took the baths at Lourdes.[34] Yet human suffering is amenable to human succor. There is a second kind of pain that does not submit to such therapy. This other disease has its origin in agonies that are not merely human. Luther identified this second sort of pain as the bruised human conscience: it is the ache of sin and guilt and alienation from God. Its cure lies in a river other than the clay-draining stream that the preacher stands in. When Bevel Summers announces this radical cure, he does not speak for himself, therefore, but for the God of the gospel. Hence the remarkable conflation of his own voice with another Voice: "If you ain't come for Jesus, you ain't come for me." As with the apostles and the prophets, so with Summers: he preaches with utmost authority. He does not speak in the subjunctive mood about what ought to be or might be, but with sheer declarative force concerning what is: "Listen to what I got to say, you people."

Bevel Summers has a rich analogical imagination because his preaching is animated by the Incarnation — by the startling union of the human and the holy in the rabbi of Nazareth. Summers avoids the direct openness to God that Barth warns against, and his speech is stretched almost to the point of snapping. Summers likens Jesus' atoning blood to the red river that is his liquid pulpit. Nothing would seem to be healed or cleansed by waters so muddy or else so bloody. Yet in the world of radical Christian paradox, things are never as they seem. Summers undoubtedly knows William Cowper's poignant hymn so often sung in Southern Protestant churches. The river whose healing powers he proclaims is in fact "a fountain fill'd with blood/Drawn from Emmanuel's veins;/And sinners plunged beneath that flood,/Lose all their guilty stains." The sanguinary atonement wrought at Golgotha provides no instant holiness. Sanctification, as he solemnly declares, is as slow a pro-

---

34. She approached the prospect of a miracle with holy skepticism, confessing that she prayed more for her crippled novel than for her crippled legs. "I am one of those people," she drily commented, "who could die for his religion easier than take a bath for it" (CW, 1056). Yet she never satirized the Marian healing site, as Peter De Vries did when he created a character who develops a disease *after* visiting Lourdes.

cess as the movement of a languid Georgia river. Salvation requires the gradual and often painful conformity of sinful human wills to the sacred will, a series of lifelong conversions that issue in holy living and holy dying.

Bevel Summers's preaching is at once so richly suggestive and so starkly simple that even a child such as Harry Ashfield can comprehend it. He is the four-year-old son of secular parents who are unloving sophisticates. The only person who has ever cared for young Ashfield is Mrs. Connin, his fundamentalist babysitter. She tells him that he is not merely the product of natural causes who was brought into the world by a doctor named Sladewall, but the supernatural creation of a carpenter named Jesus Christ. Her love and teaching enable little Harry to receive, in his own childlike way, the preaching of Bevel Summers. Summers's proclamation is as succinct as Motes's nihilism is verbose. "If I Baptize you," the preacher [Summers] said, "you'll be able to go to the Kingdom of Christ. You'll be washed in the river of suffering, son, and you'll go by the deep river of life. Do you want that?" (CW, 165). Finally, Summers reduces the call of the gospel to a single question: Does the boy want to *count?* The child instinctively discerns what he is being asked. He knows that he has never really mattered to his mother and father, that everything is a joke at his house, that, if there is a God, his last name surely must be "damn." The boy has been given everything he wants, having learned to break old toys in order to get new ones. Yet in the deepest sense the boy has been given nothing. He has no life.

At first little Harry scoffs at the preacher, just as his parents have taught him; he is a smart aleck in the making. At the same time, the boy wants desperately to count. He wants to be somebody, to love and to be loved, not to remain as he is but to "go to the Kingdom of Christ." He knows instinctively that this mysterious place must not be like the loveless place where he lives. And so he says Yes to the river-preacher, and so he is baptized. Yet it is not a baptism into peace and contentment; it is an entry into the river of suffering and death that the preacher had promised. O'Connor does not narrate the inner reasoning that prompts the boy's final decision after he returns home, but the child's naïve logic is not difficult to fathom: if he were made to count so much for having stayed under the water so briefly, he could count totally if he stayed under the water permanently. Far from committing a despairing act of suicide, therefore, young Ashfield returns to the scene of his baptism to find the new life by plunging beneath the river's surface, and thus to abandon the old death by leaving his unloving parents.

Harry Ashfield is able to succeed in this act of enduring immersion only in flight from Mr. Paradise, a man who scorns Summers's river-preaching. Because he was not himself healed of a cancerous growth on his forehead, Paradise is a bitter unbeliever. He rejects all potential occasions for gratitude. He even fishes with an unbaited hook, hoping not to catch anything, lest he be caught up into a life that receives and risks everything. Like Hazel Motes, Mr. Paradise is a solitary skeptic who has sealed himself off in mockery. Only in flight from this demonic figure offering his phallic stick of candied temptation does the boy Harry at last succeed in keeping himself under the rich red river. He finds the final kingdom not by repeating his once-and-for-all sacramental baptism, but by seeking — in a watery and literal-minded way — precisely what baptism at once enables and demands: total burial with Christ. The child Ashfield enters into the community of perpetual praise by way of a supremely happy ending to a supremely happy story.

## Lucette Carmody: Child Proclaimer of a Wintry Grace

Lucette Carmody is another of O'Connor's child preachers, even younger than Bevel Summers, a crippled girl of only eleven or twelve. O'Connor dares her readers to dismiss this deformed child evangelist as the product of money-mongering parents who are cynically willing to exploit her immense rhetorical gifts. Yet no matter how corrupt her circumstances, this little light (as Lucette's name nicely indicates) brightly shines, even as her words sparkle.

> "Listen you people," she said and flung her arms wide, "God told the world He was going to send it a king and the world waited. The world thought, a golden fleece will do for His bed. Silver and gold and peacock tails, a thousand suns in a peacock's tail will do for His sash. His mother will ride on a four-horned white beast and use the sunset for a cape. She'll trail it behind her over the ground and let the world pull it to pieces, a new one every evening." . . .
>
> "The world said, 'How long, Lord, do we have to wait for this?' And the Lord said, 'My Word is coming, my Word is coming from the house of David, the king.'" . . .
>
> She began again in a dirge-like tone. "Jesus came on cold straw, Jesus was warmed by the breath of an ox. 'Who is this?' the world said, 'who is this blue-cold child and this woman, plain as the winter? Is this the Word of God, this blue-cold child? Is this His will, this plain winter-woman?'
>
> "Listen you people!" she cried, "the world knew in its heart, the same as you know in your hearts and I know in my heart. The world said, 'Love

cuts like the cold wind and the will of God is plain as the winter. Where is this summer will of God? Where are the green seasons of God's will? Where is the spring and summer of God's will?'" . . .

"You and I know," she said turning again, "what the world hoped then. The world hoped old Herod would slay the right child, the world hoped old Herod wouldn't waste those children, but he wasted them. He didn't get the right one. Jesus grew up and raised the dead." (CW, 412-13)

Like Bevel Summers, Lucette Carmody has a strong metaphorical sense rooted, quite unawares, in a sacramental imagination. She instinctively understands the whole creation as a trope of God. Not to discern analogies between the book of nature and the book of salvation is to be unfaithful to both. Lucette's rich homiletic analogies serve not as an accusation so much as a confession: she indicts her audience even as she admits her own sin. She knows, in her own childlike way, that sin is original and universal before it is personal and particular. Thus she first describes the human condition in its generality; in fact, she uses the term "world" very much as the first Johannine epistle uses *kosmos* — not as a synonym for God's good creation, but as a description of all the powers and forces that oppose God: "For whatsoever is born of God overcometh the world: and this is the victory that overcometh the world, even our faith" (1 John 5:4).

Lucette knows what the world does not know. She has met the Love that moves the sun and the other stars. Because it is the Word who has been made flesh, the Word also turns the world, the same world that Dante described as a furious threshing floor for the winnowing of souls. Lucette proclaims this Love in all of its stark offense by contemporizing the biblical story in dialogical terms: "God told the world . . . and the world said." This Word of radical demand and engagement has a transhuman authority. With utterly untutored insight, Lucette sees that the birth-narratives of the New Testament are not mere historical accounts open to the proof or disproof of scholars. As she makes clear, this Word actively and authoritatively reads its audience; it does not passively await the audience's reading of it. Lucette declares the hard truth that human hearts desire exaltation without cost: they wish to be lifted up into a life of ease, devoid of challenge and danger. A spring and summer deity would grant glory without the price of a risky relationship with either himself or others. Hence the human dread of the God whose winter will bring judgment no less than comfort, whose love not only warms and soothes but also cuts and chills with the cold wind of truth. Hence the human rejection of the homely virgin whose child is not a chubby cherub but a skinny infant shivering on the cattle-pen straw, warmed by bovine breath.

Lucette proclaims the authoritative Word not to the world in general but to Rayber, the school psychologist, in particular. The girl preacher has a preternatural ability to discern that, among her entire audience, this deaf man leaning in at the window is the one most spiritually impaired, the soul who most needs to hearken to the freeing Word. He is a listener whose deafness is the outward sign of his inward refusal to hear. Rayber will not hear because, like Dostoevsky's Ivan Karamazov and Camus's Dr. Rieux, he believes that the suffering of innocent children discredits the goodness of God.[35] Rayber's unbelief is in fact prompted by the imbecility of his own son, Bishop. Because Bishop lacks the ordinary powers of intelligence and language, Rayber considers him worthless. Speech and reason alone, according to Rayber, make for the independent and autonomous life that justifies human existence. Since Bishop is deficient in these powers — he is both literally and mentally dumb — Rayber regards his own child as a useless creature, an absurd mistake of a bungling deity.

Yet Lucette will not leave her auditor content in his anti-theism. She strikes straight at the heart of those who, like Rayber, refuse to trust God because of the Slaughter of the Innocents, whether in the first century or our own. Offering her sprightly version of the Negro spiritual that asks "were you there when they crucified my Lord?" Lucette declares that we were there even when they tried to crush him at the beginning. We hoped that Herod's henchmen would kill this one Jew-baby, says Lucette, and spare all the rest. We much prefer to theorize the problem of evil than to confront the threat of Goodness. The world doesn't truly care, she insists, about the sinless infants who were butchered. What we really want is to protect our own unbelief, so that our loveless selves might be spared such an awful Love, such an all-commanding King, so great a Savior that he raises not only dead bodies but also dead souls.

> "Jesus grew up and raised the dead," she cried, "and the world shouted, 'Leave the dead lie. The dead are dead and can stay that way. What do we want with the dead alive?' Oh you people!" she shouted, "they nailed Him to a cross and run a spear through His side and then they said, 'Now we can have some peace, now we can ease our minds.' And they hadn't but only said it when they wanted Him to come again. Their eyes were opened and they saw the glory they had killed.

35. "Ivan Karamazov cannot believe," O'Connor comments, "as long as one child is in torment; Camus' hero cannot accept the divinity of Christ, because of the massacre of the innocents" (CW, 830).

> "Listen world," she cried, flinging up her arms so that the cape flew out behind her, "Jesus is coming again! The mountains are going to lie down like hounds at His feet, the stars are going to perch on His shoulder and when He calls it, the sun is going to fall like a goose for His feast. Will you know the Lord Jesus then? The mountains will know Him and bound forward, the stars will light on His head, the sun will drop down at His feet, but will you know the Lord Jesus then?" (CW, 413-14)

Rayber will receive no such recognition at the end of time because he refuses it in the present moment. Though his instinctive love for Bishop is so deep that it sometimes makes him want to throw himself to the ground in an act of "idiot praise," he cannot honor his instinctive care for his own son. Rayber dismisses such unstinting parental love for his "useless" child as mere madness. Yet Lucette remains unpanicked by Rayber's refusal to respond to her inviting Word. She shares Barth's confidence that "God speaks and causes his Word to penetrate the hearts of the listeners by the Holy Spirit." As a result, says Barth, those who receive the proclamation of God "are placed in a totally new situation," no matter whether they desire it or not.[36] Lucette is determined, therefore, to confront Rayber with the all-demanding, all-cleansing summons of the gospel, even as she subjects herself to its stringency:

> Her eyes still fixed on [Rayber], she cried, "I've seen the Lord in a tree of fire! The Word of God is a burning Word to burn you clean!" She was moving in his direction, the people in front of her forgotten. . . . "Burns the whole world, man and child," she cried, her eye on him, "none can escape." She stopped a little distance from the end of the stage and stood silent, her whole attention directed across the small room to his face on the [window] ledge. Her eyes were large and dark and fierce. . . . Suddenly she raised her arm and pointed toward his face. "Listen you people," she shrieked, "I see a damned soul before my eye! I see a dead man Jesus hasn't raised. His head is in the window but his ear is deaf to the Holy Word!" (CW, 414-15)

Rayber's final gesture of rejection is to rip out his hearing aid. His final refusal comes after he hears the child evangelist provide her own succinct version of T. S. Eliot's fine phrase from *Four Quartets*: "We only live, only suspire/Consumed by either fire or fire." Not satisfied with her eloquent, imagi-

---

36. Barth, *Homiletics*, pp. 40, 74.

native declaratives alone, Lucette addresses Rayber with the direct imperative of the Word of God: "Be saved in the Lord's fire or perish in your own!" (CW, 415). Having been radically displaced and reoriented by Lucette's proclamation, Rayber has but a single alternative to receiving it: he must remain encased within the tomb of his own deaf and love-denying absurdism. O'Connor hints at Rayber's final fate in his very name: just as Lucette is a Word-bearing "little light," perhaps Rayber may be identified as a latter-day Lucifer seeking to curtain the Word, a bearer of rays that darken rather than illumine.

*          *          *

Whether it be Hazel Motes or his grandfather, whether Bevel Summers or Lucette Carmody, whether in announcing Jesus or denouncing him, all of Flannery O'Connor's preachers declare a singular and relentless message. They give her fiction its striking authority by proclaiming or disclaiming the Word of God. Flannery O'Connor is an exemplary artist for the contemporary church because, like Dostoevsky, she grants her atheists a full and powerful hearing. Rayber and Motes declare the antigospel with a vigor and cogency that cannot be dismissed.[37] Nor do Bevel Summers and Lucette Carmody preach an easy and comforting truth. They summon their hearers to entrust themselves to the Christ who was crucified and raised for their salvation, and who enables their own resurrection as they follow the path of the Cross. Their preaching is not a quaint Southern habit; it is the Good News, the one Word whose awful demand engenders its saving response.

37. It should be added that O'Connor's plots, if not open-ended, do not demand finalizing interpretations. The grandmother's saving gesture toward The Misfit could be read as her ultimate self-delusion; Motes's self-pummeling as mere psychotic flagellations; Harry Ashfield's baptismal drowning as a despairing suicide; and Lucette Carmody's sermon as the ventriloquism taught by her exploiting parents. Though I regard these readings as erroneous, O'Connor leaves her plots and characters sufficiently mysterious to require the reader's interpretive engagement with them.

SIX ✌ *Demonic Nihilism:*
*The Chief Moral Temptation*
*of Modernity*

"If you live today," we have heard Flannery O'Connor declare, "you breathe in nihilism. In or out of the Church, it's the gas you breathe" (HB, 97). For O'Connor, the fetid air of nihilism is morally, no less than religiously, asphyxiating: it is not an intellectual game of shifting about counters on a philosophical board; rather, it is a life-posture dedicated to the destruction of life. O'Connor agreed with Walker Percy that literary art should function as canaries once did in coal mines: when the caged bird started to cough and keel over, the miners knew that the oxygen was nearly gone and that it was time to get out. Like Percy, O'Connor forewarned against our unbreathable air by using its rightful name: it is not atheism but nihilism. The atheist may refuse to affirm the self-identifying God of Abraham, Isaac, and Jacob — the God who became flesh in Jesus Christ — but still retain an objective moral sense, as did the ancient Greeks and Romans. The nihilist, by contrast, regards religious belief and moral virtue as mere social conventions and psychological delusions, not as realities grounded in either reason or revelation. Yet O'Connor does not confine the incidence of nihilism to high secular places; it also infiltrates the church. It is present whenever Christians live, to use John Wesley's apt phrase, as if God does not matter.

O'Connor believed that the outward carnage of the modern world, as evidenced most notably in the Soviet Gulags and the Maoist Cultural Revolution, in the Holocaust and Hiroshima and Dresden, is the direct consequence of a massive inward nihilism. It shrinks souls before it destroys bodies. The moral sense can be eviscerated, O'Connor wrote Elizabeth Hester, in the same way that the wings can be bred off chickens in order to make them produce more white meat. O'Connor did not label our tribe a brood of vipers, as Jesus called his own contemporaries, but rather "a generation of wingless chickens"; and in a phrase that is ever so revealing, she added that this "I suppose is what Nietzsche meant when he said God was dead" (CW, 942). Her reference in that letter to the great Victorian nihilist nowhere recurs in her fiction. Yet she agreed with Nietzsche that, while the atheist seeks to strike at the living God like a viper, the nihilist assumes, often unawares, that God is already dead. Nietzsche said that he could smell the decaying divine corpse — chiefly in our churches.

O'Connor rightly refused to demonize Nietzsche. Like Heidegger after him, Nietzsche was not engaged in a shouting match with the Almighty. He was protesting the massive vacancy of soul that, largely unrecognized, characterizes modern religious life in the West. Nietzsche saw that the sweet deity of the complacent middle classes has little if anything to do with the startlingly strange God of Abraham, Isaac, Jacob, and Jesus Christ. The notion of the divine as a Supreme Being — one being among a myriad of other beings, differing from them not in kind but only in degree — is a largely modern notion. The belief that God is an infinite version of ourselves leads to a magical and sentimental faith. It envisions God as willfully and extravagantly violating the closed Newtonian cosmos, always for our own advantage, of course, whenever we are sufficiently pious or moral in our beseeching of his benefits. It is noteworthy that no alleged miracles of this kind occur anywhere in O'Connor's fiction. Her characters come to their revolutionary moments of grace, the utter conversion of their lives, as the extraordinary occurs within ordinary events, though they may be extreme: Hazel Motes staring at a line of trees after his Essex has been destroyed, Mrs. May facing the horns of a charging bull, the Grandmother looking down The Misfit's gun barrel, Mrs. McIntyre transfixed at the sight of a priest as he places a wafer in a dying man's mouth.

For Flannery O'Connor, the great atheist "masters of suspicion" are to be honored for having striven so mightily against the false god of our age. As Merold Westphal, Nicholas Lash, Michael Buckley, and other Christian theologians have emphasized,[1] Nietzsche and Marx and Freud sought rightly to refute the layer-cake theology of popular Christianity that envisioned God as the Grandfather of the skies, a remote deistic deity whose relationship to the

---

1. See, for example, Nicholas Lash, *A Matter of Hope: A Theologian's Reflection on the Thought of Karl Marx* (London: Darton, Longman and Todd, 1981). Lash argues that Marx's radical critique of religion, together with his vision of a future society that will be completely just and loving, stands in full accord with the gospel: "In a word, Christian theology has traditionally acknowledged that, in the Kingdom of God, there will be no place for those mediating structures of sign and symbol which constitute the human phenomenon of religion. This acknowledgement implies (and Christians have all too often lost sight of this implication) that Christianity is inherently iconoclastic, suspicious of its own anthropomorphism, because the mistaken identification of the image for the reality, the sign for the signified, the Church for the Kingdom, is the fundamental form of idolatry" (p. 158).

world is essentially extraneous and occasional. Their refusal to credit such a No-God is a huge if unwitting compliment paid to the true God described in the Book of Hebrews: "It is a fearful thing to fall into the hands of the living God" (10:31).

Over and over O'Connor lamented the magical kind of Christianity that pervades the church, envisioning the triune and unknown God as our heavenly Step'n'fetch it, the divine factotum whom William Blake called "Old Nobodaddy." Hence her lament over fellow Catholics who used their religion as a postmortem insurance policy. Here again she stands in thorough accord with the central biblical tradition. In the very first Gospel, the Markan Jesus guards against any sensationalist conception of his powers by abjuring those whom he heals and raises to retain strict secrecy about the matter. The Fourth Gospel eschews the word "miracle" altogether, instead using the word "signs." Jesus' mighty works always point away from themselves to the kingdom whose presence they manifest; they do not demonstrate his arbitrary contravention of ordinary causality. William Placher observes that, from Augustine through Aquinas to Luther and Calvin, the chief theologians of the West have a virtually unanimous view of miracles: they are God's working in and through the natural world for his own purposes. As Augustine said, the whole of creation is at once natural and miraculous. Aquinas described miracles as those events that, because their natural causes are hidden from us, excite *admiratio,* the wonder that existentially and etymologically lies at the root of the word "miracle." Calvin added that God, as the continual sustaining cause of the entire cosmos, is always acting in and on and through his universe: "If God should but withdraw His hand a little, all things would perish immediately and dissolve into nothing."[2]

Only by way of the satanic, O'Connor believed, is it possible to understand the miasma of nothingness that engulfs our churches and our culture. Accordingly, this chapter is devoted to her assessment of demonic nihilism in both her essays and her fiction, especially as it manifests itself in our culture's alleged concern for the suffering of children. Toward that end, we will examine her depiction of the devil in *The Violent Bear It Away,* before turning to her one nihilist philosopher, Hulga Hopewell in "Good Country People." It is in this latter story that O'Connor makes overt allusion to Nietzsche's chief modern apostle, Martin Heidegger. Through her reading of his work, Hulga has embraced a nihilism that is far more than a thought project; it is also a program for the moral devastation of a young Bible salesman.

---

2. Quoted in William C. Placher, *The Domestication of Transcendence* (Louisville: Westminster/John Knox Press, 1996), p. 116.

## The Deceptions of the Demonic

In his treatise on the nature of evil, Karl Barth calls it *das Nichtige*, the Nothingness. He follows Augustine in describing evil as *privatio boni*, the absence or privation of the good. Yet Nothingness is not nothing. It is an abyss, a surd, an inexplicable shadow seeking to cast its darkness over the Light. The ancient motto *E tenebris lux* is false, in Barth's view, because it envisions God's bringing light out of darkness and thus his making good depend on the prior reality of evil. The *tohu-wabohu* ("without form and void") of Genesis 1:2 is neither a primeval darkness nor an aboriginal chaos having an independent status that God must subdue to order. The Hebrew compound means literally a "desert-ocean": an absurd thing, an anti-cosmos, a caricature and mockery of the ordered world that God is always creating for good. Evil is the nonbeing that God refuses to bring into being, the sinister anti-cosmos that he refuses to create. Precisely in its non-necessity and absurdity lies the terrible power of evil. If evil were entirely explicable — as it is whenever we mistake the Creator for the creation, worshiping finite things as if they were the infinite God (Rom. 1:25) — then it could be entirely overcome. Evil works by these subtle means, but they cannot explain its unaccountable power. St. Paul thus confesses that, despite the vigor of his faith, he cannot master evil: "For the good that I would I do not: but the evil which I would not, that I do." Hence the apostle's cry of simultaneous despair and rejoicing: "O wretched man that I am! Who will deliver me from the body of this death? I thank God through Jesus Christ our Lord" (Rom. 7:19, 24-25).

Barth follows the example of Paul by locating the mystery of iniquity in the Cross. We discover the dread power of evil, he argues, not by looking at the most heinous examples of human malice and hatred, but as we behold the crucified Lord. There alone can we discern the essence of evil to be neither theft nor rape nor murder nor even genocide, but unbelief, the refusal to trust God with the totality of our lives. This is the singular sin lying at the root of all particular sins, whether great or small. Golgotha exhibits the one evil that is the measure of all other evils. The persecution and crucifixion of Jesus make manifest the full desperation of human life. There in the surrender of the Judge to the judged, in the horrible human Nay uttered to the wondrous divine Yea, evil is truly disclosed. At Calvary, Barth contends, God has revealed the nature of Nothingness by overcoming it in a totally unanticipated and unthinkable way — by subjecting himself to it.

> He whom nothingness has no power to offend is prepared on behalf of His creature to be primarily and properly offended and humiliated, attacked

and injured by nothingness. For the sake of the creature which of itself can be no match for it, He Himself is not willing to be an easy match for it. He thus casts Himself into this conflict which is not necessarily His own. Where His creature stands or succumbs, He comes and exposes Himself to the threat of the assault, to the confrontation with nothingness which the creature cannot escape and in which it falls as an easy prey. God is not too great, nor is He ashamed, to enter this situation which is not only threatened but already corrupted, to confess Himself the Friend and Fellow of the sinful creature which is not only subject to the assault but broken by it, to acknowledge Himself the Neighbor of the sinful creature stricken and smitten by its own fault, and to act accordingly He Himself inaugurates the history of the covenant with this impotent and faithless partner.[3]

Barth and O'Connor both honor the modern thinkers who have sought to deal with Nothingness — especially Nietzsche and Heidegger, Sartre and Camus. Barth salutes them for enabling Christians and secularists alike to discern "that nothingness is really present and at work. It is no mere fiction or theme of discussion. It is no mere product of our negations to be dismissed by our affirmations. It is there. It assails us with irresistible power as we exist, and we exist as we are propelled by it into the world like a projectile."[4] Not to have experienced the shock of Nothingness that continues to strike the modern world with seismic force, Barth contends, is not to be fully modern men and women. So to deal with the demonic is all the more necessary for Christians. Yet Barth doubts that our aficionados of Nothingness have confronted the abyss as thoroughly as they claim. If they had faced the full demonry of Nothingness, how could they confidently stand before it? How could they make it something fruitful and salutary for human existence? Do they not, in the name of an ultimate realism, inject a subtle kind of morphia into the human soul? Does not their brave engagement with Nothingness mark the subtle triumph of the satanic? Barth answers clearly and negatively:

> If "I" can cope with [nothingness], opposing "myself" to it victorious in defeat; if I can acknowledge and resist it by defying it, it is not true nothingness. It may well be significant, violent, threatening and extremely aggressive, but if I can confront it with sovereign power, if I can deal with it,

3. Karl Barth, *Church Dogmatics*, 4 vols., trans. Geoffrey W. Bromiley (Edinburgh: T&T Clark, 1934-69), III/3, pp. 356-57. I have dealt with Barth's complex understanding of Nothingness in *The Comedy of Redemption*, pp. 38-48.

4. Barth, *Church Dogmatics*, III/3, p. 345.

if I can even play with it in changing situations, if I can set it behind me, I cannot convince myself that I have to do with the true and deadly dangerous adversary of myself and man and life.[5]

O'Connor speaks in similar terms about the satanic presence: it cannot be routed by even the most rigorous honesty and bravery. She understands Luciferian evil in traditional terms as a personal power determined to achieve its own supremacy.[6] When Satan appears in her fiction, she candidly observed, he is not to be understood as "this or that psychological tendency" (HB, 360). She also pointed to Baudelaire's celebrated declaration that the Devil's greatest wile is to convince us that he does not exist, and she indicated his considerable success in our own time. O'Connor used a warning from St. Cyril of Jerusalem as the epigraph for *A Good Man Is Hard to Find,* her first collection of stories: "THE DRAGON IS BY THE SIDE OF THE ROAD, WATCHING THOSE WHO PASS. BEWARE LEST HE DEVOUR YOU. WE GO TO THE FATHER OF SOULS, BUT IT IS NECESSARY TO PASS BY THE DRAGON."[7] This ancient saying is probably derived from an even older caveat: "Be sober, be vigilant," declares 1 Peter, "because your adversary the devil, as a roaring lion, walketh about, seeking whom he may devour" (5:8). For O'Connor, as for the whole of the biblical tradition, evil is something far more sinister than the sum total of human ill will; it is a ravaging presence that stalks its prey like a predatory beast.

## The Stranger Who Speaks in One's Own Voice

Satan's most unmistakable appearance in O'Connor's work occurs in *The Violent Bear It Away,* a novel in which the eighty-four-year-old backwoods prophet Mason Tarwater has his grandnephew under his tutelage, wishing to commission the fourteen-year-old Francis Marion Tarwater to serve as his successor. Yet the elder Tarwater had not promised the boy a life of either glory or delight, but rather of pain and ignominy:

---

5. Ibid., p. 346.

6. She admired both Camus and Sartre for the vigor of their unbelief, urging Christians to be similarly vigorous about their belief. Thus when Sartre famously declared that the very possibility of God means the impossibility of man — for if our humanity consists in absolute autonomy, as Sartre taught, any Reality outside it would be utterly nullifying — he forces Christians to demonstrate how faith enables freedom rather than destroying it.

7. *Three by Flannery O'Connor* (New York: Signet, 1964), p. 128.

> He had schooled him in the evils that befall prophets; in those that come
> from the world, which are trifling, and those that come from the Lord
> and burn the prophet clean; for he himself had been burned clean and
> burned clean again. He had learned by fire (CW, 332).

Mason once believed that God had summoned him to prophesy destruction
against an apostate world, and so he raged against its evils, calling down divine wrath on the rotten world. To the prophet's great dismay, God did not
visit the earth with ruin. Instead, the Lord sent "a finger of fire" upon
Tarwater himself, burning not the latter-day priests of Baal but Mason's own
body and brain with the most searing truth of all: his most scorching denunciations must be directed against himself.

It is to this life of fearful suffering and awful wrestling with God that Mason has summoned young Tarwater. The boy dreads a calling that would make
him the lightning rod for earthing the divine fire. He dreams, instead, of Moses
striking water from a rock, of Joshua making the sun stand still, of Daniel staring down lions in a pit. Eager to perform such thrilling and glamorous acts of
prophecy, the young Tarwater is disappointed that old Mason orders him to
undertake far more mundane tasks. The boy's vocation as a prophet will begin,
his great-uncle has taught him, when the old man dies. The elderly Elijah instructs his would-be Elisha to bury him deep enough in the ground to prevent
the dogs from digging him up, and also to plant a cross at the head of his grave.

The boy's second prophetic task will be to baptize Bishop, the dim-witted
son of his uncle George Rayber, the school psychologist we have met in the previous chapter, a man who is a nihilist convinced that Mason invented his own
calling. Without knowing it, Rayber is a Nietzschean. He believes that Christians suffer from what Nietzsche called *ressentiment*, a deep sense of insecurity
and unhappiness at being forced to live amid the rough and tumble of a godless
universe. Rayber insists that the elderly Tarwater has invented his prophetic
calling in order to give his life the importance that it otherwise lacks. He also believes, as we have learned, that his retarded son Bishop is a worthless creature
who should have been aborted. Young Tarwater looks forward to neither of his
callings — neither the burial nor the baptism. When the old man dies, the boy
labors for a day and a half at scooping out his great-uncle's grave. Yet gradually
the gorge of rebellion rises within him. It has risen before, whenever the old
man had spoken not of the prophet's power and glory, but "of the sweat and
stink of the cross, of being born again to die, and of spending eternity eating the
bread of life" (CW, 334). The defiant youth finally abandons his spadework and
heads off to the dead man's whiskey still, there to partake of waters that will
numb his conscience, quenching neither his spiritual nor physical thirst.

Tarwater does not undertake his spiritual rebellion alone; he is aided by an inward interlocutor. O'Connor depicts this inner voice in an appropriately paradoxical way: it arises from within the boy's own rebellious will, but it also assaults him from without as a force beyond his control. Satanic evil, she demonstrates, operates not only with human permission but in violation of it as well. This subjective devil is at once Tarwater's own alter ego but also an alien and intrusive second self. Because young Francis's Christian conscience has been so deeply formed by the religious teachings of his great-uncle, the Luciferian voice at first seems strange and strident. The boy does not welcome its insults against his dead uncle's life of prophecy. Old Mason had taught young Francis to have a deep reverence for the dead, the huge silent majority who constitute our most authentic patriarchy. It is not just that they literally fathered us; their bodies also constitute the very humus beneath our feet, thus prompting, as the word suggests, an appropriate humility.

> "The world was made for the dead. Think of all the dead there are," [the old prophet had] said, and then as if he had conceived the answer for all the insolence in the world, he said, "There's a million times more dead than living and the dead are dead a million times longer than the living are alive." (CW, 339)

Gradually, however, young Tarwater comes to welcome the inward voice that enunciates the worldly contempt the old prophet had condemned. It is the voice of theological rebellion, and it speaks with Dostoevskyan clarity about the relationship between parricide and deicide: if the boy can slay his obligations to his dead great-uncle, he can be rid of ultimate constraints as well. All things will be permitted, including wanton havoc: "'Now I can do anything I want to,' he said, softening the stranger's voice so that he could stand it. Could kill off all those chickens if I had a mind to, he thought, watching the worthless black game bantams that his uncle had been fond of keeping" (CW, 345). These are the accents of nihilistic autarky, even if they are given to a fourteen-year-old backwoods youth. Once the demonic is permitted entrance, O'Connor shows, it assumes complete control. From having been an alien intruder, the devilish voice gradually becomes Tarwater's affectionate familiar:

> He didn't search out the stranger's face but he knew by now that it was sharp and friendly and wise, shadowed under a stiff broad-brimmed panama hat that obscured the color of his eyes. He had lost his dislike for the thought of the voice. Only every now and then it sounded like a stranger's voice to him. He began to feel that he was only just now meet-

ing himself, as if as long as his uncle had lived, he had been deprived of his own acquaintance. (CW, 352)

O'Connor's devil is a comic figure rather like Dostoevsky's. He is a brittle rationalist and literalist, for example, denying the bodily resurrection on the grounds that many of the dead have been so thoroughly mangled that God could not possibly reconstitute them. "And lemme ast you this: what's God going to do with sailors drowned at sea that the fish have et and the fish that et them et by other fish and they et by yet others?" (CW, 352). This countrified Satan also argues — in accord with a good deal of modern politics and psychology — that young Tarwater's authentic selfhood depends on his complete independence and sufficiency. He must deny all transcendent power and authority, and since the demonic is also a transcendent presence, he must deny the devil himself.

> The way I see it, [the inner voice] said, you can do one of two things. One of them, not both. Nobody can do both of two things without straining themselves. You can do one thing or you can do the opposite.
> Jesus or the devil, the boy said.
> No no no, the stranger said, there ain't no such thing as a devil. I can tell you that from my own self-experience. I know that for a fact. It ain't Jesus or the devil. It's Jesus or you. (CW, 354)

There is only a short distance, this dialogue reveals, from denying the demonic to deifying oneself. Tarwater soon follows the command of his inner voice to drink his great-uncle's homemade whiskey. At first, the satanic speaker recommends that the boy drink modestly, as if he were learning a profitable social practice, but then he urges Tarwater to take the divine draft that will enable his own self-resurrection:

> Once you pass the moderation mark you've passed it, and that gyration you feel working down from the top of your brain, he said, that's the Hand of God laying a blessing on you. He has given you your release. That old man was the stone before your door and the Lord has rolled it away. He ain't rolled it quite far enough, of course. You got to finish up yourself but He's done the main part. Praise Him. (CW, 359)

Young Tarwater soon becomes so thoroughly drunk that he is able to "finish up" by attempting the one thing his dead uncle had strictly forbidden: incinerating the old man's body by setting his house afire.

O'Connor reveals that modern notions of autonomy have satanic implications whenever they deny our accountability to anything other than the sovereign self. She also shows that evil is an insidious power that cannot be explained entirely as the force of human self-will. It is also an invasive presence that works chiefly by means of deception. And while in this case the devil defrauds only a single young hellion, O'Connor makes him the sign of a larger cultural perfidy. Tarwater's denial of his divine vocation disorders not merely his own life. To refuse obligation to God is also to abandon responsibility to others, especially to a "worthless" cretinous child whom he has been commissioned to baptize, thus declaring his absolute worth before God. Believing that he can silence his prophetic calling only by an act of violent rejection, Tarwater gives the demonic its final victory by drowning Bishop.

## A Nihilist Baptism into Eternal Life

For Flannery O'Connor, the demonic nihilism of Hulga Hopewell and George Rayber and Francis Marion Tarwater cannot be answered by recourse to a noble humanism, even of a classically Christian kind. It requires a remedy far more radical: it requires Christian conversion as signaled by the act of baptism. The alleged freedom of self-invention is, for Flannery O'Connor, the ultimate slavery, whereas the total disposal of human life into the hands of God is the ultimate freedom. From Augustine through Aquinas to Barth, the central reading of Christian freedom is that it means the liberty to do the will of God and not to do evil. To refuse God's will by committing sin is not to exercise freedom but to surrender it. To sin is not to enlarge the will but to shrink it. With every contraction, the will becomes ever more enslaved, until finally it reaches total paralysis.[8] The liberating power of Jesus' command over the enslaved will is at work everywhere in the New Testament. Never does he summon his disciples to a heart-rending decision about following him, putting before them a possibility about which they must bravely choose either Yea or Nay. As he calls, so do the disciples answer — instantly and eagerly. Far from having coerced their freedom, Jesus has enabled it. They respond with what Bonhoeffer calls "the simplicity of obedience

---

8. Analogies and examples abound, perhaps the most obvious being drug addiction: the first snort of cocaine seems a blithe and innocuous act of freedom but, with each succeeding intake of ecstasy, the road to dependency and enslavement becomes increasingly irreversible, until the window of freedom is finally shut.

[that] pulls us out of the dichotomy of conscience and sin."[9] The reality of Christ's call creates the possibility of faithful response.

The Bible's most notoriously "Pelagian" passage, a long-standing favorite of many evangelists, is found in Revelation 3:20: "Behold, I stand at the door, and knock: if any man hear my voice, and open the door, I will come in to him, and will sup with him, and he with me." Barth notes that even here the prime emphasis falls on the divine summons rather than the human answer. No one would ever consider opening (or barring) the door were it not for Jesus' quiet tapping or loud rapping, as the case may require. God's grace is always prevenient, "going before" and thus enabling our very reception of God's proffer. Far from being a hat-in-hand supplicant unable to act unless we reluctantly permit him, the risen Lord (as Barth wittily recalls certain post-resurrection events) "passes through closed doors."[10] Barth's well-taken point is that a Lord whom we would elect entirely of our own will could have no real authority over us, since he could just as easily be unelected.

Flannery O'Connor understands, in ways yet unfathomed, this paradox of the grace-produced liberty enabled by the call of Christ. In her preface to the second edition of *Wise Blood,* she deals with the question of freedom by noting that, for most of her secular readers, Hazel Motes's integrity lies in his recalcitrant resistance to his calling. For her, by contrast, Motes's failure to repudiate his vocation constitutes his real freedom. "Does one's integrity ever lie in what he is not able to do?" O'Connor asks in her note to the second edtion of *Wise Blood.* "I think that usually it does, for free will does not mean one will, but many wills conflicting in one man." Motes has stumbled backward out of his nihilism and into what St. Paul calls "the glorious liberty of the children of God" (Rom. 8:21).

O'Connor pushes the paradox of ineluctable grace to its ultimate limit in *The Violent Bear It Away.* There, as we have seen, Francis Marion Tarwater engages in a demonic and nihilistic effort to throw off the mantle of prophecy that his great-uncle has laid on him. He is determined to reject his calling with every sinew of his will. He prides himself, for example, on being able to act — unlike his secular Uncle Rayber, who can merely think. Rather than giving old Mason a reverent burial, therefore, he attempts to incinerate the old prophet; then he flees Powderhead to live in the city with the enemy himself, the secular psychologist Rayber; and finally he kills Bishop, the imbecile cousin whom he has been commissioned to baptize. Yet in the very act of

9. Dietrich Bonhoeffer, *Discipleship,* trans. Barbara Green and Reinhard Krauss (Minneapolis: Fortress, 2001), p. 76.

10. Karl Barth, *Dogmatics in Outline* (New York: Harper Torchbooks, 1959), p. 123.

drowning the child, Young Tarwater also finds himself uttering the baptismal formula — thus fulfilling, against his own defiant and nihilistic will, the vocation he has been determined to deny.[11]

This scene has left many readers perplexed, even outraged. The most livid of O'Connor's interpreters is surely the French critic André Bleikasten. He accuses O'Connor of being a misanthrope whose God is hardly distinguishable from Satan:

> O'Connor's heroes are indeed sleepers: they traverse life in a dream-like state, and with the sense of impotence and anxiety experienced in nightmares. They go through the motions of revolt, but their violent gestures toward independence are all doomed to dissolve into unreality. They are nothing more than the starts and bounds of a hooked fish. Tarwater and Motes both act out scenarios written beforehand by someone else.[12]

Not only from Bleikasten's secular viewpoint, but also for those Christians who regard conversion as an act of entirely untrammeled choice, Tarwater's will has been scripted either by a Procrustean author or else by a domineering deity. For O'Connor, by contrast, Tarwater's unintended baptism of Bishop is not a breach of his freedom so much as the enabling of it. That he cannot finally kill the seed that Mason has sown within him is good news rather than ill. It reveals the long-suffering forbearance of God. Rather than blithely abandoning men and women to their own devices, God holds his wrath in check, restraining the judgment that ought to be unleashed on

---

11. No O'Connor reader has noticed, at least to my knowledge, that the youth has apparently renamed himself. Francis Marion cannot be considered a legitimate Tarwater, for his mother was one of two children belonging to the insurance salesman George Rayber, Sr. The school psychologist of the novel, George Rayber, Jr., is the other. Even though the boy's nameless mother was made illegitimately pregnant by a nameless divinity-school lover, who killed himself, Francis Marion remains a Rayber rather than a Tarwater. Mason's children are a nameless daughter who died in a car crash and a nameless son who has "gone to the devil." Old Mason has no direct descendants. At the Cherokee Lodge, Rayber rightly registers their names, therefore, as "George F. Rayber, Frank and Bishop Rayber" (CW, 425). Though we are never told at what point young Francis Marion rejected his own matronymic for his great-uncle's name, the alteration reveals how much more profoundly he remains attached to the old man whose divine calling he spurns, than to the psychologist whose demonic atheism he seeks to adopt. Indeed, he scratches out Rayber's writing in the motel register and enters his own: "Francis Marion Tarwater . . . Powderhead, Tennessee. NOT HIS SON" (CW, 428).

12. André Bleikasten, "The Heresy of Flannery O'Connor," in *Les Americanistes: New French Criticism of Modern American Fiction*, ed. Ira D. Johnson and Christiane Johnson (Port Washington, NY: Kennikat, 1978), p. 62.

them.[13] He is the Hound of Heaven, as Francis Thompson called him, pursuing his recreant people down all the alleys of their lives, refusing to be silenced and turned aside by human rejection, seeking instead to vacate the living and present hell of its miserable occupancy, desiring nothing less than that "all men . . . be saved, and . . . come unto the knowledge of the truth" (1 Tim. 2:4).

The sovereign summons of God does not strike young Tarwater as a stone cast from heaven; he is a Christ-haunted child from the start, thanks to the inner compass for the holy that Mason Tarwater has embedded within him. Even in his most rebellious acts of defiance, the boy cannot escape the memory of the old prophet's commanding eyes, whose bulging veins seem like a fishnet meant to snare him.[14] Once Young Tarwater arrives in the city at night, he is afraid to look up at the stars: "They seemed to be holes in his skull through which some distant unmoving light was watching him" (CW, 385). Least of all can he still the voice of Mason's constant call. The old man's words are like seeds dropping into the boy's bloodstream, waiting patiently to burst into life:

> "Ignore the Lord Jesus as long as you can! Spit out the bread of life and sicken on honey. Whom work beckons, to work! Whom blood to blood! Whom lust to lust! Make haste, make haste. Fly faster and faster. Spin yourselves in a frenzy, the time is short. The Lord is preparing a prophet. The Lord is preparing a prophet with fire in his hand and eye and the prophet is moving toward the city with his warning. The prophet is coming with the Lord's message. 'Go warn the children of God,' saith the Lord, 'of the terrible speed of justice.' Who will be left? Who will be left when the Lord's mercy strikes?" (CW, 368)

That Francis Marion Tarwater is a God-starved youth — profoundly restless until he can find the Augustinian rest that he seeks even as he denies it — becomes especially clear in the climactic chapters of the novel. Once, when he spies Bishop playing innocently in a reflecting pool, he moves instinctively to baptize him, only to be stopped by Rayber. On another occasion, Tarwater tenderly ties Bishop's shoelaces, recognizing the retarded child's utter helplessness and thus ministering to him despite his scorn for the imbecile. The youth's oxymoronic freedom-in-compulsion manifests it-

13. "God therefore calls a truce against sin; he does not retaliate forthwith in executing judgment upon it; he delays the punishment" (N. H. Snaith, "FORBEAR," in Alan Richardson, ed., *A Theological Wordbook of the Bible* (New York: Macmillan, 1950), p. 85.

14. Rayber's eyes, by contrast, lack specific character, "as if the schoolteacher, like the devil, could take on any look that suited him" (CW, 365).

self most markedly in the signs of his unworldly hunger and thirst. He pauses in front of the grocery window, for example, to stare at a leftover loaf of bread. On the day before the drowning, he eats six barbecue sandwiches and drinks three cans of beer. Because he denies his insatiable spiritual appetite — not only because he gorges himself on the ultimate redneck feast — it all comes back up. "A ravenous emptiness raged in his stomach as if it had reestablished its rightful tenure" (CW, 438). Later when he obtains yet another sandwich to satisfy his rampaging hunger, Tarwater finds that he cannot eat it: "It's like being empty is a thing in my stomach and it don't allow nothing else to come down in there. If I ate it, I would throw it up" (CW, 459).

These clear markers of Tarwater's hunger for the bread of life demonstrate that the baptism he performs while drowning Bishop is not O'Connor's deus ex machina. His will is coerced neither by his author nor his Author. It is freed through a surprising double negation. Tarwater would never have baptized Bishop if Rayber had not repeatedly claimed that baptism is a vacuous rite. The "natural" means of salvation, the school psychologist insists, is "through your own efforts" (CW, 451). "If there's any way to be born again," Rayber again declares, "it's a way that you accomplish yourself, an understanding about yourself that you reach after a long time, perhaps a long effort. It's nothing you get from above by spilling a little water and a few words" (CW, 450-51). To be told not to do something — especially not to do it because it is stupid — is a sure incitement to action. If only in a reflexive denial of Rayber's denial, Tarwater utters the triune baptismal sentence as he holds Bishop under the water.

Far from being an empty act, the sacrament proves splendidly performative: it literally produces what it sacramentally signifies. To be baptized is to be plunged into the aboriginal chaos out of which God fashioned the cosmos, and thus to be drowned and buried with Christ in a watery grave. It is also a resurrection from death, as the new creation emerges from the waters of life as a babe in Christ. That Bishop was biologically destined to remain a lifelong imbecile makes his baptismal death not altogether tragic, therefore, but comic in a precise Dantesque sense. He dies exactly as he would have lived — as a perpetual child in the body of Christ.[15]

---

15. Young Tarwater's unworthiness to perform this baptism has nothing to do with its authenticity, not even for Catholics: "In case of necessity, any person, even someone not baptized can baptize, if he has the required intention. The intention required is to will to do what the Church does when it baptizes, and to apply the Trinitarian formula" (*Catechism of the Catholic Church* [Mahwah, NJ: Paulist, 1994], p. 320). Whatever his intention, Tarwater utters the Trinitarian formula while plunging Bishop beneath the lake water. He also performs the most ancient and expressive form of baptism as it was practiced for more than a millennium of the church's life, only to be taken up again by latter-day Baptists: "In Christian antiquity and in mediaeval

O'Connor elects not to narrate the novel's horrible and wondrous climax directly, lest it seem mechanical and coerced, thus justifying the charge that her fiction enfleshes a divinely oppressive vision of reality. Instead, she has Tarwater gradually recall what happened. This is the only way he can discover that he has been delivered from evil at the same time that he also committed murder, his freedom being preserved rather than annihilated. Tarwater learns this paradoxical truth after hitching a ride with a truck driver who asks the boy to explain his soaked pants. He arrogantly replies that he has just finished drowning a boy. In one of O'Connor's most hilarious lines, the truck driver responds: "Just one?" Bishop's baptism is a joking matter for Young Tarwater as well, as he once again parrots Rayber's claim that baptism is a meaningless act and that we are born only once.

Yet when the driver pulls off the road to sleep for a while, the boy cannot avoid his dream-vision of what actually happened as he and Bishop went boating on the lake beside the motel. As if in virtual solicitation of his baptism, Bishop had fixed his eyes on Tarwater and then crawled onto the boy's back as Tarwater stood beside the boat in shallow water, virtually inviting a baptismal plunge. Tarwater's demonic "friend" gives him Nietzschean encouragement throughout the scene, urging him to "be a man" and to drown the dimwit. The dream-recollection makes Tarwater a virtual spectator to his own act, as he is shown what he could not possibly recall through his own self-interested memory. He sees with his inward eye and reenacts with his outward voice the undeniable truth: he has served as the agent of eternal life even as he has also brought death into the world. "Suddenly in a high raw voice the defeated boy cried out the words of baptism, shuddered, and opened his eyes. He heard the sibilant oaths of his friend fading away on the darkness" (CW, 463).

Despite her scorn for Calvinism, it is clear that Flannery O'Connor understands divine sovereignty in ways that are reminiscent of Calvin. She rejects double predestination, of course, especially as it became a prime doctrine for hyper-Calvinists; but she affirms the essentials of Calvin's reading of divine action.[16] The doctrine of sovereign election is not, in fact, a uniquely

---

times up to the 13th century, Baptism was usually administered in the form of immersion" (Ludwig Ott, *Fundamentals of Catholic Dogma*, first pub. in German in 1952, trans. Patrick Lynch [Rockford, IL: Tan, 1955], p. 352).

16. "The doctrine of double predestination," she observed, "is a strictly Protestant phenomenon." She complains that it destroys human freedom, cuts the nerve of moral choice, and renders life dramatically uninteresting. Like many others, O'Connor confuses predestination with fatalism: "I don't think literature would be possible in a determined world" (HB, 88-89). Bunyan's *Pilgrim's Progress* is a notable disproof of her argument that belief in double predestination would make literature impossible.

Calvinist doctrine. That Israel is God's elect people, chosen not for its merit or even with its deliberative consent, is a fundamentally biblical claim. That Jesus is God's chosen messiah for the salvation of the whole world is the very essence of the Good News. And that in him all believers are undeservedly elected by the very God who has undeservedly refused to reject them — this is the very essence of the gospel. "You have not chosen me, but I have chosen you" (John 15:16).

The question of Tarwater's freedom as he baptizes Bishop while drowning him concerns the proper relationship of divine initiative and human response. It is the question of Who calls and who answers, Who gives and who receives, Who both authors and finishes, and therefore who is both authored and finished. Because O'Connor always places the emphasis on the first of these pairings, her Catholicism is sometimes described as Jansenist. This is too complex a historical matter to adjudicate here. Yet it is fair to say that she would have wholly concurred with the greatest of Jansenist thinkers, Blaise Pascal, when he said that we would not seek God unless he had already found us. For Francis Marion Tarwater to have been defeated in doing evil is not a sign that he has been divinely coerced but a revelation that the seeds of freedom have been planted irrepressibly deep within him. "Election," writes the Catholic theologian Hans Urs von Balthasar, is "the effect of [the divine] call on the freedom of the person called. This freedom remains, even if it seems to be submerged under the weight of God's take-over . . . it surfaces again in the awareness that, by being servants of our mission, we enjoy a freedom that is boundless."[17] Even Tarwater's furious rebellion is the paradoxical result of his having been ineluctably called by God.

That Tarwater's baptism of Bishop was no "empty act" is indicated by the sibilance of the demonic voice as it angrily flees in frustration at losing yet another soul. The rebel prophet himself is given a vision of the child's ultimate state as, still thirsting for the water of life, Tarwater plunges his entire head into a well-bucket: "He looked down into a grey clear pool, down and down to where two silent serene eyes were gazing at him" (CW, 466). Though the lake will have to be dragged the next day in order to find Bishop's body, the child is not dead but alive with eternally tranquil eyes. He has not been annihilated but born to eternal life. And Tarwater himself, as we shall discover, is not far from his own conversion from death-dealing nihilism to a life of prophetic Christian faithfulness.

---

17. Hans Urs von Balthasar, *Theo-Drama: Theological Dramatic Theory*, Vol. III, *The Dramatis Personae: The Person in Christ*, trans. Graham Harrison (San Francisco: Ignatius Press, 1992), p. 266.

## The Pain of Children that Arouses Nihilist Temptation

Much of George Rayber's refusal to believe in God stems from the birth of the feeble-minded Bishop. This brain-stunted child proves, according to Rayber's reasoning, that the universe is an unsponsored and undirected flux, the product of absurd chance. If there is a God, Rayber concludes, he is a ham-fisted creator formed in Bishop's imbecilic image. In Rayber, O'Connor creates a latter-day Ivan Karamazov, since he too denies the divine goodness because of the world's wanton and unrelieved suffering. Karamazov creates a virtual phantasmagoria of misery from instances of human barbarity that he has discovered in Russian newspapers: Turkish soldiers cutting babies from their mothers' wombs and throwing them in the air to impale them on their bayonets; enlightened parents stuffing their five-year-old daughter's mouth with excrement and locking her in a freezing privy all night for having wet the bed, while they themselves sleep soundly; Genevan Christians teaching a naïve peasant to bless the good God even as the poor dolt is beheaded for thefts and murders which his ostensibly Christian society caused him to commit; a Russian general, offended at an eight-year-old boy for accidentally hurting the paw of the officer's dog, inciting his wolfhounds to tear the child to pieces; a lady and gentleman flogging their seven-year-old daughter with a twigged birch rod until she collapses while crying for mercy, "Papa, papa, dear papa."[18]

Such evils cannot be justified, Ivan argues, either by religious arguments based on history's beginning or by secular arguments that look to its end. Edenic liberty to eat the forbidden fruit and thus to bring evil into the world is not worth the tears of even one little girl shivering all night in a privy and crying from her excrement-filled mouth to "dear, kind God" for protection. Yet neither will Ivan accept the Hegelian-Marxist thesis that the harmonious final outcome of history negates its present evils. The notion that such savagery reveals the necessary consequences of human freedom or that it contributes to history's ultimate victory is, to Ivan, a moral and religious outrage. Neither is he satisfied with the conventional doctrine of final perdition, which holds that the monsters of torment will themselves be eternally tormented. Hellish punishment for heinous malefactors would not restore their victims, Ivan rightly argues. The impaled babies would not be brought back to life, nor would their mothers be consoled; the dismembered boy would not live out his missing years; nor would the weeping girls dry their tears.

---

18. Fyodor Dostoevsky, *The Brothers Karamazov*, trans. Richard Pevyear and Larissa Volonkhonsky (New York: Vintage, 1991), p. 241.

Ivan rejects all such theodicies because, in belittling innocent suffering, they commit unforgivable sacrilege against innocent sufferers. With a dramatic metaphor drawn from the romantic poet Schiller, he refuses to offer his hosanna for such a world: he returns his ticket to such a life.

In addition to creating, in Rayber, a character who shares Ivan's sentiments, O'Connor addresses the problem of the suffering of innocents in her introduction to *A Memoir of Mary Ann,* a deeply-moving account, written by Dominican nuns, of the life and death (at age twelve) of a girl who had been sent to live with them as she died. Though Mary Ann had suffered from incurable cancer since birth and though her face was grotesquely disfigured — a neuroblastoma had required the removal of one eye — she lived a radiantly happy life. Her unwarranted suffering was of the same kind that prompted Ivan Karamazov to deny the goodness of God. O'Connor does not dismiss Ivan's argument, knowing well that there are many millions who do not live radiantly but who, in response to similar misery, survive only by leading what Thoreau called "lives of quiet desperation." Nor did Dostoevsky turn lightly away from Ivan's nihilism. But while he makes no philosophical refutation of Ivan, Dostoevsky shows that his nihilism, while thinkable, is not livable. It leads him to a calloused unconcern for others, even as it also leads him to poison the mind of his half-brother Smerdyakov, turning him into a cold and calculating parricide. It also leads Ivan to make political arguments that are frighteningly prophetic of modern totalitarianism.[19]

Like Dostoevsky, O'Connor attempts no intellectual answer to the problem of evil. Innocent suffering cannot and must not be justified, if such justification exonerates God at the expense of blameless victims. Instead, she is concerned about our proper response to inexplicable horrors suffered by the world's wretches, and she gives an answer that many readers have found disconcerting:

> One of the tendencies of our age is to use the suffering of children to discredit the goodness of God, and once you have discredited his goodness, you are done with him. The Alymers[20] whom Hawthorne saw as a menace have multiplied. Busy cutting down human imperfection, they are

19. I have sought to show that, in viewing Dostoevsky through Western eyes rather than the lens of his own Eastern Orthodoxy, we have consistently misread the political implications of Ivan's nihilism, especially as expressed in his parable "The Grand Inquisitor." See "Ivan Karamazov's Mistake," *First Things* 128 (December 2002): 29-36.

20. In Hawthorne's story "The Birthmark," a scientist named Alymer decides that the small blot on the face of his lovely wife Georgiana is an unpleasant reminder of her mortality and thus should be eradicated. She dies as a result of his chemical attempt to remove it.

making headway also on the raw material of good. . . . In this popular pity, we mark our gain in sensibility and our loss in vision. If other ages felt less, they saw more, even though they saw with the blind, prophetical, unsentimental eye of acceptance, which is to say, of faith. In the absence of this faith now, we govern by tenderness. It is a tenderness which, long since cut off from the person of Christ, is wrapped in theory. When tenderness is detached from the source of tenderness, its logical outcome is terror. It ends in forced labor camps and in the fumes of the gas chambers. (CW, 830-31)

Because there seems to be a great distance from the advocacy of tenderness to the burning of Jews at Auschwitz and Dachau, humanists and advocates of other religious traditions have objected to O'Connor's assertion that secular pity is likely to turn murderous. But when one examines the argument that precedes and follows O'Connor's controversial claim, it carries considerable weight. Her worry about the abstract character of modern science, especially when it trenches on human life, is shared by many secular critics of modern culture. Philip Rieff and Christopher Lasch, for example, have lamented the triumph of a subhuman science that turns everyone into a pitiable victim requiring the therapy that an omnicompetent state is all too eager to provide.[21] George Steiner also traces the cold efficiency and mechanical heartlessness of the death camps, at least in part, to the theoretical sciences and high culture that were the glory of Europe; for such achievements are built on a process of objectification and distancing that can numb our response to ordinary human need and suffering:

> Utmost bestiality and the systematic dehumanization of man arose from within, and were enacted amid, the high places and institutions of European culture. The cellars for torture, the concentration camps, operated within easy reach of the concert-halls, museums and universities. The great libraries remained open; scholarship, literature, and the arts flourished as the death-trains rolled past. Men and women, apparently sane, could flog and incinerate innocent victims during their working day and recite Rilke, play Schubert, or sing Christmas carols with their loved ones in the evening.[22]

21. Philip Rieff, *The Triumph of the Therapeutic: Uses of Faith after Freud* (New York: Harper and Row, 1966); Christopher Lasch, *The Culture of Narcissism: American Life in an Age of Diminished Expectations* (New York: Norton, 1978).

22. George Steiner, "Remembering the Future," *Theology* (November/December 1990): 439.

Not for O'Connor alone, but for much of Western history and culture as well, the chief guard against such deadly abstraction from the life of concrete goods and virtues has been the conviction that the triune God has given true pity its incarnate life. As himself a community of mutual surrender and self-giving, God is no abstract idea; on the contrary, he has become historical and personal in Jesus Christ. Compassion for innocent sufferers can never be removed, it follows, from God's own suffering love.

When it is so removed, the results can be sinister. A godless goodness blinds us to our own evils. We begin to sin far more egregiously in our alleged virtues than in our obvious vices. Thus do Christians put a drastic qualification on doing good, lest it become a subtle means of exalting the helpers and trampling the helped, making them the mere means for our own righteousness. Precisely because evil is so demonically subtle, goodness must always remain "something under construction" (CW, 830). It is achieved neither easily nor quickly; on the contrary, it is the slow work of suffering rightly understood and faithfully embraced. Because of our mortality, suffering is coeval with human existence: we would suffer and die even if we were not fallen.[23] The world is full of the hazards and calamities that are intrinsic to a finite creation.

Because sinfulness brings its own terrible suffering, human life remains a vexed business even at best: "Man is born unto trouble," the Book of Job declares, "as the sparks fly upward" (5:7). Because modern science has relieved much of the suffering that derives from our finitude, it has become hubristic in its attempt to remove the consequences of sin as well, thus committing new and worse sins of its own. Just as Hawthorne's Alymer thought he could eradicate his wife's birthmark with a chemical procedure, so does our culture seek to cure every evil, whether mental or physical, with an appropriate therapy. The avoidance of suffering becomes the single criterion, therefore, for determining the good, and pain becomes the chief measure of evil.

The consequence of such a transvaluation of morality is made vivid by Walter M. Miller, Jr., O'Connor's contemporary and fellow Catholic novelist. In his novel *A Canticle for Leibowitz*, there is a poignant exchange between a priest named Zerchi and a physician named Cors. The doctor holds that euthanasia is the only justifiable remedy, especially for children, when pain can no longer be relieved. Zerchi replies with a speech that is very near to

---

23. The serpent, being a literalist, convinces Eve that God had lied when he said that the primal couple would die if they ate the forbidden fruit. They eat of it but do not die — not immediately at least. But their mortality becomes a burden rather than a blessing, and the death that would have been their natural gift becomes their terrible curse — "the last enemy that shall be destroyed" (1 Cor. 15:26).

O'Connor's own position, arguing that the modern world is self-destructive precisely because of its fury against God for having created a pain-laden world:

> "To minimize suffering and to maximize security were natural and proper ends of society and Caesar. But then they became the only ends, somehow, the only basis of law — a perversion. Inevitably, then, in seeking only them, we found only their opposites: maximum suffering and minimum security."[24]

Such scientific humanists as Doctor Cors would not ask, as O'Connor points out, why Mary Ann had to die so painfully and so early, "but why she should be born in the first place" (CW, 830). Her life seems a mindless mistake of nature because it entailed so much suffering. For Christians, by contrast, Mary Ann's life is immeasurably important because the aim of life is not to avoid pain but to please God. Mary Ann offered her life to God not by becoming sweetly pious, O'Connor notes, but by making something wondrously good of her disfigured face:

> She and the Sisters who had taught her had fashioned from her unfinished face the material of her death. The creative action of the Christian's life is to prepare his death in Christ. . . . This action by which charity grows invisibly among us, entwining the living and the dead, is called by the Church the Communion of Saints. It is a communion created upon human imperfection, created from what we make of our grotesque state. (CW, 828, 831)

## Hulga Hopewell, Martin Heidegger, and the Lure of Nothingness

The unjust suffering that may prompt a nihilistic stance toward life is the focus of "Good Country People," a story that reveals the workings of O'Connor's sacramental imagination. She confessed that she never sat down to write a story with an idea in mind, but that she always began by envisioning a particular situation. O'Connor proceeded, very much in line with the biblical tradition, from the concrete and the particular to the abstract and the

24. Walter M. Miller, Jr., *A Canticle for Leibowitz* (New York: Bantam Books, 1997; first published in 1959), p. 330.

universal.[25] In this case she said that she imagined (surely from her own experience) a stuck-at-home daughter overhearing a trifling conversation between two farm women, and then she asked how this young woman got herself into such a situation and how she might extricate herself from it. In so envisioning Joy Hopewell, O'Connor created the most convincing of the several frustrated intellectuals who are confined to the restricted world of their parents. Julian in "Everything That Rises Must Converge" and Asbury in "The Enduring Chill" are in rebellion against the suffocations of small-minded mothers; but Joy Hopewell is in metaphysical revolt against the order of the cosmos itself. Nor is her nihilism a mere thought-project: she wants to annihilate the naïve faith of a Bible salesman named Manley Pointer.

Since she has considerable cause for her discontent, Joy Hopewell is far from being an entirely unsympathetic character: the lines of her life, to reverse the affirmation of the psalmist, have fallen in terribly unpleasant places. She wears a prosthesis because as a child she was accidentally shot in a hunting accident; and she has a serious heart ailment as well. Her communal existence is confined, moreover, to the presence of two grossly complacent women, her mother and a tenant farm woman named Mrs. Freeman. Their constant mouthing of clichés makes them completely immune to self-critique: "Mrs. Hopewell had no bad qualities of her own but she was able to use other people's in such a constructive way that she never felt the lack" (CW, 264). With a doctorate in philosophy from a German university, the thirty-year-old Joy is quite justified in chafing at such a trite and smug world, condemning her, as it does, to a miserably inauthentic life. She rebels, therefore, in every way that will offend her lady-like mother: by wearing childish clothes, by slouching in her chair, even by renaming herself with the ghastliest moniker she can invent — Hulga.[26] At times she cannot contain her fury, bursting forth in bilious rage, though we see and hear her outbursts from her mother's point of view, as she listens to her "girl" ventilate:

> To her own mother she had said — without warning, without excuse, standing up in the middle of a meal with her face purple and her mouth half full — "Woman! do you ever look inside and see what you are not? God!" she had cried sitting down again and staring at her plate.

25. Unlike most of her other stories, which were the products of long and arduous gestation, this one she wrote in just four days.

26. For Hulga's mother, the name conjures up "the broad blank hull of a battleship." Yet when Flannery O'Connor visited East Texas State College in November 1962, she gave her own version of the name's origin. She said that it came to her in a moment of sheer inspiration, as a hybrid between "huge" and "ugly."

"Malebranche[27] was right: we are not our own light. We are not our own light!" Mrs. Hopewell had no idea what had brought this on. She had only made the remark, hoping Joy would take it in, that a smile never hurt anyone.

The girl had taken the Ph.D. in philosophy and this left Mrs. Hopewell at a complete loss. You could say, "My daughter is a nurse," or "My daughter is a schoolteacher," or even, "My daughter is a chemical engineer." You could not say, "My daughter is a philosopher." That was something that had ended with the Greeks and Romans. (CW, 268)

O'Connor's willful autobiographical references are unmistakable. High-toned Milledgeville society was chagrined that its homegrown author wrote about such grisly subjects as the baptismal suicide of a child, the murder of an entire family by a serial killer, the deadly goring of a proper lady by a neighbor's bull. One could perhaps say in middle Georgia, "Our girl is a child psychologist," but one could not say, "Our girl is a Gothic novelist." That was something that had ended with Mary Shelley and Edgar Allan Poe. Like Hulga Hopewell, Flannery O'Connor was a well-educated woman forced back home to the rural South, there to be put under the care of her mother, when what she wanted was to live and work among fellow writers in the North. The cortisone-weakened O'Connor walked with the aid of crutches, even as Hulga relies on her wooden leg. She also altered her name by dropping the sweet-sounding and all-too-Catholic "Mary," while retaining the angular and androgynous "Flannery." Hulga is like her creator in an even more important way: she is a bookish woman whose reading is a clue to her condition, an intellectual whose ideas indeed have consequences.

When Mrs. Hopewell opens one of her daughter's books, she happens on the following passage, which Hulga has marked for emphasis:

27. This is an apt, if pretentious, allusion for Hulga the Heideggerian to make, for Malebranche stands in the Cartesian tradition that runs from Hume and Berkeley through Kant and Heidegger. Malebranche held that we do not, in fact, see by our own light but by what he called "vision in God." He was obsessed with the Cartesian problem of human knowledge about objects outside ourselves. Together with Descartes, he argued that knowledge of the world does not come from either sensation or imagination but from clear and distinct ideas perceived by the understanding. Yet unlike his master — and much closer to Spinoza — Malebranche held that "created things are in themselves causally inefficacious and that God is the sole true cause of change in the universe" (Willis Doney, "Malebranche, Nicholas," in *Encyclopedia of Philosophy*, Vol. V, ed. Paul Edwards [New York: Macmillan, 1967], p. 140). Malebranche's denial of the mind's ability to perceive truth through the natural order of things, together with his denial of secondary causes and thus of real human freedom, would make Hulga an ideal disciple of so unsacramental a thinker.

"Science, on the other hand, has to assert its soberness and seriousness afresh and declare that it is solely concerned with what-is. Nothing — how can it be for science anything but a horror and a phantasm? If science is right, then one thing stands firm: science wishes to know nothing of Nothing. Such is after all the strictly scientific approach to Nothing. We know it by wishing to know nothing of Nothing." These words had been underlined with a blue pencil and they worked on Mrs. Hopewell like some evil incantation in gibberish. She shut the book quickly and went out of the room as if she were having a cold chill. (CW, 268-69)

Mrs. Hopewell is no philosopher, but she senses that she has encountered something sinister. What she does not know, of course, is that she has encountered a passage from Heidegger's 1929 inaugural lecture at the University of Freiburg, entitled "What Is Metaphysics?" There, as elsewhere, Heidegger argues that the whole history of Western thought and life has constituted a sustained exercise in nihilism, that is, a negation of this present world for the sake of an alleged superworld. The ancient affirmations of a transcendent order existing above and over against ordinary life, whether Greek and philosophical or Christian and theological, have also been linked to oppressive social and scientific systems. According to Heidegger, the dualistic bifurcation of the cosmos into appearance and reality, accident and essence, particular and universal, makes a sham of human existence, effectively reducing it to nothingness. The conventional identification of God with true Being makes this mortal life seem a mere shadow of the real world, a realm unworthy of serious regard, a place where people of high "spiritual" knowledge and power are able to control and manipulate the merely material-minded. *Contemptus mundi* has been the motto of too many Platonists and Christians alike. Heidegger is a vigorous nay-sayer, therefore, in quest of a freer and more authentic life than traditional religion and science have afforded. He wants to reclaim the value implicit in this world, says Stanley Rosen, the value that has been "mistakenly alienated or projected into another, supersensible, trans-historical world."[28] What has been lost, according to Heidegger, is a sense of the infinite importance of this limited life that is inexorably bent toward death.

It is evident that, like Nietzsche, Heidegger was no vulgar atheist after the fashion of an H. L. Mencken or a Robert Ingersoll. He was declaring, in his own words, that "the supersensible world, especially the world of the

28. Stanley Rosen, *Nihilism: A Philosophical Essay* (New Haven, CT: Yale University Press, 1969), p. 194.

Christian God, has lost its effective force in history."[29] Heidegger believed that "the God of Augustine and Luther and Kierkegaard, the God of Pseudo-Dionysius and Meister Eckhart and St. Catherine of Siena, had been reduced to . . . the 'paymaster' from whom we receive our virtues' reward, that God with whom we 'do business.'"[30] That God is dead in this precise cultural and religious sense means, as Laurence Hemming explains, that "the human being is in some sense dead to God."[31] O'Connor agreed with Nietzsche's similar claim, saying that morally and spiritually we have become a generation of wingless chickens. With the demise of the biblical God, the world is reduced to a dead object awaiting human manipulation, especially by way of modern technology and politics. Hence her praise of Heidegger's essays on Hölderlin's poetry, where the philosopher insists that "the poet's business [is] to name what is holy" (CW, 925).

Scientists, with their vaunted analysis of external reality, ignore the dense richness of the world, pushing it through the sieve of the mind's reductive categories. In the lecture that Hulga Hopewell has marked up in her book, Heidegger insists that this pseudo-autonomous science, with its fixation on the observable world, ignores the primary question of the negative whole encompassing all that positively is. For Heidegger, the first task of philosophy is to recognize this prior and antithetical realm of nothingness that remains "the complete negation of the totality of what-is." Because Nothing is "neither an object nor anything else that 'is' at all," Heidegger maintains that we can neither grasp nor master it. Yet our encounter with this unreachable world of Nothing has a paradoxically positive effect: it returns us to the strangeness and mystery of the ordinary world. For only in thinking the unthinkable otherness of what-is-not do we discover the wondrous completeness of what-is:

> Only when science proceeds from metaphysics can it conquer its essential task ever afresh, which consists not in accumulation and classification of knowledge but in the perpetual discovery of the whole realm of truth, whether of Nature or of History.[32]

29. From Heidegger's 1945 commentary on his rectoral address of 1933, given when he joined the Nazi party and became rector of Freiburg University; quoted in Laurence Paul Hemming, *Heidegger's Atheism: The Refusal of a Theological Voice* (Notre Dame, IN: University of Notre Dame Press, 2002), p. 38.

30. Quoted in Hemming, pp. 243-44.

31. Ibid., p. 38.

32. Martin Heidegger, "What Is Metaphysics?" in *Existence and Being* (Chicago: Regnery, 1968), pp. 332, 340, 347.

O'Connor, by contrast, agreed with the ancient Greeks that the starting point of all philosophy is the unfathomable mystery that there is Something rather than Nothing. The primordial fact is not that we are encircled by a vast void but that we are the products of parents and communities and institutions, of neighbors and friends and even enemies, but supremely of the tri-une God. The cosmos exists in God. "Know ye that the Lord he is God: it is he that hath made us, and not we ourselves" is the most fundamental of all biblical declarations (Ps. 100:3). Unlike Heidegger, therefore, O'Connor held to a metaphysics of presence rather than absence. Both revelation and reason drive us to the conviction, she believed, that the realm of "what-is" is enveloped and irradiated not by "what-is-not" but by the God who disclosed himself to Moses as Yahweh: He Who Is Who He Is. She cited St. Augustine's claim that all things pour forth from God, making the entire creation a sign of God.

To attend carefully to the created order is, for her, the artist's primary responsibility. Hence her frequent recourse to Joseph Conrad's claim that the primary aim of art is "to render the highest possible justice to the visible universe." "The artist," she affirmed, "penetrates the concrete world in order to find at its depths the image of its source, the image of ultimate reality" (MM, 157). The narrator of *Wise Blood* is concerned, for example, with the wonder that Hazel Motes and nearly everyone else in the city of Taulkinham ignore. It's the same sense of astonishment at the sheer unnecessity and total gratuity of things that compelled Martin Luther to confess that God made the night sky for his own enjoyment and that, if a man were to stare at a single kernel of grain long enough, he would die of wonder:

> The black sky was underpinned by long silver streaks that looked like scaffolding and depth on depth behind it were thousands of stars that all seemed to be moving very slowly as if they were about some vast construction work that involved the whole order of the universe and that would take all time to complete. No one was paying any attention to the sky. (CW, 19)

## The Nihilist Annihilated

Hulga Hopewell pays little attention to the sky because she spends much of her time boasting that she has no illusions. Like Heidegger, she has "seen through" the world's scrim to discern that there is nothing behind it but Nothing itself: "We are all damned," she declares to Manley Pointer, "but some of us have taken off our blindfolds and see that there's nothing to see. It's a kind of salvation" (CW, 280). Nor does Hulga give heed to the natural order. "Sometimes she went for walks," the narrator sardonically observes, "but she didn't like cats or birds or flowers or nature" (CW, 268). When Manley steals her glasses, Hulga doesn't at first notice the loss because "she seldom paid close attention to her surroundings" (CW, 287). Hulga's nihilism occludes the splendors of the earth because she has descried, in good Heideggerian fashion, the skull of death lying beneath the skin of life.

Her alleged breakthrough to nihilism has precisely the deadly effect that Nicholas Boyle has observed. There are immense moral and political implications inherent in Heidegger's obsession with the accidental character of human existence. He points out that Heidegger's concern with our "thrownness,"[33] our "being-toward-death," and thus the necessary self-assertion and self-origination of our lives, ignores the most fundamental reality:

> [W]hether or not we can choose our heroes, we certainly cannot choose our parents. For most of us it is as difficult to acknowledge that we could have been born of no other parents (and were born in fact of their love) as to acknowledge that we must and shall die. The *reductio ad absurdum* of Heidegger's position is [the Nazi philosopher Ernst] Jünger's view that the ideal soldier or state functionary would have no parents at all. Denial of the past is the typical act of authoritarian Enlightenment. A theory of politics which sees our life together as emerging not (as Hegel thought) out of mutual care and the mutual satisfaction of needs but out of some individual fiat — whether of assertion or submission is immaterial — is a theory for officials. For officials are always tempted to see themselves as embodiments of the monarchical "I will," rather than servants of civil society.[34]

Hulga is not an official who can exercise her will-to-power over the masses, but she is no less determined to dominate at least one other person as proof that the cosmos is a vast amoral zero. She wants to emancipate someone who is not hopelessly inscribed with false consciousness, not a

33. Nicholas Boyle, *Who Are We Now? Christian Humanism and the Global Market from Hegel to Heaney* (Notre Dame, IN: University of Notre Dame Press, 1998). Boyle points out that *Geworfenheit* can be translated not only as "thrownness" but also as "whelpedness," thus indicating an even more Manichean notion of human life as fundamentally a bestial affair.

34. Ibid., p. 199.

guilty adult already "alienated" by moral and religious virtue but an ingenuous youth who might be permanently freed from such oppressive "projections" as good and evil, salvation and damnation. Though Hulga can remember feeling shame as a child, she has come to believe that the mores instilled by society and tradition are a dread malignancy to be excised. Hence her gratefulness that "education had removed the last traces of [shame] as a good surgeon scrapes for cancer" (CW, 281). Better still, such constraints should not be permitted to get their first grip; rather, the young should be made to see that the universe is a religious and ethical void. And so Hulga decides to make an amoralist of Manley Pointer, the Bible salesman whom she assumes to be a moral naïf, an instance of "good country people," a rural simpleton who has dedicated his life to what he calls "Chrustian service." Like a latter-day Raskolnikov murdering his landlady to prove his emancipation from all ethical norms, Hulga wants to devastate Manley's primitive faith, taking away his shame and guilt, transforming such false feelings into "something useful" (CW, 276).

Hulga's plan to "free" Manley for a utilitarian life is a completely intellectual act. She sees him as an example of the class called "dumb Christians," not as a singular and uniquely valuable person. By reducing him to an abstraction, she can better subject him to her own will. After their first meeting, Hulga lies awake "half the night" thinking of various ways she might liberate Manley. She takes herself so seriously that she cannot detect his own wicked sense of irony. During their second meeting, when the boy asks her if she has ever eaten a two-day-old chicken, Hulga ponders the question as if he had posed it "for consideration at the meeting of a philosophical association." Not averse to lying for the sake of her larger nihilistic "truth," Hulga replies with a somber Yes, "as if she had considered the matter from all angles" (CW, 275).

This intellectual with a German doctorate is undeterred by Pointer's hard humor. She dreams about sexually seducing the boy, not about arguing Manley into unbelief. A seduction will render the boy permanently immune, Hulga thinks, to the empty conventions of right and wrong. Yet this seduction must occur without passion, lest she lose her mental self-control. At their rendezvous in the barn loft, Hulga is initially unaroused by Manley's heavy kisses; instead, she converts their power into sheer intellectual energy. Though she has never before been kissed, Hulga finds the experience entirely "unexceptional": "[H]er mind, clear and detached and ironic, was regarding him from a great distance, with amusement but with pity" (CW, 278). Hulga continues to regard Manley, not as the man-child who he surely is, but as "you poor baby" (CW, 275). When at last she begins to feel passion, despite all her efforts at self-management, she transforms him from an adolescent into an infant:

> The girl did not return any of his kisses but presently she began to and af-
> ter she had put several on his cheek, she reached his lips and remained
> there, kissing him again and again as if she were trying to draw all of the
> breath out of him. His breath was clear and sweet like a child's and the
> kisses were sticky like a child's. He mumbled about loving her and about
> knowing when he first seen her that he loved her, but the mumbling was
> like the fretting of a sleepy child being put to sleep by his mother. Her
> mind, throughout this, never stopped or lost itself for a second to her
> feelings. (CW, 279).

Although there are hints of pedophilia here, Hulga acts not as a sexual predator so much as a deadly vampire who would draw the very life out of Manley. Yet he is no more impressed with her boast that she has earned sev-eral degrees than with her wearing a muscle ointment as an aphrodisiac. He discerns instinctively that the way to penetrate Hulga's virginity is not sexu-ally but intellectually. With acute moral insight, Pointer discerns what Hulga loves most: it is not her maidenhead but the emblem of her crippled condi-tion, her wooden leg. As the outward and visible sign of her bitter inward grievance, the prosthesis is far more precious than her virginity: "She was as sensitive about the artificial leg as a peacock about his tail. No one ever touched it but her. She took care of it as someone else would his soul, in pri-vate, and almost with her own eyes turned away" (CW, 281). Hulga has fetishized her resentment against God and the world. She has become like the man whom Kierkegaard described as once being offered happiness on a proverbial silver platter, only to reply, "How dare you take away my unhappi-ness, my only raison d'être?"

Pointer knows, in the darkened heart of his own nihilism, that to steal Hulga's wooden leg is to inflict the utmost devastation: it is to destroy the very icon of her faith. At first she tries to console herself that, in removing her wooden appendage, she is performing an act of secular self-liberation akin to salvation: "It was like losing her own life and finding it again, miraculously, in his" (CW, 281). But Pointer knows better than to hallow the raw sensate act he hopes to perform with her. Seeing that Hulga has ludicrously deified herself, Manley spreads before her the condoms and pornographic cards and whis-key flask contained in his hollowed-out version of the Bible. The narrator de-scribes him as "one presenting offerings at the shrine of a goddess" (CW, 282). Pointer is not about to genuflect before this Heideggerian priestess; her wooden limb is but another trophy — akin to the glass eye he stole from another woman — to be added to the bizarre prizes he has seized in exercising his will-to-power. Horrified at her discovery that Manley is no gullible Christian, she pushes him off her. Yet he is able to relish a triumph over Hulga far more pleasurable than sex, as he declares his nihilistic unbelief to the virginal nihilist:

> "I may sell Bibles but I know which end is up and I wasn't born yesterday and I know where I'm going! . . . And I'll tell you another thing, Hulga," using the name as if he didn't think very much of it, "you ain't so smart. I been believing in nothing ever since I was born!" (CW, 283)

Next to The Misfit's final judgment of the Grandmother in "A Good Man Is Hard to Find" and the Wellesley student's calling Ruby Turpin a warthog who should "go back to hell where you came from" in "Revelation," this is perhaps the most celebrated line in all of O'Connor's work. It reveals that the core of nihilism is no mere mental worldview but a calloused way of life, a cold and heartless bent toward annihilation. Whereas the ineffectual Hulga can merely *think* the nihilism she has learned from Heidegger, the monstrous Manley brashly *enacts* his deadly philosophy. He sees that a universe whose basis lies in what-is-not invites a dreadful negation of what-is, and so he delights in sheer self-assertion and destruction. If Manley were not such an obstreperous individualist, this hick Heideggerian might become one of the parentless officials whom Ernst Jünger envisioned as operating the Nazi state. And if he did not have utter scorn for her whining self-pity, Hulga might have become his secretary.

Because he has a perverse sort of integrity, Manley Pointer will probably become a successful confidence man. Hulga, by contrast, faces even worse humiliations than she has already suffered, for she will have to yell down for her mother and Mrs. Freeman to come rescue her. They will no doubt utter new and worse banalities about the real trouble that this "girl" has gotten herself into. Their prim moralizing may drive Hulga into an even deeper nihilism of perpetual victimhood. We last glimpse her as she lies stranded in the hayloft, her churning face and bewildered eyes squinting after Pointer as he flees across the field. In her blinded vision, he appears to be a water-walking Christ: "She saw his blue figure struggling successfully across the green speckled lake" (CW, 283). Like The Misfit, Hulga may discover that Manley's final taunt fills her brain-tree like a flock of crows cawing out to her, not in japing mockery but redeeming comedy. Pointer is, in fact, Hopewell's unintentional savior, having stolen not so much her wooden leg as her false faith. It's an irony that Hulga may finally celebrate if she begins reading Reinhold Niebuhr rather than Martin Heidegger:

> What is funny about us is precisely that we take ourselves too seriously. We are rather insignificant little bundles of energy and vitality in a vast organization of life. But we pretend that we are the very center of this organization. This pretension is ludicrous; and its absurdity increases with our lack of awareness of it. The less we are able to laugh at ourselves the more it becomes necessary for others to laugh at us.[35]

The narrator, often assuming Mrs. Hopewell's viewpoint, laughs at Hulga throughout the story by referring to her as "the girl." Though no analyst of the human condition, Mrs. Hopewell herself knows that there is something childish and ludicrous about her daughter's thought and behavior. "It seemed to Mrs. Hopewell that every year [Joy-Hulga] grew less like other people and more like herself — bloated, rude, and squint-eyed" (CW, 268). Having neither church nor creed to give her life moral formation and thus communal shape, Hulga has descended into an uglifying solipsism. Now at last she has the chance to become what she and all others are called to be, a creature utterly unlike her innately sinful self. She has suffered a blessed loss, a saving devastation, a deflowering not of her sexual virginity but of her virginal nihilism. If only by the negation of her Nothingness, she has been potentially freed for a positive life of communion with God and her mother — and perhaps even with the small-minded Mrs. Freeman.

## The Primal Relation: Parents and Children

The question of suffering was, for Flannery O'Connor, never a theoretical concern to be examined at a safe critical distance. She spent her last fourteen years dying from the acute lupus erythematosus that she had inherited from her father. It required her to give up her independent life in the North, to return to the South, to live in a small Georgia town, and to be put under the care of her unintellectual mother. "This is a Return I have faced," she wrote to a friend pondering a similar recourse southward, "and when I faced it I was roped and tied and resigned the way it is necessary to be resigned to death, and largely because I thought it would be the end of any creation, any writ-

---

35. Reinhold Niebuhr, "Humour and Faith," in *Discerning the Signs of the Times* (New York: Charles Scribner's Sons, 1946), p. 120.

ing, any WORK from me" (HB, 224). O'Connor had cause for her fears: she was confined in frightful isolation from the intellectual currents wherein she had hoped to live and work. To one friend she wrote, ever so poignantly, that she was "afflicted with time" (HB, 91). To another she offered sardonic comment on her life at Andalusia, the grandiose name of her family's ordinary farm outside Milledgeville: "This season we have had three peachickens hatch and have killed one rattlesnake. Otherwise nothing goes on around here" (HB, 336). Yet in only a single published letter does O'Connor confess her frustration: "Cheers and Screams," it is signed (HB, 240).

O'Connor's impatience was prompted, at least in part, by the lack of comprehension of her work shown by her widowed mother, Regina Cline O'Connor. Though she was a woman of enormous practical skills, Mrs. O'Connor offered her daughter little spiritual and cultural companionship. When she once asked her daughter whether she was making the best use of her talent, since so few people could enjoy and be inspired by her books, O'Connor raged at her mother's blindness: "This always leaves me shaking and speechless, raises my blood pressure 140 degrees, etc. All I can ever say is, if you have to ask you'll never know" (HB, 326). Yet the note of complaint is sounded only rarely in her letters. Wry acceptance is her ordinary response. O'Connor explains her mother's slow progress through *The Violent Bear It Away* in expressions of self-irony: "All the time she is reading I know she would like to be in the yard digging. I think the reason I am a short story writer," she concludes, "is so my mother can read my work in one sitting" (HB, 340). Once when my professor and friend, the late Paul Wells Barrus, was visiting the O'Connors at Andalusia, Flannery invited him to attend the evening service of Benediction. As they arrived at the Sacred Heart Church, Barrus assumed that Regina would park the car and then join them for the service. Instead, she deposited them at the church and summarily announced, "Y'all go pray while I get the groceries."

Several of O'Connor's stories feature frustrated intellectual sons or daughters (usually in their thirties and thus well past the age when they should still be dependent on parents) living at home in reliance on their mothers: Julian in "Everything That Rises Must Converge," Hulga in "Good Country People," Asbury in "The Enduring Chill," Wesley and Schofield in "Greenleaf." Because most of these mothers are culturally uncouth and racially benighted, some critics have made a Freudian reading of Flannery's relationship with her mother, interpreting the stories as the covert confession of her own Electra complex. An atheist spinster such as Hulga Hopewell thus becomes a secret cipher of O'Connor's deep sexual frustration and bitter hatred of both God and her mother. These critics regard O'Connor's waspish intellectuals who chafe against parental provincialism as an unwitting act of self-disclosure, the confession of an aesthetic and personal martyrdom at the hands of a philistine mother. Yet when Betty Hester sought to read O'Connor's work in these reductive psycho-sexual terms, O'Connor replied wisely if tartly that her fiction could meet the test of authenticity only if it revealed "something about life colored by the writer, not about the writer colored by life" (HB, 158).

Insofar as O'Connor's stories are in fact confessional, the chief target of her satire is surely the ungrateful sons and daughters, not their well-meaning mothers. O'Connor may have come to understand the theological quality of the parent-child relation through her reading of Dostoevsky. For him, it is the primal relationship: our regard for our parents is the most fundamental index of our moral and religious character. Though old Fyodor Karamazov is a despicable creature in nearly every way, deserving the scorn that three of his four sons have for him, he nonetheless remains their father. To kill him in thought or word or deed is to slay the very source of their being and, in a very real sense, to kill God as well. In Dostoevsky's world, parricide is always tantamount to deicide: it is the ultimately nihilistic act.

Many of O'Connor's protagonists are tempted by such nihilistic and parricidal attitudes. Like O'Connor herself, they are free of all the more obvious sins — racism, hypocrisy, bigotry, and the like — but they are devoured by the primal sin of wanting to kill off a parent. If O'Connor's fiction reveals anything "about the writer colored by life," it discloses that she came to see herself as occupying a spiritual condition far deadlier than her mother's: she was tempted by the nihilistic desire to scorn the woman to whom she owed her very existence. It is thus O'Connor's brainy young ingrates, not their small-minded mothers, who receive the most terrible comeuppance in her stories. While her fiction contains a few unflattering likenesses of Regina Cline O'Connor, it offers far uglier likenesses of Flannery herself. She came to see, in fact, that her mother's deep and lasting love was the greatest of gifts. Flannery returned it in kind, for while their relationship was no doubt tense and difficult at times, the daughter never wavered in her devotion to the mother. Having no mastery of practical things, for example, O'Connor admired her mother's savoir-faire. That Regina O'Connor could shop for a new herd bull without pondering the Freudian implications of her act was an occasion for the daughter's amusement and delight. O'Connor also relished the idea of acquiring a dog whom she would name "Spot" in order to declare, "Out, damned Spot," without her mother's catching the literary allusion. O'Connor confessed, somewhat ruefully, that her function at her mother's high-society tea parties was to cover the stain on the sofa, even as she was charmed by her mother's uncomprehending interest in literary things:

> "Who is this Kafka?" she says. "People ask me." A German Jew, I says. . . . He wrote a book about a man that turns into a roach. "Well, I can't tell people that," she says. "Who is this Evalin Wow?" (HB, 33).

If Mrs. O'Connor never mastered the names of modern writers, she displayed considerable wisdom in dealing with one of Flannery's mystically inclined friends. The visitor to Andalusia had decided to lie down on the cold November ground in the hope, she said, of obtaining a more "sacramental" perspective on the universe. Astonished at so bizarre a practice, Regina admonished the woman to get up lest she catch a death of cold: "Can't you look at things standing up?" In two days' time the guest indeed fell ill, prompting Flannery's approving remark: "You can't get ahead of mother" (HB, 438). It was with deep filial gratitude, therefore, that O'Connor confessed to Cecil Dawkins the wrongness of her early belief that she could write only at several removes from her roots. It was a notion so false and potentially nihilistic that it required a radical corrective: "I would certainly have persisted in that delusion had I not got very ill and had to come home. The best of my writing has been done here" (HB, 230).

## Suffering, Death, and the Return of Talent to God

Flannery O'Connor's mind was wonderfully concentrated by the sentence of death, as Samuel Johnson prophesied. It enabled her to see, with uncommon clarity, that to prepare for death is the greatest of privileges. She agreed with Dostoevsky that the loss of belief in immortality is the chief sign of our nihilism. Even such a non-Christian as George Orwell confessed that our assumption that life ends in nothingness has made for a terrible moral evisceration of both our public and private existence. Mortalism is the name given to our conviction, succinctly summarized by Bertrand Russell, that when we die we rot. Mortalism slides easily into nihilism. Rather than fearing God as our ancestors did, we now fear death; and so our scientific projects and materialist greed are driven by a massive dread of extinction. Hence our own personal desire to die quickly and cheaply, preferably during our sleep, and without bother to anyone else. We do not trust our families to help us die, and we do not want to make a painful preparation for death.

For Flannery O'Connor, by contrast, her fourteen-year siege of illness came as a strange blessing: it protected her against the presumption and complacency endemic to an open-ended life; it enabled her to prepare for her own dying. Hence her gnomic response to a woman perplexed by Christians who have failed to recognize that "nobody would have paid any attention to Jesus if he hadn't been a martyr but had died at the age of eighty of athletes [sic] foot." "She was orthodox and didn't know it," O'Connor replied (CW, 985). The very brevity of Christ's life, O'Connor hints, provided its enormous intensity and purpose. That Jesus set his face like flint toward Jerusalem, refusing to be turned aside even by his chief disciple, reveals that he would bring in his kingdom of life even at the cost of his death. In a similar way, O'Connor's certain terminus served to focus her own life: it enabled her, in the fine old Catholic phrase, to make a good death. "I have never been anywhere but sick," she wrote to Betty Hester in 1956. "In a sense sickness is a place, more instructive than a long trip to Europe, and it's always a place where there's no company, where nobody can follow. Sickness before death is a very appropriate thing and I think those who don't have it miss one of God's mercies" (HB, 163). O'Connor's letters reveal the immense courage with which she faced the inexorable course of her illness. The sound of self-pity is never to be heard. What we find, instead, is a sardonic sense of acceptance, as in this jaunty letter to Maryat Lee in 1958:

> You didn't know I had a Dread Disease didja? Well I got one. My father died of the same stuff at the age of 44 but the scientists hope to keep me here until I am 96. I owe my existence and cheerful countenance to the pituitary glands of thousands of pigs butchered daily in Chicago Illinois at the Armour packing plant. If pigs wore garments I wouldn't be worthy to kiss the hems of them. They have been supporting my presence in this world for the last seven years. (CW, 1063)

Robert Lowell recognized this same angularity of mind and spirit during their time together at Yaddo in the late 1940s. He observed that, as a writer in her early twenties suffering from unidentified aches, O'Connor had already "found her themes and style, knew she wouldn't marry, would be Southern, shocking and disciplined. . . . In a blunt, disdainful yet somehow very unpretentious and modest way . . . she knew how good she was." When O'Connor died in 1964, Lowell remembered her, despite her fifteen years of confinement in Milledgeville under the watchful care of her mother, as "less passive and dependent than anyone" else he knew. She remained for him a "commanding, grim, witty child, who knew she was destined to live painfully and in earnest, a hero, rather like a nun or Catholic saint with a tough innocence, well able to take on her brief, hardworking, hard, steady, splendid and inconspicuous life."[36]

O'Connor refused to make her illness the defining event of her life, a condition to be endlessly mined as the ore of her fiction. Nor did she approach her dying by way of a sentimental piety, rolling her eyes heavenward in glib affirmation that the will of God must be done, no matter the cost to her. To one of her last letters she added a poignant postscript: "Prayers requested. I am sick of being sick" (HB, 581). Her lupus was a harsh destiny that she could accept only with appropriate irony. "I can with one eye squinted take it all as a blessing," she declares. "What you have to measure out, you come to observe closer, or so I tell myself" (HB, 57). The final phrase acknowledges the doubt that is never far from true faith. "When I ask myself how I believe, I have no satisfactory answer, no assurances at all, no feeling at all. I can only say . . . Lord, I believe, help my unbelief. All I can say about my love of God, is, Lord, help me in my lack of it" (HB, 92).

O'Connor was especially short-fused with anyone who attributed saintliness to her suffering. When an overzealous correspondent declared O'Connor to be near to the crucified Christ for being stricken ill, she replied firmly that affliction afforded her no special occasion for her own *imitatio Christi*: "I guess what you say about suffering being a shared experience with Christ is true, but then it should be true of every experience that is not sinful" (HB, 527). Two of her most revealing confessions came near the end of her life, as she comically confessed that she would never become a little old lady in tennis shoes. "I haven't suffered to speak of in my life," she declared, "and I don't know any more about the redemption than anybody else" (HB, 536). Writing to Roslyn Barnes, a young Catholic lay volunteer disappointed with her teaching mission in South America, O'Connor penned a remarkable testament of faith in the midst of spiritual suffering and physical anguish: "The Lord will have something to teach you there. I have never been anywhere in my life that it wasn't the place I was supposed to be — no matter how it looked at the time." Hence her deep conviction that life is not a Sophoclean tragedy but a Dantesque comedy, as she explains to a friend:

> Naw, I don't think life is a tragedy. Tragedy is something that can be explained by the professors. Life is the will of God and this cannot be defined by the professors; for which all thanksgiving. I think it is impossible to live and not to grieve but I am always suspicious of my own grief lest it

36. Quoted in Paul Mariani, *Lost Puritan: A Life of Robert Lowell* (New York: W. W. Norton, 1994), p. 327.

be self-pity in sheeps [sic] clothing. And the worst thing is to grieve for the wrong reason, for the wrong loss. Altogether it is better to pray than to grieve; and it is greater to be joyful than to grieve. But it takes more grace to be joyful than any but the greatest have. (CW, 928-29)

Not the least remarkable quality of Flannery O'Connor's faith in the face of illness is her joyful humor. Asked about her story title "The Lame Shall Enter First," O'Connor replied that the halt and the crippled will approach the kingdom ahead of everyone else by knocking them aside with their canes and crutches and wheel chairs. To a reporter who asked, with astonishing stupidity, whether O'Connor's illness was of any consequence to her fiction, she replied, "No, since for my writing I use my head and not my feet." Even on her deathbed she remained alert to life's madcap comedy. Though she complained that hospital food tasted like stewed Kleenex, she found one of her nurses, whose favorite grammatical construction was "it were," to be hysterically funny. The nurse made O'Connor laugh so hard that she could not decide "whether the Lord is giving me a reward or a punishment. She didn't know she was funny and it was agony to laugh and I reckoned she increased my pain about 100%" (HB, 569). On another occasion, when she was rendered so weak and giddy by loss of blood that she thought she was actually dying, O'Connor reported hearing not the celestial choruses of Palestrina but the idiotic lines of a folk song: "Wooden boxes without topses,/They were shoes for Clementine" (HB, 578).

O'Connor's letters collected in *The Habit of Being* have been compared to Keats's as among the most important works in our entire epistolary tradition. Like his, her letters reveal both the character and the intention of the writer's art. This collection must also be numbered as one of the most spiritually astringent books of our time. To read O'Connor's letters is to follow her remarkable progress toward death and to encounter the thorny wisdom that she derived from it. As the end nears, O'Connor becomes ever briefer but never less tough-minded. Writing to Janet McKane, a primary school teacher in New York whom O'Connor had known only through her letters, she offers thanks at her final Christmas in 1963 "for everything, mostly for being" (HB, 555). Less than six weeks before her death, she displays a clear-eyed realism: "They expect me to improve, or so they say. I expect anything that happens" (HB, 587).

O'Connor described death as "the most significant position life offers the Christian" (MM, 110). She confessed that most of her stories end in death because "death has always been a brother to my imagination." There is nothing macabre about this conviction, nor can it be dismissed as an obsession produced by her father's early death and her own fatal illness. O'Connor had finished all but the final revisions of *Wise Blood,* a novel that ends with two gruesome deaths, by the time she discovered her disease in 1952. The claims she made about the centrality of death for the Christian life are but standard biblical teaching: "LORD, make me to know mine end, and the measure of my days, what it is; that I may know how frail I am" (Ps. 39:4). "So teach us to number our days," the psalmist again petitions, "that we may apply our hearts unto wisdom" (90:12).

To prepare for our death, by the ordering of our loves to the love of God, is to prepare not only for true life in eternity but also for right living in this present world. It is also to acquire the one antidote against the nihilism that engulfs modern life. O'Connor found that her own Christian existence as an artist was figured profoundly in Jesus' parable of the man who multiplied his gifts, so that when his master returned he was able to give good account of them. Not, of course, that we can give anything to the God who, as the giver of "every good . . . and perfect gift" (James 1:17), is the fount of all bounty; but that, just as this God gives himself in his gifts, so can we give ourselves to him in rightly returning them. "The human comes before art," O'Connor wrote to Elizabeth Hester. "You do not write the best you can for the sake of art but for the sake of returning your talent increased to the invisible God to use or not use as he sees fit. Resignation to the will of God does not mean that you stop resisting evil or obstacles, it means that you leave the outcome out of your personal considerations. It is the most concern coupled with the least concern" (HB, 419).

"It seems to me," Flannery O'Connor declared, "that all good stories are about conversion, about a character's changing" (HB, 275). Whether secular or religious in their origins and intentions, novels and stories having lasting merit always depict characters faced with moral challenges and spiritual quandaries that demand their transformation. Whether these tests are met for good or ill, the characters are changed: they are converted. The New Testament word for conversion — *metanoia* — literally means to alter one's mind, to revolutionize the entire course of one's life, to turn around, to travel in the opposite direction. In most of O'Connor's stories the central characters undergo a painful confrontation with their own pride and presumption, behold themselves in the blinding light of divine grace and, if only at the last moment of their lives, come to radical conversion. Neither in her novels nor her stories does she take her protagonists beyond their sudden and drastic conversion; we are rarely shown the consequences of this total turnabout in their lives.

O'Connor had a good deal of Christian tradition on her side. Most conversion narratives, whether fictional or historical, end with the life-changing reversal. St. Augustine concludes the biographical section of his *Confessions* with his conversion in the Milan garden, his baptism shortly thereafter, his mystical experience at Ostia with his mother, Monica, and, finally, with her death and burial. Augustine apparently felt no need to recount the character of his life beyond his all-determining reversal in the year 432. Likewise, John Henry Newman finishes the monumental account of his conversion from Anglicanism to Catholicism, *Apologia Pro Vita Sua*, by declaring: "From the time I became a Catholic, of course, I have no further history of my religious opinions to narrate." Newman confesses that his mind has been theologically active during the intervening years, but that he is finally done with doubt — at least with any doubt that could undermine his faith or require him to alter his theology in fundamental ways.[1] The small and large acts of charity, the daily yieldings and resistances to temptation, the incremental gains and losses that characterize the Christian life — these he deemed of interest only to himself and God, and thus unworthy of public display.[2] So it is in Evelyn Waugh's *Brideshead Revisited:* Lord Marchmain's deathbed return to the Catholic faith brings the novel to its climactic conclusion.

Yet Flannery O'Connor was far from uninterested in the transformed life that conversion prompts. She lived, as we have seen, with extraordinary Christian devotion, both as writer and believer. She regarded both her writing and her believing as intrinsic to her vocation, which she understood to mean two noncontradictory things: the general summons to cast everything aside and to follow Jesus Christ, as well as the particular call to work out one's salvation amid the often fearful circumstances of one's own life — in her case, through the discipline of her art. This double understanding of vocation accords with the church's teachings, and it also illuminates her fiction. The aim of this penultimate chapter is to trace Flannery O'Connor's understanding of vocation by way of six particular emphases: (1) that Christian vocation acquires a new urgency with the collapse of the old Christendom, an opportunity to recover its original meaning as a call to the Christian life itself; (2) that O'Connor's uncouth prophet Mason Tarwater responds to this urgency with the requisite vehemence and intolerance, at once outward and inward, required at this late hour; (3) that Tarwater's nephew George Rayber rejects such an intolerant vocation as unmitigated madness; (4) that Rayber's intolerant kind of humanism has been produced by a disturbing convergence of Enlightenment political and religious forces; (5) that, against the grain of her age, O'Connor was willing to give drastic witness concerning abortion; and (6) that she called her audience not only to a willing mortification of the sinful flesh but also to the purity of heart that enables true sexuality.

1. John Henry Newman, *Apologia Pro Vita Sua,* ed. David J. DeLaura (New York: W. W. Norton, 1968), p. 184.

2. Bunyan is a notable exception to this rule. He wrote a long "relation" of his 12-year imprisonment in the Bedford jail, and the final page of his conversion narrative contains a remarkable confession of his constant need for reconversion: "I have sometimes seen more in a line of the Bible than I could well tell how to stand under, and yet at another time the whole Bible hath been to me as dry as a stick; or rather, my heart hath been so dead and dry unto it, that I could not conceive the least drachm of refreshment, though I have looked it all over" (John Bunyan, *Grace Abounding* [New York: Dutton, 1966], p. 102).

## The Collapse of Christendom and the Vocation to Radical Testimony

"When you can assume that your audience holds the same beliefs you do," O'Connor opined in one of her most celebrated pronouncements, "you can relax a little and use more normal means of talking to it; when you have to assume that it does not, then you have to make your vision apparent by shock — to the hard of hearing you shout, and for the almost-blind you draw large and startling figures" (MM, 34). O'Connor was referring not only to her secular audience as needing to be startled into attention; she was no less worried about her churchly readers. In reviewing a novel by Paul Horgan, a fellow Catholic who wrote from a Christian humanist viewpoint, O'Connor observed that "he seems able to assume an audience which has not lost its belief in Christian doctrine."[3] For O'Connor, such an assumption is long past. Christian humanism may have once had the power to disperse the enveloping miasma, especially as Eric Voegelin recounts its rise and fall in his massive *Order and History*. In her reviews of his work, O'Connor commends Voegelin for discerning the deep complementarity between God's miraculous self-identification in Israel and the church on the one hand, and pagan culture's natural longing for a return to its source on the other.[4] Yet she had little hope of finding a new medieval synthesis for our age. The hour is far too late, she confessed, for anything so serene and sensible. Grace does not complete and perfect nature in a smooth and seamless way, as Aquinas is sometimes wrongly interpreted; the image of God in man must be wrenched from its unnatural thralldom to false lords in both the church and the world. Vocation, the summons to live out the privileges and requirements of the Christian faith, is the point of this most radical wrenching.

Karl Barth notes that our understanding of vocation as a calling fit only for pastors and missionaries, for priests and monks and nuns, is largely the product of the phenomenon that we have come to call Christendom.[5] Once Christianity had triumphed in the West, especially after Constantine had made it the official religion of the Roman Empire, the gospel became a natural inheritance that one received unconsciously, almost by osmosis, through the very fact of one's birth:

---

3. *"The Presence of Grace" and Other Book Reviews*, compiled by Leo J. Zuber (Athens, GA: University of Georgia Press, 1983), p. 19.

4. Ibid., pp. 60-61, 67-68, 70-71.

5. It could be argued that this division of Christians into two tiers was but the initial step toward the later reduction of vocation to mere career choice.

> [T]o be a Christian was to live in the tradition which was shaped, or par-
> tially shaped, by Christianity. It was to be brought up and educated in the
> context of the history in which, side by side with the ancient world and
> the different national traditions, side by side with ancient and modern
> learning as it grew and blossomed and bore fruit on this soil, Christian
> influences also helped to shape and determine society in a more or less
> penetrating way. To be a Christian was thus to share the inheritance visi-
> ble in the variously described complex of Christian ideas, principles,
> habits and customs, or in the circle of the Christian Church. It was to take
> these seriously and to find nourishment also in these elements of the na-
> tive background.[6]

Barth does not dismiss the rich legacy of Christendom. It gave entire
nations and peoples what he calls "a very positive relation to Christianity."
Being a good citizen and being a good Christian became deeply intertwined,
and they were high callings indeed. Nor were the accomplishments of Christendom confined to the medieval Catholic world alone. Liberal Protestantism achieved its own version of Christendom throughout much of Europe
and the United States in the nineteenth century. Many of the benefits that we
take for granted — education for the masses, prison and labor reform, humane treatment for the mentally ill, the abolition of slavery, and the freeing
of women from stereotyped roles — were the products of Protestant Christendom. Yet these enormous triumphs were bought at considerable cost. It
eventually meant that no real vocation was required of Christians, no living
faith that must be radically renewed in the church and perpetually given by
God, rather than naturally received and culturally bestowed. Being Christian
became an attachment, says Barth, "implicitly and secondarily to Jesus
Christ, but explicitly and primarily to a family, nation, culture and civilization."[7] The most fundamental definition of vocation was lost: "vocation as
the process in which man becomes a Christian."[8] A massive Christian atheism has been the result, a church living amidst a culture that has effectively
edged the triune God off the scene.

> The idea of Christianity which is automatically given and received with
> the rest of our inheritance has now become historically impossible, no

6. Karl Barth, *Church Dogmatics*, 4 vols., trans. Geoffrey W. Bromiley (Edinburgh: T&T
Clark, 1934-69), III/2, p. 522.
7. Ibid.
8. Ibid., p. 513.

matter how tenaciously it may linger on and even renew itself in various attempts at restoration by the Church and the world. The Christian West, i.e., the society in which Christian and non-Christian existence came together, or seemed to do so, no longer exists in the city or in the peace of the most remote village hamlet. Even in Spain it no longer exists. Hence [one] can no longer be brought up as a member of it. [One's] Christianity can no longer derive from the fact that [one] is a member of it. . . . It may be argued that to-day even from the historical standpoint there can be no escaping the startling recognition that [one's] being as a Christian is either grounded in [one's] vocation or it is simply an illusion which seems beautiful perhaps in the after-glow of a time vanished beyond recall.[9]

Longer and perhaps more fully than anywhere else — longer even than in Italy or Spain, more fully even than in Ireland or Poland — old-fashioned Christendom held fast in the American South. William Willimon wittily suggests that its demise occurred only in 1963, when the Fox Theater in his hometown of Greenville, South Carolina, refused to close on Sunday evenings to accommodate the local Protestant churches. It was not latter-day Visigoths and Vandals who invaded and overwhelmed Christendom; instead, the local outpost of Hollywood won this skirmish to determine who would provide the essential formative ethos for the young. Willimon joins Stanley Hauerwas in confessing that a religious sea change had occurred:

[O]ur parents had never worried about whether we would grow up Christian. The church was the only show in town. On Sundays, the town closed down. One could not even buy a gallon of gas. There was a traffic jam on Sunday morning at 9:45, when all went to their respective Sunday schools. By overlooking much that was wrong in that world — it was a racially segregated world, remember — people saw a world that looked good and right. In taking a child to Sunday school, parents affirmed everything that was good, wholesome, reasonable, and American. Church, home, and state formed a national consortium that worked together to instill "Christian values." People grew up Christian simply by being lucky enough to be born in places such as Greenville, South Carolina, or Pleasant Grove, Texas.[10]

9. Ibid., pp. 524-25.
10. Stanley M. Hauerwas and William H. Willimon, *Resident Aliens: Life in the Christian Colony* (Nashville: Abingdon, 1989), p. 16.

When being Christian becomes the natural and obvious and expected thing, then the gospel becomes the wallpaper of one's life, the religious equivalent of background music. Vocation, in turn, is transformed into a "special" calling: to enter "full-time Christian service" or else to make one's witness in the spare time that is left over from one's secular trade or profession. What is far worse, it becomes entirely secularized into a synonym for one's career. In all three cases, the central meaning of vocation is largely lost. In the Bible, by contrast, vocation is the call of God to do his will in the world, making witness to his kingdom. The scriptural pattern is quite straightforward: it always entails an utter surprise, as God lays his claim on people quite without regard to their preparation or even their qualifications. Abraham, the wandering Aramaean shepherd, is summoned to leave his native country and to become the father of a "new people"; the stammering Moses is called to lead Israel out of Egyptian slavery; the boy Samuel is chosen rather than the elderly priest; Gideon is surprised by an angel while he is thrashing wheat; Amos the Tekoan tender of mulberry trees and sheep is commanded to prophesy against his own people; Elijah throws the mantle of prophecy over the startled Elisha while he is plowing; Jeroboam and Jehu are unexpectedly anointed to become kings by God's own command; Isaiah and Ezekiel are given sudden visions of the Lord's majesty; the stuttering Jeremiah is addressed by a heavenly voice.

The New Testament pattern is much the same. Jesus himself has no calling, since his identity as the incarnate Son is already in full accord with his vocation from the Father. Instead, he calls others to be his disciples and apostles. Barth observes that Jesus does not even summon them to salvation in the popular sense; he does not offer them an invitation to gain paradise and avoid perdition,[11] at least not in any selfish sense. Jesus' summons is at once simple and scandalous: he calls men and women to lay aside all else and to join in the movement of his kingdom. Simon, Andrew, James, and John are not asked — as fishermen — to find their calling by way of their particular occupation, worthy as it is, but to "thow away everything" (as The Misfit puts it) and to follow him. They are to regard their entire lives as their vocation. As Christ's witnesses, they will possess an entirely new profession: they will become "fishers of men" (Matt. 4:19). The Fourth Gospel lacks

---

11. "Can the community of Jesus Christ . . . really be only, or at any rate essentially and decisively, a kind of institute of salvation? . . . Is not every form of egocentricity excused and even confirmed and sanctified, if egocentricity in this sacred form is the divinely willed meaning of Christian existence and [if] the Christian song of praise consists finally only in a many-tongued but monotonous *pro me, pro me,* and similar possessive expressions?" (Barth, *Church Dogmatics,* IV/3, Part 2, p. 567).

even such verbal summonses to the disciples. The sheer presence of Jesus suffices for them to know they have been called. Never is vocation a matter of talent or merit. Like Sarah before them, Hannah and Elizabeth are equally unsuited for becoming mothers of the "sons of promise," and so is the untutored Mary supremely unqualified to become the Mother of God. Their radical receptivity to the divine call is what sets these women apart. Even in the most dramatic of the New Testament conversion accounts, Saul's being struck blind on the road to Damascus, there is no emphasis on his credentials, much less on any existential crisis of decision. Saul knows that he is totally unworthy, since he was a persecutor of the church and thus of Christ himself. Yet his own sinfulness counts for nothing as compared to the calling of the newly named Paul: "But when it pleased God, who separated me from my mother's womb, and called me by his grace, to reveal his Son in me, that I might preach him among the heathen; immediately I conferred not with flesh and blood" (Gal. 1:15-16). Though he is a tentmaker rather than a fisherman or carpenter, Paul's vocation is to be an apostle, a witness to the gospel. He is to call others into the kingdom.

The scriptural pattern of vocation never entails anything akin to modern notions of private choice or personal preference. In each of the cases we have considered, the Word of the Lord was announced and heard and heeded. The resulting formula — "Thus saith the Lord" — is not an arrogation of authority to those who listened and followed, but exactly the opposite. It marks their acceptance of his Word as the only basis for their own preaching and teaching and writing. They are called to proclaim mercy and judgment that the world cannot proclaim to itself: "Eye hath not seen, nor ear heard, neither have entered into the heart of man, the things which God hath prepared for them that love him" (1 Cor. 2:9). Such untrammeled good news puts much less emphasis on the called than the Caller, as Hans Urs von Balthasar declares:

> Scripture's central concern is solely with God's operation, with the way he overcomes people and seizes them. Only occasionally, incidentally, does it record man's reaction; man's freedom becomes particularly visible when he hesitates, prevaricates, actually resists or, having laid hold of his mission, turns aside from it. Saul and Judas turn aside utterly, but David, Peter, and no doubt Jeremiah, turn aside to some extent, only to be recaptured by the power of their vocation. If this is possible in the case of the great vocations [which] they serve as the pillars of salvation history, it stands to reason that, out of the wealth of vocations stirred up by the Word, very many, indeed a vast number, may meet with no re-

223

sponse. [Hence] Jesus' saying, "Many are called, but few are chosen" (Mt. 20:16; 22:14).[12]

Flannery O'Connor's chief interest lies with characters who have met their vocations with positive, albeit agonizingly difficult, responses. Among the vast millions who have been summoned, they are the few who constitute Christ's "little flock" (Luke 12:32). After the collapse of American Christendom, first in the nineteenth-century North and then in the twentieth-century South, the summons to become and to remain a Christian cannot be anything other than wrenching. No longer can the Christian life be taken for granted; such a notion leads, as we have seen, to a churchly kind of atheism. Vocation to the life of faith entails an inward wrestling and sometimes even an outward violence.

## Mason Tarwater: Violent Prophet of the Kingdom of God

The figure of Mason Tarwater in Flannery O'Connor's second novel, *The Violent Bear It Away,* is her most convincing fictional portrait of Christian vocation as a summons to make startling witness for Christ in the world. The old man is obsessed with his vocation as a prophet. Like a latter-day Jonah, he urges God to rain down his wrath on a world that has forsaken its savior. He warns this "generation of vipers," as Jesus called it, "to flee from the wrath to come" (Matt. 3:7). To Tarwater's immense disappointment, the world does not listen. Far worse, even the Lord himself seems oblivious to Mason's reproaches. The flames do not fall, nor do the wicked writhe. Instead, the sun "rose and set, rose and set, on a world that turned from green to white and green to white and green to white again" (CW, 332). It is not the words of Matthew but of the book of Ecclesiastes that seem to disclose the divine inaction: "The sun also riseth, and the sun goeth down . . . and there is no new thing under the sun" (Eccles. 1:5, 9).

In his own primitive way, Tarwater is forced to confront the problem of historicism — the terrible successiveness of human events. History seems altogether as heartless as nature, a repetitive round whose only significance lies in the patterns we impose on it. Far from being a perplexity intrinsic to modernity, the bootlessness of history was an assumption that the early Christians took for granted. Paul, for example, believed that all events were

---

12. Hans Urs von Balthasar, *Theo-Drama: Theological Dramatic Theory,* Vol. III, *The Dramatis Personae: The Person in Christ,* ed. Graham Harrison (San Francisco: Ignatius Press, 1992), p. 265.

mysteriously linked, yet not forming any chain of unbroken progress but rather constituting a steady deterioration and imminent collapse. Christian vocation was and remains, against all assumptions about order and progress, a summons to a drastically different reading of history, as William Beardslee makes clear:

> Paul does not think of Christ as calling men to find meaning in or to renew the vitality of that pattern of human tradition and life which we call 'culture'. The social, intellectual, moral and aesthetic forms which constitute culture were for him primarily manifestations of the 'wisdom of this world', and stood in opposition to the new life given by Christ. . . . For him, men cannot find life through culture, or through its enrichment or renewal. Not only individual loyalties, but all the interlocking structures of power and of standards and values stand under the condemnation of God.[13]

Mason Tarwater's condemnations would seem, in their unremitting gloom, to be thoroughly Pauline. Yet they are not. Paul does not regard the divine Word as relentlessly negative and admonitory. Pauline censures are directed only at the sinful and collapsing world; he also insists that God is positively at work within history. First in the Hebrew and Jewish people, then in the life and death and resurrection of Christ, God acts within space and time. Since the very origin of things, the Father and Son and Spirit have been creating the one universal community. The scope of divine action has an ever-narrowing focus, until it arrives finally at Golgotha; for this tenanted tree of divine mercy and judgment has roots deep enough to encircle all the dead and arms wide enough to embrace all the living. The old prophet's "rage of vision" was not given, he learns, in order to incinerate the unfaithful and to vindicate himself. As his name indicates, Mason is meant to build up and not to tear down, to construct something good with the stones of redeemed human recalcitrance. He is called, as the narrator makes evident, for a life devoted to "saving and not destruction. . . . He had learned enough to hate the destruc-

---

13. William A. Beardslee, *Human Achievement and Divine Vocation in the Message of Paul* (Naperville, IL: Alec. R. Allenson, 1961), p. 12. Beardslee does not deny, of course, that the propagation of the gospel requires Christians to make use of the many goods that civilization provides. The spread of the gospel can thus have the secondary effect of renewing culture, even when this is not its primary intention: "Paul's thought cannot provide a base from which to justify Christianity as something which might 'save civilization'. It can, however, suggest the possibility that work done for other than cultural goals may also set free forces which will, incidentally to their conscious purpose, effect a partial renewal of the patterns of cultural activity" (p. 13).

tion that had to come and not [to hate] all that was going to be destroyed" (CW, 332-33).

As a lone prophet who belongs to no visible church, this proclaimer of a radically communal kingdom appears to be a contradiction in terms. Yet he recognizes that, unlike any benefit the world might bestow, the baptism of his two nephews will make them members of the universal Christian family, his kinsmen in faith far more than blood. Just as one does not elect one's parents, neither can one choose God as the ultimate parent. The triune Lord sovereignly wills not to confine his communal life within the Godhead but to gather a people unto himself. Even when baptism is a freely chosen deed rather than the decision of parents and godparents, it signifies much more than one's own decision to follow Jesus. Baptism is for Christians what circumcision is for Jews: a public sign that the universal God of Israel and Christ and the church has claimed believers for life in a particular community that lives by its outward and visible practices. Baptism is thus a political act through and through: it is a radical transfer of allegiance and citizenship from one regime to another, from a polity that is corrupt and perishing to the only one that is being redeemed and shall stand forever. Not even the gates of hell will be able to prevail against its onrushing power. Baptism is a sacramental and regenerative rite precisely because it is not a merely human choice; it is God's own adoption of his people into his community.

St. Augustine learned this difficult truth in the summer of 382, after he had embraced a neo-Platonic kind of Christianity but remained undecided about his baptism. He recalled the story of two friends who had disputed this very question. Victorinus had mastered the Scriptures and studied all the Christian books, yet Simplicianus insisted that he would not consider him a Christian until he was baptized into Christ's body. "Then do walls make Christians?"[14] Victorinus impatiently and perhaps mockingly asked. The popular assumption of our time, shared by many Catholics no less than most Protestants, is that the answer is negative. The future bishop of Hippo, by contrast, remembered this story because he knew that Simplicianus required a positive response. The walls of the church — a metaphor for Christ's visible and earthly body — do in fact make Christians.

Mason Tarwater is no Augustine, but he would know from his reading of John 3:5 that Christians are initiated into the community of Christ's permanent and indelible life by being born not of flesh and blood, nor of inward and private conversion alone, but "of water and of the Spirit." This

14. Saint Augustine, *Confessions*, trans. Henry Chadwick (New York: Oxford University Press, 1992), VIII.ii.4: 136.

curmudgeonly Christian's first community of baptismal witnesses must be his own family, and so the old man seeks to propagate the gospel by inculcating it in his nearest kinfolk, especially the young. Tarwater wants to baptize children and to school them so deeply in Christian things that their character will be formed in the image of Christ, making them "laborers together with God" (1 Cor. 3:9). Yet his own children are beyond saving: his daughter has died in a car crash, and his only son has "gone to the devil." The old man has thus concentrated his prophetic vocation on his nephew Rayber, kidnapping him when he was only four. He immediately baptized the child in the hope of training him in Christian knowledge and wisdom. Though he was rescued after only four days, the adult Rayber remains embittered about his baptism at the hands of the old prophet. This school psychologist is determined, therefore, to give young Francis Marion Tarwater, the orphaned son of his late sister, a thoroughly unbaptized and secular upbringing.

Equally bent on taking this second child in the opposite direction — baptizing and forming him into a Christian — Mason Tarwater has again resorted to abduction. To ensure that the seven-year-old Francis will receive a vocation in the deepest Christian sense, the elderly prophet sequesters him at his remote rural outpost, a farm where faith is such an explosive fact that the place is appropriately named Powderhead. As if this abduction were not sufficient proof of his seriousness, Mason acts like a late incarnation of the Apostle Peter when Rayber comes to rescue the child. With the schoolteacher in the role of Malchus, Tarwater does not swing a sword but fires his shotgun, wounding Rayber in the leg, taking a wedge out of one ear, and leaving him perpetually hard of hearing.[15]

Having soon baptized Francis Marion, the prophet has also instructed the boy in the fundamentals of the faith. The uncouth prophet does not accept the attempt of modern education to produce future autonomous adults who will make up their own minds, deciding and defining things for themselves. Such training is not meant to form moral character but to produce a good consumer, a chooser of one's own "lifestyle" from a smorgasbord of options where Christian faith becomes merely another "preference." The prophet Tarwater seeks, instead, to help his grandnephew become faithful to the commitments that are intrinsic to baptismal life in Christ. He believes that time has order and meaning because God is orchestrating the true course of history — from creation through redemption to consummation.

---

15. This incident reminds me of a North Carolina radio evangelist whom I once heard commenting on this incident in Gethsemane. "It wasn't Peter's fault that old Malchus ducked," said the preacher, "'cause he shore wasn't aiming for no ear!"

Yet this positive temporal line has its negative counterpart, the horrendous legacy of evil. Like the divine, the demonic also embodies itself in specific individuals and events. The prophetic task of discernment, Mason teaches, is to identify the divergent lineages: the bright red line of redemption that is the boy's true legacy, and the dark arc of evil that would lead to his utter damnation. Accordingly, Tarwater has taught the boy "two complete histories, the history of the world, beginning with Adam, and the history of the schoolteacher . . ." (CW, 366).

Mason Tarwater is too orthodox a Christian to grant evil any sort of dualistic equality with good. He has not schooled the younger Tarwater in the full ancestry of the world's evildoers but rather in the strong roll call of biblical figures who have been radically summoned by God: "Abel and Enoch and Noah and Job, Abraham and Moses, King David and Solomon, and all the prophets, from Elijah who escaped death, to John whose severed head struck terror from a dish" (CW, 340).[16] That this list does not consist of the morally pure, but of a drunk and a doubter and a deceiver, a whiner and an adulterer and a schemer, reveals Mason Tarwater's profoundly biblical understanding of vocation. To be called as a Christian is not to become an ethically untainted person, much less the well-adjusted anthropoid that Rayber regards as a true human being. It is to become a person who lives *coram Deo*, constantly before God, in repentance and conversion.[17]

Like Jesus and the prophets, therefore, old Tarwater retreats to the wilderness for direct engagement with the Lord. O'Connor's narrator reports that he emerges from the forest looking "as if he had been wrestling with a wildcat." Like a latter-day Ezekiel, he is "full of the visions he had seen in [the wildcat's] eyes, wheels of light and strange beasts with giant wings of fire and four heads turned to the four points of the universe" (CW, 334). Whether in prophets ancient or modern, such dreadful confrontations cannot be discounted as wish projections. Young Tarwater recognizes this terrible truth

---

16. O'Connor agreed with Mason's approach to education:

Ours is the first age in history which has asked the child what he would tolerate learning. . . . In other ages the attention of children was held by Homer and Virgil, among others, but, by the reverse evolutionary process, that is no longer possible; our children are too stupid now to enter the past imaginatively. No one asks the student if algebra pleases him or if he finds it satisfactory that some French verbs are irregular, but if he prefers [John] Hersey to [Nathaniel] Hawthorne, his taste must prevail. . . . And if the student finds that [Hawthorne, for example] is not to his taste? Well, that is regrettable. Most regrettable. His taste should not be consulted; it is being formed. (MM, 137, 140)

17. This is Barth's interpretation of Genesis 17:1: "I am the Almighty God; walk before me and be thou perfect." See *Dogmatics in Outline* (New York: Harper Torchbooks, 1959), p. 49.

when the old prophet returns from one of his wilderness wrestlings with the Lord: "There was no fire in his uncle's eye and he spoke only of the sweat and stink of the cross, of being born again to die, and of spending eternity eating the bread of life . . ." (CW, 334). Mason Tarwater is like Ezekiel in another regard. Whether the captive Israelites heed or spurn his message matters much less than that God's presence be decisively marked: "And they, whether they will hear, or whether they will forbear, (for they are a rebellious house) yet shall know that there hath been a prophet among them" (Ezek. 2:5). Mason wants young Tarwater to be that prophet and to enact his own Christian vocation by baptizing Rayber's imbecilic son, Bishop.

Since Southern fundamentalism has not produced many pedobaptists, readers are often puzzled by the obsession of this backwoods John the Baptist with baptizing children. Why is he not an itinerant evangelist urging adults to repent of their sins and follow Christ in their own individual lives? Perhaps Tarwater is a paleo-Methodist who has retained John Wesley's belief in baptismal regeneration. Wesley himself declared, for example, that with baptism "a principle of grace is infused that cannot be lost except through long-continued wickedness."[18] The more profound reason for Mason's fanatical baptizing, however, lies in his radical sense of the Christian life as an outward affair of distinctive habits and practices far more than an interior life of individual spirituality. We never hear Mason urge any private conversion of the emotions. Whatever is emotionally born can emotionally die. Vocation, the old man understands, is an indefectible calling that is publicly signified through baptism, the irreversible act of incorporation into the body of Christ.

## George Rayber and the "Madness" of Prophetic Intolerance

George Rayber believes that a violent, kingdom-seizing prophet such as Mason Tarwater is certifiably insane. To Rayber, the very idea of vocation is fraudulent because there is no God to summon us to any task beyond our own desires. He scorns baptism as mere superstition, as veritable hocus-pocus — "only an empty act" (CW, 450). A man in his late thirties, Rayber

18. Methodist theologian Stephen Blakemore points out that, for Wesley, baptism unites children to the body of Christ by making them prevenient participants in salvation. The church's other practices are yet further means of grace — "grace upon grace" is the Methodist phrase — for enabling the Christian faith of young people to become fully their own in confirmation, thus being propelled toward a life whose aim is perfection and entire sanctification.

remains angrily obsessed with his childhood abduction and baptism, even though his parents rescued him from Tarwater after only four days. Convinced that his fundamental autonomy had been violated and thus that he is permanently scarred, he is determined to refute everything his Uncle Mason stands for. He is bitterly opposed, for example, to Jesus' insistence that the little ones should be allowed to approach him, since their simplicity and forthrightness are the material of the kingdom (Mark 10:14), complaining instead, "Children are cursed with believing" (CW, 376). They are not yet independent creatures capable of giving their informed consent. Personal formation must remain entirely the result, in his view, of one's own preferences rather than the guidance of families and churches and other character-shaping institutions.

Through an act of sheer will, Rayber boasts, he has disinfected himself of "the idiot hopes" and the "foolish violence" that old Mason had instilled in him. It would be better still for the world's children if they were never bothered with religion at all. Left to their own devices, they would become like him: adults who have been freed from the counterfeit need for a vocation. "The great dignity of man," Rayber declares, offering his latter-day version of Pico della Mirandola's sixteenth-century oration, "is his ability to say: I am born once and no more. What I can see and do for myself and my fellowman in this life is all of my portion and I'm content with it. It's enough to be a man" (CW, 437). Thus has Rayber set his intolerant humanism like flint against Old Tarwater's intolerant Christianity, and O'Connor requires the reader to choose between them.

As a school psychologist, George Rayber approaches his scientific studies with dispassionate analysis, not allowing any ties of gratitude or familial concern to limit his research. In the name of charity, he has invited the old prophet to live in his home. But for three months Rayber has covertly analyzed Mason, observing all his actions and asking sly questions, as the prophet later recognizes, "that meant more than one thing, planting traps around the house and watching him fall into them . . ." (CW, 331). Rayber's cold conclusion, duly published in a scholarly journal, is that the elderly prophet is a throwback to a primitive age, "a type that [is] almost extinct" (CW, 178). In perhaps his most heartless act, Rayber asks the unsuspecting Mason to read the conclusion of his report: "This fixation of being called by the Lord had its origin in insecurity. He needed the assurance of a call and so he called himself" (CW, 378).

Mason Tarwater is enraged by this verdict on his divine vocation, the conclusion that, fearing subconsciously that his life lacked significance, he had manufactured his calling. The prophet is convinced, on the contrary, that his vocation springs from his painful encounter with the transcendent and unknown God who has miraculously identified himself in Israel and Christ. Mason is thus intolerant of those who ignore or deny this most profound of mysteries. He complains, for instance, that Rayber is cursed for not knowing that there are things he doesn't know. Just as a reverence for mystery opens life to infinite possibility, so does a repudiation of mystery produce a closed cosmos and a clamshell existence. It also reduces others to ciphers. Rayber's denial of the mystery of vocation leaves Old Tarwater feeling paralyzed, trapped, even mummified:

> For the length of a minute, he could not move. He felt he was tied hand and foot inside the schoolteacher's head, a space as bare and neat as the cell in the asylum, and was shrinking, drying up to fit it. His eyeballs swerved from side to side as if he were pinned in a straight jacket again. Jonah, Ezekiel, Daniel, he was at that moment all of them — the swallowed, the lowered, the enclosed. (CW, 378)

But Mason remains undaunted by Rayber's attempt to reduce his vocation to mere psychological need. For all his ranting, the old prophet goes to the heart of Christian vocation as Dietrich Bonhoeffer described it in his most celebrated single statement: "Whenever Christ calls us, his call leads us to death."[19] Rarely does the Christian life constitute a call to physical death by way of the world's obloquy and persecution; but it is always a summons to die to one's own arrogant presumptions. Old Mason confesses that he has faced both kinds of death, as divine judgment has seared his conscience like a branding iron:

> "Called myself!" the old man would hiss, "called myself!" This so enraged him that half the time he could do nothing but repeat it. "Called myself. I called myself. I, Mason Tarwater, called myself! Called myself to be beaten and tied up. Called myself to be spit on and snickered at. Called myself to be struck down in my pride. Called myself to be torn by the Lord's eye. Listen boy," he would say and grab the child by the straps of his overalls and shake him slowly, "even the mercy of the Lord burns." (CW, 341-42)

19. Dietrich Bonhoeffer, *Discipleship*, trans. Barbara Green and Reinhard Krauss (Minneapolis: Fortress, 2001), p. 87. This is a more faithful rendering of "Jeder Ruf Christi fährt in den Tod" than Reginald Fuller's more famous and dramatic version: "When Christ calls a man, he bids him come and die."

After beholding his great-uncle in his moments of high inspiration, young Francis Marion Tarwater believes that he too would like to become a prophet. But if vatic ecstasies were the essence of Christian vocation, Rayber's reductionist critique would surely be right: self-generated exultant visions would justify the charge that Mason has called himself. Yet the old prophet's vocation produces experiences that are far from gratifying. In these miserable encounters, Mason is much like the prophet Jeremiah, who makes even worse allegations against Yahweh than did Job. Jeremiah accuses God of having deceived him. More bitterly still, Jeremiah complains that he is unable to prevent God from speaking through him: "Then I said, I will not make mention of him, nor speak any more in his name. But his word was in mine heart as a burning fire shut up in my bones, and I was weary with forbearing, and I could not stay" (Jer. 20:9).

The elder Tarwater learned the hard consequences of his unapologetic and intolerant faith when he was sent to a prison for the insane to serve a four-year sentence for abducting the youthful Rayber. He could have been released much earlier had he been keen enough to recognize that his prophesying on the psychiatric ward served to prolong his incarceration. Yet the prophet's problem was not a mere lack of perception, as Young Tarwater thinks. Like John Bunyan, Mason Tarwater had too much integrity to seek his release at the cost of his witness. His vocation is as tough as an oak knot, and he is determined to fulfill his divine vocation with St. Paul's disregard for outward conditions. As a preacher of the Word, he is "instant in season, out of season" (2 Tim. 4:2). Adrienne von Speyr, a Swiss Catholic mystic and collaborator in Hans Urs von Balthasar's theological work, declares that Christ's disciples have no holidays from proclaiming the Word, no permission to take time out.[20]

## The Enlightenment Forces that Make for Secular Intolerance

Old Tarwater's violent life of baptismal prophecy would seem to be another example of the "barbaric grotesquerie" that H. L. Mencken lamented in Southern fundamentalists. Many of O'Connor's early critics were astonished — just as many later readers have been offended — to find that, while she hardly sanctioned Mason Tarwater's bloody-mindedness, she regarded him

---

20. Adrienne von Speyr, *They Followed His Call: Vocation and Asceticism*, trans. Erasmo Leiva-Merikakis (San Francisco: Ignatius, 1986), p. 60.

as a Christian of her own kind. Of her grotesque characters she observed that "their fanaticism is a reproach, not merely an eccentricity" (MM, 44).[21] It is a reproach chiefly to Enlightenment notions of tolerance built on the increased hegemony of the omnicompetent secular state and the diminished status of religion to a matter of mere private preference.

William Cavanaugh maintains that the standard accounts concerning modern tolerance are wrongheaded. We have been taught that the sixteenth- and seventeenth-century "wars of religion" required the state to intervene among the fighting Christians, and thus to take matters of religious doctrine and practice out of the public realm lest all of Europe be bathed in blood. Cavanaugh shows, on the contrary, that the alleged religious wars were the birthpangs of the sovereign modern state, the centralizing power that has "a monopoly on violence within a defined territory." Public discourse was secularized during the Enlightenment, Cavanaugh argues, in order to save the state from the threat it feared from the church: "Christianity produces divisions within the state body precisely because it pretends to be a body which transcends state boundaries." Even law itself becomes a thing to be "'made' or legislated by the state rather than 'disclosed' from its divine source through the workings of custom and tradition."[22]

John Locke's principle of toleration reduces religious doctrine and practice to mere private opinion; it eliminates "the Church body as a rival to the state body by redefining religion as a purely internal matter, an affair of the soul and not of the body." The rise of the sovereign secular state is predicated on an elevation of the isolated individual, moreover, a propertied creature having relation to other individuals only by means of self-protecting contracts rather than mutual covenants devoted to common ends. Locke thus reverses the venerable Christian tradition that holds that the degrada-

---

21. That Mason Tarwater operates an illegal whiskey still and is given to bouts of wild doubt about God serves only to confirm his calling as a prophet. The stronger one's faith, the greater one's sense of God's absence. If the old prophet had been a Catholic, he would surely have belonged to those rigorous defenders of church teaching who constitute Opus Dei. (Their ascetic practices include self-flagellation and the wearing of hair shirts. Their arrogant and often ill-tempered founder, Josemaria Escriva de Balaguer, was canonized on October 6, 2002.) Or if Tarwater had been a Dutch Calvinist, he might have become another Abraham Kuyper, not because of Kuyper's remarkable fifty-seven-year career as minister and politician devoted to "bringing all things captive to Christ," but because on three occasions Kuyper suffered nervous breakdowns. Nor should it be forgotten that Dietrich Bonhoeffer, in participating in the plot to assassinate Hitler, sought not to take a wedge out of the *Führer's* ear nor merely to wound him in the leg.

22. William T. Cavanaugh, "The City: Beyond Secular Parodies," in *Radical Orthodoxy*, ed. John Milbank, Catherine Pickstock, and Graham Ward (New York: Routledge, 1999), pp. 191, 189, 190, 192.

tion of our common life into rival groups and competing individuals was the chief result of the Edenic calamity. For Locke, such contentions are the norm:

> But the depravity of mankind being such that they had rather injuriously prey upon the fruits of other men's labours than take pains to provide for themselves, the necessity of preserving men in the possession of what honest industry has already acquired and also of preserving their liberty and strength, whereby they may acquire what they farther want, obliges men to enter into society with one another, that by mutual assistance and joint force they may secure unto each other their properties, in the things that contribute to the comfort and happiness of this life, leaving in the meanwhile to every man the care of his own eternal happiness, the attainment whereof can neither be facilitated by another man's industry, nor can the loss of it turn to another man's prejudice, nor the hope of it be forced on him by an external violence.[23]

In their desire to occupy the high ground above all competing religious claims and proselytizing confessions, the framers of the American Constitution sought to occupy a position of neutrality toward them. Yet their moral vision, despite its alleged impartiality, constitutes a very specific kind of civil religion, as we have seen. Its occlusion of all historically rooted confessional faith makes it "not only not particularistic," as Sidney Mead observed, but "designedly anti-particularistic."[24] Nowhere does this anti-particularism become more evident than in the triumph of the idea of individual freedom of conscience. It is a principle endorsed even by the Second Vatican Council in its *Declaration on Religious Freedom:* "The truth cannot impose itself except by virtue of its own truth, as it makes its entrance into the mind at once quietly and with power. Religious freedom, in turn, which men demand as necessary to fulfill their duty to worship God, has to do with immunity from coercion in civil society."[25] Freedom of conscience, in this Catholic formulation, is

23. In this same "Letter Concerning Toleration," Locke makes ever so clear that the state alone, not the church, has any concern to establish a commonwealth: "The care of each man's soul belongs only to himself." Jefferson voices similar sentiments in his *Notes on Virginia*, declaring that "the legitimate powers of government extend to such acts only as are injurious to others. But it does me no injury for my neighbor to say there are twenty Gods, or no God. It neither picks my pocket nor breaks my leg."

24. Quoted by Richard T. Hughes, *How Christian Faith Can Sustain the Life of the Mind* (Grand Rapids, MI: Eerdmans, 2001), p. 23.

25. *The Documents of Vatican II*, ed. Walter M. Abbott, S.J. (New York: Guild Press, 1966), p. 677. John Courtney Murray praised the Declaration for clearing up a long-standing ambigu-

based on the dignity of every person as a creature made by and for God.[26] Its American version inscribed in the First Amendment was designed to protect the church against the intrusions of the state, not permitting it to open a window into men's souls and thus to coerce belief.

Public life in late-modern America is the product of a remarkable convergence of forces: the sovereign secular state as managing the affairs of propertied individuals; the principle of tolerance as a "live and let live" policy that relegates religion to the private sphere; and the notion of free conscience as operating in the autonomous individual, immune from any communally determined ends. By 1995, when UNESCO issued its *Declaration of Principles*, a thoroughly individualistic idea of society had triumphed, though the declaration's key sentences offer an important caveat:

> Consistent with respect for human rights, the practice of tolerance does not mean toleration of social injustice or the abandonment or weakening of one's own convictions. It means that one is free to adhere to one's own convictions and accepts that others adhere to theirs. It means accepting the fact that human beings, naturally diverse in their appearance, situation, speech, behavior and values, have the right to live in peace and be as they are. It also means that one's views are not to be imposed on others. . . . Tolerance is the responsibility that upholds human rights, pluralism (including cultural pluralism), democracy, and the rule of law.[27]

The upshot of this unprecedented conjunction of Enlightenment forces is the radically oxymoronic idea of private morality. *Roe v. Wade*, the 1973 Supreme Court decision reversing at least two millennia of sanctions against abortion, was based entirely on the notion of privacy. Justice Anthony Kennedy, in his majority opinion for *Planned Parenthood v. Casey*, the 1992 Supreme Court decision upholding the 1973 ruling, clearly articulated the privatism and subjectivism that virtually rule American life: "At the very heart of liberty," wrote Justice Kennedy, "is the right to define one's own concept of existence,

---

ity: "The Church does not deal with the secular order in terms of a double standard — freedom for the Church when Catholics are a minority, privilege for the Church and intolerance for others when Catholics are a majority" (ibid., p. 673).

26. John Courtney Murray assured Pope Paul VI that this sure foundation would prevent the Declaration from being abused, since the phrase "freedom of conscience" is itself "dangerous" (quoted in John T. McGreevy, *Catholicism and American Freedom: A History* [New York: W. W. Norton, 2003], p. 265).

27. Quoted in A. J. Conyers, *The Long Truce: How Toleration Made the World Safe for Power and Profit* (Dallas: Spence, 2001), pp. 42-43, 194-95.

of meaning, of the universe, of the mystery of human life." As the sovereign secular state leaves the public square vacant of shared moral content and common ethical ends, citizens are required to find their personal identity almost entirely in private associations: families, friends, civic clubs, and so forth. Once these "voluntary" groups are relegated to the sphere of personal preference, dislodged from their intended status as vital communities and life-sustaining institutions, they soon wither and die — unless they cultivate their own deliberately countercultural existence. The church, by contrast, is the one institution that, for all its failings, is not moribund, but only because it is sustained by the God whose own communal life it seeks to embody.

## The Death of Innocent Bodies and Guilty Souls

Already in the 1950s, Flannery O'Connor had the prophetic insight to discern that the American version of the Enlightenment would become a serious stumbling block to Christian faithfulness. She discerned that the church would be required to resist the twentieth-century *Pax Americana,* just as the early church found it necessary to oppose the pretensions to ultimacy made by the first-century *Pax Romana.* Georges Florovsky notes that Rome viewed itself as "the City, a permanent and 'eternal' City, *Urbs aeterna,* and an ultimate City also. In a sense, it claimed for itself an 'eschatological dimension.' It posed as an ultimate solution to the human problem." It was necessary for the church to challenge this Roman claim to be the one universal commonwealth, embodying the decisive expression of what constitutes "humanity," offering to all over whom it exercised authority the only lasting and genuine peace. The first Christians rightly opposed this Roman pretense to an all-encompassing competence over human affairs that also demanded the complete and unconditional allegiance of its subjects. Florovsky concludes: "The Church was a challenge to the Empire, and the Empire was a stumbling block for the Christians."[28] In a similar way, St. Augustine insisted that the church must resist the state whenever it impedes obedience to the supreme and true God.

> The Heavenly City . . . knows only one God as the object of worship, and decrees, with faithful devotion, that he only is to be served with that ser-

---

28. Georges Florovsky, "Empire and Desert: Antinomies of Christian History," *Greek Orthodox Theological Review* 3 (Winter 1957): 133-34. I gratefully acknowledge my debt to my colleague Barry Harvey for this reference and for his many other insights concerning the church's moral and political life.

vice which the Greeks call *latreia,* which is due to God alone. And the result of this difference has been that the Heavenly City could not have laws of religion common with the earthly city, and in defence of her religious laws she was bound to dissent from those who thought differently and to prove a burdensome nuisance to them. Thus she had to endure their anger and hatred, and the assaults of persecution.[29]

Five centuries before Augustine, the Roman playwright Terence voiced a sentiment that has become the virtual motto of modern secular humanism: *Homo sum; humani nihil a me alienum puto* (I am a man; nothing human can be alien to me). Flannery O'Connor confessed, on the contrary, that a great number of things were alien to her, in fact were abominations to her in the literal sense: they were *ab-homine* — against the human. In her first novel, *Wise Blood,* O'Connor revealed, in Sabbath Lily Hawks, one of these antihuman forces that would come to dominate late modern life. She is the daughter of the fake evangelist Asa Hawks, the one who preaches salvation in Christ but who has failed to blind himself in proof of his so-called faith. Though Sabbath appears to be a nymphomaniac, there is a certain innocence about her sexuality. She wants to seduce Hazel Motes because she secretly suspects that his anti-gospel is just as fraudulent as her father's evangelism. She thus plays the role of the hell-bound slattern who might as well enjoy the ride. We can surmise that Sabbath Hawks is far from an erotomaniacal nihilist because of the fierce and instructive ghosts, as O'Connor called them, that still haunt her. She is obsessed, for example, with the murder of a child, a killing she reports as though it belonged to someone else, when it clearly pertains to her own experience:

> "Listen," she said [to Motes] in a louder voice, "this here man and woman killed this little baby. It was her own child but it was ugly and she never give it any love. This child had Jesus and this woman didn't have nothing but good looks and a man she was living in sin with. She sent the child away and it come back and she sent it away again and ever' time she sent it away, it come back to where her and this man was living in sin. They strangled it with a silk stocking and hung it up in the chimney. It didn't give her any peace after that, though. Everything she looked at was that child. Jesus made it beautiful to haunt her. She couldn't lie with this man without she saw it, staring through the chimney at her, shining through the brick in the middle of the night." (CW, 28).

29. Augustine, *Concerning the City of God against the Pagans,* trans. Henry Bettenson, ed. David Knowles (Baltimore: Penguin, 1972), p. 878.

It strains credulity to imagine this story's being literally true — that two lovers once hid their murderous act by suspending their dead baby like a smoked ham in a chimney — though the Holocaust allusion may be apt. Yet it is altogether plausible to believe that Sabbath and some anonymous lover have killed their infant. And since Sabbath lives with her failed preacher-father, the baby may have been the product of incest. If so, Sabbath is herself a victim of the worst kind of sexual abuse. In either case, she discerns the moral nihilism of a culture that will destroy a human life when it gets in the way of erotic charm and "good looks." Sabbath Hawks's obsession with a murdered child is more than a macabre vignette. It's Flannery O'Connor's prophetic anticipation, in the early 1950s, of the sexual abandonment that would begin in the 1960s and then become a world pandemic. Twenty percent of all pregnancies now end in abortions, more than fifty million per year.[30]

Abortion-on-demand is the American signature on what, in *Evangelium Vitae*, Pope John Paul II calls our "culture of death": "The twentieth century will have been an era of massive attacks on life," he writes, "an endless series of wars and a continual taking of innocent human life."[31] In the opening of his hallmark encyclical, the pope observes the huge irony that, in an Enlightenment era priding itself on the discovery of inviolable human rights, "the very right to life is being denied or trampled upon, especially at the more significant moments of existence: the moment of birth and the moment of death."[32] Once a transgressive hedonism and materialism have triumphed, John Paul declares, the body itself becomes perverted in the most fundamental way:

> Within this same cultural climate, the body is no longer perceived as proper personal reality, a sign and place of relations with others, with God and with the world. It is reduced to pure materiality: it is simply a complex of organs, functions and energies to be used according to the

---

30. "The World in Numbers: Abortion Decisions," *Atlantic* (April 2003): 38. Far from being medically "necessary," many of these abortions are performed as a means of birth control or else for sex selection: "A 1986 survey found that of 8,000 abortions performed in a Bombay clinic, all but three involved female fetuses" (ibid., p. 39). Abortion is also the leading cause of death among blacks, roughly 1500 per day, as Damon Owens reports: "More black babies are killed in a three-day period by abortion than were ever lynched in the history of America" (quoted in Elizabeth Fox-Genovese, "Deadly Choice: Abortion as a War Against Women," *Touchstone* [September 2003]: 39).

31. *Evangelium Vitae*, 1.17.

32. Ibid., 1.18.

sole criteria of pleasure and efficiency. Consequently, sexuality too is depersonalized and exploited: from being the sign, place and language of love, that is, of the gift of self and acceptance of another, in all the other's richness as a person, it increasingly becomes the occasion and instrument for self-assertion and the selfish satisfaction of personal desires and instincts. Thus the original import of human sexuality is distorted and falsified, and the two meanings, unitive and procreative, inherent in the very nature of the conjugal act, are artificially separated: in this way the marriage union is betrayed and its fruitfulness is subjected to the caprice of the couple. Procreation then becomes the "enemy" to be avoided in sexual activity: if it is welcomed, this is only because it expresses a desire, or indeed the intention, to have a child "at all costs," and not because it signifies the complete acceptance of the other and therefore an openness to the richness of life which the child represents.[33]

Sabbath Hawks's pained conscience reminds her that the slain baby "had Jesus" and thus had life that its killers could not kill. However fraudulent her father's preaching, it gave her a morally formed imagination, thus justifying John Paul's hope that nothing can extinguish the sense of right and wrong. Because the triune God has profoundly united himself with every human being — from the creation of the cosmos, but explicitly in Israel and Christ and the church — our human kind cannot be so falsely reconstructed as to elide the distinction between good and evil: "All the conditioning and efforts to enforce silence [about the taking of innocent life] fail to stifle the voice of the Lord echoing in the conscience of every individual: it is always from this intimate sanctuary of the conscience that a new journey of love, openness and service to human life can begin."[34]

Conscience operates in Ms. Hawks yet again when Hazel Motes seeks to convert Sabbath to his nihilistic conviction that "[e]verything is all one" and thus that all moral distinctions are delusory. His attempt to silence Sabbath's

---

33. Ibid., 1.23. As evidence for the pope's fear that human life is being horribly dishonored, consider the claims of the feminist Eileen McDonagh, who speaks of "the coerced imposition of pregnancy": "The fetus is not innocent but aggressively intrudes on a woman's body so massively that deadly force is justified to stop it" (quoted in J. Budziszewski, "The Furies of Conscience: Denial & the Wages of Sin," *Touchstone* [September 2003]: 34).

34. *Evangelium Vitae*, 1.24. The unconverted Motes performs his own act of symbolic infanticide when he snatches the mummified Jesus that Sabbath is cradling in her arms and smashes it against a wall. Again, Sabbath is the voice of truth: "I knew when I first seen you you were mean and evil. . . . I seen you wouldn't let nobody have nothing. I seen you were mean enough to slam a baby against a wall" (CW, 106-7).

guilt only exacerbates it as she tells yet another story about a child who was cast off, not by a young mother as before, but by a neglectful grandmother. Perhaps this abused and unwanted child was Sabbath herself, and perhaps she has perpetuated the cycle of destruction by aborting her own baby. In any case, Sabbath can discern the signs of a guilty conscience, even when its only register is a grandmother's allergies:

> "There was this child once . . . that nobody cared if it lived or died. Its kin sent it around from one to another of them and finally to its grand-mother who was a very evil woman and she couldn't stand to have it around because the least good thing made her break out in these welps. She would get all itching and swoll. Even her eyes would itch her and swell up and there was nothing she could do but run up and down the road, shaking her hands and cursing and it was twicet as bad when this child was there so she kept the child locked in a chicken crate. It seen its granny in hell-fire, swoll and burning, and it told her everything it seen and she got so swoll until finally she went to the well and wrapped the well rope around her neck and let down the bucket and broke her neck." (CW, 69)

The treatment of the utterly helpless and vulnerable was, for Flannery O'Connor as for all Christians, the index of a church's or a culture's moral life. This was not a matter of her mere opinion but of her deepest conviction, and here she stood with the central Christian tradition. Whereas Scripture itself remains silent about abortion and infanticide, Christian tradition is astonishingly vocal. From the very beginning, Christians were known as the people set apart from their pagan neighbors by not killing their allegedly unwanted babies. By the time of the *Didache,* the early summary of Christian doctrine and practice recorded in the late first or early second century, the church had made explicit the rule that had always been implicit: "You shall not murder a child by abortion nor kill that which is born." Convinced that they were meant to live against the grain of their own ancient culture of death, these early Christians repudiated the common Greco-Roman practice called "exposure." Readers of Sophocles' *Oedipus the King* will remember that, in the ancient Mediterranean world, unwanted babies — in Oedipus' case, a club-footed infant — were taken to remote places and left to die from exposure to the ravages of either wild animals or inclement weather. In writing his *First Apology* sometime around 155, Justin Martyr vehemently commands Christians to reject infanticide in all its forms, especially exposure. Justin points out that the sex-traders of his day — akin to those of our own time, it might be said — were seizing abandoned babies and raising them to become prostitutes.

Though Flannery O'Connor's death came more than a quarter-century before Walker Percy's, the latter shared her worry about the nihilistic gas that is asphyxiating our church and culture alike. Percy believed that it was having an especially deadening effect on certain souls who sit in the high places of American cultural and ecclesiastical power. Only two years before his own death in 1990, Percy wrote a letter to *The New York Times,* which it refused to publish. That our national "newspaper of record" refused to run a plea voiced by one of our major novelists makes the letter all the more worth hearing:

> The most influential book published in German in the first quarter of [the twentieth] century was entitled *The Justification of the Destruction of Life Devoid of Value.* Its co-authors were the distinguished jurist Karl Binding and the prominent psychiatrist Alfred Hoche. Neither Binding nor Hoche had ever heard of Hitler or the Nazis. Nor, in all likelihood, did Hitler ever read the book. He didn't have to. . . .
>
> I would not wish to be understood as implying that the respected American institutions I have named [*The New York Times,* the United States Supreme Court, the American Civil Liberties Union, the National Organization of Women] are similar or corresponding to pre-Nazi institutions.
>
> But I do suggest that once the line is crossed, once the principle gains acceptance — juridically, medically, socially — [that] innocent human life can be destroyed for whatever reason, for the most admirable socio-economic, medical, or social reasons — then it does not take a prophet to predict what will happen next, or if not next, then sooner or later. At any rate, a warning is in order. Depending on the disposition of the majority and the opinion polls — now in favor of allowing women to get rid of un-born and unwanted babies — it is not difficult to imagine an electorate or a court ten years, fifty years from now, who would favor getting rid of useless old people, retarded children, anti-social blacks, illegal Hispanics, gypsies, Jews. . . .[35]

35. Walker Percy, *Signposts in a Strange Land,* ed. Patrick Samway (New York: Farrar, Straus & Giroux, 1991), pp. 350-51. The Canadian moral philosopher George Grant has voiced similar concerns: "One can foresee a time when before one can qualify for rights a kind of Means Test may be used: 'Are you human in the fullest sense of the word?' 'Are you still enjoying the quality of life?' And here is the crunch; as the foetus loses out on this ethic, so will all the weak, the aged, the infirm, the unproductive. If we come to believe that we are not creatures, but acci-

Like Percy, O'Connor discerned that our consumerist culture that is centered on advertising and entertainment would end by killing bodies no less than souls. The crime of doing away with an unwanted child, together with its hellish consequences, arises not only in *Wise Blood* but, as we have seen, in *The Violent Bear It Away* as well. To speak of abortion as a reproductive right and of euthanasia as a private choice — as if killing were the equivalent of shopping for clothes or selecting an automobile — is to turn our moral life into a consumer's existence. But all the things that count, especially all Christian things, are matters of communal obligation and obedience, not of private preference or choice. For each person to determine the moral meaning of the universe for himself is a recipe not only for individualist anarchy and social chaos but also for what Christians have defined as slavery. True liberty is found, as Christ and all the saints have expressed with relentless monotony, not when we define reality for ourselves but when we conform ourselves to the reality that God has established in Israel and Christ and the church. *The Book of Common Prayer* gives this free and faithful life its proper name — "the service which is perfect freedom." For Cranmer and the sixteenth century, the word "service" retained its Latinate sense: it did not and does not mean anything akin to civic club volunteerism, but joyful slavery to the triune God.

## Mortifying the Flesh and Cultivating Purity of Heart

Francis Marion Tarwater discovers such glad obedience only after he has drowned Rayber's idiot child named Bishop. Tarwater is blessedly saved, as we have seen, from having committed unadulterated murder, since he baptized Bishop even as he killed him. Even so, the youth believes that he has once and for all repudiated his call to prophecy. For he is still accompanied by the demonic stranger who, having successfully urged him to drown Bishop, speaks no longer as a stranger but as his "friend." Tarwater plans to take possession of the farm where, as he wrongly believes, he left the old man incinerated. There he will rule in sheer autonomy, free from the shackles of both the school psychologist and his prophet-uncle.

On this final trip to the country, Tarwater is accompanied, not by an inner voice of demonic temptation, but by a man who has given him a ride. He

dents, rights will no longer be given in the very nature of our legal system. The most powerful among us will then decide who is to have rights and who is not" (George Grant, *Technology and Justice* [Toronto: Anasi, 1986], p. 126).

drives a lavender car, wears a lavender shirt, carries a lavender handkerchief, and has lavender eyes — eyes that watch Tarwater "with what might be a leer" (CW, 471). After rendering Tarwater unconscious with a drugged drink, he sodomizes the boy. Although O'Connor does not directly depict the pedophilic rape, her narrator makes clear that it is not only a sexual but also a demonic and vampiric act. Just as Hulga Hopewell had tried to suck the life out of Manley Pointer with her kisses, this man's "delicate skin had acquired a faint pink tint as if he had refreshed himself on blood" (CW, 472).

That O'Connor depicts the Devil as a leering pedophilic rapist obsessed with the color purple is uncharacteristic of her art. Though she resorted to "large and startling figures," her grotesques are rarely caricatures and her moral outlook is never propagandistic. Rather are her religious convictions stitched into the fabric of her fiction. To create a satanic figure who is a homosexual predator, by contrast, is to make evil obvious rather than subtle. Yet O'Connor believed that she could not have had Tarwater discover the real horror of evil in any other way:

> The man who gives [the boy] the lift is the personification of the voice, the stranger who has been counseling him all along; in other words, he is the devil, and it takes this action of the devil's to make Tarwater see for the first time what evil is. He accepts the devil's liquor and he reaps what the devil has to give. Without this experience of evil, his acceptance of his vocation in the end would be merely a dishonest manipulation by me. Those who see and feel what the devil is turn to God. Tarwater learned the hard way but he has a hard head.[36]

Young Tarwater has believed that his inner voices are merely the promptings of his own sweet will, when in fact the stranger-become-friend is a satanic power who, as O'Connor says, "suggests possibilities to all of us" (HB, 375). The murderous youth has to be shown that he has yielded his will to an invasive and transcendent evil who embodies himself in a moral perversion that Tarwater can recognize. In drowning Bishop, he has denied what John Paul II calls "the incomparable value of every human person." The boy must discover, alas, what it means for his own body and person to be violated. He has made such violent rejection of his divine calling that it takes an

---

36. Quoted in Richard Giannone, *Flannery O'Connor and the Mystery of Love* (Urbana, IL: University of Illinois Press), pp. 255-56. It is also worth noting that, in the story entitled "The River," the solitary and scoffing Mr. Paradise, the nihilist who fishes with a wormless hook, tempts Harry Ashfield with a phallic candy cane.

equally violent act of abuse for him to learn that human life, in the pope's words, "remains *a sacred reality* entrusted to us, to be preserved with a sense of responsibility and brought to perfection in love and in the gift of ourselves to God and to our brothers and sisters."[37]

Here, as in so many other ways, Flannery O'Connor proved herself to be a prophetic writer. She saw, with uncanny foresight, the rise of a hyper-eroticized culture in which human identity would be defined ever less in relation to God, community, and society and ever more in terms of personal sexual fulfillment. O'Connor is not suggesting that modern nihilism shows itself primarily in homosexual rapists, especially since her century of unprecedented carnage was hardly the work of pedophiles. As a single woman who had several lesbian friends, O'Connor had no desire to demonize homosexuality. The church catholic has regarded it as one sin among many, and far from the most egregious. Yet neither was O'Connor willing to deny the witness of both Scripture and tradition concerning the teaching of Romans 1, which Richard Hays has succinctly clarified:

> Paul singles out homosexual intercourse for special attention because he regards it as providing a particularly graphic image of the way in which human fallenness distorts God's created order. God the creator made man and woman for each other, to cleave together, to be fruitful and multiply. When human beings engage in homosexual activity, they enact an outward and visible sign of an inward and spiritual reality: the rejection of the Creator's design. They embody the spiritual condition of those who have "exchanged the truth about God for a lie."[38]

The divine summons to mortify the sins of the flesh and to vivify the gifts of the spirit is also central to "A Temple of the Holy Ghost." There O'Connor has an anonymous twelve-year-old girl confront a hermaphrodite who has dealt with his malformity in a deeply liberating way. As the child learns how he has redeemed his bodily life, she is able to overcome her own terrible sins of the spirit, which are also linked to her two chief personal traits — her intellectual brilliance and her religious insight. This brainy girl likes to make fun of everyone dimwitted, particularly the two country boys who have come to court her two visiting cousins. In their love of sentimental gospel songs, the Wilkins brothers know nothing of the mystical faith and exultant hymnody of the young girl's own Catholicism. She scorns their mem-

---

37. *Ev. Vit.*, Intro., 2; italics in the original.
38. Richard Hays, "Awaiting the Redemption of Our Bodies," *Sojourners* (July 18, 1991): 19.

bership in the Church of God, even as she mocks the Baptist preacher who offers pious prayers at her school. The story's precocious young protagonist thus makes the two gifts that one cannot possibly earn or deserve — native intelligence and religious faith — into a cause for spiritual pride. She is, in fact, a little monster of presumption.

Yet this smart alice is a complicated creature, for she also possesses an acute religious sensibility. At night she makes a dogged effort at her prayers, racking her conscience and recalling at least a few of her sins. She thinks of Christ on the road to Calvary, falling under the weight of his crushing cross. Knowing that she lacks such spiritual powers of endurance, she hopes instead to become a martyr — "if they killed her quick" (CW, 204). Like the rest of her society, the girl wants to avoid suffering, especially the long suffering of the saints. Yet this little woman-child is religiously reflective in a way that gives her a potential for spiritual excellence that her pubescent cousins lack. She is outraged, for example, at their mockery of the nun who has given them a formula from 1 Corinthians 6 to fend off fresh young men in the back seats of cars. Sister Perpetua has told the girls to say, "Stop sir! I am a Temple of the Holy Ghost." Groping boys, so the nun taught, would then surely desist! Such unworldly advice strikes the two cousins as hilariously wrong-headed. The sexually innocent child, by contrast, is touched by the news that she is nothing less than the dwelling place of God. It "made her feel as if somebody had given her a present" (CW, 199).

O'Connor once observed that this story was her single attempt to write about what she called "the most mysterious of the virtues" — purity (CW, 970). The nameless girl learns the meaning of purity only after her cousins return from a freak show at the local fair. They tell the curious child about the hermaphrodite whom they have seen: he earns his living by exhibiting his sexually mixed features to voyeurs wanting to confirm that they are not as he is.[39] Yet he makes the spectators' perverse frisson into the occasion for his own confession: "God made me thisaway and if you laugh He may strike you the same way. This is the way He wanted me to be and I ain't disputing His way. I'm showing you because I got to make the best of it. I expect you to act like ladies and gentlemen. I never done it to myself nor had a thing to do with it but I'm making the best of it. I don't dispute hit" (CW, 206).

---

39. I refer to the hermaphrodite as "he" even though the two cousins use the pronoun "it." Their neutered word reveals, all too clearly, that they have thoughtlessly transformed a God-imaged person into an impersonal thing. Medical dictionaries also indicate that there is no pure hermaphroditism, no fully developed genitalia of both kinds, but always a predominance of one set of gender traits over the other. And since this particular hermaphrodite ends by playing a priestly role, it seems appropriate to envision his character in masculine terms.

The town's Protestant preachers are so scandalized by this sexually em-bodied person who contravenes the ordinary norms that they have the freak show shut down. Yet O'Connor's Catholic child is not offended by this hybrid creature with his strange creed. Perhaps because she has seen crucifixes that are beautiful even in their ugliness, she responds to her cousins' report with neither pity nor horror, but with a reverie that ends in reverence. She dreams that the freak is the liturgist in a service of worship, leading the people in a lit-any of radical injunction and affirmation:

> "God done this to me and I praise Him."
> "Amen. Amen."
> "He could strike you thisaway."
> "Amen. Amen."
> "But he has not."
> "Amen."
> "Raise yourself up. A temple of the Holy Ghost. You! You are God's temple, don't you know? Don't you know? God's Spirit has a dwelling in you, don't you know?" (CW, 207)

By the story's end, the proud little protagonist has begun to be trans-formed. Her humbling has begun with her perception of the holy within the hermaphrodite. In her childlike way she has come to see that the freak's de-formity defeats standard definitions of formliness, even as his faith exposes the terrible inadequacy of conventional belief. He enables her to discern the mysterious frontier that lies between the known and the unknown, the per-ceived and the unperceived. He represents what the narrator calls an "answer to a riddle that was more puzzling than the riddle itself" (CW, 206). The rid-dling answer is that the freak, in faithfully embracing his suffering, inhabits the deepest realm of mystery. He dwells there not in spite of his disfigure-ment but because he humbly accepts it. Deprived of the sexual satisfaction that many of us moderns regard as the defining center of our being, the her-maphrodite has cause to adopt a nihilist view of the universe. Yet he never complains about his condition. He avoids the twin sins of hard pride and soft self-pity because he has access to an anti-nihilist conception of reality: his faithfulness enables him to see that he is no mere genetic accident. For while he may indeed be a freak of nature, his life is first and last the will of God.[40]

40. The uneducated hermaphrodite has no way of knowing the important theological distinction between first and second causes. He does not understand, therefore, that not all nat-ural events can be ascribed directly to the will of God. Nor does he know that the divinely or-

Feminist critics have complained that O'Connor does not honor her own sexuality but adopts, according to them, a patriarchal and masculinist aesthetic — with its emphasis on objective narrators, withering satire, impersonal tone, and cold antisentimentality.[41] Louise Westling argues, for example, that O'Connor gives the child a religious vision of the hermaphrodite that "erases the distinction between the sexes and thus relieves her of the necessity of accepting her own femininity and joining the rites of adolescent courtship which she finds so disgusting as she watches her cousins perform them."[42] It is true that O'Connor generally avoids sexual relationships in her fiction and that she never writes about romantic love at all. She explained to Betty Hester that she did not write about a subject that would require her own intimate experience of it: "I've always believed there were two [sexes] but generally acted as if there were only one" (CW, 985).

This is not O'Connor's shocking denial of her own sexuality so much as it is a statement of her deepest conviction about human nature. Our creation in God's image, she suggests, affords us an unbreakable mutuality with every other person — a solidarity that, while not denying our sexuality, enables our humanity to transcend it. We are full human beings not only in and through, but sometimes even apart from, our genital condition.

> On the subject of the feminist business, I just never . . . think of qualities which are specifically feminine or masculine. I suppose I [divide] people into two classes: the Irksome and the Non-Irksome without regard to sex. Yes and there are the Medium Irksome and the Rare Irksome. (HB, 176)

O'Connor's feminist critics lack her humor. They are thus unable to honor the profound truth of her claim about the hermaphrodite: "There is certainly

---

dered cosmos has room for chance, so that his deformed bodily condition could be the result of nature's impersonal probabilities, even as his life itself remains the direct intention of the personal God. The hermaphrodite is surely right to insist, however, on the Prime Causality providentially ruling over all things, making even chance events cohere with the sovereignty and goodness of God. His faith enables him to see that he is not a mere physical body, as modern naturalists hold, but an inspirited body whose incorporeal soul provides him enormous moral freedom within the limits of his malformed sexual state.

41. For book-length examples, see Katherine Hempel Prown, *Revising Flannery O'Connor: Southern Literary Culture and the Problem of Female Authorship* (Charlottesville, VA: University Press of Virginia, 2001); and Sarah Gordon, *Flannery O'Connor: The Obedient Imagination* (Athens, GA: University of Georgia Press, 2000).

42. Louise Westling, "Flannery O'Connor's Revelations to 'A,'" *Southern Humanities Review* XX, no. 1 (Winter 1986): 18.

a more poignant element of suffering in this [man's state]," O'Connor observes, "than in anything else one could find at a fair." He becomes Christ-like — and thus fully and completely human — in the one way that is available to everyone: through faithful submission to his suffering. Such resignation, O'Connor adds, "is one of the fruits of the Holy Ghost" (CW, 925).

Among the gifts of the Spirit, purity of heart (Matt. 5:8) is usually linked with chastity of body no less than wholeness of mind and will. Given this connection, there is little wonder that O'Connor called purity the twentieth century's "dirty word" (CW, 925). The Catholic Catechism rightly ties it to modesty, a virtue not notably present in late-modern life:

> Purity requires modesty. . . . Modesty protects the intimate center of the person. It means refusing to unveil what should remain hidden. It is ordered to chastity to whose sensitivity it bears witness. It guides how one looks at others and behaves towards them in conformity with the dignity of the persons and their solidarity.[43]

The slam-bang brashness of Flannery O'Connor's fiction is no contradiction of her modesty. On the contrary, the integrity of her "intimate center," her refusal to reveal what should remain hidden, were the marks of a modesty that was at once religious and sexual. That she sought to remain perpetually prepubescent was not a denial of her sexuality so much as an attempt to redirect it toward higher ends, as she confessed in a touching letter to Betty Hester:

> The things you have said about my being surprised to be over twelve, etc., have struck me as being quite comically accurate. When I was twelve I made up my mind absolutely that I would not get any older. I don't remember how I meant to stop it. There was something about "teen" attached to anything that was repulsive to me. I certainly didn't approve of what I saw of people that age. I was a very ancient twelve; my views at that age would have done credit to a Civil War veteran. Anyway. I went through the years 13 to 20 in a very surly way. . . . I am much younger now than I was at twelve or anyway, less burdened. The weight of centuries lies on children, I'm sure of it. (CW, 985)

This remarkable confession reveals the essence of O'Connor's understanding of purity. It does not mean an unsullied innocence but rather a re-

43. *Catechism of the Catholic Church* (Mahwah, NJ: Paulist Press, 1994), p. 604.

demptive and uncorrupting knowledge of the world's evils. Hence her description of lesbianism as a condition akin to "any other form of uncleanness" (CW, 925). Again anticipating the church's future teaching, O'Connor regarded homoerotic yearnings as sinless unless acted upon. Like all other inherited conditions that tempt us to transgression, abnormal sexual proclivities must be resisted, disciplined, mortified. O'Connor was too deep a Christian to accept what Richard Hays calls "the apparently common sense assumption that only freely chosen acts are morally culpable." "Quite the reverse," Hays explains: "The very nature of sin is that it is not freely chosen. We are in bondage to sin but still accountable to God's righteous judgment of our actions. . . . [I]t cannot be maintained that homosexuality is morally neutral because it is involuntary."[44] What we all have in common, whatever our sexual condition, is the duty to struggle with it and to purify it. Thus the Catholic catechism makes clear that, while homosexual orientation is not inherently sinful, "homosexual acts are intrinsically disordered":

> The number of men and women who have deep-seated homosexual tendencies is not negligible. They do not choose their homosexual condition; for most of them it is a trial. They must be accepted with respect, compassion, and sensitivity. Every sign of unjust discrimination in their regard should be avoided. These persons are called to fulfill God's will in their lives and, if they are Christians, to unite to the sacrifice of the Lord's Cross the difficulties they may encounter from their condition.
>
> Homosexual persons are called to chastity. By the virtues of self-mastery that teach them inner freedom, at times by the support of disinterested friendship, by prayer and sacramental grace, they can and should gradually and resolutely approach Christian perfection.[45]

*     *     *

It may seem that we have removed ourselves a considerable distance from the subject of vocation. But for Flannery O'Connor there is a profound connection between huge genocidal horrors and individual sinful acts: they are both defects in vocation, whether corporate or personal. The church is complicit in evils both great and small, she suggests, whenever it fails to teach and preach "the gospel of life," as Pope John Paul II calls it. For this gospel alone

44. Hays, p. 20.
45. *Catechism*, p. 566.

creates what Stanley Hauerwas calls "a community of character,"[46] namely, a church consisting of believers who have been habituated to following the Christ who both commands and enables them to accept death willingly rather than to take life innocently. To have purity of heart is to refuse to kill innocent bodies but rather to mortify one's own sinful flesh. Even for a woman who would die at age thirty-nine — her bud "no sooner blown than blasted," as Milton says of Lycidas — the life of faithfully accepted suffering was not a grim stoic existence but a thing of supreme joy. Hence her reply to a woman who had complained that Catholic Christianity is too easy: "You are quite right that it is easier to be a Catholic than something else. It is easier than anything else and if any Catholic should tell you otherwise, you can tell him to go to the devil. The Church does not demand any sacrifice out of proportion to what she gives" (CW, 928).

---

46. Stanley Hauerwas, *A Community of Character: Toward a Constructive Christian Social Ethic* (Notre Dame, IN: University of Notre Dame Press, 1981).

EIGHT ❧ *Climbing into the Starry Field*
*and Shouting Hallelujah:*
*O'Connor's Vision of the World to Come*

"If Christianity be not altogether thoroughgoing eschatology, there remains in it no relationship whatever with Christ." This peremptory claim by Karl Barth would seem to guarantee sure dismissal in our time. Ours is an anti-eschatological age. The word "eschatology" itself seems to posit an unhealthy dualism between this present suffering world and a putative ideal world. Christians who still believe in heaven often envision it sentimentally as the place where all good people go, where we ourselves will be united with our friends and families, where we shall enjoy personal bliss bye and bye. Such is the hope of many conservative Christians who regard salvation almost entirely as an affair of "getting us to Heaven." They ignore John Wesley's wise counter-conviction that the chief purpose of the Christian life is to get heaven into us — and thus to get the hell out, as certain wags have suggested. From the Renaissance through the nineteenth century, there arose a new and optimistic eschatology that became the hope of many liberal Christians. They believed that the kingdom of God was progressively being realized on earth. They held the fond hope that wars would soon cease, that hunger and disease would be conquered, that homelessness and poverty would be overcome, that the kingdom of heaven would indeed occur on earth, under the fatherhood of God and the brotherhood of man — specifically in the neighborhood of Boston, the real locus of the liberal outlook. Even if it now seems a hopelessly naïve and old-fashioned vision, such liberal Christianity still thrives among a small band of believers who populate the old-line Protestant churches. They devote themselves to correct causes in the conviction that, if the kingdom doesn't occur here and now, it will never occur at all.

Conservative and liberal eschatologies are equally sub-biblical. They justify the critique of Marx and Nietzsche that Christianity is a slave religion of the weak, an opiate for those who cannot face the unrequited injustices of human existence and the utter finality of death. Whether by casting their eyes to the sky in post-worldly hope, or by grinding away at their bootless attempts to correct all social ills, both conservatives and liberals seem equally opaque to the bright hope of Christian faith and the dark pathos of our time. The calamities of our disastrous age seem to vindicate the great nineteenth-century nay-sayers. An ominous, end-of-the-world atmosphere pervades human life in our late age. The planet seems burdened with ecological damages that it cannot much longer bear. Disease and starvation ravage entire continents. Nationalism, tribalism, and terrorism seem to know no limits, producing a suicidal warfare that has compunction against neither biological nor nuclear weapons. Whether Christian or pagan, most of us have become secularists in the literal sense: we believe that the *saeculum* — this present age — will be succeeded by no others. It matters little whether it ends with a bang or a whimper.[1]

The early Christians had neither the postmillennial hopefulness of conservatives nor the premillennial laboriousness of liberals. Facing a world altogether as bleak as ours, they were prepared to answer both the overeager enthusiasts and the world-weary cynics of their own age. They had a thorough-going eschatological faith. They believed that the world had already ended and that Christ would return in order to complete the new age that his life, death, and bodily resurrection had inaugurated. Rather than canceling the importance of earthly life, their eschatological faith drastically enhanced it, as Karl Löwith explains:

> Nothing in the New Testament warrants a conception of the new events that constituted early Christianity as the beginning of a new epoch of secular developments within a continuous process. For the early Christians the history of this world had rather come to an end, and Jesus himself was seen by them not as a world-historical link in the chain of historical happenings but as the unique redeemer. What really begins with the appearance of Jesus Christ is not a new epoch of secular history, called "Christian," but the beginning of an end. The Christian times are Christian only insofar as they are the last time. Because the Kingdom of God, moreover, is not to be realized in a continuous process of historical de-

---

1. Otto Weber makes the shrewd observation that our desperate this-worldliness has caused suicide and capital punishment to exchange places on the scale of dread and horror. Our medieval ancestors regarded suicide as the unforgivable sin, since it presumed upon the prerogative that belongs to God alone; on the other hand, they considered capital punishment wholly acceptable, because God could correct in the next life whatever miscarriages of justice might occur on earth. But with the collapse of eschatological faith, suicide has become a virtual right and capital punishment a dubious penalty.

velopment, the eschatological history of salvation also cannot impart a new and progressive meaning to the history of the world, which is [already] fulfilled by having reached its term. The "meaning" of the history of this world is fulfilled against itself because the story of salvation, as embodied in Jesus Christ, redeems and dismantles, as it were, the hopeless history of the world.[2]

Flannery O'Connor's eschatological vision serves both to redeem and dismantle the hopelessness of our time. Far from debasing human existence, her belief in the Life beyond life gives a sharp urgency to ordinary experience. Her fiction summons people of all kinds and conditions to an eschatological life here and now. Her characters learn either wondrously to live out their salvation, or else miserably to fall away into damnation. This drastic either-or does not mean that the alternatives are equal. The first and last word spoken by Christians to the world, whether in art or in the church, must be Yes rather than No: "Do I make my plans like a worldly man," asks Paul, "ready to say Yes and No at once? As surely as God is faithful, our word to you has not been Yes and No. For the Son of God, Jesus Christ, whom we preached among you, Silvanus and Timothy and I, was not Yes and No; but in him it is always Yes. For all the promises of God find their Yes in him. That is why we utter the Amen through him, to the glory of God" (2 Cor. 1:17b-20, RSV).

To declare any other gospel is to betray the word itself, turning glad tidings into baleful and admonitory news. Most of O'Connor's stories end, therefore, in a glad moment of grace, as the gift of salvation comes to her protagonists amidst a blinding blaze of revelation, at once disclosing the horror of sin but also overcoming the horror with hope. If it is only at the point of death, most of her characters acknowledge the redeeming paradox announced by Mason Tarwater: "Even the mercy of the Lord burns."

## The Perdition That Feels No Pain

While the preponderance of Scripture is devoted to the proclamation of a kingdom that is at once already present and yet to be manifest, there is no denying that both the first and second comings of Christ bring judgment. The threat of holy wrath bears down on the world with a fearful urgency. Hans Urs

---

2. Karl Löwith, "History and Christianity," in Charles W. Kegley and Robert W. Bretall, eds., *Reinhold Niebuhr: His Religious, Social, and Political Thought* (New York: Macmillan, 1961), p. 283.

von Balthasar explains: "Love itself, as the utmost gift, is also the utmost demand."[3] The seventeenth-century Anglican divine Jeremy Taylor offered a similar admonition: "[God] threatens terrible things if we will not be happy."[4] The mystic Marie des Vallées speaks even more darkly: "God['s] love is more terrible, and better understands how to make us suffer, than his justice. . . . I love his divine justice and find it wonderful, mild and pleasing, but [divine] love is relentless and frightful in a cruel way."[5] This strange saying points to Christ's agony on the cross: the hellish torment of his seeing, from the viewpoint of absolute Love, the entire human race turning away and crucifying it.

The plain biblical fact of God's judgment cannot be denied. Admonitions about the sheep and the goats, the right hand and the left hand, the everlasting lake of fire, the weeping and wailing and gnashing of teeth are far too prominent, in both Scripture and Christian tradition, to be dismissed by recourse to a spongy universalism.[6] Though Karl Barth is sometimes accused of being a universalist, he adamantly insists on the Last Assize: "That which is not of God's grace and right cannot [finally] exist," Barth warns. "Infinitely much human as well as Christian 'greatness' perhaps plunges there [at the Last Judgment] into the outermost darkness."[7]

There is a frightening possibility that the last divine word could be a final negation uttered in answer to our final impenitence. There is no doubt about our own capacity to end in rebellion. In one of her most famous pronouncements, O'Connor confessed that "man [is] so free that with his last breath he can say No" (MM, 182). Persistent rejection of God's grace ends in "the pain of absolute loss," as Roman Catholics succinctly define the meaning of hell. This rejection and loss have consequences here and now, not only in the life to come. Adrienne von Speyr describes what happens to the person who silences the divine summons by putting God off, as if the Lord of the cosmos could be made permanently to wait. The negligent creature becomes a frightening figure, says von Speyr, "a permanently marked man."

3. Hans Urs von Balthasar, *Dare We Hope "That All Men Be Saved"?*, trans. David Kipp and Lothar Krauth (San Francisco: Ignatius, 1988), p. 41.

4. Quoted in C. S. Lewis, "Preface" to *George MacDonald: An Anthology* (New York: Macmillan, 1978), p. xxxi.

5. Quoted in von Balthasar, *Dare We Hope*, p. 108, n. 20.

6. It is best to treat such heavy matters with a little levity. Martin Luther opined that the real question is not whether we are sheep or goats, but whether God is herbivorous or carnivorous. If it's the latter, no one shall go undevoured. There was a Scots Presbyterian minister who was asked how the bare-gummed will be able eternally to gnash their teeth. The dour Scot is said to have replied: "Teeth will be provided."

7. Karl Barth, *Dogmatics in Outline* (New York: Harper Torchbooks, 1959), pp. 135-36.

He is and remains recognizable. He has pushed aside the experience of his life. In the future he remains embittered, dissatisfied, sarcastic, fault-finding, and he never grows tired of exposing his reasons, just concealing a sense of "knowing better" and trying to prove the impossibility of discipleship. But he is marked in advance; his words are superfluous.[8]

George Rayber is this marked man. Like Ivan Karamazov, he is not an atheist so much as an anti-theist. He believes that, if there is a God at all, he is surely a monster. Rayber is as determined as Karamazov is to deny and refute this evil deity, this gnostic demiurge. This school psychologist has become a secular monk, ascetically denying himself the world's pleasures, lest they soften his stiff will not to believe: "He slept in a narrow iron bed, worked sitting in a straight-backed chair, ate frugally, spoke little, and cultivated the dullest of friends" (CW, 402). The single chink in Rayber's secularist armor is his unaccountable love for his retarded son, Bishop. Precisely in his "uselessness," his innocence, his obliviousness to insult and scorn, this mindless child stirs an "irrational" love in Rayber. Bishop is a sign of the sheer gratuity of all created things, the stark and utter unnecessity of every living creature, the knee-bending astonishment that there is something rather than nothing at all. Even so convinced an atheist as George Eliot could not help but observe, in *Middlemarch*, that "if we had a keen vision and feeling of all ordinary life, it would be like hearing the grass grow and the squirrel's heart beat, and we should die of that roar which lies on the other side of silence. As it is, the quickest of us walk about well wadded with stupidity."

Rayber is an atheist whose mystical sense of the world as a total gift makes him fear that his "horrifying love" for Bishop, if left uncontrolled, might become all-encompassing, taking in the whole cosmos:

> Anything [Rayber] looked at too long could bring it on. . . . It could be a stick or a stone, the line of a shadow, the absurd old man's walk of a starling crossing the sidewalk. If, without thinking, he lent himself to it, he would feel suddenly a morbid surge of the love that terrified him — powerful enough to throw him to the ground in an act of idiot praise. It was completely irrational and abnormal.
>
> He was not afraid of love in general. He knew the value of it and how it could be used. He had seen it transform [people] in cases where nothing else had worked. . . . The love that would overcome him was of a different

8. Adrienne von Speyr, *They Followed His Call*, trans. Erasmo Leiva-Merikakis (San Francisco: Ignatius, 1986), p. 31.

order entirely. It was not the kind that could be used for the child's improvement or his own. It was love without reason, love for something futureless, love that appeared to exist only to be itself, imperious and all-demanding, the kind that would cause him to make a fool of himself in an instant. And it only began with Bishop. It began with Bishop and then like an avalanche covered everything his reason hated. (CW, 401)

Like few other rationalists, Rayber understands the real meaning of divine love. Precisely because Bishop's "uselessness" makes him incapable of any reciprocal exchange, any return of the love that he might receive, Rayber sees the boy as an unbidden gift. Just as God has freely loved his utterly unlovable people, asking not even their gratitude, much less their repayment in kind, so does the divine gratuity make every living thing infinitely valuable. All things are precious, Rayber understands, not chiefly for what they might become, but simply for what they are. Like Ivan Karamazov, with his inexplicable love for the sticky little leaves in spring even as he chooses to turn back his ticket to life, Rayber the nihilist has a mystical desire to love everything absolutely and without qualification.

Yet spiritual love can become sentimental and self-indulgent; authentic love is always costly, at once "imperious and all-demanding." If Rayber expressed his unstinting love for the feeble-minded Bishop, he would appear foolish before the hard gaze of the utilitarian world. A culture of efficiency and productivity honors only those lives that "contribute to society." To avoid the "madness" of such useless love, and to maintain perfect mastery over his desires, Rayber is determined to steer a narrow course between equally perilous chasms: the "idiocy" of loving Bishop and giving gratitude to God, and the "emptiness" of not loving his son and thus descending into the void. Rayber is too honest to seek any middle way between the absolute alternatives. He knows that, in ultimate matters, there are only two options: transcendent faith and utter nothingness. When the time comes to make the bitter choice between the two abysses, he vows to maintain his integrity by electing nothingness rather than love of God and child.

Rayber has already sought, on at least one occasion, to choose the void. He attempted to drown Bishop in the ocean, only to suffer a last-minute failure of nerve that led him to have the unconscious child revived. The schoolteacher doesn't miss his second opportunity. Even though it does not come by Rayber's hand, he is clearly complicit in the drowning of Bishop. Despite having heard Francis Tarwater's repeated claim that, unlike his weak-willed kinsman, he himself can act, Rayber allows the boy to take Bishop boating. This is a virtual invitation to murder. When Rayber first hears the drowning Bishop bellow out his protest, he is initially stricken with horror. But the hard rationalist gradually regains self-control, steeling himself against grief. So thoroughly has Rayber succeeded in silencing the repeated call of the ultimate Voice that he hears its final echo — in Bishop's dying scream — as if it were a remote occurrence happening to someone else. With chilling candor, O'Connor's narrator sets forth the pain of absolute loss, the damnation of being unable to love:

> The machine [his hearing aid] made the sounds [of Bishop's cry] seem to come from inside him as if something in him were tearing itself free. He clenched his teeth. The muscles in his face contracted and revealed lines of pain beneath harder than bone. He set his jaw. No cry must escape him. The one thing he knew, the one thing he was certain of was that no cry must escape him. . . .
>
> He stood there trying to remember something else before he moved away. It came to him finally as something so distant and vague in his mind that it might have already happened, a long time ago. It was that to-morrow they would drag the pond for Bishop.
>
> He stood waiting for the raging pain, the intolerable hurt that was his due, to begin, so that he could ignore it, but he continued to feel nothing. He stood light-headed at the [motel] window and it was not until he realized there would be no pain that he collapsed. (CW, 456)

Because Rayber has allowed the final summons of Bishop's love to go unanswered, that love has torn itself free from the man's heart. Our final assessment of Rayber depends on our reading of his collapse after he hears Bishop's drowning scream. It may be regarded as his final descent into permanent perdition, his uncoerced election of nothingness, his entry into the unrecognized hell that he has repeatedly vowed he would choose over "idiot" love when the time at last came. To dwell in absolute spiritual vacuity, as Rayber does, is the precise meaning of damnation as Dostoevsky's Father Zosima describes it: the hell of being unable to love. Yet a more positive reading of Rayber's fate is also possible. That Rayber is not able to rejoice at Bishop's death — glad at last to be rid of his useless son — may augur a more hopeful future for the school psychologist. It may demonstrate the final defeat of his cold-hearted atheism. Like Mrs. McIntyre after her collapse in "The Displaced Person," the deaf and disabled Rayber may have crumpled into the beginning of his salvation.[9] Even so, it is clear that we have witnessed a man's

---

9. O'Connor hedges on Rayber's ultimate state. On the one hand, she says that he "wins" his battle against the grace of God and thus damns himself (HB, 488); on the other

damnation, at least in this present life, as O'Connor reveals hell to be an existential reality, not some far-off state of timeless punishment. To define either salvation or damnation entirely in post-temporal terms, O'Connor teaches, is to miss the real import of Christian eschatology. The end has already come, the Kingdom is in our midst, and we are already dwelling in various states of paradise or perdition. The new life is now present because the world's reconciliation has already taken place in Jesus Christ; or else the old death, which has been brought to its term, is passing ever more rapidly away into nothingness, seeking to sweep souls such as Rayber along with it.

## The Paradise Whose Silence Is Broken
## Only by Shouting the Truth

To confess with the Apostles' Creed that Jesus Christ "is coming to judge the quick and the dead" is to expect nothing other than the Apocalypse. The word itself, which means to "uncover" or "reveal," makes clear that this event will not constitute some entirely unheard-of thing, but rather the final disclosure and universal manifestation of the kingdom of God that is already in our midst. Just seven years before his death, perhaps thinking of his own coming encounter with the living Lord, Karl Barth described to a friend what he took to be the essence of eschatology:

> "Eternal" life is not another, second life beyond our present one, but the reverse side of this life, as God sees it, which is hidden from us here and now. It is this life in relationship to what God has done in Jesus Christ for the whole world and thus also for us. So we wait and hope — in respect of our death — to be made manifest with him (Jesus Christ who is raised from the dead), in the glory of judgment, and also of the grace of God. That will be the new thing: that the veil which now lies over the whole world and thus over our life (tears, death, sorrow, crying, grief) will be taken away, and God's counsel (already accomplished in Jesus Christ) will stand before our eyes, the object of our deepest shame, but also of our joyful thanks and praise.[10]

---

hand, she holds out the extratextual hope that Rayber's collapse, like Mrs. McIntyre's at the end of "The Displaced Person," may signal "that he is not going to be able to sustain his choice" (HB, 484).

10. Quoted in Eberhard Busch, *Karl Barth: His Life from Letters and Autobiographical Texts,* trans. John Bowden (Philadelphia: Fortress, 1976), p. 488.

O'Connor's confessed affinity for Karl Barth would surely have extended to Hans Urs von Balthasar had his work been translated into English before her death in 1964. Von Balthasar makes clear his conviction that hell is a state and not a place, and thus a present as well as a future reality. He cites St. Augustine's commentary on Genesis: "There is, then, definitely a real hell, but I take it to affect the imagination, not the body."[11] Von Balthasar also shows that, as with Rayber's collapse into total insensibility, evil always turns inward and consumes itself, making it incapable of real community or friendship. Since personhood entails a positive engagement with other persons, damnation produces what Cardinal Joseph Ratzinger calls a terrible kind of unpersonhood, "a decomposition and denigration of being a person."[12]

Yet the self-destructive powers of evil are never the main focus of Christian witness. For while the church has specified many saints, it has never declared anyone definitively damned. Dante places Judas in the lowest pit of Hell, but von Balthasar regards Jesus' betrayer as a figure who stands near rather than far from us; he is "the representative example for something of which all sinners are also guilty."[13] The real issue, von Balthasar argues, is not Judas's final state but our own present hope. How can we live truthfully and redemptively if we are assured that a great deal — perhaps most — of God's good creation will be irretrievably lost, that the preponderance of human effort and culture will be swallowed up in the swirling abyss? Considering our utter failure to meet the demands of divine love, would not the ultimate abuse and denial of God's love lie precisely in hoping for ourselves what we refuse to hope for all others? Could we ever assume the final abandonment of any other person besides ourselves? Would not this assumption that even one other person might dwell forever beyond the pale of divine mercy also cut the cord of our own unreserved love for him? Would not such a conclusion sever the demand that, as Jürgen Verweyen puts it, we "have a patience that absolutely never gives up but is prepared to wait infinitely long for the other"?[14]

These are the questions that two eschatological scenes in O'Connor's fiction serve to answer. The first occurs when young Tarwater, having drowned Bishop and having himself been sodomized by the devil's agent, angrily purges the satanic presence by setting the woods afire. He heads home

11. Quoted in von Balthasar, *Dare We Hope*, p. 127.

12. Quoted in ibid., p. 145.

13. Ibid., p. 187. He adds, somewhat ominously, that "[t]he certainty that a number of men, especially unbelievers, must end in hell we can leave to Islam" (p. 213).

14. Quoted in ibid., pp. 78-79.

for Powderhead, expecting to meet the awful judgment that he deserves for having incinerated — so he believes — his great-uncle. The farmhouse does lie in ashes, but the corn crop has been freshly laid by. To his immense astonishment and even greater gratitude, Tarwater finds a newly mounded grave with a crude cross planted at its head. Buford, a black farm worker, has dragged the huge prophet from the burning house and given him the reverent burial the old man had requested. This utterly unbidden and unmerited gift of grace, an act of sheer transcendent mercy that spares the boy a lifetime of overwhelming guilt, at last frees Tarwater to become the prophet that he is meant to be. The flaming woods that he has set on fire no longer betoken the heat of his anger but the ardor of God's summons: "He knew that this was the fire that had encircled Daniel, that had raised Elijah from the earth, that had spoken to Moses and would in the instant speak to him. He threw himself to the ground and with his face against the dirt of the grave, he heard the command. GO WARN THE CHILDREN OF GOD OF THE TERRIBLE SPEED OF MERCY" (CW, 478).

That prophets repent in sackcloth and ashes, abasing themselves in abject humility, does not make them immune to being killed by the very people whom they are sent to save. In a letter commenting on Francis Marion Tarwater's postfictional fate, O'Connor observed that "the children of God . . . will dispatch him pretty quick" (HB, 342). Even if the young evangelist dies in order to realize his mission, his death will not invalidate his calling. He has seen what ultimately counts: that the cross is not a knife driven into the heart of the world to rend its life, but the tree, as O'Connor confessed, whose roots encircle all the dead and whose branches embrace all the living. In the end, Tarwater's vision reaches even to paradise, for he is given a glimpse of Old Mason feeding eagerly among the great throng of the redeemed, as the multiplied loaf is passed among them. The boy knows that this hunger for the Bread of Life is also his, that it belongs not to him alone but to every living soul, and that no one can rest, as St. Augustine said, until the craving is satisfied:

> He felt his hunger no longer as a pain but as a tide. He felt it rising in himself through time and darkness, rising through the centuries, and he knew that it rose in a line of men whose lives were chosen to sustain it, who would wander the world, strangers from that violent country where the silence is never broken except to shout the truth. (CW, 478)

That O'Connor can envision the realm of the blessed dead as being inhabited by "violent" men who are strangers on the earth reveals her abiding fear that ours is an age of the mediocre and the flaccid, of the pusillanimous and the falsely satisfied. It also displays her conviction that paradise is not a static condition. This is a central Christian conception, from the Book of Revelation through Dante and modern theologians such as Barth and von Balthasar, both of whom eschew the term "eternity" because it evokes an absence of movement and energy in the divine life and thus misconstrues our own participation in it. They are all agreed with Gregory of Nyssa's contention that "eternal bliss means a dynamic, never-ending movement toward the center in God; never-ending because God's essence can never be fully reached."[15]

This "dynamic, never-ending movement toward God" lies at the center of the vision granted to Ruby Turpin at the end of "Revelation," O'Connor's most winsome story. Mrs. Turpin is a complex character, at once frighteningly complacent about her own life and yet engagingly open to the truth. Convinced that Jesus has given her everything — a faithful husband, Claud, a prosperous sanitary hog farm, and a prominent standing in society — Ruby thanks Christ at night for all her blessings, naming them one by one. In fact, she falls asleep by imagining the kind of person Jesus could have made her into — a Negro, for example — if he had not created her to be the excellent person that she is. Since most of the "colored people" she knows are "trashy," Mrs. Turpin remains assured that Christ "would have made her a neat clean respectable Negro woman, herself but black" (CW, 636). Such musings, though racist, seem more amusing than vicious, until Ruby remembers that there are genteel whites who have lost their possessions, even as there are prosperous black doctors who own expensive homes and cars and cattle. These counter-indicators upset Ruby Turpin's ranking of the good and the bad. That she has a hierarchical imagination is not itself evil, but that her hierarchy is humanly constructed rather than divinely revealed makes it potentially fascist: "Usually by the time she had fallen asleep all the classes of people were moiling and roiling around in her head, and she would dream they were all crammed in together in a box car, being ridden off to be put in a gas oven" (CW, 636). Ruby Turpin lives in the shadow of the Holocaust, and she obscurely senses her link to it, even if she cannot articulate her feelings in historical terms. The Hitlerian horror was undergirded by the assumption that, in the absence of transcendent moral order, human life becomes as disposable as vermin. The Jews violated Hitler's hierarchy, just as well-off blacks disrupt Ruby's conviction that the social order must be arranged according to her own norms. And since the world refuses to conform to her vision of it,

15. Ibid., p. 245.

she dreams of having everything dissolved in the flaming chaos of the death camps.

Mrs. Turpin meets her avenging angel of judgment in the person of an acne-faced Wellesley student, who confronts her in a medical waiting room. Mary Grace is not an echo of either the Virgin Mary or any of the Marys who are central to Jesus' ministry. She is a secular bearer of the grace that O'Connor described as having to wound before it can heal.[16] Outraged at Ruby's litany of thankfulness for all the good things Jesus has given her, Mary Grace flings a huge psychology textbook at the self-congratulating Turpin, striking her over the eye. The demon of wrath then shoves Ruby roughly to the floor, pounces astride her, and screams out a memorable imprecation: "Go back to hell where you came from, you old warthog" (CW, 646). Because she is a Christ-haunted Southerner, Mrs. Turpin is unable to dismiss this vicious attack as the work of a mere madwoman. Just as the Grandmother in "A Good Man Is Hard to Find" recognizes The Misfit as someone she has known from the foundation of time, so does Ruby instantly discern that she has been sent a dread message from her Lord. At first she tries to deny the truthfulness of the judgment that has befallen her by extolling her own good works: "It's no trash around here, black or white, that I haven't given to. And break my back to the bone every day working. And do for the church." Then she becomes snide and sarcastic about God's having directed his ire not at "rednecks" or "niggers," as she would have called them, but at a "neat, clean respectable woman" such as herself. Hence her fury at a deity who shows himself to be no respecter of persons but sends his condemnation on a decent white lady. She reminds God that, unlike those who deserve divine reproach, she does not lie down in the middle of the street and stop traffic like black civil rights demonstrators, or "dip snuff and spit in every puddle and have it all over [her] face" like white trash. She concludes her Job-like complaint by confessing, with unrecognized verbal irony, "I could be nasty" (CW, 652).

Even if Christ has totally overturned her hierarchy, putting the first last and making the wise foolish, Ruby Turpin determines to maintain the proper social distinctions: "Call me a warthog from hell. Put that bottom rail on the top. There'll still be a top and a bottom." When none of Ruby's self-justifications proves satisfying, she grows ever more desperate, defying God with more Job-like taunts: "Who do you think you are?" (CW, 653). But unlike Job, who acquires a certain dignity in contending with God, Mrs. Turpin becomes increasingly childish and futile in her rage. Her last query comes re-

---

16. O'Connor often observed that all of her major characters were versions of herself, and we will recall that her full name was Mary Flannery O'Connor.

bounding back to her in the form of an echo, as if God were asking Ruby who she considers herself to be. As almost always in O'Connor's work, the answer occurs through silence. This talky woman who has raged against God receives no divine lecture but an eschatological vision. With the sky darkening toward sunset, Ruby stares down at an old sow who feeds her suckling piglets in utter disregard for her own welfare. This scene of unstanched giving and vibrant receiving enables Ruby to gaze "through the very heart of mystery." She seems, in fact, to be "absorbing some abysmal life-giving knowledge" (CW, 653). Then she lifts up her eyes to the heavens, where the disappearing sun has left only a long purple streak in the sky. There, with her hands raised in a priestly gesture, she beholds a purgatorial vision that redeems even as it judges:

> She saw the streak as a vast swinging bridge extending upward from the earth through a field of living fire. Upon it a vast horde of souls were rumbling toward heaven. There were whole companies of white-trash, clean for the first time in their lives, and bands of black niggers in white robes, and battalions of freaks and lunatics shouting and clapping and leaping like frogs. And bringing up the end of the procession was a tribe of people whom she recognized at once as those who, like herself and Claud, had always had a little of everything and the God-given wit to use it right. She leaned forward to observe them closer. They were marching behind the others with great dignity, accountable as they had always been for good order and common sense and respectable behavior. They alone were on key. Yet she could see by their shocked and altered faces that even their virtues were being burned away. (CW, 653-54)

This momentary eschatological disclosure concerns not only Ruby's future life in a paradise but also her present life in a small Southern town. In one of her angriest queries, Ruby Turpin had asked God, "How am I a hog and me both? How am I saved and from hell too?" (CW, 652). Here in an apocalyptic vision she finds her answer. Both the question and the reply are central to the Christian faith: How can one be the reborn child of God while remaining a miserable offender? Luther struck at the core of the matter when he declared that Christians are *simul justus et peccator*. We are simultaneously justified by Christ's life and death and resurrection, said Luther, while remaining dreadful sinners who must work out our salvation in fear and trembling. Far from sanctioning the status quo by means of what Bonhoeffer called "cheap grace" — a reliance on Christ's forgiveness as the unguent for a complacent life — eschatological faith enables true transformation.

Ruby Turpin's hopeless world must be both dismantled and redeemed. Everything is thus turned upside down in her final eschatological vision, for she is made to see things as God sees them. Now she must learn, however painfully, to live in the revolutionary new age that God is inaugurating by way of the redemption already wrought in Christ, even as it awaits its final fulfillment beyond time. She has seen that the divine mercy is like the refiner's fire, cleansing rather than consuming her spurious goodness. Her pride of place and position is being purged by this incandescent sight of all the world's "inferior" folk entering the kingdom ahead of her. O'Connor does not suggest that society's outsiders are intrinsically noble. But like the New Testament "publicans and sinners" who are so welcoming to Jesus, the emarginated are not inclined toward Ruby's self-justifying righteousness, if only because they have so little cause to think highly of themselves. Mrs. Turpin also discovers that, while her small virtues of "good order and common sense and respectable behavior" are necessary to social existence, they are not the keys of the Kingdom. And when such miniscule virtues lead to moral arrogance and spiritual presumption, as they have in her case, they become more pernicious than the common vices.

O'Connor never ends her stories with easy victories, since neither good art nor authentic faith is ever less than arduous and exacting. Ruby Turpin is still far from salvation. Her false goodness will not be easily cleansed. Even in receiving her divine vision, she retains her tone of arch condescension: she and Claud "always had a little of everything and the God-given wit to use it right." Yet neither will she be able to forget what she has glimpsed. The good news that she is included in the heavenly procession, not because of her gleaming good works but by God's burning mercy alone, promises to put constraints on her presumption. That she and Claud are at the rear of the train is meant as a positive spur to a new kind of excellence and joyfulness, as she is called to conform her sinful life to the gracious life of the triune God. Mrs. Turpin receives a hint of what such a redeemed life is meant to be as she trudges home in the darkness, for she does not hear wails of damnation but songs of jubilation: "In the woods around her the invisible cricket choruses had struck up, but what she heard were the voices of the souls climbing into the starry field and shouting hallelujah" (CW, 654).

\*        \*        \*

Flannery O'Connor's South was Christ-haunted, as she repeatedly emphasized, though not Christ-centered. But to be haunted by the ragged figure of the Nazarene who swings from limb to limb in the great tree of Southern cultural and religious life is to be given a gift of immense proportion. Walker Percy offers thanks for this gift at the end of his apocalyptic novel of 1971, *Love in the Ruins*. Percy's protagonist-antagonist, Dr. Thomas More, seeks to unite both the Christians and secularists, the liberals and conservatives, the blacks and whites of his region to serve the common good. More's organization wittily parodies the anti-Catholic society that rose to prominence in the 1950s and that was called "Protestants and Other Americans United for the Separation of Church and State" (POAU). It's far too late for Protestants and Catholics to be set against each other, More suggests, when church and culture are both in a state of collapse. Dr. More slyly calls his group "Southerners and Others United to Preserve the Union in Repayment of an Old Debt to the Yankees Who Saved It Once Before and Are Destroying It Now" (SOUP).[17]

The Yankee gospel of progress and enlightenment that once saved the nation from ruin, insisting that no human being can ever be regarded as mere chattel and that peoples of all creeds and colors are due basic fairness and justice, has largely cut itself off from Christian confession and tradition. There is no longer a Southern problem or a Northern problem or even a California problem. Severed from the biblical story and the institutions it once sustained, the Divided States of America will founder and sink into the abyss that eventually will engulf all nations and cultures.[18] Yet hope remains, the eschatological hope that Ruby Turpin encountered, the hope that God's burning mercy hurries terribly and wonderfully near. Flannery O'Connor's work both enlivens and extends this hope because it was inspired by a terribly and wonderfully Christ-haunted region.

---

17. Walker Percy, *Love in the Ruins: The Adventures of a Bad Catholic at a Time Near the End of the World* (New York: Farrar, Straus & Giroux, 1971), p. 401.

18. When *Love in the Ruins* won the National Book Award in 1971, Walker Percy was asked what if any "message" his apocalyptic novel enshrines. Percy's answer made ironically clear that our plight is a not a regional epidemic but a national pandemic: "If my novel has any message, it is probably this: Don't give up, New York, California, Chicago, Philadelphia. Louisiana is with you. Georgia is on your side."

# Index of Names and Subjects

# Index of Scripture References